The Real Thing

The Real Thing

TESTIMONIAL DISCOURSE AND LATIN AMERICA

Georg M. Gugelberger, Editor

Duke University Press   Durham & London

1996

© 1996 Duke University Press   All rights reserved

Printed in the United States of America on acid-free paper ∞

Typeset in Garamond with Gill Sans display, by Keystone Typesetting, Inc.

Library of Congress Cataloging-in-Publication Data appear on

the last printed page of this book.

Contents

Acknowledgments

I would like to gratefully acknowledge the following people. Christopher Wise, a former student of mine and now professor of English at West Georgia College, as well as my students Robert d'Alonzo and Chris Mahoney, for helping with proofreading and editorial matters in the early stages of this book. At Duke University Press, my thanks to Paul Kelleher for a superb job in copyediting, Jean Brady for her timely management of this book's production, and Reynolds Smith for his continuous support. Further, I thank Fredric Jameson for originally suggesting that I submit a proposal to Duke University Press for this collection of essays. I would also like to acknowledge the anonymous readers who supported this book, whose many valuable suggestions I hope to have incorporated in one way or another. I thank Doris Sommer for revising her essay, so that it could be better included in a collection of essays that focuses on the debates about and within *testimonio* criticism. Finally, my thanks to John Beverley for writing a new essay especially for this collection.

I am grateful to the following journals for granting permission to reprint these previously published articles: John Beverley, "The Margin at the Center: On *Testimonio* (Testimonial Narrative)," *Modern Fiction Studies* 35, no. 1 (spring 1989): 11–28; George Yúdice, "*Testimonio* and Postmodernism," *Latin American Perspectives* 18, no. 3 (summer 1991): 15–31; Margaret Randall, "Reclaiming Voices: Notes on a New Female Practice in Journalism," *Latin American Perspectives* 18, no. 3 (summer 1991): 103–13; Barbara Harlow, "*Testimonio* and Survival: Roque Dalton's *Miguel Mármol*," *Latin American Perspectives* 18, no. 4 (fall 1991): 9–21; Marc Zimmerman, "*Testimonio* in Guatemala: Payeras, Rigoberta, and Beyond," *Latin American Perspectives* 18, no. 4 (fall 1991): 22–47; Elzbieta Sklodowska, "Spanish American Testimonial Novel: Some Afterthoughts," *New Novel Review* 1, no. 2 (April 1994): 32–41.

Georg M. Gugelberger Introduction:

Institutionalization of Transgression

Testimonial Discourse and Beyond

The need for a relatively more unbuttoned, unfixed, and mobile mode of proceeding—that's why the Deleuzian idea of the nomadic is so interesting—is to me a much more useful and liberating instrument. Much of what we are talking about is essentially unhoused. You might say the real conflict is between the unhoused and the housed.
—Edward Said (Sprinker 1992, 231)

"**W**hat is left of the desire called testimonio?" John Beverley asks at the conclusion of his essay in this collection, which he appropriately entitles "The Real Thing." Indeed, what is left of that which the academic Left had considered for so long as exemplary of a "poetics of solidarity," a possible center of "resistance literature" (Barbara Harlow)? Recently the Chilean daily *La Epoca* printed the following wedding announcement: "La premio Nobel de la Paz guatemalteca, RIGOBERTA MENCHU, esté feliz de haber contraído matrimonio y espera procrear dos hijos con su esposo ANGEL FRANCISCO CANIL. . . . Menchú dijo estar 'muy contenta' de haberse casado con alguien de su mismo grupo étnico, un compañero de lucha a quien definió como un 'gordito encantador, cariñoso y simpático' . . . "[1] It all sounded so familiar, just like the ending of a soap opera. What had happened to our "icon" with a secret? Obviously the euphoric "moment" of the testimonio has passed, and it is now time to assess in a more self- and metacritical spirit its reception by the critical and academic disciplines. The year 1989 witnessed the fall of many walls, not only the most symbolic one in Berlin. The "cruce divisorio Primer mundo/Tercer mundo"[2] long since had turned into a "cruce divisorio" Third World/ postcolonial. Obviously more is at stake here than changes in terminology. The desire called testimonio was the desire called Third World literature. With the replacement of the Third World metaphor by the metaphor of postcoloniality, testimonio critics could not remain unaffected. When the margin moves to the center and loses its counter-hegemonic quality a different assessment is required. As John Beverley observes in his essay "Postmodern Music and Left Politics," "Whatever the problem with the concept of the Third World, it can no longer mark an 'other' that is radically outside of and different from Contemporary North American or European society" (Beverley 1993a, 139).

The testimonio—generically hybrid, "homeless" and "unheimlich" (literally unhomed rather than uncanny), extraliterary and even post-literary in the opinion of some critics—found its institutional home during the (in)famous canon debates. It was not left outside, but rather was invited in, albeit in a co-opted form that accompanied the increasing interest in the genre of the autobiography. The cannons of canonization shoot differently these days; everything expressed orally or in writing, painted, filmed, videotaped, performed, or danced, is bound to become "canon fodder" and will find a place in institutional discourse or in disciplinary and/or interdisciplinary studies. Only rarely are the implications of disciplinary or the weight of the "inter" (as in-between-ness) in "interdisciplinary studies" brought to the fore. Entering disciplinarity, then, shall be the focus of some of the essays, especially in the second part of this collection. The movement traced by these essays is from the early and euphoric moments of solidarity and redemption to a period when critics are more suspicious about the "outsider's" wedding to a new canon. The question to be asked is, What happens when modes of transgression become sanctioned and canonized, even auratized (to borrow Walter Benjamin's familiar and often misconstrued concept)?

Outside in the Teaching Machine, the felicitous and Deleuzian title of Gayatri Chakravorty Spivak's latest book, echoes our dreams and our failures. We wanted to have it both ways: from within the system we dreamed about being outside with the "subaltern"; our words were to reflect the struggles of the oppressed. But you cannot be inside and outside at the same time. You cannot be nomadic and sedentary at the same time. If you are housed in academia, you will have lost the power to be "unheimlich." This is even more so now, in these days that Sande Cohen has described provocatively and not unjustifiably in his book *Academia and the Luster of Capital.* And obviously, at least since John Guillory's study, we should be familiar with the concept of "cultural capital." The testimonio and the ensuing testimonio criticism obviously are part of such cultural capital.

We must have known from Walter Benjamin's failing dream about the salvational potential of photography and film—already frowned upon by Theodor W. Adorno—that deauratization hardly ever is possible. More recently Deleuze and Guattari have reflected convincingly on the deterritorializing nomadic and rhizomatic possibilities that, nevertheless, always will be reterritorialized by the state machine. Deauratization is linked to reauratization as deterritorialization is linked to reterritorialization; they are the intrinsic aspects of how capital actually functions. What at first appears salvational is all too soon turned into a monument. In every new constitution, be it of a genre or a discipline, resides some restitutional power. The "auratic" is intrinsically connected to capital and the State Apparatus. Only temporarily do deauratizing and rhizomatic moments "subvert" the dominating power of the state and the institution. Neither photography nor movements in art that negated the museum and the aura, such as Dada, Concept Art, Fluxus, and others, could resist the power of capital, which always reauratizes, exhibits, documents, puts into galleries and museums. The recent growth of museum culture (museums increasingly designed and signed by famous architects) is like the literature in the declining stage, which Roland Barthes has described as being like phosphorus: it shone the brightest just before it became extinct. Dreams of deauratization and deterritorialization, the fight against our various disciplines from within, the desire to change them, may actually have given way to their strengthening. By fighting what constitutes a discipline, something always is restored to the discipline. No one has demonstrated this better than Alberto Moreiras, whose essay appears in this collection.

This collection includes some of the major essays on testimonio writing of the first phase; in addition, it reflects on those and with those subsequently involved in the numerous testimonio debates. At least since the enemies of the classics became the classics themselves in high modernism, we know that counterdiscourse has become institutionalized. This is where we are now. However, and this strikes me to be potentially as significant as the production of the testimonio itself, it appears that we would not be able to see our impasse as clearly were it not for the testimonio that, in its ensuing metacritical phase, also has become a testimony to our own critical malaise. While not necessarily making the subaltern "visible," testimonio has helped to make ourselves visible to ourselves.

The painter Paul Klee once said, and the antiphilosopher Gilles Deleuze more recently has reasserted, that the task is not to render/ reproduce but to make visible (Boundas 1993, 19). In these words the fate and the history of the testimonio are encapsulated. Testimonio, together with Holocaust writing, led to the perhaps too rapid conclusion that we are in the age of the testimony (Felman and Laub 1992, 5). Perhaps we should not yet give the age another name. We also should not necessarily identify testimonio with testimonial literature (in English the word "literature" was added but was not implied in the Spanish original[3]) or testimonio with testimonial discourse, which obviously came later and at the crucial point when the genre found its home in Western and particularly "Unitedstatian"[4] institutions. Most certainly we do not wish to identify Holocaust testimonies, which are basically documentary, with the testimonio that wants to effect change and is quite different from documentary writing. The one has no audience, or perceives its audience as having vanished apocalyptically, while the other definitely lives from the hope and will to effect change or at least raise consciousness. Witness the original title of Rigoberta Menchú's work, *Me llamo Rigoberta Menchú y así me nació la conciencia.*

Understanding and consciousness raising begins with the name, the politics of labeling, with what Gayatri Chakravorty Spivak means when she emphasizes the need for reflecting on the rhetorical figure of the catachresis. Suffice it to say that interest in this genre/anti-genre, in this literature that does not want to be literature, occurred at a crucial and critical moment of our history, shortly before and soon after the date that led to the misnomer of the "new world order," which is another metaphor for world disorder.

Originally, this collection of essays had been envisioned as a reprint of the essays included in the special issue on Latin American testimonio of the journal *Latin American Perspectives* (1991) and a selection from a collection of essays in Spanish in the *Revista de crítica literaria latino-americana* (1992). Some of the essays in the two collections overlapped; also, essays were in English in one collection, while they were in Spanish in the other. The two special issues reflected a high point in the discussion of the late eighties and very early nineties. In the process, this plan significantly changed when it became only too apparent that fundamental changes in the reception and discussion of the "new" genre had occurred. The issues of authenticity and salvationality, the poetics of solidarity as Moreiras has called it, became critically investigated, and new social movements approached political reality differently. Furthermore, the acceptance of the icon of testimonio writing, Rigoberta Menchú's narrative, into an expanded canon (witness the by now [in]famous Stanford debate on great books, in addition to Menchú's receiving the Nobel Peace Prize) numbed to a certain degree the counterdiscursivity of the genre. In short, a reconsideration is at hand. Numerous new people have entered the debate that previously centered on John Beverley, George Yúdice, Margaret Randall, Doris Sommer, and others. This collection of essays seeks to be more representative and show not only the early stages of the debate but also the "sliding into the beyond" of testimonial discourse during the early and mid-nineties.

The title of this collection is not merely a borrowing of John Beverley's essay contribution. It is a reflection on the dilemma of present critical discourse that is so much engaged with issues of representationality, realism, truth, etcetera. Testimonio, perhaps more than any genre in the past, has foregrounded the issue of what is "real" and has been defined by Jara as "una huella de lo real," a trace of the real (Jara and Vidal 1986, 2). The "real" thing is also the thing with the real, the issue of what is and can be real. At first the genre of the testimonio was a Latin American "thing," originating in Cuba in the immediate years of the revolution, then manifesting again in Bolivia before it became nearly a Central American genre. The second stage was the critical response to the testimonio by "progressive" intellectuals in the United States, a majority of whom were women, just as the majority of the producers of the testimonio were women. The third stage in the development of testimonio was the response of critics in the United States, many of whom were of Latin American origin, who struggled with the issues of "lo real" and started to refute the presumed "left" "poetics of solidarity," going "beyond" the unconditional affirmation of the genre as represented in this collection by Barbara Harlow and in the Latin American Perspectives collection by the majority of the contributors. Marc Zimmerman was one of the first to use the term "beyond," in the course of looking at the implications of the testimonio in Guatemala; Zimmerman found that what is said in the "classic" by Rigoberta Menchú is not necessarily confirmed by Payeras and others. Doris Sommer located the silences of Menchú's text and started an ambiguous project of drawing conclusions about these "secrets." Critics such as Beverley,

Sklodowska, Moreiras, and Williams responded differently. In short, most of these essays continue a lively debate between those who saw in testimonio a salvation, almost the proof that the subaltern can speak, and those who saw in the first wave of reception a flawed affirmation giving way to an implicit restitution of precisely that discipline that the originators of the discourse considered as being challenged by the testimonio (see Moreiras's essay in this volume). Most of them have turned from discussions of the testimonio toward a discussion of institutional agency. Gareth Williams and Fredric Jameson extensively discuss the "transfer" of the genre from the Southern hemisphere to the Northern hemisphere.

The emergence of the "Third World" genre of the testimonio on the (largely academic) markets of the First World has been, to say the least, ambiguous and complex. Hailed at first as salvational and authentic by those with "*testimonio*-seeing eyes" (Sklodowska's words), it more recently—after institutional canonization and appropriation—has been rightfully reassessed. When a genre of the oppressed becomes part of the self-styled abject (Julia Kristeva via Gareth Williams), in other words, when Third World salvational discourse is transformed into cultural capital (by way of canonization), we should become more vigilant.

"The fact that we, the interpretative community of academic critics, have agreed to 'recognize' testimonio and give it institutional legitimation is, arguably, one of the most important events of the past two decades in Spanish American literary history" (Sklodowska, this volume, 84). And we should add to Elzbieta Sklodowska's observation that the fact that this genre has been taken so seriously beyond Latin American studies is itself a significant turn from formalist literary concerns toward a greater opening of literature to the world. The institutional legitimation, always lagging behind in time of the production of the work itself, has had three significant moments: (1) the collection of essays entitled *Testimonio y literatura* (1986) edited by René Jara and Hernán Vidal; (2) the Georg Gugelberger and Michael Kearney collection of essays in two issues of *Latin American Perspectives* under the title *Voices of the Voiceless in Testimonial Literature* (1991); (3) the special edition, *La voz del otro: Testimonio, subalternidad y verdad narrativa,* of the *Revista de crítica literaria latinoamericana* (1992) edited by John Beverley and Hugo Achugar. The present collection of essays on the genre of the testimonio is an attempt, not so much to strengthen an institutional legitimation, but rather to problematize precisely the implication of this institutionalization.

The publication of this collection clearly comes at a time when the initial interest in the genre has begun to fade, perhaps due to the developments since 1989 that took down the wall between an outdated binary. With this decline in interest came a larger move, which is discussed in an exemplary fashion in John Beverley's appropriately titled *Against Literature*, a fundamental rethinking of what we do in institutions when we "preach" and teach literature, albeit with our problematizing and historicizing imperatives in mind. Why was the testimonio considered to be so interesting? It was at the crossroads of all the discourses of institutional battles in recent years: postcolonial and/ versus postmodern; genre versus non-genre; interest in autobiography; the function of the canon; authenticity/realism; the debates on subalternity; othering discourse; orature/literature; dual authorship; editorial intervention; margin/center; race/class/gender; feminisms (some apparently unjustifiably declared the testimonio women's discourse); minority discourse; Third World writing; the post-boom novel; Latin Americanism; questions of disciplinarity; and so on. Testimonio has been the salvational dream of a declining cultural left in hegemonic countries, comparable to what Walter Benjamin expected from photography and film when he reflected on his famous auratic theory. While the literary/ formal "value" of the genre may be negligible, its tremendous implicit trajectories continue to deserve attention.

Let us assume, and I think correctly, that the end of this century and years into the next will be characterized by migrations unforeseen in the past (Hans Magnus Enzensberger's "Grosse Wanderung"), due to a combination of technological facility and the politics of hunger and death. Then it might be proper to ask how this scenario bears on literature and theory, not so much how it is reflected in literature but rather how literature and theory can function in a responsible and perhaps even rehumanizing way. The othering discourse, as it has been called among other things, has permutated since the sixteenth century as rapidly as definitions of literature. The process has increased in speed since events around the year 1989. Othering was that willful attempt— often seriously meant but nonetheless always biased and based on what Spivak calls the Western "error as truth" (Spivak 1987, 101)[5]—to grasp the other (also fabricated as the "exotic") from the sixteenth century to colonialism and beyond, mainly in anthropology and literature. It is safe to postulate that it was largely through literary "disciplines" that all areas of institutionalized discourse were affected. Through the control of education, the state held on to its gains from nation to colony, from metropolis to periphery.

Literature, we know all too well, has been deeply implicated in those processes of state formation and colonial expansion that have defined Europe and its other. For instance, Edward Said has critiqued powerfully the genre of the novel (unthinkable without the expansion of capital and the empire) and the "making" of the "Orient" by Western writers. We are too familiar with the white male "field worker" (alias anthropologist) or traveler who went to a faraway place, settled down in comfort for a year, and then gave us the "truth" (usually a lie) about the other and the other society. One only has to think of such titles as *Travels into the Interior Districts of Africa, Narrative of an Expedition to the Zambesi, 17 Jahre in Yoruba Land, How I Found Livingston,* and hundreds of dime novels that sketch "the Africa that never was" and leave us with the by now irritating—but, of course, they were not always perceived as irritating—unpopulated and edenic landscapes.[6]

Out of the ruins of the "scramble for Africa" (and more recently the so-called Third World in general, since roughly the coining of the term "tiers monde" by Alfred Sauvy in the fifties) came the field of Third World literary studies. More recently, in the wake of a newly colonizing postmodernism, the Third World's potential enemy "postcolonial studies"[7] was invented in the eighties. It is in the years between the creation of the term *Third World* and its decline that the genre of the testimonio came into being and found its problematic reception. The genre came into existence due to the Cuban Revolution, more specifically due to Miguel Barnet's recording of the life story of Esteban Montejo under the title *Biografía de un cimarrón/The Autobiography of a Runaway Slave* (1966). In the sixties and seventies numerous testimonios were published. In the late eighties progressive critics proposed new theories of representationality and authenticity based on the increasing publication of testimonios. This happened precisely at a moment when poststructuralism and deconstruction eroded all hopes for representation and referentiality in literature. Thus, the testimonio becomes interesting not so much for what it says and how it says it (as literature per se), but rather for how it entered critical discourse and the institutional centers of higher learning, thereby dismantling our treasured notions of literature.

Let me cite two by now famous definitions of testimonial discourse, as given by John Beverley and George Yúdice. In his article on "The Margin at the Center," which he later revised for inclusion in his book *Against Literature,* John Beverley writes:

By *testimonio* I mean a novel or novella-length narrative in book or pamphlet (that is, printed as opposed to acoustic) form, told in the first person by a narrator who is also a real protagonist or witness of the event he or she recounts, and whose unit of narration is usually a "life" or a significant life experience. *Testimonio* may include, but is not subsumed under, any of the following categories, some of which are conventionally considered literature, others not: autobiography, autobiographical novel, oral history, memoir, confession, diary, interview, eyewitness report, life history, *novela-testimonio,* nonfiction novel, or "factographic literature." . . . The situation of narration in *testimonio* has to involve an urgency to communicate, a problem of repression, poverty, subalternity, imprisonment, struggle for survival, and so on. (Beverley 1989, 12–13)

Further, George Yúdice has defined the genre as: "an authentic narrative, told by a witness who is moved to narrate by the urgency of a situation (e.g., war, oppression, revolution, etc.). Emphasizing popular, oral discourse, the witness portrays his or her own experience as an agent (rather than a representative) of a collective memory and identity. Truth is summoned in the cause of denouncing a present situation of exploitation and oppression or in exorcising and setting aright official history" (Yúdice 1991a, 17; also this volume, 44). Despite these relatively clear definitions, Elzbieta Sklodowska rightfully insists that *"testimonio* remains undefined" (this volume, 84). Let me also quote a familiar and powerful passage from one of these testimonios, perhaps the best known and undoubtedly the icon of the genre, *Me llamo Rigoberta Menchú y así me nació la conciencia* (1983), whose title is significantly shortened in English as *I, Rigoberta Menchú: An Indian Woman in Guatemala* (1984). The page from which I am quoting is a long, detailed, and painful passage *representing* what happened to Rigoberta's mother:

My mother was kidnapped. And from the very beginning she was raped by the town's high-ranking army officers. And I want to say in advance that I have in my hands details of every step of the rape and torture suffered by my mother. . . . My mother was raped by the kidnappers, and after that they took her down to the camp. . . . They have a lot of pits there where they punish the people they have kidnapped and where my little brother was tortured as well. They took my mother to the same place. There she was raped by the officers commanding the troops. After that she was subjected to terrible tortures. The first day they shaved her head, put a uniform on her and then they said: "If you are a guerilla why don't you fight us here." . . . While they beat her, they asked her where we were. . . . She pretended she knew nothing. . . . On the third day of her torture, they cut off her ears. They cut her whole body bit by bit. . . . They began with small tortures, small beatings and worked up to terrible tortures. . . . From the pain, from the torture all over her body, disfigured and starving, my mother began to lose consciousness and was in her death throes. . . . They gave her food. Then they started raping her again. She was disfigured by those same officers. She endured a great deal, but she didn't die. . . . They left her there dying for four or five days, enduring the sun, the rain and the night. My mother was covered in worms, because in the mountains there is a fly which gets straight into any wound. . . . Since all my mother's wounds were open, there were worms in all of them. She was still alive. My mother died in terrible agony. When my mother died, the soldiers stood over her and urinated in her mouth; even after she was dead! (Menchú 1984, 198–99)

After such a passage, Doris Sommer reminds us: "To doubt referentiality in testimonials would be an irresponsible luxury given the urgency of the call to action" (Sommer 1992, earlier unpublished version of the essay included in this volume). But the reception of Rigoberta Menchú and the continuing poststructuralist theorizing that defers referentiality and representationality engaged precisely in such luxury and celebrated increasingly virtual reality games. This clearly showed once again that whatever literature is or might be, it hardly will be able to instigate action and effect deeply needed change. This also demonstrates, among other things, that whatever literature is not, we (in the institution) can make it into literature and by doing so destroy its essence. This usually happens in the so-called canon debates. Santiago Colás, in his contribution to this collection, extensively pursues the question, "What's Wrong with Representation?"

The testimonio is placed at the intersection of multiple roads: oral versus literary (which implies questioning why the literary has always colonized the oral); authored/authoritarian discourse versus edited discourse (one author or two authors?: is the text a product of Rigoberta Menchú or rather of her editor Elisabeth Burgos-Debray?); literature versus anthropology; literature versus non-literature, or even against literature; autobiography versus demography (people's writing); the battle of representationality; the canon debate (is this a work that should be integrated into the canon and what happens if it is?); "masterpiece" of literature versus minority writing; and issues of postmodernity versus postcoloniality. The scandal of the assignment of Rigoberta Menchú's testimonio in one of the required courses at Stanford University becomes a central focus for the neoconservative assaults on multicultural education and political correctness. What is the place of such a text in tertiary education generally (regardless of discipline)? And what happens if we use such a text? Few genres have begged as many questions and interpellated mainstream discourse to such a degree.

Representative of the oppressed subaltern, the repressed and homeless, the exiled and the migrant, this genre, which at first resisted a place in the house of genology (the study of literary genres), is so mobile that permitting it entry into the institution of higher learning makes the process of learning indeed "unheimlich" (uncanny). The literary nomad or subaltern speech as that which cannot be really spoken is always outside of the home/base/canon. Its battlefield is the border area between transgression and acceptance. If we accept, that is, integrate, the outside work into the home of the canon, we violate the authenticity of the genre. Yet, if we do not integrate such genres, we are forced to continue policing the canon with the most conservative policies. The implications of dealing with this at first harmless genre thereby become paradigmatic for the situation of the intellectual in today's institution.

The genre of the testimonio seemed at first to cling steadfastly to representationality and to be outside canonized literature—a nomadic and homeless genre with the hope for solidarity and community not only in Latin America. It is the homelessness of an unplaceable genre between disciplines (e.g., literature and anthropology), on the verge of being autobiography without being autobiography, authored without having an author. It is the genre that reflected homelessness and poverty and suddenly found an institutional home in the expanded canon. The genre of the oppressed, of the migrating and impoverished Indian in Guatemala, turned into (un)comfortable reading material for those in centers of higher learning. In other words, it changed from product to commodity.[8] But it did not do so because of its content alone, but rather for its perhaps too easy assimilation into mainstream discourse. When counterdiscourse is co-opted by mainstream discourse, new problems arise. These problems urgently require to be addressed.

Where do we go from here? If, as indeed it can be shown with ease, institutionalized literary discourse fights for expansion of the canon (correctly, we might add, but only to a certain degree) without being fully aware of the implications that canonization entails (such as merely creating new can[n]on fodder), where do we go if we still hope to regain use-value for literature rather than the generic exchange-value of increasing commodification? The answer must be a continuous search for ways of subverting the history of mere canonization reform. In other words, we must look for new ways of understanding this process of co-optation, unless we are satisfied with previous avant-garde methods of strange-making (Shklovsky's *ostranenija*). One way to do this certainly is to constantly historicize the process of canon expansion and integration, restoring to the work that has become a harmless masterpiece a harmful allegorical quality. And we must continuously find ways to render nomadic discourses that are homebound; we must keep them nomadic; we must not allow their return home; we must leave them as "unheimlich" and threatening.

For this necessary interpellation, we can learn from Gilles Deleuze and Félix Guattari how to turn the teaching machine into the "war machine."[9] Deleuze and Guattari are very aware of the need for nomadic erosion, of how nomadic deterritorialization is constantly reterritorialized by the state (machine) and the teaching machine. Implicit in my remarks about the subversive elements of the testimonio, which has become reterritorialized in the canon debate (canon = Institutional State Apparatus), is the expressed need for changing the paradigms of literary expectancy. If canon equals state and if the masterpieces (of literature) strengthen the state, the emphasis must be on finding the *Sprengsätze,* the dynamite of otherness that nomadic discourse can provide.

What are "we" to do in "the teaching machine," we who came from the intrinsic study of literature and moved toward a liberating discourse, from there even moved "against literature," once we became aware of the implications of what we had fought for originally (namely, the expansion of the canon, introduction of marginal discourses, interest in minority, Third World, and postcolonial literatures, feminisms and marxisms)? Has the struggle been to achieve merely another list of required readings? Voices of a new disciplinary mapping already assume with confidence that "[t]he frontiers in our profession seem to exist only to be endlessly crossed, violated, renegotiated" (Greenblatt and Gunn 1992, 7). We must monitor the system's ever increasing capability and capacity to always turn the "anti" into the "pro," counterdiscourse into discourse, the anticanonical into the requirement. Needless to say, the first thing is to stay alert, the second is to historicize rather than to interpret. We need to show in testimonial discourse specifically, as in Third World literature and minority discourse in general, how this movement from an authentic margin has been betrayed by inclusion in the Western canon, which can be considered as yet another form of colonialization.

But is this all? I propose that we learn more from this: namely, that we not develop an aesthetic methodology akin to the various avant-gardisms of modernism and most certainly not the ludic pastiche that characterizes postmodernism, but that we construct and search for the *Sprengsätze* of the nomadology Deleuze and Guattari envision. That would imply a continuously shifting emphasis on different discourses and a willingness to move from a once potentially liberating discourse to another once it becomes obvious that the integration into the institution has de-energized the former discourse. This enlarged understanding of how capital works forces those who had illusions about an all too easy redemption (from Benjamin to the present) to once again realistically assess the situation of how literary discourse functions within the state.

The increasing co-optation of everything into an irritating, bestselling pluralism of all disciplines—for example, institutionalized Cultural Studies (see Fredric Jameson as discussed by John Beverley in these pages)—is akin to reterritorializing everything that previously was deterritorialized. This process is the taming of the nomad by the sedentary, the continuous alienation of dis-alienational moments. But the margin at the center may not be the answer to the problem.

The rhizomatic thought of Deleuze and Guattari is an important instrument for the conception of the antistructured, the antisystemic, and the antihierarchical. This mode of thought is associated with the minor and with certain minority literatures (from Kafka to Ouologuem). The rhizome is the antigenealogical. Akin to a virus, it is the opposite of the organic and the arboresque (with its bifurcating roots, stem, and branches). The rhizome is the opposite of the Western binary: always in-the-middle, intermezzo, in-between-ness. In other words, it is the anticanonical. Deleuze and Guattari propose "The war machine-book against the State apparatus-book" (Deleuze and Guattari 1991, 9). The nomadology of Deleuze and Guattari has little to do with the Western picturesque images of wandering Tauri on camels in the Sahara. It is a strategy of mentally undoing that which becomes too quickly reterritorialized by institutional action. "The outside (homeless) is not another site, but rather an out-of-site that erodes and dissolves all other sites," as Constantin V. Boundas has said appropriately about Deleuze (Boundas 1993, 15). As painful as it may have been to give up the attachment to representationality (and implicitly to realism from Lukács to Brecht and beyond), the gains of this loss are potentially empowering. Concluding his *Culture and Imperialism,* Edward Said invokes Paul Virilio as well as Deleuze and Guattari, and then states: "Yet it is no exaggeration to say that liberation as an intellectual mission, born in the resistance and opposition to the confinements and ravages of imperialism, has now shifted from the settled, established, and domesticated dynamics of culture to its unhoused, decentered, and exilic energies, energies whose incarnation today is the migrant, and whose consciousness is that of the intellectual and artist in exile, the political figure between domains, between forms, between homes, and between languages" (Said 1993, 332). One way of heeding the advice by Deleuze and Guattari with regard to the consequences drawn from the reterritorialization of the testimonio in institutions of "higher learning" is to go beyond this genre, learn from the implications of the discourse that accompanied it, and find other developments that now have the potential the testimonio had years ago. This kind of search is done by Javier Sanjinés C who studies the developments in Bolivia in the post-Domitila period. His interest in the non-literary, in graffiti and popular TV programs, is strengthened by the ability to perform new readings of what was previously rejected, following the insights gained from studying the testimonio. Of all the contributors in this collection he perhaps has gone the furthest in developing new grounds for critical thought.

Most of the contributors to this collection are well known in the extensive debates on testimonio. Many of the essays included here continue a dialogue, and some of the papers respond to each other. While reprinting in part 1 of this collection a few essays of the first phase of testimonio criticism—such as those by John Beverley, George Yúdice, Barbara Harlow, Margaret Randall, Fredric Jameson, Marc Zimmerman, and Doris Sommer (albeit a significantly modified version)—I also have included new material that pushes the debate further. The change is perhaps most visible when one contrasts John Beverley's opening and foundational essay, "The Margin at the Center," with his concluding essay on "The Real Thing." The essays in part 2 reassess newer developments, but even in part 1 some cautionary notes already can be heard in the essays by Sklodowska and Sommer. Sklodowska is represented by a key essay that holds a distinctly different position within the first phase of testimonio discourse. One of the major critics unfortunately omitted in both the *Revista* and *Latin American Perspectives* collections, Sklodowska discusses Miguel Barnet's testimonio-novel from a new perspective. Doris Sommer has pursued the "secrets" so "openly" hidden in Rigoberta Menchú's discourse and now explains how minority texts "manipulate" a reader who is presumed to know better. With the help of Mechú, or due to the insights gained from struggling with the literary/ antiliterary in Menchú's testimonio, Sommer elaborates the strategic importance of "secrets" to show how positionality is announced in Third World texts. Her essay on Toni Morrison and Rigoberta Menchú in *Cultures of United States Imperialism* (1993) exemplifies another direction she has taken in this discourse. By studying the planted silences in Rigoberta Menchú's text against easy appropriations of Otherness into manageable universal categories, Sommer marks a turning point between the essays in part 1 and part 2 of this collection, and she keeps vital a discussion with the majority of testimonio critics, especially with John Beverley.

Alberto Moreiras and Gareth Williams, who obviously have learned much from Fredric Jameson, move the debate to another level while speaking to/with Beverley, Yúdice, Sommer, and each other. Their essays demonstrate clearly shifting disciplinary paradigms and contain similarities and supplementary thoughts. In a LASA (Latin American Studies Association) panel in Atlanta, in March 1994, titled "Testimonio y abyección," Moreiras summarizes the present situation: "The solidarity movement has today almost waned, but testimonio criticism has come to be an important academic activity in the context of Latin

American literature and cultural studies departments." Moreiras perceives the "radical break" between testimonio's subject and the enunciating subject of testimonio criticism "that does not bear comparison with the merely positional distance between the literary author and its paraphrastic or exegetic critic." Revising Walter Benjamin's notion of the auratic, Moreiras postulates the testimonio as postauratic, but its critical reception as auratic. This is the "abjection" he describes and the problem resulting from this situation. He can see the testimonio as an "aesthetic fix" that cannot produce solidarity but only a poetics of solidarity. Since the function of solidarity would be a break from poetics/aesthetics, the celebration of the testimonio is something highly uncanny. "In the hands of testimonio critics," Moreiras reminds us, "testimonio loses its extraliterary force, which now becomes merely the empowering mechanism for a canonized reading strategy." The discourse of Moreiras reminds us once more of Spivak's insight that the subaltern cannot speak.

The issues of subalternity and testimonio are addressed by Gareth Williams, who provides us with an analysis of the "Founding Statement" of the Latin American Subaltern Studies Group (whose members include John Beverley, Robert Carr, and Javier Sanjinés C, to name only those who have extensively addressed testimonio issues before). The Latin American Subaltern Studies Group obviously is an outgrowth of developments on the Indian subcontinent and the extensive writings by Indian critics such as Ranajit Guha, Gayatri Chakravorty Spivak, and others. Gareth Williams speaks of the need to mediate rather than dominate discourses of cultural exchange between Third World cultural production and First World institutional sites of theorization and appropriation. The subaltern, according to Williams, "either protagonizes or falls victim to the conditions of exchange that mediate both its social existence and its increasing presence in radical institutional critiques in the First World" (this volume, 226). Without criticizing the efforts of the Subaltern Studies Group, Williams reminds us of the task, which is not only of how to represent the Latin American subaltern, "but equally how to represent ourselves—our own positionality . . . within metropolitan processes of Latin American subaltern re-representation" (228). Gareth Williams tries to provide us with "a symptomatic reading of identity/solidarity–based Latinamericanism's contemporary strategies of engagement with the subaltern subject: a reexamination of academic processes of objectification and 'otherization' that addresses the specific agency of normative positioning (center-periphery thinking), of disciplinary fantasy, and of Latinamericanist enjoyment of the subaltern" (232). The icon of salvational discourse, the testimonio, in this new phase of metacritical assessment presents itself no longer as icon but rather as another fetish, a product of "disciplinary fantasy," merely another commodity. We act, Gareth Williams fear-lessly reminds us, "as if Latin American subalternity were not, in the very practice of cultural exchange, inevitably submitted to discursive commodification" (234). The former salvational genre here has become the contradictory utopian project of the metropolitan intellectual.

With such grave insights we now face a situation that hardly is pleasing. As mentioned above, I believe that Deleuze and Guattari, barely invoked in testimonio criticism, can provide us with a way out of the dilemma. Deauratization and deterritorialization should not be re-garded as something stable. They are moments in a process that changes rapidly. And any critical theory needs to be aware of this before it postulates another aesthetic fix. If we assess the situation as Robert Young recently has done in his book on hybridity, we perhaps can avoid many moments of self-doubt and utopian wrong desires. Young simply went beyond what Deleuze and Guattari stated, not thought, by pro-claiming that deterritorialization and reterritorialization are two faces of the same coin, the essence of late capital.

What, then, we must insist, has been that desire called testimonio? John Beverley interestingly cites Slavoj Žižek's observation on the Lady in medieval "courtly love poetry," who "becomes the mirror onto which the subject projects his narcissistic ideal." Similarly, the testimonio progressive critics of the first phase projected their desire for a poetics of solidarity and resistance onto the new genre. Now it clearly seems to have lost the energy to significantly alter institutional discourses. The critical discourse focusing on testimonio is shifting elsewhere. The icon has been unmasked as another fetish. But, and this cannot be empha-sized strongly enough, without the insights gained and problems faced while discussing the testimonio, we hardly would be where we are now, looking for new ways of expression that deterritorialize our disciplines and breathe new life into them. At the same time we are able to give up illusionary desires when facing reality. Deterritorialization is bound to be reterritorialized; every anti-discourse is bound to be co-opted; there always is restitution, even in subversion. But we cannot stop pointing out the reinvigorating struggle that is behind such restitution. And we have to live with the fact that the intellectual too has blinders. The task we can learn from our experience with the testimonio is a strategy of dis-closure, a new vigilance. The going beyond testimonio is also the call for the going beyond theory. Every interpretation is a falsification, every truth an error. The subaltern may not write, but the subaltern undoubtedly will act. May we learn to observe more critically even if the institutionalized bars behind which we work make the communication very difficult, almost impossible. Pointing to this possibility of the impossible, realizing what we cannot do—namely, to identify with the subaltern in a gesture of solidarity—is a worthy experience of learning. This new objectivity we can learn from Deleuze and Guattari. Robert J. C. Young has pointed out that Deleuze and Guattari (in particular their *Anti-Oedipus*) are virtually absent from discussions of postcolonial theory. By linking with Deleuze and Guattari we will see the "capitalist machine" for what it is, "the twofold movement of decoding or deterritorializing flows on the one hand, and their violent and artificial reterritorialization on the other" (cited in Young 1995, 169). Young remains suspicious even of Deleuze and Guattari's idea that "nomadism is a radically anti-capitalist strategy; nomadism is, rather, one brutal characteristic mode of capitalism itself" (Young 1995, 173). We may not like this outcome but we can hardly avoid its implications. In the end there is only "mourning," "travail du deuil" as Jacques Derrida has called it, or the famous "Trauerarbeit" of which Walter Benjamin already had spoken.

Notes

1. *La Epoca,* 29 March 1995.
2. See Carr 1992. In Europe the attachment to the Third World paradigm seems to continue less disturbed than in the English-speaking world. See, for example, the recent study in Moura 1992 and the older German study in Sareika 1980. Is it proper to ask why the dissatisfaction with the term "Third World" is so characteristic of some U.S. scholarship?
3. Throughout this introduction I have preferred to use the Spanish term *testimonio* rather than the English *testimonial literature*. In the Spanish term the potential anti-literary quality is preserved, which is lost in the oxymoronic

testimonial literature. Suffice it to say that, for example, in German one would never speak of *Zeugnisliteratur*. On the other hand, part of the objective of this essay is to demonstrate how *Zeugnis*/testimonio/witnessing has procreated (*gezeugt*) a new discourse of disciplinary self-reflexivity.

4. I use the term *Unitedstatian* in the sense developed in Kearney 1991. It obviously is drawn from the Spanish *estadounidense*.

5. It is in the essay "Reading the World: Literary Studies in the Eighties" (Spivak 1987) where Spivak speaks of "our ideological acceptance of error-as-truth."

6. On this topic see Hammond and Jablow 1970, and Pratt 1986, 1992.

7. For a brief overview of "Postcolonial Cultural Studies" see my entry under this title in Groden and Kreiswirth 1994. For one of the best analyses of the present intentional terminological confusion, see Dirlik 1994.

8. Perhaps we should remember Karl Marx's statement in the *Grundrisse*: "A man who produces an article for his own immediate use, to consume it himself, creates a product, but not a commodity" (quoted in Kamenka 1983, 396). Is not the testimonio, after it has moved as a product out of its immediate community into the Western academic discourse market, related to this development?

9. Part of Gilles Deleuze and Félix Guattari's *A Thousand Plateaus* was originally published in English under the title *Nomadology: The War-Machine*.

PART

I

John Beverley   *The Margin at the Center*

On Testimonio *(Testimonial Narrative)*

> The deformed Caliban—enslaved, robbed of his island, taught the language by Prospero—rebukes him thus: "You taught me language and my profit on it/Is, I know how to curse."
> —Roberto Fernández Retamar, *Caliban*

Do social struggles give rise to new forms of literature, or is it more a question of the adequacy of their representation in existing narrative forms such as the short story or the novel, as in, for example, Gayatri Spivak's articulations of the stories of the Bengali writer Mahasweta Devi or the debate around Fredric Jameson's notion of national allegory in Third World writing?[1] What happens when, as in the case of Western Europe since the Renaissance, there has been a complicity between the rise of "literature" as a secular institution and the development of forms of colonial and imperialist oppression against which many of these struggles are directed? Are there experiences in the world today that would be betrayed or misrepresented by the forms of literature as we know it?

Raymond Williams formulated a similar question in relation to British working-class writing:

> Very few if any of us could write at all if certain forms were not available. And then we may be lucky, we may find forms which correspond to our experience. But take the case of the nineteenth-century working-class writers, who wanted to write about their working lives. The most popular form was the novel, but though they had marvelous material that could go into the novel very few of them managed to write good or any novels. Instead they wrote marvelous autobiographies. Why? Because the form coming down through the religious tradition was of a witness confessing the story of his life, or there was the defence speech at a trial when a man tells the judge who he is and what he had done, or of course other kinds of speech. These oral forms were more accessible

forms centered on "I," on the single person. . . . The novel with its quite different narrative forms was virtually impenetrable to working-class writers for three or four generations, and there are still many problems in using the received forms for what is, in the end, very different material. Indeed the forms of working-class consciousness are bound to be different from the literary forms of another class, and it is a long struggle to find new and adequate forms. (Williams 1980, 25)

Let me set the frame of the discussion a bit differently than Williams does. In the period of what Marx describes as the primitive accumulation in Western Europe—say 1400 to 1650—which is also the age of the formation of the great colonial empires, there appears or reappears, under the impetus of humanism, a series of literary forms such as the essay, the short story of *novela ejemplar,* the picaresque novel, the various kinds of Petrarchan lyric including the sonnet, the autobiography, and the secular theater. These forms, as ideological practices, are also a *means* of these economic developments (in the sense that they contribute to the creation of the subject form of "European Man"). By the same token, then, we should expect an age such as our own—also one of transition or the potential for transition from one mode or production to another—to experience the emergence of new forms of cultural and literary expression that embody, in more or less thematically explicit and formally articulated ways, the social forces contending for power in the world today. I have in mind here, by analogy to the role of the bourgeoisie in the transition from feudalism to capitalism, not only the struggle of working people everywhere against exploitation, but also in contingent ways movements of ethnic or national liberation, the women's liberation movement, poor and oppressed peoples' organizations of all types, the gay rights movement, the peace movement, ecological activism, and the like. One of these new forms in embryo, I will argue, is the kind of narrative text that in Latin American Spanish has come to be called *testimonio*.

By *testimonio* I mean a novel or novella-length narrative in book or pamphlet (that is, printed as opposed to acoustic) form, told in the first person by a narrator who is also the real protagonist or witness of the events he or she recounts, and whose unit of narration is usually a "life" or a significant life experience. Testimonio may include, but is not subsumed under, any of the following textual categories, some of which are conventionally considered literature, others not: autobiography, autobiographical novel, oral history, memoir, confession, diary, interview, eyewitness report, life history, *novela-testimonio,* nonfiction novel, or "factographic literature." I will deal in particular with the distinctions between testimonio, life history, autobiography, and the all-encompassing term "documentary fiction."[2] However, because testimonio is by nature a protean and demotic form not yet subject to legislation by a normative literary establishment, any attempt to specify a generic definition for it, as I do here, should be considered at best provisional, at worst repressive.

As Williams suggests, testimonio-like texts have existed for a long time at the margin of literature, representing in particular those subjects—the child, the "native," the woman, the insane, the criminal, the proletarian—excluded from authorized representation when it was a question of speaking and writing for themselves. But for practical purposes we can say that testimonio coalesces as a new narrative genre in the 1960s and further develops in close relation to the movements for national liberation and the generalized cultural radicalism of that decade. Testimonio is implicitly or explicitly a component of what Barbara Harlow has called a "resistance literature." In Latin America, where testimonio has enjoyed an especially rich development, it was sanctioned as a genre or mode by two related developments: the 1970 decision of Cuba's Casa de las Américas to begin awarding a prize in this category in their annual literary contest, and the reception in the late 1960s of Truman Capote's *In Cold Blood* (1965) and Miguel Barnet's *Autobiography of a Runaway Slave (Biografía de un cimarrón)* (1966).[3]

But the roots of testimonio go back to the importance in previous Latin American literature of a series of nonfictional narrative texts such as the colonial *crónicas,* the *costumbrista* essay (*Facundo, Os sertoes*), the war diaries (*diarios de campaña*) of, for example, Bolivar or Martí, or the Romantic biography, a key genre of Latin American liberalism. This tradition combined with the wide popularity of the sort of anthropological or sociological life history composed out of tape-recorded narratives developed by academic social scientists such as Oscar Lewis or Ricardo Pozas in the 1950s.[4] Testimonio also drew on—in my opinion much more crucially—the sort of direct-participant account, usually presented without any literary or academic aspirations whatever (although often with political ones), represented by a book such as Che Guevara's *Reminiscences of the Cuban Revolutionary War* (1959), one of the defining texts of 1960s leftist sensibility throughout the Americas. The success of Che's account (with its corresponding manual, *Guerrilla Warfare*) inspired in Cuba a series of direct-participant testimonios by combatants in the 26 of July Movement and later in the campaigns against the counterrevolutionary bands in the Escambray mountains and at the Bay of Pigs. In a related way (in some cases directly), there began to emerge throughout the Third World, and in very close connection to the spread of armed struggle movements and the Vietnam War, a literature of personal witness and involvement designed to make the cause of these movements known to the outside world, to attract recruits, to reflect on successes or failures of the struggle, and so on.[5]

The word *testimonio* translates literally as testimony, as in the act of testifying or bearing witness in a legal or religious sense. That connotation is important because it distinguishes testimonio from simply recorded participant narrative, as in the case of "oral history." In oral history it is the intentionality of the *recorder*—usually a social scientist—that is dominant, and the resulting text is in some sense "data." In testimonio, by contrast, it is the intentionality of the *narrator* that is paramount. The situation of narration in testimonio has to involve an urgency to communicate, a problem of repression, poverty, subalternity, imprisonment, struggle for survival, and so on, implicated in the act of narration itself. The position of the reader of testimonio is akin to that of a jury member in a courtroom. Unlike the novel, testimonio promises by definition to be primarily concerned with sincerity rather than literariness. This relates testimonio to the generic 1960s ideology and practice of "speaking betterness," to use the term popularized in the Chinese Cultural Revolution, evident for example in the "consciousness raising" sessions of the women's liberation movement; Fanon's theory of decolonization; the pedagogy of Paolo Freire (one of the richest sources of testimonial material has been the interaction of intellectuals, peasants, and working people in literacy campaigns); Laingian, and in a very different way Lacanian, psychotherapies. Testimonio, in other words, is an instance of the New Left and feminist slogan that "the personal is the political."[6]

Because in many cases the narrator is someone who is either functionally illiterate or, if literate, not a professional writer, the production of a testimonio generally involves tape-recording and then transcription and editing of an oral account by an interlocutor who is an intellectual, often a journalist or a writer. (To use the Russian formalist term, testimonio is a sort of *skaz,* a literary simulacrum of oral narrative.) The nature of the intervention of this gathering and editing function is one of the more hotly debated theoretical points in the discussion of the genre, and I will come back to it. What needs to be noted here is that the assumed lack of writing ability or skill on the part of the narrator of the testimonio, even in those cases where it is written instead of narrated orally, also contributes to the "truth-effect" the form generates.

The situation of narration in the testimonio suggests an affinity with the picaresque novel, particularly with that sense of the picaresque that sees the hero's act of telling his or her life as yet another picaresque act. But testimonio, even where it approximates in content a kind of neo-picaresque, as it does quite often, is a basically different narrative mode. It is not, to begin with, fiction. We are meant to experience both the speaker and the situations and events recounted as real. The "legal" connotation implicit in its convention implies a pledge of honesty on the part of the narrator, which the listener/reader is bound to respect.[7]

Moreover, testimonio is not so much concerned with the life of a "problematic hero"—the term Lukács used to describe the nature of the hero of the bourgeois novel—as with a problematic collective social situation that the narrator lives with or alongside others. The situation of the narrator in testimonio is one that must be representative of a social class or group; in the picaresque novel, by contrast, a collective social predicament such as unemployment and marginalization is experienced and narrated as a personal destiny. The "I" that speaks to us in the picaresque or first-person novel is in general precisely the mark of a difference or antagonism with the community, in the picaresque the *Ichform* (Jauss's term; see Jauss 1959) of the self-made man: hence the picaresque's cynicism about human nature, its rendering of lower-class types as comic, as opposed to the egalitarian reader-character relation implied by both the novel and testimonio. The narrator in testimonio, on the other hand, speaks for, or in the name of, a community or group, approximating in this way the symbolic function of the epic hero, without at the same time assuming his hierarchical and patriarchal status. René Jara speaks of an "epicidad cotidiana," an everyday epicality, in testimonio (Jara and Spadaccini 1989, 2). Another way of putting this would be to define testimonio as a nonfictional, popular-democratic form of epic narrative.

By way of example, here is the opening of *I, Rigoberta Menchú,* a well-known testimonio by a Guatemalan Indian woman:

My name is Rigoberta Menchú. I'm 23 years old. This is my testimony. I didn't learn it from a book and I didn't learn it alone. I'd like to stress that it's not only my life, it's also the testimony of my people. It's hard for me to remember everything that's happened to me in my life since there have been many bad times but, yes, moments of joy as well. The important thing is that what has happened to me has happened to many other people also: My story is the story of all poor Guatemalans. My personal experience is the reality of a whole people. (Menchú 1984, 1)

Rigoberta Menchú was and is an activist on behalf of her community, the Quiché-speaking Indians of the western highlands of Guatemala, so this statement of principles is perhaps a little more explicit than is usual in a testimonio. But the metonymic function of the narrative voice it declares is latent in the form, is part of its narrative convention, even in those cases when the narrator is, for example, a drug addict or criminal. Testimonio is a fundamentally democratic and egalitarian form of narrative in the sense that it implies that *any* life so narrated can have a kind of representational value. Each individual testimonio evokes an absent polyphony of other voices, other possible lives and experiences. Thus, one common formal variation on the classic first-person singular testimonio is the polyphonic testimonio made up of accounts by different participants in the same event.

What testimonio does have in common with the picaresque and with autobiography, however, is the powerful textual affirmation of the speaking subject itself. This should be evident in the passage from *I, Rigoberta Menchú* just quoted. The dominant formal aspect of the testimonio is the voice that speaks to the reader in the form of an "I" that demands to be recognized, that wants or needs to stake a claim on our attention. This presence of the voice, which we are meant to experience as the voice of a real rather than a fictional person, is the mark of a desire not to be silenced or defeated, to impose oneself on an institution of power like literature from the position of the excluded or the marginal. Jameson has spoken of the way in which testimonio produces a "new anonymity," a form of selfhood distinct from the "overripe subjectivity" of the modernist Bildungsroman.[8] But this way of thinking about testimonio runs the risk of conceding to the subjects of testimonio only the "facelessness" that is already theirs in the dominant culture. One should note rather the insistence on and affirmation of the individual subject evident in titles such as *I, Rigoberta Menchú* (even more strongly in the Spanish: *Me llamo Rigoberta Menchú y así me nació la conciencia*), *I'm a Juvenile Delinquent* (*Soy un delincuente*), *Let Me Speak! Testimony of Domitila, A Woman of the Bolivian Mines* (*Si me permiten hablar*), *Doris Tijerino: Inside the Nicaraguan Revolution* ("*Somos milliones . . .* ": *La vida de Doris María*). Rather than a "decentered" subjectivity, which in the current Koreanization of the world economy is almost synonymous with cheap labor, testimonio constitutes an affirmation of the individual self *in a collective mode.*[9]

In a related way, testimonio implies a challenge to the loss of the authority of orality in the context of processes of cultural modernization that privilege literacy and literature as norms of expression. Or, alternatively, it represents the entry into literature of persons who would normally, in those societies where literature is a form of class privilege, be excluded from direct literary expression, who have had to be "represented" by professional writers. There is a great difference between having someone like Rigoberta Menchú tell the story of her people and having it told, however well, by someone like, say, the Nobel Prize–winning Guatemalan novelist Miguel Angel Asturias.[10]

Testimonio involves a sort of erasure of the function, and thus also of the textual presence, of the "author," which by contrast is so central in all major forms of bourgeois writing since the Renaissance, so much so that our very notions of literature and the literary are bound up with notions of the author, or, at least, of an authorial intention. In Miguel Barnet's words, the author has been replaced in testimonio by the function of a "compiler" (*compilador*) or "activator" (*gestante*), somewhat on the model of the film producer. There seems implicit in this situation both a challenge and an alternative to the patriarchal and elitist function the author plays in class-divided and in sexually and racially divided societies: in particular, a relief from the figure of the "great writer" or writer as cultural hero that is so much a part of the ideology of literary modernism.

The erasure of authorial presence in the testimonio, together with its nonfictional character, make possible a different kind of complicity—might we call it fraternal?—between narrator and reader than is possible in, say, the novel, which as Lukács demonstrated, obligates an ironic distancing on the part of both novelist and reader from the fate of the protagonist. Eliana Rivero, writing about *La montaña es algo más que una inmensa estepa verde,* a testimonio by the Sandinista guerrilla comandante Omar Cabezas (published in English as *Fire from the Mountain*), notes that "the act of speaking faithfully recorded on the tape, transcribed and then 'written' remains in the *testimonio* punctuated by a repeated series of interlocutive and conversational markers . . . which constantly put the reader on alert: 'True? Are you following me? OK? So . . . ' " She concludes that the testimonio is a "snail-like discourse [*discurso encaracolado*] which turns on itself and which in the process totally de-automatizes the reaction of the reader, whose complicity it invites through the medium of his or her counterpart in the text, the direct interlocutor" (Rivero 1985, 218–28).

Just as testimonio implies a new kind of relation between narrator and reader, the contradictions of sex, class, race, and age that frame the narrative's production can also reproduce themselves in the relation of the narrator to this direct interlocutor. This is especially so when, as in *I, Rigoberta Menchú,* the narrator is someone who requires an interlocutor with a different ethnic and/or class background in order first to elicit the oral account, then to give it textual form as a testimonio, and finally to see to its publication and distribution. (In cases where testimonios are more directly a part of political or social activism, for example in the use of testimonio in liberation theology–based community dialogues or as a kind of cadre literature internal to left or nationalist groups, these editorial functions are often handled directly by the party or movement in question, constituting then not only a new literary form but also new, noncommoditized forms of literary production and distribution.)

I do not want to minimize the nature of these contradictions; among other things, they represent the possibility for a depoliticized articulation of the testimonio as a sort of *costumbrismo* of the subaltern or for the smothering of a genuine popular voice by well-intentioned but repressive (Stalinist, humanist, and so on) notions of political "correctness" or pertinence. But there is another way of looking at them. It is a truism that successful revolutionary movements in the colonial and postcolonial world have generally involved a union of working-class, or to use the more inclusive term, popular, forces with a radicalized intelligentsia, drawn partly from formally educated sections of the peasantry and working class but also from the petty bourgeoisie and déclassé bourgeois or oligarchic strata that have become imbued with socialist ideas, organizational forms, culture, and so on. (Lenin was among the first to theorize this phenomenon in *What Is To Be Done?*) In this context, the relation of narrator and compiler in the production of a testimonio can function as an ideological figure or *ideologeme* for the possibility of union of a radicalized intelligentsia and the poor and working classes of a country. To put this another way, testimonio gives voice in literature to a previously "voiceless," anonymous, collective popular-democratic subject, the *pueblo* or "people," but in such a way that the intellectual or professional, usually of bourgeois or petty-bourgeois background, is interpolated as being part of, and dependent on, the "people" without at the same time losing his or her identity as an intellectual. In other words, testimonio is not a form of liberal guilt. It suggests as an appropriate ethical and political response more the possibility of solidarity than of charity.[11]

The audience for testimonio, either in the immediate national or local context or in metropolitan cultural centers, remains largely that reading public that in presocialist societies is still a partially class-limited social formation, even in the "advanced" capitalist democracies. The complicity a testimonio establishes with its readers involves their identification—by engaging their sense of ethics and justice—with a popular cause normally distant, not to say alien, from their immediate experience. Testimonio in this sense has been important in maintaining and developing the practice of international human rights and solidarity movements. It is also a way of putting on the agenda, within a given country, problems of poverty and oppression, for example in rural areas that are not normally visible in the dominant forms of representation.

The compiler for Rigoberta Menchú's testimonio, Elisabeth Burgos-Debray, was a Venezuelan social scientist living in Paris at the time she met Menchú, with all that implies about contradictions between metropolis and periphery, high culture and low culture, dominant and emergent social formations, dominant and subaltern languages. Her account of the relationship she developed with Rigoberta Menchú in the course of doing the testimonio forms the preface to the book, constituting a sort of testimonio about the production of a testimonio. One of the problems the two women encountered is that Menchú had to speak to Burgos-Debray in Spanish, the language for her of the *ladinos* or mestizos who oppressed her people, which she had just and very imperfectly learned (the conflict in Guatemala of Spanish and indigenous languages is in fact one of the themes of her narrative). In preparing the text, Burgos-Debray had to decide then what to correct and what not to correct in her recorded speech. She left in, for example, repetitions and digressions that she considered characteristic of oral narrative. On the other hand, she notes that she decided "to correct the gender mistakes which inevitably occur when someone has just learned to speak a foreign language. It would have been artificial to leave them uncorrected and it would have made Rigoberta look 'picturesque,' which is the last thing I wanted" (Menchú 1984, xx–xxi).

One could speak here, in a way familiar from the dialectic of master and slave or colonizer and colonized, of the interlocutor manipulating or exploiting the material the informant provides to suit her own cosmopolitan political, intellectual, and aesthetic predilections. K. Millet makes the following argument, for example, about the testimonio of an indigenous woman, *Los sueños de Lucinda Nahuelhual,* compiled by the Chilean feminist activist, Sonia Montecino Aguirre:

> *Los sueños de Lucinda Nahuelhual* is not a narrative about a Mapuche Indian woman, but rather it is a textualizing of Ms. Sonia Montecino Aguirre and her political sympathies. . . . From the moment of the narrative's inception, the figure of "the other," Lucinda Nahuelhual, is only that, a figure, an empty signifier, a narration constructed on the significance of Ms. Aguirre's own political agenda. . . . [T]he idea of "elevating" the Mapuche woman, Lucinda, to the status of a signifier of an urban feminist movement where power is maintained primarily within the hands of "enlightened" women from the hegemony requires that the indigenous woman accept a position of loss in order to signify meaning to her audience of "sisters." (Millet 1987, 425, 427)

Because I have not read *Los sueños,* I cannot comment on the specifics of Millet's critique. But although it is true that there are possibilities of distortion and misrepresentation involved in testimonio, the argument here seems to reject the possibility of any textual representation of an "other" as such (all signifiers are "empty" unless and until they signify something for somebody) in favor of something like a (liberal?) notion of the irreducible particularity of the individual. In a situation like that of Chile today, politically the question would seem not so much to insist on the *difference* in the social situations of the direct narrator and the interlocutor but rather on the possibility of their articulation together in a common program or front.

In the creation of the testimonial text, control of representation does not just flow one way as Millet's argument implies: someone like Rigoberta Menchú is also in a sense exploiting her interlocutor in order to have her story reach and influence an international audience, something that as an activist for her community she sees in quite utilitarian terms as a political task. Moreover, editorial power does not belong to the compiler alone. Menchú, worrying, correctly, that there are some ways in which her account could be used against herself or her people (for example, by academic specialists advising counterinsurgency programs such as the one the CIA set up in Guatemala), notes that there are certain things—her Nahuatl name, for example—she will *not* speak of: for example, "I'm still keeping my Indian identity a secret. I'm still keeping secret what I think no-one should know. Not even anthropologists or intellectuals, no matter how many books they have, can find out all our secrets" (Menchú 1984, 247). Although Burgos-Debray does the final selection and shaping of the text, the individual narrative units are wholly composed by Menchú and as such depend on her skills and intentionality as a narrator. An example of this may be found in the excruciating detail she uses (in chapters 24 and 27 of her book) to describe the torture and murder of her mother and brother by the Guatemalan army, which gives the episodes a hallucinatory and symbolic intensity different from the matter-of-fact narration one expects from testimonio. One could say this is a kind of testimonial expressionism or "magic realism."

Perhaps something like Mao's notion of "contradictions among the people" (as opposed to contradictions between "the people" as a whole and, for example, imperialism) expresses the nature of the narrator/compiler/reader relations in the testimonio, in the sense that there are deep and inescapable contradictions involved in these relations, contradictions that can only be resolved on the level of general structural change both on a national and a global level. But there is also a sense of sisterhood and mutuality in the struggle against a common system of oppression. Testimonio is not, in other words, a reenactment of the anthropological function of the colonial or subaltern "native informant," about which Gayatri Spivak (1983) among others has recently written. Hence, although one of the sources and models of the testimonio is undoubtedly the ethnographic "life history," it is not reducible to that category (nor, as I noted above, to oral history).

One fact that is evident in the passage from *I, Rigoberta Menchú* we have been discussing is that the presence of a "real" popular voice in the testimonio is in part at least an illusion. Obviously, we are dealing here, as in any discursive medium, with an effect that has been produced, in the case of a testimonio both by the direct narrator—using devices of an oral storytelling tradition—and the compiler who, according to norms of literary form and expression, makes a text out of the material. Although it is easy to deconstruct this illusion, it is also necessary to insist on its presence to understand the testimonio's peculiar aesthetic-ideological power. Elzbieta Sklodowska, developing a point about the textual nature of testimonio that can be connected with the argument made above by Millet, cautions that

it would be naive to assume a direct homology between text and history. The discourse of a witness cannot be a reflection of his or her experience, but rather a refraction determined by the vicissitudes of memory, intention, ideology. The intention and the ideology of the author-editor further superimposes the original text, creating more ambiguities, silences, and absences in the process of selecting and editing the material in a way consonant with norms of literary form. Thus, although the *testimonio* uses a series of devices to gain a sense of veracity and authenticity—among them the point of view of the first-person witness-narrator—the play between fiction and history reappears inexorably as a problem. (Sklodowska 1982, 379; my translation)

What is at stake, however, is the *particular* nature of the "reality effect" of the testimonio, not simply pointing out the difference between (any) text and reality. What is important about testimonio is that it produces if not the real then certainly a sensation of *experiencing the real* and that this has determinate effects on the reader that are different from those produced by even the most realist or "documentary" fiction. "More than an interpretation of reality," notes Jara in a useful corrective to Sklodowska's point, the testimonio is "*a trace of the real,* of that history which, as such, is inexpressible" (Jara and Vidal 1986, 2).

Sklodowska is no doubt right about the interplay between real and imaginary in testimonio. But to subsume testimonio under the category of literary fictionality is to deprive it of its power to engage the reader in the ways I have indicated here, to make of it simply another form of literature, as good as but certainly no better than and not basically different from what is already the case. This seems to me a formalist and, at least in effect, a politically liberal response to testimonio, which tolerates or encourages its incorporation into the academically sanctioned field of literature at the expense of relativizing its moral and political urgency.[12] What has to be understood, however, is precisely how *testimonio puts into question* the existing institution of literature as an ideological apparatus of alienation and domination at the same time that it constitutes itself as a new form of literature.

Having said this much, however, I now need to distinguish testimonio from (1) that central form of nonfictional first-person narrative that is autobiography and cognate forms of personal narrative such as memoirs, diaries, confessions, reminiscences, and the like; and (2) Barbara Foley's articulation of the category of "documentary fiction" in *Telling the Truth*. Autobiography first, with the proviso that some forms of "documentary fiction" Foley considers are autobiographical or pseudo-autobiographical. The dividing line is not always exact, but the following might represent the general case: even in, for example, nineteenth-century memoirs of women or ex-slaves (that is, texts where the narrator writes clearly from a position of subalternity), there is implicit an ideology of individualism in the very convention of the autobiographical form that is built on the notion of a coherent, self-evident, self-conscious, commanding subject that appropriates literature precisely as a means of "self-expression" and that in turn constructs textually for the reader the liberal imaginary of a unique, "free," autonomous ego as the natural form of being and public achievement. By contrast, as I have suggested, in testimonio the narrative "I" has the status of what linguists call a shifter—a linguistic function that can be assumed indiscriminately by anyone. Recalling Rigoberta Menchú's narrative proposition, the meaning of her testimonio lies not in its uniqueness but in its ability to stand for the experience of her community as a whole. Because the authorial function has been erased or mitigated, the relationship between authorship and forms of individual and hierarchical power in bourgeois society has also changed. Testimonio represents an affirmation of the individual subject, even of individual growth and transformation, but in connection with a group or class situation marked by marginalization, oppression, and struggle. If it loses this connection, it ceases to be testimonio and becomes autobiography, that is, an account of, and also a means of access to, middle- or upper-class status, a sort of documentary bildungsroman. If Rigoberta Menchú had become a "writer" instead of remaining as she has a member of, and an activist for, her ethnic community, her narration would have been an autobiography. By contrast, even where its subject is a person "of the left," as for example in Agnes Smedley's *Daughter of Earth,* Trotsky's *My Life,* or Neruda's *Memoirs,* autobiography and the autobiographical novel are essentially conservative modes in the sense that they imply that individual triumph over circumstances is possible in spite of "obstacles." Autobiography produces in the reader, who, generally speaking, is already either middle or upper class or expecting to be a part of those classes, the specular effect of confirming and authorizing his or (less so) her situation of relative social privilege. Testimonio, by contrast, even in the cases of testimonios from the political right, such as Armando Valladares's prison memoir *Against All Hope* or Solzhenitsyn's *Gulag Archipelago,* always signifies the need for a general social change in which the stability of the reader's world must be brought into question.[13]

I am generally sympathetic with the project Barbara Foley has staked out in *Telling the Truth.* In particular, her deconstruction of what she calls "the fact/fiction distinction" and her emphasis on the inevitable historicity of literary categories are useful for conceptualizing some aspects of the testimonio, including its peculiar truth-claim on the reader. She writes, for example, of a "mimetic contract" (that is also a historically specific form of social contract) in terms of which "any given element in a narrative . . . must be scanned and interpreted as either factual or fictive in order to be read and understood" (Foley 1986, 40). As against the claim (in, for example, speech-act theory) that fictional mimesis has no "propositional power" in relation to the real, Foley argues that "rather than retreating from the task of formulating propositions about the historical world, mimesis possesses, if anything, an intensified propositional power" (66). To wit: "[W]hen the fictional world reconcretizes actual processes and structures in the historical world, it attempts to persuade the reader of the legitimacy of the author's specific conceptions of these processes and structures" (85). It follows that "the knowledge that fiction conveys is the knowledge of the contradictory and subjective appropriation of an objective social reality" (96), and that fictional modes of all sorts "are equally autotelic (configurational) and referential (analogous) at the same time. All are, moreover, equally assertive" (72).[14]

What Foley is *not* doing in *Telling the Truth,* however, is producing an account of testimonial narrative as such. Although some of the texts she discusses in her chapter on Afro-American narrative are testimonios in the sense outlined here, Foley herself prefers to deal with them through the somewhat different category of the documentary novel. But this is to make of testimonio one of the mutations the novel has undergone in the course of its (European) evolution from the Renaissance on, whereas I have wanted to suggest here that it implies a radical break (as in the structuralist notion of *coupure*) with the novel and with literary fictionality as such. In other words, *the testimonio is not a form of the novel.* It cannot be adequately theorized therefore by the sort of argument Foley develops, which is, on the other hand, very useful for understanding certain forms of fiction and fictionalized autobiography that depend on the semiotic intensification of a reality-effect.[15]

If the novel is a closed and private form in the sense that both the story and the subject end with the end of the text, defining that auto-referential self-sufficiency that is the basis of formalist reading practices, the testimonio exhibits by contrast what Jara calls a "public intimacy" in which the distinction between public and private spheres of life essential in all forms of bourgeois culture and law is transgressed. The narrator in testimonio is a real person who continues living and acting in a real social history that also continues. Testimonio can never in this sense create the illusion of that textual "in-itselfness" that has been the basis of literary formalism, nor can it be adequately analyzed in these terms. It is, to use Umberto Eco's slogan, an "open work" that implies the importance and power of literature as a form of social action but also its radical insufficiency.

In principle, testimonio appears therefore as an extraliterary or even antiliterary form of discourse. That, paradoxically, is precisely the basis of both its aesthetic and political appeal. As Foley suggests, in literary history the intensification of a narrative or representational reality-effect is generally associated with the contestation of the dominant system and its forms of cultural idealization and legitimation. This was certainly the case of the picaresque novel and *Don Quijote* in relation to the novels of chivalry in the Spanish Renaissance. What happens, however, when something like testimonio is appropriated by "literature"?

Does it involve a neutralization of its peculiar aesthetic effect, which depends, as we have seen, precisely on its status outside accepted literary forms and norms? In relation to these questions and the discussion of Foley above, I need finally to distinguish *testimonio* from testimonial *novel*. Miguel Barnet called his *Autobiography of a Runaway Slave* a "testimonial novel" (*novela-testimonio*), even though the story was nonfictional. He wanted to emphasize how the material of an ethnographic "life history" could be made into a literary form. But I would rather reserve the term *testimonial novel* (or Capote's "nonfiction novel") for those narrative texts where an "author" in the conventional sense has either invented a testimonio-like story or, as in the case of *In Cold Blood* or *Woman at Point Zero* mentioned above (or Barnet's own later work, such as *Canción de Rachel*), extensively reworked, with explicitly literary goals (greater figurative density, tighter narrative form, elimination of digressions and interruptions, and so on), a testimonial account that is no longer present as such except in its simulacrum. If the picaresque novel were the pseudoautobiography of the lower-class individual (inverting thus a "learned" humanist form into a pseudopopular one), we might observe in recent literature: (1) novels that are in fact pseudo-testimonios, inverting a form that grows out of subaltern experience into one that is middlebrow (an example might be the Mexican novel *El vampiro de la Colonia Roma,* which purports to be the testimonio of a homosexual prostitute); (2) a growing concern on the part of contemporary novelists to produce something like a testimonial "voice" in their fiction, with variable political intentions (for example, Mario Vargas Llosa's *The Story of Mayta* on the right, Manlio Argueta's *One Day of Life* on the left); and (3) a series of ambiguous forms located between the novel and testimonio, such as *Woman at Point Zero* or the very intriguing novel/memoir of the Cultural Revolution, *A Cadre School Life,* which is a testimonio rendered in the mold of a narrative genre of classical Chinese literature.

But if the testimonio comes into being necessarily at the margin of the historically given institution of literature, it is also clear that it is becoming a new postfictional form of literature with significant cultural and political repercussions. To return to our starting point: if the novel had a special relationship with humanism and the rise of the European bourgeoisie, testimonio is by contrast a new form of narrative literature in which we can at the same time witness and be a part of the emerging culture of an international proletarian/popular-democratic subject in its period of ascendancy. But it would be in the spirit of testimonio itself to end on a more skeptical note: literature, even where it is infused with a popular-democratic form and content, as in the case of testimonio, is not itself a popular-democratic cultural form, and (pace Gramsci) it is an open question as to whether it can ever be. How much of a favor do we do testimonio by positing, as here, that it has become a new form of literature or by making it an alternative reading to the canon (one track of the new Stanford civilization requirement now includes *I, Rigoberta Menchú*)? Perhaps such moves preempt or occlude a vision of an emergent popular-democratic culture that is no longer based on the institutions of humanism and literature.

Notes

1. See Gayatri Spivak's *In Other Worlds* (1987), Fredric Jameson's "Third World Literature" (1986), and Aijaz Ahmad's article and Jameson's rejoinder in *Social Text* (1987).
2. I will touch on Barbara Foley's work later. Testimonio is difficult to classify according to standard bibliographic categories. To what section of a library or a bookstore does a testimonio belong? Under whose name is it to be listed in a card catalog or database? How should it be reviewed: as fiction or non-fiction?
3. The definition of *testimonio* in the rules of the Casa de las Américas contest is as follows: "Testimonies must document some aspect of Latin American or Caribbean reality from a direct source. A direct source is understood as knowledge of the facts by the author or his or her compilation of narratives or evidence obtained from the individuals involved or qualified witnesses. In both cases reliable documentation, written or graphic, is indispensable. The form is at the author's discretion, but literary quality is also indispensable." On the Latin American reception of *In Cold Blood,* see Ariel Dorfman (1966).
4. Pozas and Lewis were actually reviving a form that had been initiated in the 1930s by University of Chicago anthropologists and had then fallen into disuse during the period of academic McCarthyism of the Cold War.
5. Thus, there are Palestinian, Angolan, Vietnamese, Irish, Brazilian, South African, Argentinian, Nicaraguan, and other such testimonial literatures. On guerrilla testimonio, see Barbara Harlow (1987) and Juan Duchesne (1986).
6. One of the most important protagonists of the testimonio was the North American socialist-feminist poet Margaret Randall, who played a major role in

developing the form in Cuba in the 1970s and then in Nicaragua after 1979 where she conducted a series of workshops to train people to collect their own experience and begin building a popular history written by themselves. She is the author of a handbook on how to make a testimonio: *Testimonios: A Guide to Oral History* (1985b).

7.   The reception of testimonio thus has something to do with a revulsion for fiction and the fictive as such, with its "postmodern" estrangement. Testimonio, if you want to look at it that way (and you are certainly not obliged to), could be seen as a form of postmodern narrative closely related to established U.S. forms like drug or gay narratives, of which William Burroughs's *Junky* is perhaps the classic case, or black, Chicano, and Puerto Rican autobiography (*The Autobiography of Malcolm X, Down These Mean Streets*), John Rechy's work, and so on. But, as George Yúdice has argued, "first world postmodernism feeds off of and is at the expense of an occluded third world warrant" in any case (Yúdice 1985b).

8.   In a lecture at the University of Pittsburgh, March 1987. See also the idea he advances in a subsequent interview of a postbourgeois *"collective subject, decentered but not schizophrenic . . .* which emerges in certain forms of storytelling that can be found in third-world literature, in testimonial literature, in gossip and rumors, and in things of this kind. It is storytelling that is neither personal in the modernist sense, nor depersonalized in the pathological sense of the schizophrenic text" (quoted in Stephanson 1987, 45).

9.   The most dramatic instance of this affirmation of the self I know of occurs in the Egyptian testimonial novel *Woman at Point Zero* where the narrator, Firdaus, is a young prostitute about to be executed for murdering her pimp. Her interlocutor, the Egyptian feminist writer, Nawal el Sa'adawi, was at the time working in the prison as a psychiatrist. Firdaus begins by addressing this person, who represents, albeit in benevolent form, the repressive power of both the state and the institution of literature, as follows: "Let me speak! Do not interrupt me! I have no time to listen to you. They are coming to take me at six o'clock this evening" (el Sa'adawi 1983, 11). Barbara Harlow notes that al-Saadawi was herself imprisoned by the Sadat regime for feminist activities some years later and wrote an account of her experience in *Memoirs from the Women's Prison* (Harlow 1987, 139–40).

10.   A kind of anti-testimonio, for example, is Richard Rodríguez's *Hunger of Memory,* which is precisely a bildungsroman of the access to English-language literacy—and thence to middle-class status—by a Chicano from a working-class background. Because one of its themes is opposition to official bilingualism, it has become a popular text for neoconservative initiatives in education. Paradoxically it is also used frequently in English writing classes by persons who would otherwise probably not identify with neoconservatism to indoctrinate students into the ideology of "good writing."

11. Testimonio in this sense is uniquely situated to represent the components of what Sandinista theoreticians Roger Burbach and Orlando Nuñéz have called the "Third Force" in their potential linkage with working-class issues and movements: that is, middle-class intellectuals and sections of the petty bourgeoisie, marginalized social sectors, and what have come to be known as "new social movements" (religious *communidades de base,* feminist groups, ecology organizations, human rights groups, and so on). See especially Burbach and Nuñéz 1987, 63–79.

12. This seems in particular the outcome of Roberto González Echevarría's influential discussion of Barnet's *Autobiography of a Runaway Slave.*

13. I have perhaps overstated here the distinction between testimonio and autobiography. I am aware, for example, of the existence in certain forms of women's writing, and in U.S. black, Latino, and gay literature, of something that might be called "popular" autobiography, somewhere between autobiography—as I characterize it here—and testimonio as such. Moreover, in Latin American writing autobiography often has a direct political resonance. (See Sylvia Molloy 1991). This is a good place to note that testimonio offers one kind of answer to the problem of women's access to literature. Sidonie Smith, in a paper on women's autobiographies at the Stanford conference on autobiography, argued that every woman who writes finally interrogates the ideology of gender that lies behind the engendering of self in forms such as the novel or autobiography. She alludes to the notion that the institution of literature itself is phallocentric. On the other hand, repressing the desire for power in order to avoid complicity with domination is a form of female self-effacement sanctioned by the patriarchy. How do we find forms of expression that break out of this double bind? Many of the best known testimonios are in the voices of women, yet because of the narrative situation we have identified, testimonio does not produce textually an essentialized "woman's experience." It is a (self-conscious) instance of what Gayatri Spivak has advocated as "tactical essentialism" in feminist political practice.

14. I am indebted for this summary to Eric Heyne's review (1987).

15. Foley claims that the documentary novel "locates itself near the border between factual discourse and fictive discourse, *but does not propose an eradication of that border.* Rather, it purports to represent reality by means of agreed-upon conceptions of fictionality, while grafting onto its fictive pact some kind of additional claim to empirical validation" (Foley 1986, 25; italics mine).

George Yúdice Testimonio and

Postmodernism

Whom Does Testimonial Writing Represent?

More than any other form of writing in Latin America, the *testimonio* has contributed to the demise of the traditional role of the intellectual/artist as spokesperson for the "voiceless." As some major writers—most notably Octavio Paz and Mario Vargas Llosa—increasingly take neoconservative positions and as the subordinated and oppressed feel more enabled to opt to speak for themselves in the wake of the new social movements, Liberation Theology, and other consciousness-raising grassroots movements, there is less of a social and cultural imperative for concerned writers to heroically assume the grievances and demands of the oppressed, as in Pablo Neruda's *Alturas de Macchu Picchu* (1946): "From across the earth bring together / all the silenced scattered lips / and from the depths speak to me . . . / Speak through my words and my blood" (38–39).

In contrast, the *testimonialista* gives his or her personal testimony "directly," addressing a specific interlocutor. As in the works of Elvia Alvarado (1987), Rigoberta Menchú (1983), and Domitila Barrios de Chungara (1977), that personal story is a shared one with the community to which the testimonialista belongs. The speaker does not speak for or represent a community but rather performs an act of identity-formation that is simultaneously personal and collective. For example, Domitila Barrios (1977, 13) tells Moema Viezzer, her interlocutor: "I don't want the story I am about to tell to be interpreted as a personal matter. Because I think that my life is related to my people. What has happened to me may have happened to hundreds of others in my country. . . . That's why I say that I do not want to simply tell a personal story, I want to speak of my people. I want to bear witness to all the experiences that we have gained through so many years of struggle in Bolivia and thus contribute a tiny grain of sand to the hope that our experience will contribute in some way to the new generation."

Testimonial writing is animated by a popular perspective that contrasts markedly with Georg Lukács's idea that the professional writer who attempts to represent the "whole people"—he has the historical novelist Walter Scott in mind—is the best spokesperson for the popular. The true "popular portrayer of history" is not a person of the people but rather a mediator who "bring[s] to life those objective poetic principles which really underlie the poetry of popular life and history" (Lukács 1983, 56). Although it is true that the French Revolution made history a "mass" experience—with the creation, for example, of mass armies— in the period Lukács writes about, neither the novelists nor Lukács could conceive of the popular elements themselves as the enunciators of history. No doubt, such a rejection stems from the acceptance of a Hegelian conception of the "Historical Spirit," which, despite Lukács's marxism, must rise to the highest consciousness or, in other words, rise "above" the material vulgarity of the "presentation of history from 'below'" (Lukács 1983, 283).

The position adopted by Neruda in the passage quoted above is akin to the one Lukács attributes to the historical novelist: "mediator between 'below' and 'above,' between the immediacy of reaction to events and the highest possible consciousness" (1983, 288). This mediator is the "world-historical individual" who guides the historical novel through its representation of "the complex, capillary factors of development of the whole society" such that "the significant features of the 'world-historical individual' not only grow organically out of this development, but at the same time explain it, give it consciousness and raise it to a higher level" (Lukács 1983, 127).

In effect, what Lukács defines as the "world-historical individual" is the novelistic device that is also employed by poets like Neruda by means of which the gap—the Hegelian alienation—between consciousness and materiality, conceived here as the popular, is bridged, thus providing the grounds for a universal disalienation and emancipation. In the case of testimonial writing, on the other hand, no claims are made for such a universal emancipation. Testimonial writing, in this respect, coincides with one of the fundamental tenets of postmodernity: the rejection of what Jean-François Lyotard (1984) calls grand or master narratives, which function to legitimize "political or historical tele-ologies, . . . or the great 'actors' and 'subjects' of history—the nation-state, the proletariat, the party, the West, etc." (according to Jameson 1984b, xii).

The rejection of the master narratives thus implies a different sub-ject of discourse, one that does not conceive of itself as universal and as searching for universal truth but, rather, as seeking emancipation and survival within specific and local circumstances. Following the studies of Barnet (1969, 1981), Fornet (1977), González Echevarría (1980), and Casas (1981), testimonial writing may be defined as an authentic narrative, told by a witness who is moved to narrate by the urgency of a situation (e.g., war, oppression, revolution, etc.). Emphasizing popular, oral discourse, the witness portrays his or her own experience as an agent (rather than a representative) of a collective memory and identity. Truth is summoned in the cause of denouncing a present situation of exploita-tion and oppression or in exorcising and setting aright official history.

Testimonial writing is quite heterogeneous; critics—for example, Foster (1984) and the essayists in Jara and Vidal (1986)—have included works as diverse as Augusto Roa Bastos's *Yo el Supremo,* the journalistic books of Eduardo Galeano, personal accounts of social struggle or war like those of Domitila Barrios (1977) and Omar Cabezas (1983), and so on. My argument regarding testimonio and its challenge to master discourse relies on those texts that are written as collaborative dialogues between activists engaged in a struggle and politically committed or empathetic transcribers/editors. The reason for this is that many texts do not really abandon the forms of subjectivity inscribed in certain master discourses.

Cabezas's *La montaña es algo más que una inmensa estepa verde,* for example, easily accommodates the subjective structures provided by patriarchy. Cabezas's "new man," which some critics—for example, Du-chesne (1986)—describe as a "new subject," repeats patriarchal priv-ilege in the guise of a Sandinista uniform. The epic hero of the narrative is empowered and legitimized to embody the authority to govern by means of a series of paternal figures who relay that authority from the original revolutionary, Augusto Sandino. "When don Leandro speaks to me in that way . . . giving me his sons and speaking to me of Sandino and the Sandinista struggle I suddenly feel don Leandro as a father. I realize that, in reality, he is the father, that don Bacho and don Leandro are the fathers of the fatherland. Never before have I felt more a son of Sandinismo . . . I found my history through him, my tradition, the essence of Nicaragua, my genesis, my forefathers" (Cabezas 1983, 252–53).

Similarly, the testimonios collected and anthologized around the events of the Mariel exodus attempt to recreate the "epic" heroism of the "people" during the invasion of Girón (the Bay of Pigs) almost two decades before. If the earliest manifestations of Cuban popular testimonio tended to enshrine Fidel, Ché, and others in a revolutionary pantheon, the texts dating from Girón have served the function of constituting a national identity by rallying against the external enemy and its internal accomplices. Rather than aggrandized heroes, we see everyday people—militiamen, jet pilots, soldiers, and civilians, among others—expressing their experiences at Girón. They constitute a "people" in the populist sense of the word.

This constitution of the "people" by rallying against a common enemy has even found residence in a museum, a "testimonial museum." The *marielitos* who first gathered at the Peruvian Embassy in Miramar can now be seen in floor-to-ceiling-size photographs. They are described as *escoria,* or "scum." We read that this scum is composed of "homosexuals, lesbians, pederasts, . . . *santeros,* dope fiends and prostitutes, counterrevolutionary ex-cons, Jehovah's Witnesses, etc." (Hernández Pérez 1983, 8). Reflecting on his experience, the writer of this testimonio makes clear the interpellative mission of the genre: to recuperate "the potentialities of the people" by reliving the 1960s, years in which the "people" constituted themselves in the process of their own defense. After going through his experience, Secret Agent César offers the ideological satisfaction to his readers: "ideologically I feel more fulfilled and more committed to my all in order to defend this people to whom I have the honor to belong" (Hernández Pérez 1983, 20).

But rather than a testimonial process generated from the bottom up by the people themselves, there seems to be no doubt that *La leyenda de lo cotidiano,* in which this and other similar testimonios are found, is an attempt on the part of the state to consolidate a national subject by means of the testimonial process. Likewise, *Dice la paloma,* whose editors include Mirta Aguirre, Angel Augier, Roberto Fernández Retamar, and Onelio Jorge Cardoso, brings together a series of military testimonios as a paean to their "heroic epic."

In contrast, those testimonios that emerge from the consciousness-raising experiences of the Christian Base Community movement, for example, undermine rather than reconsolidate patriarchal and paternalistic master narratives. Even Catholicism and Marxism deconstruct each other's overriding legitimacy and take a subordinate position within the struggle for survival as just two among several other "popular weapons" of self-defense (Menchú 1983, 270).

Literary critics—for example, González Echevarría (1980)—have been quick to discard the testimonialista's claim to authenticity, based on the age-old literary premise that narrative voice is always a persona that does not coincide with the individual narrating. I do not claim that testimonial writing suffers no problems of referentiality, but I do point out that it is not so much a representation of a referent (say, the "people" or Lukács's "typical" man) but a practice involved in the construction of such an entity. That is, testimonial writing is first and foremost an act, a tactic by means of which people engage in the process of self-constitution and survival. It is a way of using narrative discourse whose function is not solely pragmatic (that is, for the purposes of self-defense and survival) but just as significantly aesthetic (insofar as the subjects of the testimonial discourse rework their identity through the aesthetic), though that aesthetic does not usually correspond to the definitions of the literary as legitimized by dominant educational, publishing, and professional institutions.

It could be said, of course, that we are not comparing equivalent types of discourse, that the work of the historical novelist or the heroic poet is literary and that of the testimonialista is something else, a form of oral history, "new" journalism, or political activism. In fact, Miguel Barnet, the most important writer and theorist of the testimonial in its early period (1960s and 1970s), eventually rejected the label *testimonio* for his own work because he did not want it to be identified with "nonliterary" forms of writing (see Yúdice 1986, x). In other words, he continues to subscribe to the premises by means of which the above mentioned institutions legitimize themselves.

The ambiguity and confusion over the status of the testimonial is very significant because it indicates that there is a shift taking place in the very notion of the literary. Not only are nonprofessionals—testimonialistas—becoming writers (and here we should include the participants in the Nicaraguan popular poetry workshops—for example,

Pring-Mill 1983), concomitant institutional changes also have taken place that affect conditions of publication and distribution. Political organizations, ranging from human rights groups to solidarity networks and sympathizing alternative publishers and media producers, in and outside of Latin America, have promoted these texts in ways that blur the boundaries between social science, political activism, and literature. In the United States, for example, testimonial writing is taught in literature as well as anthropology, sociology, and political science courses, thus requiring new methodologies of interpretation and analysis that fall outside the purview of prevailing disciplinary classifications.

Testimonial Writing and the Challenge to Literature

Testimonial writing thus fits into and contributes to the ongoing challenge to the literary, which is no longer understood simply as an autonomous cultural activity conditioned by social and political factors. While the generic norms to which any text conforms are still regarded as "relatively autonomous"—that is, they hold across diverse contexts—they are now also understood to have a social and political function, which ranges from the reproduction of hegemony to pragmatic intervention in the organization of society.

The modern institution of literature traditionally has functioned as a gatekeeper, permitting certain classes of individuals to establish standards of taste within the public sphere and excluding others. This explains why contestatory writers such as Neruda or Gabriel García Márquez, trained within the institution, have had no trouble performing in the literary sphere and why the expression of those deemed nonliterary—by the standards of that same institution—has been assigned to the genres of other disciplines—oral history, ethnography, and so on—or to substandard discursive forms—folktale, gossip, legend, and so on.

The shift marked by the growing importance of the testimonial does not mean, however, that the "people" have taken expression into their hands. Who writes, when and where and by what means, is never determined unilaterally by any one class or group, much less the individual. The particular arrangement of institutions in a given society serves to channel and constrain expression (the state-sponsored Cuban testimonios on the Mariel exodus, discussed above, provide a good example). This does not mean that only "infrastructural" factors can produce changes in this arrangement and, consequently, in the modes and means of expression. Aesthetic factors, such as those based in the ethos of given groups or communities, can also act to alter institutional authority by changing the rules of the games by which expression is monitored.

I use the concept *aesthetic* independently of the particular acceptation given to it in bourgeois modernity, that is, the freedom inherent in form, the "lawfulness without a law," which Kant (1952, 86) describes in his *Critique of Judgment* (1790). As Terry Eagleton explains:

From the depths of a benighted late feudal autocracy, a vision could be projected of a universal order of free, equal, autonomous human subjects, obeying no laws but those which they gave to themselves. This bourgeois public sphere breaks decisively with the privilege and particularism of the *ancien régime,* installing the middle class, in image if not in reality, as a truly universal subject, and compensating with the grandeur of this dream for its politically supine status. What is at stake here is nothing less than the production of an entirely new kind of human subject—one which like the work of art itself, discovers the law in the depths of its own free identity, rather than in some oppressive external power. (Eagleton 1990, 19)

The history of interpretations of the aesthetic is too long to summarize here, but it will suffice to make two important points. First, the aesthetic only rarely has been understood as completely autonomous or independent of social and political factors in Latin America. This is explained by the fact that early writers were also statesmen; in fact, the foundation of national states in the nineteenth century was paralleled and supported by foundational novels such as José Mármol's *Amalia* ([1851] 1971), José de Alencar's *O Guarani* ([1857] 1960), Alberto Blest Gana's *Martín Rivas* ([1862] 1977), and Manuel de Jesús Galván's *Enriquillo* ([1882] 1976), in which all obstacles are overcome, thus establishing a discourse of national consolidation (see Sommer 1989). As for a truly autonomous literature (that is, whose inner dynamics preclude any possibility of authentically representing "external," or worldly, circumstances), it begins to emerge with *modernismo* but is not fully theorized as such until Jorge Luis Borges's *Ficciones* (1955) and the "novel of language" of the "boom" years with such exemplary "self-referential" texts as Salvador Elizondo's *Farabeuf* (1965) and Severo Sarduy's *Cobra* (1972).

Second, the history of modern aesthetics is characterized by a countermovement that has sought to reunite art (which had been institutionally severed from life practices), aesthetics, and life. This latter tendency takes at least two forms: on the one hand, the attempt to aestheticize life, as in the avant-garde arts of the early part of the twentieth century, which continued to laud the practice of vocationally dedicated artists. This explains why even contestatory artists and writers continually reproduced the institutional constraints of the artistic and literary systems, which, by defining what the aesthetic is, determine who has access to aesthetic "capital." On the other hand, movements like testimonial writing have made an effort to recognize and valorize the aesthetics of life practices themselves. It is in this latter sense that I should like to present the importance of testimonial writing for an era—often referred to as postmodernity—in which the master discourses attaching to prevailing institutional arrangements are being dismantled.

Testimonial Writing and the Aesthetics of Hegemonic Postmodernism

Testimonial writing shares several features with what is currently called postmodernity: the rejection of master discourses or prevailing frameworks of interpreting the world and the increasing importance of the marginal. However, there are significant differences in the ways in which "hegemonic" postmodern texts and testimonial writing approach this emergent fragmentation and marginality. Even though one of the projects of certain postmodern texts is to dismantle the classics of Western tradition, their purview remains, unsurprisingly, Western.

Deconstructionists' (for example, Jacques Derrida's) attempts to demonstrate that supposed supplements (writing as supplement to speaking, culture as supplement to nature, foreplay or masturbation as supplements to procreative sex, etcetera) and marginalized elements (the savage as foil to the civilized, the female as backdrop against which models of justice and right are constructed, figurative language as necessary evil in philosophical enterprises to establish objective models for determining truth, and so on) are the condition of possibility for the constitution of prevailing frameworks of conduct, sociality, thought, explanation, and so on (see Derrida 1976, 1980). These attempts, however, do not provide the marginalized elements with their own specificity outside of hegemonic discourse; they exist as the hidden fuel with which that discourse reproduces itself.

The task of the deconstructionists has not been to vindicate or emancipate the marginalized elements but rather to detect the traces left behind as they are consumed in the projection of "natural," "rational," and "logical" states of affairs. They delight in the contradictory exposure of what their own culture attempts to conceal. In contemporary postmodern discourse, these concealed, marginalized elements are usually referred to as "alterity," "other," or "otherness." But "the other does not exist," to paraphrase Jacques Lacan's (1983, 144) notorious statement: "There is no such thing as *The* woman, where the definite article stands for the universal. There is no such thing as *The* woman since of her essence . . . she is not at all." In other words, the other has no existence except as the absence that difference establishes with respect to the subject of discourse—the *is not*: (Western) Man, the subject of hegemonic discourse, *is not* woman.

As Gayatri Spivak (1983, 174) explains, the "female element" (or more generally the "other" or marginalized element) does not signify "female person" (or "other person"). Thus not only does hegemonic discourse displace the other or marginalized element but, more importantly for the comparison and contrast of testimonial writing and "hegemonic" postmodernism, deconstruction only recuperates the other as absence, the *is not* against which the subject of discourse *is*.

One major reason why neither traditional hegemonic discourse nor postmodern discourse can "take the place of the other" is that, in the terms of one dominant perspective (French poststructuralism), they operate according to a logic of representation and displacement that posits the very definition of literature at the (dis)juncture of the two. For Michel Foucault (1977, 57), for example, the "ontology of literature" inheres in the "limiting otherness" (in this particular case, the other is identified with "death") "to which language addresses itself and against which it is poised." Because the "other" is "that absence in the interior from which the work paradoxically erects itself" (Foucault 1977, 66), it does not exist. On this view, the aesthetic is the experience of this generalized limit that takes on the guise of woman, death, monster, savage, "heart of darkness," in sum, all that is abject: "abject and abjection are my safeguards. The primers of my culture. . . . The abject is lined with the sublime" (Kristeva 1982, 2, 11).

The experience of the abject is, perhaps, hegemonic postmodernism's privileged aesthetic principle. It is the experience of the ineffable, often referred to as *jouissance*, at the limits of reality, the "violence of mourning for an 'object' that has always already been lost" (Kristeva 1982, 15). In our electronic, postindustrial order, in which "the real has been supplanted by the signs of the real" (Baudrillard 1978, 7), resulting in the waning of affect, psychic fragmentation, the displacement of anxiety as psychic warrant, the random oscillation between euphoric highs and lows, the supersession of the aesthetic of expression, the abolition of critical distance, and the eclipse of historicity (Jameson 1984a), we are no longer capable of representing ourselves, thus losing ourselves (expelling ourselves, according to Kristeva) in the hyperreal space of death, where the corpse nourishes the representation (the "Symbolic," in her terminology).

When Kristeva celebrates the corpse, "the utmost of abjection," which infects/"feeds" life, she is speaking metaphorically of the experience of *écriture,* a writing that "feeds off" the otherness that resides at the limits of language. Kristeva (1982) presents her concept of writing as the violence to the limiting otherness that "safeguards" her (hegemonic) culture. This does not mean, however, that she is interested in violence done to marginalized persons.

It is this same aesthetic that makes possible postmodern texts like Joan Didion's *Salvador,* in which the only interest is in the short circuit—the horror—that such violence produces in the hegemonic subject. In *Salvador,* the experience of limits has nothing whatsoever to do with any empathy with the marginalized persons to whom violence is done. El Salvador—"terror is the given of the place" (Didion 1983, 14)—is Didion's "heart of darkness," as one jacket blurb acknowledges.

In this place the identityless corpses of utmost abjection proliferate with a hallucinatory, anaesthetic reproducibility: "These bodies . . . are often broken into unnatural positions, and the faces to which the bodies are attached (when they are attached) are equally unnatural, sometimes unrecognizable as human faces, obliterated by acid or beaten to a mash of misplaced ears and teeth or slashed ear to ear and invaded by insects" (Didion 1983, 16–17). Didion's (hegemonic) postmodern experience is evident in her capacity to immerse herself in the abject, this cadaverous and obscenely anonymous other (an experience that Kristeva might celebrate) without registering any affect whatsoever. On the contrary, in a parody of touristic advertising language, which may not be ironic (for then she would concede its meaningfulness and human relevance), she describes body dumps as "visitors' must-do, difficult but worth the detour" (Didion 1983, 20). Indeed, she comments on her own alienation by rejecting the irony of the existence of a futuristic shopping mall in the midst of this "place [that] brings everything into question" (which deconstructs everything?): "I wrote it down dutifully, this being the kind of 'color' I knew how to interpret, the kind of inductive irony, the detail that was supposed to illuminate the story. As I wrote it down I realized that I was no longer much interested in this kind of irony, that this was a story that would not be illuminated by such details, that this was a story that would perhaps not be illuminated at all, that this was perhaps even less a 'story' than a true *noche obscura*" (Didion 1983, 36).

This uninterpretable "story"—it is, in fact, a form of the sublime, a grotesquely mystical noche obscura—is a prelude to Didion's attempts to describe the inconceivability of Salvadoran reality. It cannot be represented because language has ceased to refer. Hence the displacement of language to meaningless numbers as an attempt to capture the "ineffable" (Didion 1983, 61). Reality is abolished and replaced with an obscene simulation by the proliferation of meaningless trumped-up documents and the adoption of solutions "crafted" in the language of advertising in Washington or Panama or Mexico (Didion 1983, 65).

If the "texture of life in such a situation is essentially untranslatable" (Didion 1983, 103), it is because Didion has refused to become involved in what is all around her: "As I waited to cross back over the Boulevard de los Heroes to the Camino Real I noticed soldiers herding a young civilian into a van, their guns at the boy's back, and I walked straight ahead, not wanting to see anything at all" (Didion 1983, 36). Indeed, she is quick to see "cultural impotence" but not one single counterhegemonic expression. No doubt its human relevance and its eccentricity to the hegemonic postmodernist lens, which does not register meaningfulness, preclude interviews with mass organizations of peasants, workers, students, and women or a visit to the guerrilla zones of control.

In other words, the aesthetic-ideological underpinnings of her putative "testimonial" reportage transform her testimony into a self-reflection on her own alienated vision. She cannot "see" the subjects of the counterhegemonic project because they are marginal and such marginalized elements appear in hegemonic postmodern texts only as the horror that excites the writer. With the "other" thus neutralized, it becomes indistinguishable from the oppressors; both, according to Didion, wield the same reality-defying strategies, the same "problem solving" name-changes that make it impossible to know what is what. The renaming of the "Human Rights Commission" of the Archdiocese, virtually indistinguishable by name from the government's "Commission on Human Rights," signals, for Didion, "the presence of the ineffable" (1983, 64), that is, the charge that provides her aesthetic fix.

Testimonial Writing and the Aesthetics of Solidarity

Didion thrives on the ineffable while Salvadoran "natives" wallow in their "cultural impotence." On the one hand, all that is important is the horror that extinguishes the reality that the hegemonic postmodern artist finds boring. On the other hand, the "natives" are truly unimportant because, as real persons, they are part of what is found to be boring. Had Didion been able to empathize with and chronicle the "natives'" own interpretations, she might have encountered a different account of reality; their "impoverished" cultural performances might have been seen as a refusal to embody the types that governmental, educational, and church institutions forced on them.

Seen in this light, it becomes possible to interpret such everyday practices in terms of the struggle for hegemony. Against the injunctions of such hegemonic institutions, popular sectors in turn resignify their patterns of production and consumption, their ethnic customs, their culinary and religious practices, their sexual relations, and so on. As regards literary production, testimonial writing provides a new means for popular sectors to wage their struggle for hegemony in the public sphere from which they were hitherto excluded or forced to represent stereotypes by the reigning elites.

During the 1960s social changes were taking place, such as Paulo Freire's consciousness-raising literacy movement, the formation of Christian Base Communities, and peasant and worker mass organizations, which were totally absent from the canonical texts of the literary "boom." The "popular" was either essentialized in the petty-bourgeois recreations of peasant and indigenous speech and culture (for example, Salarrué in El Salvador, Asturias in Guatemala) or pawned off as mass culture (Fuentes, Puig, Sarduy). There were testimonial narratives before and during the "boom," but they were not brought into the literary sphere. It is not until after the creation of a literary award for testimonial literature by Cuba's major cultural institution, Casa de las Américas, that the genre, with its attendant emphasis on the marginal and the popular, is recognized as such. It is significant, as regards global hegemonic struggles, that the prize was instituted after the break with liberal Latin American intellectuals over the "hardening" of the Soviet line of the Cuban government. This was clearly a contestatory and a positive move on the part of the Cubans, for with it they helped erode the "boom" canon, which cultivated self-referentiality, simulation, and poststructuralist écriture.

Testimonial writing, as the word indicates, promotes expression of personal experience. That personal experience, of course, is the *collective* struggle against oppression from oligarchy, military, and transnational capital. Like the Christian Base Communities—grassroots movements in which popular (that is, exploited) sectors reread the gospel as the "good news" of the coming of the Kingdom of God here on earth— testimonial writing also emphasizes a rereading of culture as lived history and a profession of faith in the struggles of the oppressed. Indeed, the two come together in Ernesto Cardenal's Christian community in Solentiname, where he led Bible discussions—rereadings, reinterpretations—and recorded the peasants' applications of their interpretations to their own lives both in a three-volume "popular treatise" on the Gospel and in the poetry workshops conducted by Mayra Jiménez (see Cardenal 1978; Jiménez 1980).

Christian Base Communities, like Liberation Theology, operate in accordance with an amalgam of marxism and Christianity. The former offers a class analysis of oppression whose inherent instrumental rationality (the will to power) is tempered by the latter's message of love for and solidarity with the poor. Proposing the "people" (the poor) as the active subject and agent of history, Liberation Theology conceives of culture as the poor living their freedom, in all social spheres (economically, politically, religiously, etcetera). Where Liberation Theology departs from conventional marxist thought is in the renunciation not only of private property but also of elitism as regards knowledge and power (see Scannone 1979). Liberated consciousness is free of such elitism, according to Menchú's testimonial narrative, to which I now turn.

"My name is Rigoberta Menchú. I am twenty three years old. I would like to give this living testimony which I have not learned in a book nor by myself, for all of this I have learned with my people. . . . My personal situation encompasses the entire reality of a people" (Menchú 1983; my translation). Consciousness-raising is what Menchú has experienced in a lifelong struggle for survival against the military lackeys of a rapacious land-owning class with close ties to U.S. and transnational capital. Her mother, father, and brother were murdered or disappeared; she herself had to flee her Indian community in order to stay alive. Throughout her life in Guatemala, however, she learned who she was by participating in a collective struggle for material and cultural survival. She identifies herself as one of the "people," meaning by this all who are exploited: "I can say that I had no formal education for my political formation but that I attempted to turn my own experience into the general situation of the people. I was happiest when I realized that my problem was not only mine. That my anxieties were . . . also the anxiet[ies] of all who face a bitter life" (Menchú 1983, 144; my translation). She clearly conceives of her testimonial as a kind of gospel, a performative speech for which, to carry it out, she had to learn Spanish, leave her country, travel the world over testifying for human rights organizations and solidarity groups. Popular culture is thus constituted, not as the persistence of timeless customs, but as the adaptation to historical circumstances in order to survive and prosper. She begins her narrative with an account of her family, their customs and cultural practices.

As an Indian, Menchú gives an account of "native" customs from the perspective of one who uses them as "popular weapons" for survival. Her description of the planting ceremony and the significance of the seed and the earth for her Indian community reveals an ethic-aesthetic of solidarity that is made possible by her social context. In a society in which production is intimately connected to the body, in which the body itself bears the mark of creative substances—"we're made of white and yellow corn" (Menchú 1983, 81)—in which nature is the source of all beings, "representation" is not born of the exclusion of the "limiting otherness"—in this case, the *nahual*—but, rather, by dialogue and interaction with it. "For us the *nahual* is a representative of the earth, a representative of the animals and a representative of the water and sun. And all of this induces us to form an image of that representative" (Menchú 1983, 39; my translation).

Again, in contrast with the hegemonic postmodern text, in which the "I" is expelled as vomit, in which the body transforms into vomit that which is expelled, separating it from nature (mother and father), thus making dialogue impossible—"I abject *myself* within the same motion through which 'I' claim to establish myself" (Kristeva 1982, 3)— Menchú's text is, rather, a testimonial of incorporation, embodiment.

Representation for Menchú, then, is something quite different from classical political representation or the aesthetic reflective mimesis of nineteenth-century European realist fiction. The nahual, more than a representation, is a means for establishing solidarity. It projects the absence of domination in early Christian lore, whose significance also lies in the body, that is, Christ's embodiment of love. This is precisely the sense in which Menchú's community fuses Christianity with its own rituals in a syncretic body of practices for survival.

Their first contacts with Christianity had been through the conservative and orthodox Catholicism of Acción Católica, which, dispensed like a "soporific," only made it easier for the ruling class of large landowners to exploit them (Menchú 1983, 148). Thus, Indians came to distrust those priests who, like other *ladino* (Westernized *mestizo*) denigrators of the indigenous population, lived apart, rejecting Indian customs (Menchú 1983, 160).

Religion, like other cultural practices, is a form of social reproduction. Thus when Menchú argues that the objective of Christianity is to create God's kingdom here on earth she means that it "will exist only when we all have enough to eat" (Menchú 1983, 160). It is precisely in that practical use of religion that Catholicism is reconcilable with traditional Indian practices. The significance of all Indian expression is to embody the image of the earth (Menchú 1983, 107). Indian religiosity emanates from Indian culture, which in turn is considered to be a product of a dialogical relationship with the earth and nature. Land, and nature in general—which not only provide material sustenance but also embody *Dios Mundo* (earth god)—must not be owned or exploited instrumentally. The child undergoes certain rites to purify his hands so that he may never rob (that is, take from the community, the social body) nor "abuse nature" (that is, the natural body; Menchú 1983, 32). The Indian analysis of existential and social strife, then, begins with the condemnation of private or state ownership of the land (Menchú 1983, 142).

Indians turn to Christianity (in its "primitive" mode) as a means to express their desire to maintain an integrated social harmony (Menchú 1983, 106). When their view of this harmony is upset by instrumental reason and economic exploitation of land and labor, they convoke religious meetings in which they appeal to both God and nature and use Catholicism's sacred texts as "popular weapons" for vindication: "We began to study the Bible as a principal document. The Bible has many stories like ours regarding our ancestors. . . . The important thing is that we have begun to integrate that reality as our own reality" (Menchú 1983, 156; my translation).

Menchú's testimonio does not fetishize otherness as do the hegemonic postmodern texts referred to above. Instead, she gives a personal specificity to those marginalized and oppressed elements of which she herself is one. She is not an elite speaking for or representing the "people." Her discourse is not at all about representation or about deconstructing representation by the violence to the marginal. Instead, it is a practice, a part of the struggle for hegemony. In embracing Christ as the symbol of revolutionary consciousness and conscience, Menchú's community also embraces him as the most important of a panoply of "popular weapons" (Menchú 1983, 160), which include both Christianity and Marxism, two master discourses that in the struggle for survival are made to yield their overriding authority. It is the practical aesthetics of community-building, of solidarity, that determines how and to what extent such master discourses are brought into the service of recognition and valuation of the marginalized: "In the revolutionary process we have to defend ourselves against the enemy but we also have to defend our faith as Christians, and we also have to think ahead to after victory when we'll have many great tasks before us as Christians to bring about change. . . . Together we can build a popular Church, a real church, not a hierarchy nor a building, but a change for us as persons. I have taken that option as a contribution to the popular war of the people. And I know and I am confident that the people are the only ones capable . . . of transforming society. And that's not a theory (Menchú 1983, 270; my translation).

Notes on a New Female Practice in Journalism

I'd been in El Salvador two weeks and I was walking home one day when I heard shots. There were tanks all along the block, and some fifty soldiers and police. They had mortars, machine guns, and they were attacking one house in particular. It was incredible, because they had all this trained on just one house, and the only thing you could hear coming from inside the house were the shots of a small caliber pistol. Then the shots from inside were heard no more. Everything grew quiet. The smoke cleared and the first group of policemen and journalists entered the house. There was a young man dead in the bathroom. And there was a woman, maybe forty or forty-five, wearing an apron and with a kerchief around her head. She was lying in a pool of blood. . . . I was the only woman in the group, and the only journalist from the U.S. who had stayed in El Salvador for more than a couple of days that month. And I just couldn't believe what happened next: the Chief of Police went into another room and got a machine gun. He knelt beside the older woman and placed it in her hand. "This was the weapon, this was the machine gun she used against us," he said. He got a box of bullets, unused bullets still wrapped in paper, and he threw them on the floor on top of her blood. "Those were her bullets," he said. And the international press took photos and they said, "Right, right," and they took notes: " . . . she had a machine gun, she was shooting at the Government Forces, terrorist, guerrilla" and so on. (Ann Nelson, quoted in Randall 1985b, 56)

There was something wrong with "free journalism."
To begin with, many of us were unable to correctly formulate the questions, much less pretend to evolve answers. We came from countries where freedom of the press existed. We could write and publish anything. Yet in the 1960s and 1970s when our hometown newspapers filtered back to us in Mexico, Cuba, and Nicaragua, much more

often than not the news we read was unrecognizable as having anything to do with the reality we saw around us. Who wrote those feature stories? What world did they inhabit?

Inhabit might have been the key word. Although we lived in these places, relating to situations of everyday life as workers or as mothers with school-aged children, most journalists came, stayed a few days in the local luxury hotel, and left. Much of their "news" came from conversations over drinks at that hotel's Americanized bar. We guessed you had to inhabit a place to know it.

There were six women working in production here in Jibacoa. Today eighty-six percent of the women in this community are working. We owe this in great measure to the theater. . . . Our experience with the play about sexism was tremendous. We criticized the man who thinks his wife is a submissive object in the home, and we showed how women can't and mustn't accept that. . . . We dramatized cases we have right here. (testimony from Jacinta Odilia Orozco, in Randall 1981a, 65)

If you didn't understand the language, if you didn't speak Spanish, how could you really communicate? How could you listen? To report accurately on a given part of the world, we decided, you must live and work in that place, speak its language, get to know its people and their culture.

That's when we began to understand the more subtle nature of free press. For many of us *did* live and work in the countries whose news we cared to tell. Many of us learned to speak the language, involved ourselves deeply in the culture, listened. But the truer our stories, the more they had to do with what was really going on, then the fewer possibilities we had for getting them published.

Our knowledge and experience pushed us to take sides. We were no longer "impartial," and in punishment we were relegated to speak only to each other. In our country with its loudly touted freedom of the press, we had no trouble seeing our work in print. But publication was limited to journals that reached a few hundred at best; no threat at all to a population of 220 million.

I'm not going to pursue this line of very obvious analysis. It's been done a thousand times by historians, sociologists, social anthropologists, political scientists, as well as many journalists. I'm more interested, here, in talking about another way of telling the story, a way evolved and explored mainly by women: the first-person narrative, testimony, or oral history.

In the late 1960s and early 1970s two important forces came to bear on the work of a number of women who lived in and wrote out of Latin America. The first was a disparate but growing awareness of the relationship between U.S. government foreign policy and the reality of life for most Third World peoples. It wasn't difficult for us to understand why real news about these people did not, for the most part, find its way into the mainstream U.S. press.

The second important force was feminism. It exploded across our collective consciousness, catching each of us wherever in our own lives we happened to be standing. As women reevaluating our present we began to realize we had a past, a history hidden or distorted, a memory we needed—for our own health and well-being—to retrieve. As writers, as journalists, we gradually came to feel it was no longer satisfying to try to "write like the men." We were no longer sure we accepted male criteria for what good writing, or accurate journalism, was. We began to listen to our own voices, play by our own rules.

The change was sometimes uneven, an ascending spiral rather than an immediate shift. Some of us wrote essays about our discoveries. Others were less analytical, more intuitive. We learned to trust our—and each other's—analyses *and* intuitive powers. Our work changed.

Social life: none. It was a neglected life. The people were traditionalist, poor, peasants. There was a solidarity among the families, and a lot of camaraderie among the women. When one woman was going to give birth another one would be with her. The women didn't smoke or drink. Those who had a bit of food would help out another who didn't have anything, even in poverty. That's how we were. When I was growing up and even after I got married there was still no school here. (testimony by Olivia Silva, in Randall 1983, 50)

We began to understand that our collective as well as our individual memories have been invaded, raped, erased. Recreating these memories has been an ongoing concern, taking place in many ways and in a number of disciplines. Listening—to ourselves as well as to our grandmothers, mothers, sisters, and to women of different histories, ethnicities, social classes, and cultures—has been important in the context of this changed vision.

A new practice of listening and telling is sometimes called oral history. Sometimes it's called testimony, or testimonial journalism. Some people refer to it more simply as in-depth interviewing. Whatever the label, it has created a body of voice and image, a new resource literature—much of it from the so-called Third World and much of it from and about women. This new literature provides a whole other way of listening to and looking at life in places like Latin America.

Although the best of this work crosses genre lines, for the moment and for the purpose of these notes I would like to consider it as journalism. I would also like to look at some of the things that set it apart from journalism of the more conventional type.

In the first place, I have not casually called it a *practice*. This way of telling a story is not product-oriented like the traditional (male-defined) news story, balanced on "events" and portraying them as static. When we tell our stories, or make ourselves vehicles for others to do so, we offer process. We are interested in what was, what is, and what may be in the future. We are interested in *how* and *why* our informants did what they did, and what contradictions or complexities were a part of that.

We began to be clear about who did what, and to whom. People were not massacred. The army massacred them (or the police, or whoever). Battles did not take place. Named forces waged them, against named victims.

It was at one of our first union meetings. A few of the key members were late . . . so we started the meeting without them. By the time they arrived we had made a number of important decisions. I was supposed to report these decisions and started off by saying, "Well, comrades, this was a great meeting. We did all we had to do. We changed our executive in a diplomatic way." I was then informed that the word was democratic, not diplomatic. "No problem," I said. I never was one for shutting up. I always went right ahead and made my mistakes so they could teach me how it was supposed to be done. That's how I learned. (testimony by Gladys Baez, in Randall 1981b, 169)

We based our choice of informants on criteria different from the usual journalistic guidelines. We didn't go to the "spokesperson" (too often the spokes*man*), we tended not to ask "officials." We began to do our own thinking about who makes history, and noticed they are usually ordinary working people, women, often children. We believed it was important to present different views of an event or conflict. We went to people with contrasting viewpoints and consulted as well the more traditional sources. But we chose our central voices from those centrally involved.

Memory was vital. It occupied a new, almost sacred, place in our writing: in our poetry, prose, essays, journalistic efforts; even in our images: photography and other visual art forms. We came to understand how a retrieval of our own memory was essential, not simply for the language of our lives, but for the very meaning of that language, the nurturance of life itself. We gave thought to ways in which we might uncover, discover, recreate the memories of those whose voices we passed on. It was not a matter of remembering more. It was a matter of remembering differently, unfettered by what men have deemed worthy of recording, unaltered by male interpretation, uncluttered by the male system of rewards for achievement according to their values.

We were bringing back our own voice. We learned to listen. We were unafraid to present our voices in all their unaltered richness, with respect for culture, with respect for wisdom even when that wisdom assumed forms as yet unnamed among us, with respect for language. Language, for us, was not some abstract object to be "closely read" in the ahistoric manner of the new criticism. Language lives intimately linked to time and place, is informed by history and ideology, music and meaning. A new and evolving understanding of language has enabled us to hear our multiple voices and offer them (often in translation) to others.

As feminism pushed us to question our assumptions on all levels, we tended to bring fewer of these assumptions, cultural or otherwise, to bear on the way we conducted an interview. Most of us tried to practice a humility and respect for people's differing histories, customs, dreams. An honoring of our differences as well as of our commonalities became a goal among us as feminist women; such an honoring naturally found its way into our work as transmitters of our sisters' lives.

. . . how to retain the vitality, and often beautiful simplicity, of Rigoberta's words, but aim for clarity at the same time. . . . I've left the repetitions, tense irregularities, and sometimes convoluted sentences which come from (her) search to find the right expression in Spanish. Words have been left in Spanish or Quiché. (Ann Wright, translator's preface, in Menchú 1984)

... my cause ... born out of wretchedness and bitterness ... radicalized by the poverty in which my people live ... the oppression which prevents us from performing our ceremonies, and shows no respect for our way of life ... it's not easy to understand, just like that. And I think I've given some idea of that in my account. Nevertheless, I'm still keeping my Indian identity a secret. I'm still keeping secret what I think no one should know. Not even anthropologists or intellectuals, no matter how many books they have, can find out all our secrets. (last lines of Menchú's narrative, 1984, 246–47)

Just as we gave thought to *how* to present other women's stories, we also understood it may not be desirable, or even possible, for us to do this alone, assuming the role of unique or only scribe. Sometimes we worked collectively, attempting to free ourselves of the competitiveness so prevalent among our male colleagues. At times we felt it particularly important to involve the informant, facilitating to the protagonist the role of writer and/or analyst rather than guarding that jealously for ourselves.

Our work attracted people, often eager to tell their stories through us. In the mid-1970s, living in Cuba, I was approached by Dominga de la Cruz, an elderly Puerto Rican woman who had become a well-known figure in Havana. Often referred to as "the woman who picked up the flag during the Ponce Massacre in 1937," most people ignored her personal history before and after that historic act. Dominga asked me to write her story; "so I can leave it to the young ones," was the way she put it. I felt honored. Faced with an ongoing exile, saddened by years of oppression in her native Puerto Rico, I thought her involvement in the research and writing might give Dominga stimulus and hope. It did, to the extent that she was still able to take those tasks on. The attempt, inconclusive as it was, nevertheless made for a very different kind of book than the one I would have written had I been satisfied to do it in the more conventional way (Randall 1979).

Sometimes these attempts were more successful. It is important to say that we women who in the 1970s began exploring the possibilities of oral history in Latin America, listened to men as well as women (to an infinitely greater degree than the men had ever listened to us). Naturally, as we perceived the ways in which we had been historically silenced, we were especially interested in reclaiming women's voices. But we were also interested in our brothers, particularly when they were from the working poor, peasants, or other neglected groups.

In Cuba in 1975 I began work on a book about an elderly farmer who, although he formally had no more than a third-grade education, wrote verse plays about life in the countryside and had organized a local theater group to produce them. *El guajíricantor,* as he called himself, took a very active role in telling his story. He made his testimony more vivid with gesture, and even theater. He sent me scraps of paper on which he recorded his dreams. And he found working on the manuscript itself exciting. The form of that book was richly shaped by our collaboration (Randall with Moreno 1979).

The different phases of listening, recording, and transmitting others' voices had become a new field—oral history—rich in experiment and producing discussion about ethics, responsibility, and additional creative possibilities. When I began, in 1969, on what would be my first book involving this approach (Randall 1972), I was all pragmatism, solving problems as they arose. Oral history was already an incipient discipline among U.S. and European academics, with its attendant conferences, journals, discussion, techniques. In Latin America, several movements for social change had produced what would be called *testimonio* (a new form that crossed the boundaries of literature and journalism). But I did not pay much attention to any of this. By that time I was living in Cuba, which, because of the cultural blockade, was relatively isolated from the latest literary trends. My first contact with the term *oral history* occurred when the Mexican oral historian Eugenia Meyers visited the island in the mid-1970s. To my surprise she told me that my work to that point was considered pioneering in the field![1]

When I had been working in this vein for a number of years, however, I began to experiment more. Process was always an important part of this experimentation. I had begun by wondering how physically to use a tape recorder, how to record a voice without technology getting in its way; in short, how to put people who had never had contact with recording devices at ease in their presence.

Then I began to do my own photography. Now the problem was multiple: how to attend to the voice at the same time as I concentrated on the images; and how to move between one and the other so as not to diminish either but enrich both. Later these issues arose not only in the interviewing, but in the subsequent work of editing transcripts and printing photographs.

I remember how excited I was when I discovered that "listening" again to a voice, recreating the person's actual presence through rereading the interview transcript, influenced the way I might print that person's image in the darkroom; and that the act of seeing, the way an image came up through the developer, also influenced exactly how I might edit a transcript. This first happened during the making of *Sandino's Daughters,* and became much more conscious in later work.

I went in (to the hospital room) . . . Alma heard me arguing and began shouting, "Mom, here I am." So the doctor said "Look, it's against the rules but that voice deserves an answer. You can see her for a minute." He was impressed by how young she was. He asked me, "How did they bring her to the hospital? They say it was a bomb." . . . I went in to see her and I'll never forget it. I wasn't crying but I was done in. I didn't cry so as not to upset her, right? When the doctor opened the door, she lifted her two stubs, wrapped in gauze, and said, "Look, mom, I'm alive! You see, they didn't kill me. They dropped the big bomb on me but they didn't kill me. Life is what matters, so don't worry yourself." . . . Already planning her cover. (testimony from Zulema Baltodano, in Randall 1981b, 77)

The learning process was not always limited to conscious investigation and subsequent conclusions. On an invitation from the Vietnamese Women's Union I visited what was still North Vietnam in the fall of 1974. It was six months before the Vietnamese victory of April 1975. I didn't speak the language, so I had to conduct my interviews through interpreters. I remember once, at a divorce hearing in Hanoi, my translator—herself a young woman—burst into tears and found it impossible to continue speaking. She explained that the very idea of divorce so shocked and saddened her that she couldn't abstract herself from the proceedings. I learned about custom and culture that day, in a way I would not have had I stuck to straight or "impartial" reporting. My interpreter's manner itself taught me much about women in Vietnam.

I can reminisce about my experience, but I don't want to give the impression that I was the only woman doing oral history and using it in reporting of one kind or another—in so-called straight journalism, in poetry, or in prose. In Latin America there were many writers working in this way. Prominent among them were a number of women whose work has been central to a real understanding of life in those countries. They include the Brazilian Moema Viezzer, the Venezuelan Elisabeth Burgos-Debray, the Mexican Elena Poniatowska, the Cuban Nancy Morejón, Laurette Séjourné—a French anthropologist who has lived for many years in Mexico—and North Americans like Karen Wald and Medea Benjamin.[2]

Women have not only retrieved and recreated the memory of language, of the voice; they have also worked with visual images in a particularly relevant way. The North American photographer Susan Meiseles is noteworthy in this respect.[3]

But I will take discussion of my own work one step further, and speak of what can happen—what *has* happened to me—when U.S. government officials decide to retaliate against those of us who tell it like it is. When I returned to the United States in January of 1984, the U.S. Immigration and Naturalization Service (INS) denied my petition for residency. They invoked the 1952 McCarran-Walter Act and initiated deportation proceedings against me explicitly based on the critical nature of my writings. In citing offensive or "subversive" texts, an immigration judge actually and primarily quoted from the women in my books. After almost five years of struggle, successive defeats, and appeals, I finally won my immigration case in August of 1989.

In searching for reasons why I have been singled out in this way, I have come to the conclusion that central among them is the fact that I have transmitted the voices of ordinary people—perhaps specifically ordinary women—from countries the U.S. government must lie about in order to justify its outrageous foreign policy.

Through a systematic campaign of dehumanizing the people in "alien" nations, our government can keep us feeling those people are *other*. It's one of the ways they perpetuate racism and keep us apart. If we hear those people's real voices, there is always the risk that we will discover we are not so different. We may not have to hate them after all.

I wrote a poem, at the height of my struggle with the INS, which speaks from my conviction that central among my "sins" has been the transmission of peoples' voices, the re-creation of popular memory. In this context, I feel that it's not only me but the women in my books who are under attack by the INS. I'd like to close with this poem, in homage to the women and their voices.

Under Attack[4]

Listen. These voices are under attack.

Ismaela of the dark tobacco house, Grandma,
a maid her lifetime of winters, granddaughter of slaves.
Straight to my eyes:
"My mama used to tell me, one of these days
the hens gonna shit upwards!
And I'd stare at those hens' asses, wondering
when *will* that happen?
When we pushed the big ones down
and pulled the little ones up!"

"For Mama, Papa, and Blackie" she wrote
on the poem she left to say goodbye.
Nicaragua, 1977.
Disappear or be disappeared.
Dora Maria whose gaze
her mother always knew.
She trembled at her first delivery,
then took a city fearlessly.

Rain and the river rising. Catalina
chases her ducks that stray.
"And my months," she cries,
on that platform with poles, a house
to do over and over.
"My months gone in the hospital at Iquitos
and the full moon
bringing a madness to my head."
Her body is light against my touch.
A woman's voice, parting such density of rain.

Xuan, my cold hand in hers,
evokes the barracks.
"Soldiers who were our brothers."
Night after night, village by village

Quang Tri, 1974.
Gunfire replaced by quiet conversation.
The work of women.
Xuan's history, too, is under attack.

Dominga brings her memory down
from the needle trade, Don Pedro,
her own babies dead from hunger.
"I want to tell you my story," she says,
"leave it to the young ones
so they'll know."
We are rocking. We are laughing.
This woman who rescued the flag at Ponce,
Puerto Rico, 1937.
Known by that act alone,
until a book carries her words. Her voice.

I bring you these women. Listen.
They speak but their lives are under attack.

They too are denied adjustment of status
in the land of the free. In the home of the brave.
—*Hartford, Connecticut   Winter 1988*

Notes

1. By this time I had done oral history with Cuban, Vietnamese, Chilean, Peruvian, and Nicaraguan women, some of it published in book form, some of it in magazines.
2. Moema Viezzer gave us the testimony of Domitila (Barrios de Chungara 1978), and Elisabeth Burgos-Debray that of Rigoberta Menchú (1984). Elena Poniatowska was the first to publish the story of what really happened on the night of 1 October 1968 in Mexico City (1971). Nancy Morejón recorded the stories of Cuban nickel miners; Laurette Séjourné recreated the experience of the ground-breaking Cuban theater group (1977) and also collected testimony by Cuban women (her work is so far untranslated). Karen Wald first shed light on education in Cuba (1978), and Medea Benjamin has most recently published the testimony of Elvia Alvarado (1987).

3. U.S. photographer Susan Meiseles was among the first to record the Nicaraguan war, and her pictures are history in her book (1981) as well as in magazines around the world. The *way* she made her images, and the images themselves, I would argue, come from a specifically female eye. In El Salvador she continued to make images, and produced a book of pictures by the thirty photojournalists then most active in that country.

4. "Under Attack" by Margaret Randall copyright © South End Press, 1988, reprinted by permission.

Barbara Harlow Testimonio *and Survival*

Roque Dalton's Miguel Mármol

It is enough to understand, for example, what it means for a writer and a Salvadoran militant to receive detailed information (and to be authorized to transmit it publicly) from an eyewitness, a survivor, of the great anti-communist massacre of 1932 in El Salvador.
—Roque Dalton (1987, Introduction)[1]

In January 1932, following an aborted peasant uprising planned in large part by the recently formed Communist Party of El Salvador and supported by peasant organizations and trade unions, the military and police forces of the Salvadoran government under the presidency of General Maximiliano Hernández Martínez massacred over 30,000 civilians. At the time of the *matanza*,[2] as the massacre is popularly known, Miguel Mármol was twenty-seven years old, a shoemaker, labor organizer, and member of the Communist Party. He survived the brutal repression of 1932, and three-and-a-half decades later, in Prague, he told his story to his young compatriot Roque Dalton. Dalton, who was born three years after the matanza, had become a member of the Communist Party in 1955. A militant and a poet who won the Central American Poetry Prize in the same year that he joined the party, Dalton was executed in 1975 by a faction within his own Ejército Revolucionario del Pueblo (People's Revolutionary Army, or ERP). Meanwhile, Mármol in his ninth decade lived in exile in Cuba, where he recently died.

What then is asked for by Dalton in the "enough" that comes from understanding what is meant by the testimony entrusted to him by the older Communist and fellow Salvadoran? Three historical narratives, at least, intersect in often conflicting ways in the collaborative work of the two men: the significance of the year and the events of 1932 for the history of El Salvador; the complicated relationship of Mármol to Dalton, of Dalton to Mármol, with its contradictory implications for representing, both descriptively and prescriptively, the role of the intellectual within oppositional movements; and the emergence, consolidation, and fragmentation over half a century of the Communist Party in El Salvador. This article proposes to examine some of the strategic ways whereby *Miguel Mármol* opens a critically discursive site in which these issues of continuing crucial consequence for political and cultural resistance are raised and negotiated.

Miguel Mármol is Mármol's story of his fifty years as a political activist, beginning with his earliest memories of childhood poverty in the village of Ilopango and provisorily concluding with union organizing in Guatemala in 1954, as told to Dalton for a reading public. The telling took place in Czechoslovakia and began in an expensive restaurant when a Czech journalist who had been interviewing the older man became bored and took leave of the two Salvadorans just as the "conversation became anecdotal" and "before Mármol could finish relating the adventures of his execution" (Dalton 1987, 34). Dalton, however, was "transported back to [his] country, the heaven-and-hell where [his] revolutionary ideals were born" (Dalton 1987, 34), and with the plan of writing a "narrative article, a story or something along that line," Dalton, according to his own account, arranged to meet his colleague for their first working session together on 14 May 1966, his thirty-first birthday. Questions of politics, poetry, theory, and practice proliferated and the anecdotal narrative expanded until the young poet discovered that he would have to rethink his project as a book: "I began to realize that to write about Mármol I'd have to go into—and not superficially—the history of the Salvadoran workers' movement and the CP of our country, and that to go into that I'd have to try to 'dismantle' the image of the government of the Laborite Araujo, to reconsider the government of Martínez (about which we militants of my generation have a view that begins in 1944, precisely with its overthrow), to delve into the international situation during a period of world crisis, into several decades of history. And that couldn't be done in a couple of articles. It was then that I began thinking about a book" (Dalton 1987, 35). That book, *Miguel Mármol,* was to take on some of the pressing historical and political imperatives for which both Dalton and Mármol, in their critically different but reciprocal ways, lived, participated in the Salvadoran resistance struggle, and eventually faced execution(s).

Dalton refers to that book as a *testimonio* and as such it fits within the generic configurations of cultural resistance currently emerging from the contemporary historical circumstances of anticolonial and anti-imperialist struggles. The testimonio, according to John Beverley, is a "novel or novella-length narrative in book or pamphlet (that is, printed as opposed to acoustic) form, told in the first person by a narrator who is also the real protagonist or witness of the events he or she recounts and whose unit of narration is usually a 'life' or a significant life experience" (Beverley 1989, 12–13; also this volume, 24). More important, however, than these apparently formal criteria, which suggest the testimonio's identification with the autobiography, are the specific historical conditions that inform the testimonial composition and determine its interventionary challenge to the dominant institutions of literature as these are underwritten by ascendant conventions of authorship and disciplinary strictures and definitions. Crucial to the testimonio is the antiauthoritarian relationship between the narrator and the compiler or "activator" of the narrator-protagonist's account of the events to which she or he bears witness. This counterhegemonic relationship in turn implicates the reader, both in the events and in their retelling. Although the "intervention of this gathering and editing" is, as Beverley points out, "one of the most hotly debated theoretical points in the discussion of this genre" (1989, 15), the collaborative nature of the project reworks the hierarchical structures of power implicit in literature as a cultural institution. Much as Scheherazade, through her appropriation of the storytelling function in the *Arabian Nights,* transformed the autocratic structures of the sultan Shahryar's rule and at the same time saved her sisters in the kingdom from her lord's despotism, so too the necessary participation of the testimonial narrator-activist in literary production historicizes and politicizes the traditional claims to an aesthetic autonomy of culture made by its institutionally sanctioned and credentialed attendants. Rather than acting as gatekeepers to the halls of learning, authors and other "professionals," often the "traditional intellectuals" in the Gramscian sense of the term, become instead the amanuenses in a new collaborative project enabling the "voices of the dispossessed" to penetrate international media circuits and information networks.

Like other testimonios, such as those by Domitila Barrios de Chungara in Bolivia (1977), Rigoberta Menchú in Guatemala (1983), Leila Khaled in Palestine (1973) and Elvia Alvarado in Honduras (1987), Miguel Mármol's public "life" or "life experience" is rendered into literary form by another participant in the testimonio project. Each of these narrators, as organizer and activist among her or his own peoples and even in international forums, has an already articulate political voice. The testimonio, then, transgressing distinctions of discipline and genre, introduces that politically conscious, strategically developed, even militant articulation into an isolationist literary arena and collapses its self-protective defenses. Unlike other testimonios, however, whose narrators are, according to convention, attributed author status, *Miguel Mármol* presents itself on the title page as the work, not of its protagonist Miguel Mármol, but of Roque Dalton, its *compilador* (compiler). Nor does the relationship between the two participants in the volume derive from the anthropological paradigm of ethnographer/"native informant" or the geopolitical model of metropolitan researcher/peripheral subject. Rather, the collaboration of poet-revolutionary and Communist Party organizer, with their militancy in common, proposes a radical reordering of literary and political priorities that engages internal party debates, historical and generational affiliations, no less than generic dispositions. Each of the participants is reidentified in the process, as Roque Dalton insists in the conclusion to his introduction to the testimonio: "Therefore, in the face of Miguel Mármol's testimony, I rejected the first trap suggested by my writing vocation: that of writing a novel based on him, or of novelizing the testimony. I quickly realized that the direct words of the witness for the prosecution were irreplaceable. Especially since what most interests us is not to portray reality, but to transform it" (Dalton 1987, 40). Indeed, the conventional subject-author identification of the book—Roque Dalton, *Miguel Mármol*—might well be read against convention, as Roque Dalton–Miguel Mármol, a single volume with two authors, or two protagonists and no author at all. This reordering of hierarchical distinctions is itself informed by the combined difference and shared collective commitment of the two participants.

Mármol opens his testimony, ostensibly answering a question posed to him by his interlocutor and collaborator: "You're asking me if everything I've done and experienced was already written in my destiny? Only an academic would ask that kind of question, and it makes me think of that song about 'what might have been and never was' " (Dalton 1987, 45). The direct address form, the immediate invocation of a partner in dialogue, establishes a profound reciprocity between Mármol and Dalton and implicates as well their eventual readers in the exchange. At the same time, however, it proposes another adversarial and conflicted relationship among them that will require a mutual elaboration in the testimony to follow: "only an academic would ask that kind of question." Mármol is not an academic, he claims, but, he insists almost accusatorily, Dalton is. This distinction is more than a personal difference between the two men, and it will have fundamental polemical consequences for Mármol's narration of his biography and his attendant analysis of the contested history of the Communist Party in El Salvador.

Mármol, who began his own political career as an artisan and a shoemaker, argues the importance of working-class origins for the Salvadoran Communist Party: "We're not distorting our country's history when we say our Communist Party is the child of the Salvadoran working class, since you won't find any instances, as occurred in other countries, where the CP was primarily organized in the university or among the petty-bourgeois intelligentsia" (Dalton 1987, 140). Mármol's identification of himself, positively, as an artisan and member of the working class, and his denigration of (the role of) academics and intellectuals, is critically thematized in the course of his narrative. It figures both in his analyses of the historical conditions of the Salvadoran struggle in 1932, as when he denies sounding like a professor or academic (Dalton 1987, 290), and again in his injunctions to other colleagues in the party to fulfill the tasks assigned them by their own class positions. Discussing the case of Agustin Farabundo Martí, the early leader of the Salvadoran Communist Party who was executed by a firing squad following the 1932 massacre, Mármol criticizes, for example, the "lack of serious studies of Martí's life, which is the fault of us revolutionaries," but he goes on to assert that "within the framework of this conversation, I wouldn't dare presume to expound on the significance of el Negro Martí in our history. That's something for communists who have had time to go to the university to do" (Dalton 1987, 173).

The insistence on the "framework of [that] conversation," the dialogue, that is, between Mármol, the older party organizer, and Dalton, the younger university-educated poet, even as it emphasizes their shared commitments, further problematizes the collaborative relationship between the two Communists. It raises too the contested question about the function of intellectuals within the party's organizational apparatus and their role in the revolutionary struggle. The argument, however, is not an essentialist one, and to construe it as such would be, as Gramsci has pointed out, to mistake questions of personal identity for political analysis: "The most widespread error of method seems to me that of having looked for this criterion of distinction [of intellectuals] in the intrinsic nature of intellectual activities, rather than in the ensemble of the system of relations in which these activities (and therefore the intellectual groups who personify them) have their place within the general complex of social relations" (Gramsci 1983, 8). The distinction that Mármol repeatedly draws between the working-class artisan and the academic or intellectual functions particularly in the critical efforts to reconstruct the events leading to the 1932 matanza and to analyze historically the reasons for and the contributions of the Communist Party to the failure of the peasant uprising with its disastrous aftermath of widespread death and destruction wreaked on the civilian population and on the party's own organizational structures and capacities.

The year 1932 and the matanza are radically decisive not only for the historical ordering of El Salvador's recent past but for the analysis of its present conditions and for the more visionary projections of its future political trajectory. The year, so important to Salvadoran political self-analysis, is no less a part of its literary history. Its decisiveness is underscored, for example, in Dalton's poem "All," where he writes:

> We were all born half-dead in 1932
> we survived but half-alive
> each of us with an account of thirty thousand massacred.
> ("All" in Dalton 1984, 42–43)

The year 1932 figures just as critically in Manlio Argueta's novel *One Day of Life* (1983), where Lupe remembers a time when the bodies of the massacred were being found almost as indiscriminately as they had been murdered; the year structures again the narration of the present in Argueta's subsequent novel *Cuzcatlan: Where the Southern Sea Beats* (1987), which sees the contemporary death squads in El Salvador as direct descendants of General Martínez's military forces. The attempted effacement of the year 1932 from the official record of Salvadoran history is then a massacre of another sort, the annihilation of the historical memory and thus a popular contribution to articulating a vision of the future. According to Argueta, writing in the prologue to the English translation of Dalton's *Miguel Mármol,* "The insurrection of 1932 has recently ended. The massacre is repeated, and silence and terror imposed. No one dares to deal with it, to analyse it, the facts are hidden, including the newspapers in the archives of that period. But the story is kept alive by word of mouth, from ear to ear" (in Dalton 1987, xiii). For Mármol himself, 1932 remains the point of departure and continues as the central moment of his historical narrative: "After that damned year all of us are different men and I think that from then on El Salvador is a different country. El Salvador is today, before anything else, a creation of that barbarism" (Dalton 1987, 305).

The focus of Mármol's testimony in its elaboration by Dalton cannot escape the relentless pressures exerted by 1932. The narrative's very structure and retrospective sequencing are constantly coerced by the year, the events, and the critical demand these persist in making on the rendering of Mármol's life story as a party militant: "And one thing is certain: that the communist who doesn't have the problem of '32 in his mind, cannot be a good communist, a good Salvadoran revolutionary" (Dalton 1987, 317–18). Was the party sufficiently prepared, materially and ideologically, to lead an uprising? Had the leadership adequately estimated the ripeness of the conditions for insurrection? Was the focus on the peasantry correct? Was the urban working class ready? Were the leaders right in postponing—even for a few days—the beginning of the revolt? The continuing conflicted analysis of the events and the aftermath of 1932 divides the Salvadoran Communists in particular and the left more generally among themselves, creating divisions that are decided along generational lines as well as according to ideological, partisan, or sectarian positions. For Mármol, these differences function in terms of the background or previous training of the party member and the determining effect that this necessarily has on the critique of the early leaders of the Communist Party in El Salvador, its structures and its strategies: "To throw all the blame on the communist leaders who didn't make a successful insurrection was and continues to be a prejudiced point of view, proper to reactionary or petty-bourgeois mentalities, to intellectuals isolated from reality, who, after the events, come up with the most intelligent analyses in the world that don't serve anyone to take a step forward" (Dalton 1987, 391).

Although Mármol may critique both the form and the substance of later—as well as much of contemporary—analyses of the circumstances and events of 1932, he nonetheless reiterates the urgent necessity of continuing the analytical enterprise. For Mármol, such a project requires that it be carried out, not through private introspection on the part of any of the surviving participants, nor in the exclusive terms of individual castigation or judgmental reproaches, but collectively, as a historically critical project integral to the very functioning of the party's organization and its continued active operations:

I don't think it's my job to go into a deep analysis and a whole critique on this subject. I've only wanted to put forth a series of facts for the most part unfamiliar to Salvadorans, so that they can be examined by our youngest comrades and be made use of for an analysis. I don't have the sufficient capacity or knowledge. And I don't think this is the job for any one person alone, no matter how capable, no matter how well-versed in Marxism they may be. The result of an individual analysis of a problem so complex and so deliberately confused and distorted will always be partial. We're talking about a task for a revolutionary organization, for the Party, which we communists haven't yet fulfilled. (Dalton 1987, 321–22)

The furtherance of such an analysis is crucial to Mármol's record of his own participation and survival in the 1932 insurrection, and the imperative of its pursuit confers on his personal testimonio its larger historical and political significance. Thus he goes on: "But nevertheless, I insist that it is an indispensible revolutionary task. As for me, I'm not in any way afraid of it. On the contrary, I believe that I'll only die in peace when my Party and my people demonstrate they have learned the fundamental lessons of the slaughter of '32" (Dalton 1987, 322).

The vocational differences between Mármol and Dalton and their political ramifications for their collective struggle, activated by Mármol in the opening lines of his testimonio and pursued between the rest of the lines of his account of the history of the Salvadoran Communist Party, are reiterated from an alternative perspective and based on other critical premises by Dalton in his introduction (1987). For Dalton, theoretical training must eventually allow for the transformation of class origins into revolutionary practice. His account of Mármol's political position speaks as well to the contradictions raised by his own generational and class specificities: "in accordance with the deformed structure of the working class in a country such as El Salvador—whose history is a long progression from one dependency to another—the proper class location of Mármol is ambiguous and, in any case, to conceptualize it we would need a composite definition. . . . To all this has to be added that in the course of his revolutionary development, Miguel Mármol had but sporadic opportunities to engage in more or less profound, prolonged Marxist studies" (Dalton 1987, 25). Dalton goes on in his reading of Mármol's autobiographical and ideological positioning: "it is clear that the level of education received by one means or another didn't diminish in any appreciable way his, I repeat, almost exclusively practical revolutionary nature. Even, let's say once and for all, a relatively *empirical* nature" (Dalton 1987, 26).

The critical differences between the two Salvadoran Communists, and the political distances that these produce, are historical as well as class based. Mármol insists, even if at times with the nostalgia that comes of retrospection and a consciousness of the historical limitations of his own seniority, on the active agency of history in the formation of the party and its cadres. "We were truly beginners," he recalls, "beginners in 1930, which isn't the same as being beginners in these modern times, now when there's so much experience within the grasp of revolutionary youth" (Dalton 1987, 197). Nonetheless, with his testimonio now almost complete and thus too his critique, Mármol returns to the historical continuity of these successive beginnings, which narrate the solidarity between himself and the younger poet: "we began as leaders during a historical stage that has not ended" (Dalton 1987, 466). But even while emphasizing the constitutive effects of history and chronology, Mármol refuses to overlook what he sees as the originating class position of his testimonial colleague and Salvadoran Communist compatriot.

The implicit analysis that Mármol elaborates throughout his testimonio about his interlocutor's theoretical position is explicitly rendered posthumously—and self-critically, the effect perhaps of the experience of the testimonio—in an interview in 1986 with the English translators of *Miguel Mármol*: "Roque," Mármol tells them, "had his conceptions of the past and I had mine. Roque was an intellectual of petty-bourgeois origin. An intellectual comrade is always more radical and extreme than a worker" (Dalton 1987, 492). Dalton himself, however, had continued to assume in radically critical ways in his writing the burden of class as determined by his own social background. In *Poetry and Militancy in Latin America,* the poet attempted to theorize the political contradictions posed by the "personal circumstances in which [he] engage[s] in creative work": his "long and deep bourgeois formative period" and the "long communist militancy . . . held to for so many years now" (Dalton 1981, 10). The burdens of class are to be understood historically, not essentially, or even literarily, according to Dalton, and it is less his own personal identity that it is at stake than the Gramscian "complex of social relations." "Now then," he writes, "what I cannot do . . . is cross out the present effects [of the past] with the stroke of a pen" (Dalton 1981, 11). His role as militant and revolutionary is rather to alter the very definition of poetry:

> Poetry
> pardon me for having helped you understand
> that you are not made of words alone.
> ("Ars Poetica 1974" in Dalton 1984, 58)

And his role as a revolutionary poet is to "transform reality" and the nature of the poet:

> That was when he began writing on the walls
> in his own handwriting
> on fences and buildings
> and on the giant billboards.
> The change was no small thing
> quite the contrary
> in the beginning
> he fell into a deep creative slump.
>
> It's just that sonnets don't look good on walls
> and phrases he was mad about before, like
> "oh abysmal sandalwood, honey of moss"
> looked like a big joke on peeling walls.
> ("History of a Poetic" in Dalton 1984, 79)

Mármol's personal itinerary, as he reports it to Roque Dalton for publication, spans a historical period of half a century. The focus or emphasis of the Dalton-Mármol testimonial remains, however, that of the "political" over the "personal" in terms that too often occlude issues of gender and the need for the party to participate in social and political restructuring of the traditional society and its attendant gender roles, which, in Mármol's analysis, continue despite the competing historical pressures for change from both progressive and reactionary forces. Mármol's account of his relationship with his wife, in particular, as well as with other women whom he encountered on his revolutionary way, suggest some of the problematic and contradictory parameters of his critique of women's growing influence in political activity and within the party, especially as he confronted this structural change following his release from prison. A reading of *Miguel Mármol* in the context provided by the testimonios of women activists such as Domitila Barrios de Chungara, Doris Tijerino, Elvia Alvarado, and Rigoberta Menchú would in turn further the possibilities for (self-)critical social and political analysis already opened in the collaboration between Dalton and Mármol.

Rather than critically addressing the complications in his personal life caused by his political activity, Mármol instead counterpoints dramatically the significant events of his biography with the electoral and governmental history of El Salvador, its center wrought asunder by the repressive rule of General Martínez from 1932 to 1944, and with his growing affiliation with international Communism, first adumbrated in his trip to the Soviet Union in 1930 as a Salvadoran delegate to the World Congress of Red Trade Unions (PROFINTERN). That journey, which took Mármol by ship with Yugoslavs, Germans, and other Europeans across the Atlantic and brought him together with other Latin American Communists gathered in the Soviet Union, resulted in an evolving internationalist consciousness and a consolidation of his own Central American commitments. It served as well to establish his public identity as a Communist. Mármol's brief internment in Cuba en route back to El Salvador initiated him into the experience of prison and political detention, which were to continue through subsequent years in El Salvador, as well as in Guatemala, and were to punctuate his alternating periods of active labor organizing and clandestine party work. Miguel Mármol is, according to Manlio Argueta, a "living document" (Dalton 1987, xvii), and *Miguel Mármol,* in the words of Margaret Randall, is one of those "books that are records," the "books without which the understanding of a particular time or place would not be complete" (Dalton 1987, ix). And according to the poet and *compilador* of Mármol's testimony, Roque Dalton, who, like Mármol, sees the year 1932 as a constitutive date in Salvadoran history, "no one can inform us better about a massacre than the survivors" (Dalton 1987, 38–39).

Roque Dalton did not ultimately survive the internal debates over armed struggle and militarism in the Central American context within his own political organization, debates that had found another kind of forum in the Dalton-Mármol testimonio. Dalton was executed in 1975 together with another comrade identified only as "Pancho" by a faction of the Ejército Revolucionario del Pueblo. In Ecuador in February 1976, on hearing the details of that execution, Eduardo Galeano, the Uruguayan writer and historian, reflected on the bitterly conflicted circumstances of Dalton's death: "We all meet death in a way that resembles us. Some of us, in silence, walking on tiptoe; others, shrinking away; others, asking forgiveness or permission. There are those who meet it arguing or demanding explanations, and there are those who make their way slugging or cursing. There are those who embrace death. Those who close their eyes; those who cry. I always thought that Roque would meet death roaring with laughter. I wonder if he could have. Wouldn't the sorrow of being murdered by those who had been your comrades have been stronger?" (Galeano 1984, 96). As Mármol himself had maintained a decade earlier in the last pages of his testimonio to Dalton and speaking of his own premature experience of posthumous celebration, "my best memories are of the moments that followed the imminent danger of death, those moments when you realize you've been reborn" (Dalton 1987, 482). Those memories were not vouchsafed to Roque Dalton, but to Mármol, whose life, the "living document," is, as Galeano described it, a series of "resurrections" (Galeano 1987), twelve in all, the most spectacular of which remains, once and forever, the "resurrection" from his own execution in 1932 by General Martínez's firing squad.

Roque Dalton and Miguel Mármol shared finally in the experience of death as they had shared in the re-creation of historical life through the testimonio. Their mutual and unrelenting concern with a political analysis of that life at the expense even of their personal identities animates the testimonio and continues after the fact to rework the genre itself. Mármol insists throughout his narration on reconstructing his personal history as a political analysis. "You see," he told Dalton and his readers, "I don't like to dwell so much on this aspect of the persecutions [the difficulties of family life], because this isn't an adventure story, but simply notes of my most general recollections in the hope that they will maybe be of some use to today's young revolutionaries. And because I realize that true revolutionaries never like to dwell too much on their misfortunes" (Dalton 1987, 157). In this demand for an uncompromising political analysis, Mármol is reciprocated by his collaborator: "to study this [mind] I would need to have more than a layman's knowledge of ethnology and psychology. And then there would be too much about a very complex area that I prefer to maintain in the narration simply as shading, at a level that won't disturb the essentially political intentions of comrade Mármol's deposition and of my elaborative work" (Dalton 1987, 30). Until, finally, Mármol demands of Dalton, "You ask who am I to talk this way, like I'm giving a lesson to the whole world? Well, simply and humbly, one old communist among millions of communists, who's risked his skin, and not just once, for the revolution, for the communist movement, and who's not talking at the moment for philosophers, for deep intellectuals, but only and exclusively for everyday revolutionaries, plain and simple" (Dalton 1987, 475).

It is that question, posed by Mármol the party militant, and Dalton's answer, as revolutionary poet, through their shared work in the testimonio itself, that distinguish *Miguel Mármol* not only as testimonio, as historical genre challenging the institutions of literature, but as political analysis challenging the course of history and the reductivist attempts to reappropriate its analysis according to what Dalton would later dismiss as "crock logic."

> Criticism of the Soviet Union
> can only be made by one who is anti-Soviet.

> Criticism of China
> can only be made by one who is anti-China.

> Criticism of the Salvadoran Communist Party
> can only be made by an agent of the CIA.

Self-criticism is equivalent to suicide.
("Crock Logic" in Dalton 1984, 67)

Is it enough, in the end, just to understand?

Notes

1. This and other quotations from Dalton are © Curbstone Press, 1987, and are used here by permission.
2. For one, albeit flawed by its anti-Communist bias, account of the massacre, see Thomas Anderson (1971). Claribel Alegría and Darwin J. Flakoll's recently translated novel *Ashes of Izalco* (1989) offers a powerful reconstruction of the events and aftermath of January 1932.

Elzbieta Sklodowska

Spanish American Testimonial Novel

Some Afterthoughts

It has been long recognized that we cannot understand the specificity of various discourses without an appreciation of the role that interpretive communities play in producing meanings. In his well-known article, "How to Recognize a Poem When You See One," Stanley Fish develops an argument that "acts of recognition, rather than being triggered by formal characteristics, are their source. It is not that the presence of poetic qualities compels a certain kind of attention but that the paying of a certain kind of attention results in the emergence of poetic qualities" (Fish 1981, 105).

In this paper I will argue that in the context of Spanish American literature of the last two decades, "paying of a certain kind of attention" to some of the previously neglected forms of nonfiction has resulted in the emergence of *testimonio* as a literary genre in its own right. Some rarely explored islands of Spanish American letters, such as women's writing, subaltern autobiography, and minority experience, have come to be evaluated with "*testimonio*-seeing" eyes and the presence of the term itself in the language of literary criticism has become ubiquitous. The fact that we, the interpretive community of academic critics, have agreed to "recognize" testimonio and give it institutional legitimation is, arguably, one of the most important events of the past two decades in Spanish American literary history. I insist on the word "recognize," because the presence of testimonial qualities has been a time-honored trait of Spanish American writing since its inception, and one could easily make a case for viewing it, along with realism, as a perennial mode of Western letters.

Despite all the critical attention it has received, *testimonio* remains undefined. In this case, the notion of genre is clearly "historically derived" rather than "logically prescribed" (Lohafer 1983, 11), and testimonio serves as a shorthand for a whole spectrum of narrative conventions. According to some critics, testimonio may show "family resemblance" to more established literary forms, such as the picaresque narrative and the bildungsroman. The new "genre," we are told, also relies on specifically forensic patterns of argumentation as well as on the narrative conventions of autobiography and the traditional realist novel. With the former it shares the split identity of the narrating/ experiencing self, while with the latter it assumes an empiricist position. Unlike most classic autobiographies, however, it does not focus on the inner self, but on communal experience.

On the other hand, testimonio's creative use of the "life story" formula—as we know it from the studies of Oscar Lewis—places it within the tradition of the Chicago school of sociology with its concern for retrieving voices of people who had seldom been heard. In fact, the demarcation between testimonio and the life story is the most nebulous, and L. Langness's definition of life story as "an *extensive* record of a person's life told to and recorded by another, who then edits and writes the life as though it were autobiography" (1965, 4–5) applies to testimonio as well.

Testimonio inevitably positions itself around the shifting borders of a well-known but elusive genre: the novel. As a matter of fact, for some testimonial writers, like Miguel Barnet, terms such as *testimonio* and *novela testimonial* become interchangeable. On the other hand, we have to recognize the fact that since the mid-1970s Spanish American testimonio ("raw" testimonies devoid of aesthetic elaboration) has had an important impact on shaping up the explicitly "literary" novels.[1]

By establishing an explicit interplay between factual and fictional, between aesthetic aspirations to literariness and scientific claims to objectivity, testimonio has consistently defied the critics by departing from a traditional system of assumptions about truth and falsity, history and fiction, science and literature. While it is clear that an unambiguous definition of *testimonio* keeps eluding us, amid the debates still resonating in the field of Latin American testimonio criticism there must be, one should assume, a fairly general agreement as to what testimonio represents. After all, if testimonio was given an identity in our recent (re)readings of Spanish American letters, this rereading must have been informed by a common understanding of what counts as testimonio.

I propose to look at two definitions of *testimonio* in order to approach this question. I start with these conceptualizations for two reasons. First and foremost, what they propose are true definitions and not simply a list of more or less distinct traits and relations. Second, these definitions stand out as the most ingenious attempts to break both the deadlock of "family resemblance" and the Aristotelian dichotomy between fiction and history. For George Yúdice, "Testimonial writing may be defined as an authentic narrative, told by a witness who is moved to narrate by the urgency of a situation (e.g., war, oppression, revolution, etc.). Emphasizing popular, oral discourse, the witness portrays his or her own experience as an agent (rather than a representative) of a collective memory and identity. Truth is summoned in the cause of denouncing a present situation of exploitation and oppression or in exorcising and setting aright official history" (Yúdice 1991a, 17; also this volume, 44). When answering the question, "What exactly is a testimonio?" John Beverley and Marc Zimmerman write:

a novel or novella-length narrative, told in the first person by a narrator who is also the actual protagonist or witness of the events she or he recounts. The unit of narration is usually a life or a significant life episode (e.g., the experience of being a prisoner). Since in many cases the narrator is someone who is either functionally illiterate or, if literate, not a professional writer or intellectual, the production of a testimonio generally involves the recording and/or transcription and editing of an oral account by an interlocutor who is a journalist, writer, or social activist. The word suggests the act of testifying or bearing witness in a legal or religious sense. (Beverley and Zimmerman 1990, 173)

To any poststructuralist, post-boom, or postmodern reader the giveaway in Yúdice's definition is the notion of "authentic narrative." The critic succumbs to what Foucault calls "the will of truth" and finds testimonio's authenticity in an unquestioned origin of the word. We find ourselves in the heartland of phonocentrism, as Christopher Norris has explained it, following Derrida: "*Voice* becomes a metaphor of truth and authenticity, a source of self-present 'living' speech as opposed to the secondary lifeless emanations of writing" (1986, 28). In both definitions testimonial writing is politically principled and strongly action-oriented, which detracts from exploring its discursive armature. In strictly formal terms, it is simply perceived as a curious brand of life document, autobiography, and forensic patterns of confession, which takes the form of a novel. All this does quite a bit, but not enough, to clarify how testimonio's technique actually works. To help us delve further into the protocols governing testimonial writing and its recognition, I will focus on the intricate tension between the indeterminacy of experience and the closure of discourse, between the act of living/surviving/witnessing and the act of testifying/transcribing. I propose to test this terrain by using the notion of the *differend,* Jean-François Lyotard's felicitous term coined in his meditation on the vicissitudes of testifying in the post-Holocaust era. Lyotard gives the name of a *differend* to "the case where the plaintiff is divested of the means to argue and becomes for that reason a victim. If the addressor, the addressee, and the sense of the testimony are neutralized, everything takes place as if there were no damages. A case of differend between two parties takes place when the "regulation" of the conflict that opposes them is done in the idiom of one of the parties while the wrong suffered by the other is not signified in that idiom" (Lyotard 1988, 9).

Four instances are needed, according to Lyotard, to constitute a phrase universe of *testimonial contract* as a truth-believing paradigm. First, an addressee—someone not only willing to listen and accept the reality of the referent, but also worthy of being spoken to. Then there is an addressor, a witness who refuses to remain silent. Third, a language capable of signifying the referent. Then there is a "case" or the referent itself that "asks to be put into phrases, and suffers from the wrong of not being able to be put into phrases right away" (Lyotard 1988, 13). The referent, continues Lyotard, may be obliterated if silence results from the denial of one or several of the preceding three instances (14). In other words, testimony takes place only if the reality of a referent is established and in order for this to happen all silent negations must be withdrawn and the authority of the witness, addressee's competence, and language's ability to signify must be assured.

I am of course all the more aware that in the case of mediated testimonials Lyotard's model must be nuanced because it is further complicated by the fact that there are two levels of communication: first, the truth-believing effect has to be established between the two interlocutors and, secondly, between their collaborative text and the reader willing to approach it with *"testimonio-*seeing eyes." Hence, I will further use the notion of veridiction—a crucial concept in the semiotic theory of Algirdas Julien Greimas—in my attempt to establish what mechanisms embedded in the highly mediated genre of testimonio might have inclined us to read it as truth-saying and how this celebration of authentic representation has occurred in the heyday of postmodernism when all notions of truth and meaning have become eroded.

According to Greimas, "truth-believing must be installed at the two extremities of the communication channel," thus creating a tacit agreement, a veridiction contract between the speaker and the addressee. Since discourse is "no longer considered as the representation of a truth exterior to it," and since "the enunciator is no longer presumed to produce true discourse, but discourses producing a 'truth' meaning effect" (Greimas 1989, 657), the modern reader, Greimas contends, has to be persuaded to interpret the discourse as truth-saying.

After this theoretical detour, for the sake of brevity I will limit my discussion of the testimonial code of representation and communication to *The Autobiography of a Runaway Slave,* Miguel Barnet's/Esteban Montejo's foundational testimonio first published in Cuba in 1966 and a few years later (re)baptized as *novela testimonial* by the editor himself.[2] To simplify matters even further, I will assume that it displays in miniature the narrative powers at work in mediated testimonials. I will analyze how a signifying referent—the fundamental tenet of any nonfictional discourse—is created when the testimony of a 105-year-old illiterate former slave is transcribed by a young ethnologist of European background who has no direct knowledge of the facts he assembles into discourse.

In the introduction, Barnet, the addressee of the primary testimony, reviews his reasons, methods, and intentions in recording and editing Montejo's life story, but the primary function of these editorial remarks is to present the text that follows as truth-saying and thereby forge a tacit agreement with the reader as to its irrefutable authenticity. In order to create an illusion of seamless, mutually (re)created reality, Barnet directs our attention away from his own persona and claims that he is an unobtrusive interviewer and a self-effacing editor. His visible presence is, indeed, limited to the margins of discourse comprised by the prologue, a number of somewhat random footnotes and—in the Spanish version—a glossary of Afro-Cuban terms. These traces of presence and authority provide us with a clue to Barnet's efforts to balance the freedom of "literary" creativity with the constraint of the testimonial "discipline." The prologue also exemplifies one of the most powerful strategies to control discourse. As Michel Foucault has persuasively argued in "Order of Discourse," commentary strives to exorcise "the chance element of discourse" and to reduce chance and multiplicity from "what might risk being said" (Foucault 1981, 58).

Within the main text Barnet also follows what Greimas calls the strategy of "objectivizing camouflage" (Greimas 1989, 658) whereby all "marks of enunciation" are erased. Barnet's veridictory technique of "objectivizing camouflage" relies on the obliteration of the context of the primary discourse: the interviewer's questions are eliminated and a simulacrum of a monologue supplants the original dialogue. All this is intended to support the editor's claim that it is indeed Montejo who is "the real author of this book" (E. Montejo 1968, 8).

In terms of Lyotard's model, Barnet is the cornerstone of the bona fide testimonial contract. He can justly lay claim to being a competent addressee (a professional ethnographer), an engaged participant, whose sympathetic gaze should foster communication and eliminate silence. The actual extent to which Barnet as editor might have imposed his own choice of stylistic devices and reordered Montejo's original account is silenced and impossible to assess. Barnet admits, however, that in order to spare the reader from Montejo's rambling stories, he has had to paraphrase: "If I had transcribed his story word for word it would have been confusing and repetitive. I have kept the story within fixed time-limits, not being concerned to recreate the period in minute detail of time and place" (E. Montejo 1968, 8). Whereas interweaving the various strands of the original dialogue may be perceived as a necessary evil, Barnet's method of distilling his interlocutor's speech is rather disquieting: "I wanted his story to sound spontaneous and as if it came from the heart, and so I inserted words and expressions characteristic of Esteban wherever they seemed appropriate" (7). By sifting out data, Barnet is performing a contradictory role: on the one hand he is a researcher, an engaged participant, whose own theoretical biases and sympathetic attitude should not interfere with the making of a scientific record. On the other hand, he is a writer who—despite his explicit disavowal of all literary intentions—pursues a narrative that would retrieve the past in the guise of a readable account. And from both of these points of view Montejo's account, derived from autobiographical remembrance, requires reconfiguring.

Barnet's preface is intended to create an illusion of a common front and give unity and uniformity to a project which *ex definitione* should address the issue of difference and not erase it. Unlike historians and ethnographers who over the past thirty years have begun to break their silence on the mechanisms of discursive authority, transcription, and inscription (Hayden White, James Clifford, Clifford Geertz), Barnet makes claims to exhaustive understanding of his witness and does not view his own intervention as coercive or manipulative. Attempting to find his way between the Scylla of narrative chaos and the Charybdis of constraint, Barnet thus usurps the power as to what to reveal, how and when.

Exploring the tacit clauses of the testimonial contract, as it appears in *The Autobiography of a Runaway Slave,* makes us realize to what extent testimonio actually resembles discourses that Michel de Certeau calls "heterologies." An overriding concern that binds together discursive practices that fall into this category is that of capturing the voice reaching us from a distance: geographic, historic, cultural. In Certeau's words: "The heterological operations seem to depend on the fulfillment of two conditions: an object, defined as a 'fable,' and an instrument, translation. To define the position of the other (primitive, religious, mad, childlike, or popular) as a 'fable' is not merely to identify it with 'what speaks' but with a speech that 'does not know' what it says. . . . The 'fable' is thus a word full of meaning, but what it says 'implicitly' becomes 'explicit' only through scholarly exegesis." (Certeau 1984, 160)

Similar to the heterological mechanisms present in anthropological and psychoanalytic accounts—where the structuring force of scientific presuppositions determines inclusions and exclusions—in *The Autobiography of a Runaway Slave* it is the editor who warrants a story's "tellability" (Bruner's term). In all these cases the act of bearing witness calls for a guided dialogue. In each case the fragmentation of the original account is gradually transformed into a coherent and "complete" discourse.

Obviously, psychoanalytic, anthropological, and testimonial contracts may differ in the degree of freedom they grant their informants in controlling the final text. In the case of *The Autobiography* the informant is not really allowed to control the production of the text. He is illiterate and consequently cannot read and contest Barnet's (in)version of himself. Barnet recalls, nevertheless, Esteban's concern as he was constantly looking at the interviewer's notebook, and he almost forced his editor "to write down everything he said" (E. Montejo 1968, 8).

It may be worthwhile to compare Barnet's prefatory remarks with another heterological discourse—Freud's introduction to what is probably his best-known case history, "Fragment of an Analysis of a Case of Hysteria." As Steven Marcus has demonstrated in his article "Freud and Dora: Story, History, Case History," when Freud specifies what it is that is wrong with his patients' stories, "the difficulties are in the first instance formal shortcomings of *narrative*: the connections, 'even the ostensible ones—are for the most part incoherent,' obscured and unclear; 'and the sequence of different events is uncertain'" (Marcus 1983, 162). Among various types of narrative insufficiency, Marcus continues, Freud lists "amnesias and paramnesias of several kinds and various other means of severing connections and altering chronologies" (163). In a similar vein, Barnet underscores the problem of failing memory as related to Montejo's inability to tell a coherent, chronological story. "In many cases my informant was unable to remember precisely," he states on one occasion, to elaborate further: "Esteban's life in the forest is a remote and confused period in his memory" (E. Montejo 1968, 8). The superseding voice of the editor is supposed to bring a restoration of order to this chaos, substitute for an absent voice, secure the "tellability" of the story, as it indeed does, since one-third of *The Autobiography* deals precisely with Montejo's survival in the forest.

While Barnet is unwittingly exposing the complex relations between the researcher and the witness, he does not seem concerned about the deeply unsettling implications of this situation. Curiously enough, when filling in the interstices of Montejo's voice, Barnet not only follows the rules of narrative "tellability" and the methodological guidelines of the discipline. I would argue that he also embarks on a search for his own identity through his encounters with Montejo. This yearning to know the "other," as the authors of "The Postmodernist Turn in Anthropology" point out, is yet another heterological trait and it "can be traced to the romanticism so frequently associated with anthropologists' scholarly pursuits. Traditionally, the romantic component has been linked to the heroic quest, by the single anthropologist, for 'his soul' through confrontation with the exotic 'other'" (Mascia-Lees et al. 1989, 25).

For Barnet the result of the testimonial transcription is cathartic also in a different way: "This book helps to fill certain gaps in Cuba's history," Barnet assures his readers. "None of the orthodox, schematically minded historians would ever have bothered with the experiences of a man like Esteban. But Esteban appeared on the scene as if to show that one voice from the heart of action is worth a vociferous chorus from the sidelines" (E. Montejo 1968, 9).

I have argued elsewhere that Barnet's idea to commit Montejo's voice to paper might have been inspired by Fidel Castro's "Words to the Intellectuals."[3] In one of his three well-publicized speeches addressed to intellectuals in June of 1961, the Cuban leader recalled talking to an old woman, a onetime slave; he then confronted his audience at the National Library with the following rhetorical question: "Who could describe life under slavery better than this woman, and who can describe the present better than you?" (quoted in González de Cascorro 1978, 85). Like many other intellectuals of his generation and background, Barnet preferred to eschew the present and still keep his place "within the Revolution." Unlike Heberto Padilla or Edmundo Desnoes, who soon found themselves "out of the game," Barnet devised an acceptable formula: he became, in his own words, "a mediator for the voice of others," a scribe unveiling and reinterpreting the past on behalf of the Cuban people who, like Montejo or the old woman from Castro's anecdote, had no recorded history.

Contrasting Barnet's complaints about the incoherence of his interlocutor's story with the actual text, signals the palimpsest-like structure of testimonial writing. Even when analyzed by a well-meaning reader who—like Yúdice—wants to see testimonio as an instrument of truth, *The Autobiography of a Runaway Slave* raises numerous questions as to why certain items were excluded or included. The title itself poses a challenge to Barnet's project: Montejo's *autobiography*—called *biografía* in the original—does not cover but a fraction of Montejo's life. From the introduction we learn that Montejo was an ardent supporter of the Cuban Revolution, but we have to take Barnet's word for it, since Montejo never really states it and the story comes to an abrupt closure fifty years before the Revolution, with a brief reference to the death of Máximo Gómez in 1905. Montejo's life after Independence is for the most part a ghost chapter, which can only be partly reconstructed from allusions dispersed throughout *The Autobiography* and from Barnet's next testimonial novel, *Song of Rachel* (1969). In a structural sense *The Autobiography* reveals Barnet's failure to fill the gaps and—as in Rigoberta Menchú's case—the failure of his "seduction" of the witness.

The Autobiography shows substantial editorial manipulations in the chronological division of the text (slavery-abolition—the War of Independence) and in the way its ethnographic material is organized by different topics and punctuated with dramatic reconstructions of historical events. This "belletrization" of ethnography, blurring considerable differences between two projects, two stories, two veridictory contracts becomes legitimate in Barnet's view since he writes out of a strong identification with his witness.[4] What is puzzling in this line of reasoning, however, is that Barnet's image of Montejo is blatantly heterological. At one point Barnet refers to Montejo's beliefs in the following manner: "His vision of the creation of the universe particularly appealed to me because of its poetic, surrealist slant" (E. Montejo 1968, 8). This perception of the testimonial witness resembles the construction of the so-called magic realist narrative in that it frames the "other" as fantastically exotic. What we get instead of difference is awkwardness. The use of the term "surrealist" is so tainted with Eurocentric assumptions that its presence within testimonio is particularly disquieting. Moreover, it exemplifies the heterological practice of translation as domestication of alterity, perpetuating myths about the West and its "others."

Let us go now to the second and third instances of Lyotard's model—the witness and language. Montejo, the witness, is portrayed in the prologue as rather willing to share his experiences, but, as we have already seen, Barnet underscores the problem of his failing memory and his inability to tell a chronological story. Even though the delimitation of territories between the editor and the witness is impossible, alongside the editor's efforts at embellishment and orchestration we hear—or want to hear—a different voice resonating beyond the strictures of the form. This voice that slips beyond the control of the author/scribe will be called here Montejo's voice even though I realize it is just an echo of his voice.

First and foremost this voice challenges the editor's claim that we can reconstruct the world through accumulation of facts and their causal reordering. Montejo makes us acutely aware that the sense of totality suggested by such an approach is treacherous, and he testifies to the limits of witnessing, particularly in relation to religious tabu, traumatic experiences (such as natural disasters or collective catastrophes), and intimate personal dramas. "There are some things about life I don't understand," he admits in the opening line that sets the tone for the rest of the account. "Everything about Nature is obscure to me, and about gods more so still" (E. Montejo 1968, 15). Moreover, there is even a discrepancy between his "real" name and the one he uses: "One of my surnames is Montejo," he explains, "after my mother who was a slave of French origin. The other is Mera. But hardly anyone knows this. Well, why should I tell people, since it is false anyway? It should really be Mesa, but what happened is that they changed it in the archives." (17).

Even though some literary devices—such as irony, allegory, parables, and symbols—are predicated upon the disjunction between appearance and substance, I would hesitate to interpret Montejo's silences in terms of a rhetorical ploy. Contrary to Doris Sommer—who has convincingly studied such "literary secrets" in another testimonial text, *I, Rigoberta Menchú*—I would like to emphasize that we are dealing here with very real secrets essential to the survival of the entire culture, and not with a belletrization of narrative gaps.

Montejo's restraint in disclosing certain aspects of his life is not only consistent with his personality but with the legacy of Afro-Cuban culture as well. In his study, *Domination and the Arts of Resistance*, James C. Scott (1990) demonstrates convincingly how different systems of oppression generate practices and rituals he calls "hidden transcripts of discourse." Ciphered language, Scott argues, constitutes one of the most powerful forms of everyday low-profile resistance in cases when direct vituperation or rebellion are considered too risky. Montejo's account gives ample evidence of the functioning of such "hidden transcripts" in the Aesopic folktales typical of the Afro-Cuban oral heritage. Occasionally he is more explicit about the atmosphere of discursive resistance that pervaded the entire slave culture: "These blacks made a secret of everything," he recalls. "They have changed a lot now, but in those days the hardest thing you could do was to try to win the confidence of one of them" (E. Montejo 1968, 36). Sometimes Montejo unmasks the meaning of Afro-Cuban "public transcript," which—out of fear—was constructed to appeal to the expectations of the powerful: "*Santería* used to be a religion for Africans, and even the Civil Guards . . . would have nothing to do with it," he recalls. "They would make some remark in passing like, 'What's going on here?' and the Negroes would say, 'We're celebrating San Juan.' But of course it was not San Juan but Oggún, the god of war" (80).

This is by no means to say that Montejo's account is anti-testimonial. It is rather meta-testimonial. If indeed, as Susan S. Lanser has pointed out, the authority of a narrator hinges on his/her social identity (class, gender, race), honesty, competence, and reliability and his/her privileged access to information and narrative self-consciousness, it may be Montejo's self-conscious stance that makes us truth-believing.

Montejo's self-reflexive account, obviously, does not escape its own prisonhouse of language. While he repeatedly displays his awareness of the equivocal nature of perception, understanding, communication, and the very act of bearing witness he, nevertheless, considers himself a reliable narrator. Montejo claims he always "makes sure of the facts first" (E. Montejo 1968, 122) and is quite suspicious of other people's stories. "You cannot put much trust in people," he contends, and then goes so far as to proclaim: "The truth is I don't even trust the Holy Ghost" (59). Despite the fact that Montejo has to preserve as instrument the very same language whose truth value he dismantles, by focusing on the holes between the warp and the woof of his story rather than on the perfect design itself, unlike his editor and unlike most testimonio critics, Montejo creates an internal system of self-questioning whereby he "inoculates" his story against external critique.

The narrator's ability to construct a truth-believing pact is put to the test when the fabric of experience becomes interwoven with such supernatural phenomena as headless riders, mermaids, spirits, and demons. "I once told a young man about the little devil," recalls Montejo, "and he said I was lying. Well, it may sound like a lie, but it's the plain truth" (E. Montejo 1968, 132). His skillful persuasion in such instances bears some affinity to so-called magic realism: very much like García Márquez in his celebrated levitation episodes, Montejo surrounds non-empirical phenomena with a vast array of everyday, material details that serve as assurances of plausibility and let him remain completely calm, almost aloof. This strategy is exemplified in the following portrayal of *güijes,* whom he treats as personal acquaintances, although it is never clear whether he had actually met them or not. Montejo speaks about "little black men with men's hands and feet like . . . well, I never found out what sort of feet they had, but their heads were flattened like frogs', exactly like frogs'. Ave Maria, the fuss and commotion there was when the güijes appeared" (126). A similar technique is employed over and over again: "When witches appeared," asserts Montejo, "they took off their skins and hung them up behind the door and stepped out just like that, all raw" (127).

This rhetoric can succeed as long as he denies his audience—comprised in this case by Barnet and us, the readers—a full participatory experience. In other words, as long as we are less knowledgeable than the speaker and/or cannot verify his statements. That is why Montejo reminds us that at best we can only get one foot into his world. He first of all warns us that the ability to experience the supernatural is a privilege not everyone can enjoy. "Negroes had a natural tendency to see them," he concludes when talking about *güijes*. On a different occasion he stipulates: "People who have the gift of visions see them almost every day; people who don't can still see them from time to time, though less often. I wouldn't call myself a seer, though I have seen strange things, like a light which walked alongside me and kept stopping when it came to a place where there was buried money to be dug up, and then disappeared. . . . They don't appear now because I don't get about as much as I did, and the lights are a country thing" (E. Montejo 1968, 127). On the other hand, certain phenomena are just too rare to be verifiable. As far as the witches are concerned, for instance, Montejo explains matter-of-factly that "there aren't many of them left here, because the Civil Guard exterminated them all. They were all Canary Islanders, I never saw a single Cuban witch" (127).

Unlike his editor, who focused on the romanticized notion of bonding between the interviewer and the well-informed witness and underscored the researcher's capacity to elicit truth—Montejo is scarcely *en rapport* with anyone. His voice truly dramatizes the crisis of truth and the inevitability of (self)-deception. Moreover, Montejo's story, like that of Ginés de Pasamonte, resists closure: "I say I don't want to die, so I can fight in all the battles to come. And I'm not going into the trenches or using any of those modern weapons. A machete will do for me" (E. Montejo 1968, 223). As Shoshana Felman and Dori Laub remind us in a recent book, in the testimony, language is in process and in trial, and it does not offer a final word on anything (Felman and Laub 1992, 5). Montejo—with his awareness of the impossibility of constructing a univocal narrative—stands as a witness to Barnet's anxiety about closure, and his voice generates its own, alternative rereading.

So while Barnet's introduction with its methodological contentions is cast in the mimetic frame, Montejo's voice brings us back to the notion of *differend*:

In the differend, something "asks" to be put into phrases, and suffers from the wrong of not being able to be put into phrases right away. This is when the human beings who thought they could use language as an instrument of communication learn through the feeling of pain which accompanies silence (and of pleasure which accompanies the invention of a new idiom), that they are summoned by language, not to augment to their profit the quantity of information communicable through existing idioms, but to recognize that what remains to be phrased exceeds what they can presently phrase, and that they must be allowed to institute idioms which do not yet exist. (Lyotard 1988, 13)

Whereas Barnet wants to predispose the reader to view the text as seamless, Montejo tells us that language—including his own—reveals only inasmuch as it conceals as it thrives on dissimulation, camouflage, deceit, duplicity, and not so benign lies. Montejo's narrative logic rests on the opposition between memory and experience, presence and absence, appearing and being, witnessing and testifying.

If definitions of *testimonio* are indeed symptomatic of what we look for when we read with testimonio-seeing eyes, this brief rereading of *The Autobiography of a Runaway Slave* tells us also what we tend to overlook. Yúdice, Beverley, and Zimmerman find testimonio's authenticity in the voice of the victim, who has the unquestioned power and right to "summon truth," "denounce," "exorcise," and "set aright." But they also tend to overcompensate for the internal discord we may find in specific texts, and they direct our attention away from the problematic inscription of the *differend*. For these critics, the testimonial word that emerges from oppression is perceived as natural, pure, uniquely insightful, and immune to ideological blindness.

Let us return to the initial concern of this paper—the critical perception and reception of Spanish American testimonio within the context of the boom and the post-boom. As I hope to have shown, testimonio is constructed in such a way as to, unwittingly, direct our attention to its own fissures. How was it possible then, that Barnet's text—built as it is around so many contradictions—instead of engendering some deconstructive readings ended up serving as a propitious model for the canonization of testimonio as a neorealist super-genre, a model of an "authentic narrative" for witnessing the unspeakable and narrating the unspoken experience of the Latin American subaltern? In other words, how was it possible to canonize testimonio as a discourse inverting the paradigm of subaltern (under)representation in Latin American letters?

I do not wish to launch a diatribe against the critics who fostered this process, partly because I would also have to say mea culpa. I can attempt to solve this paradox only by arguing that most critics did not read testimonial texts—they read the official voices of these texts, confusing the tongues of the editor and his/her surrogates. It is apparent that Barnet's attempt at genre making appealed to the practitioners of testimonio and critics alike because of his attractive claim to have devised the blueprint for a genuinely democratic and uniquely Latin American literary practice of harmonious weaving and blending of divergent voices. The reception of Barnet's project follows the critical trend that views all Latin American literature as an ongoing quest, a quest for a style that not only expresses the New World on its own terms, but also demonstrates an unrelenting commitment to the subaltern other.

Second, I think that this blind spot—which has had a galvanizing effect not only on testimonio criticism but on the perception of recent Spanish American narrative in general[5]—may have to do with a very legitimate concern of invalidating testimony, of transposing the reality of human suffering into nothing more than text. "If there is nobody to adduce the proof, nobody to admit it, and/or if the argument which upholds it is judged to be absurd," Lyotard warns us, "then the plaintiff is dismissed, the wrong he or she complains of cannot be attested. He or she becomes a victim" (Lyotard 1988, 9). It is likely that any reading of testimonio against the grain of its editorial voice would have been perceived as politically dangerous. I realize that there is a fine line between invalidating testimony and acknowledging, self-critically, "that what remains to be phrased exceeds what we can presently phrase" (Lyotard 1988, 13). Nevertheless, seeing testimonio as a seamless monument of authenticity and truth deprives it, in my opinion, of the ongoing tension between stories told and remaining to be told. More to the point, perhaps it also diminishes its potential as a forward-looking discourse participating in an open-ended and endless task of rewriting human experience. This task, in Lyotard's words, implies instituting "new addressees, new addressors, new significations, and new referents in order for the wrong to find an expression and for the plaintiff to cease being a victim. This requires new rules for the formation and linking of phrases. No one doubts that language is capable of admitting these new phrase families or new genres of discourse. Every wrong ought to be able to be put into phrases" (13).

From the vantage point of today I would like to suggest that we take our cue from the voice of the witness in testimonial texts. Testimonio's literary and political power ultimately stems from the witness's ethos, which, as we have seen, remains unscathed by his or her sense of disorientation and discontinuity. I would argue that if we allow for a similar dissonance in our critical enterprise, we will help in creating a discursive space in which the voice of the *differend* will not be subjected to suffocation or cannibalization. Consequently, we will be a step closer to recognizing the fact that testimonio does not provide a solution to the problems of Latin American expression, but it continues the same old quest in a new guise. In practical terms what it means is that we as critics may also contribute to giving the *differend* its due.

One final quote from James Clifford's "Notes on (Field)notes" may help my conclusion here concerning the critical operations performed on testimonio: "I am reminded of Roland Barthes' image of the sauce or glaze, the *nappe,* which the French cuisine smoothes over and hides the productive, transformative processes of the cooking. Barthes makes this into an image for ideological, naturalizing discourse. I have the impression that I can sometimes see through the *nappe* of the finished ethnography—beneath the unifying glaze, chopped meat" (Clifford 1990, 64). Ultimately, however, as any discourse, testimonio triggers its own rereading. And then, beneath the unifying glaze of the editorial remarks and critical commentaries, we can sometimes see, if not chopped meat, at least rice and beans.

Notes

Earlier versions of parts of this paper were read at the MLA convention in San Francisco, December 1991, and the Twentieth Century Spanish and Spanish-American Literature International Symposium at the University of Colorado, Boulder, November 1993.

1. When referring to Gustavo Pellón's chapter on "The Spanish American Novel: Recent Developments 1975 to 1990," Donald Shaw indicates that "the

three most obvious new directions in the Post-Boom novel are the historical novel, the documental novel and the hard-nosed detective novel" (Shaw 1993, 70). In my *Testimonio hispanoamericano: Historia, teoría, poética* I argue that "en la década del ochenta el contrato testimonial se convierte en el recurso retórico más socorrido por los escritores más reconocidos del *boom*—basta citar *Crónica de una muerte anunciada* de Gabriel García Márquez e *Historia de Mayta* de Mario Vargas Llosa. En ambos casos la apropiación del formato testimonial es, en realidad, una desmitificación del mismo" (Sklodowska 1992, 180).

2. See the English version of Barnet's "manifesto," "The Documentary Novel" (1981).

3. See my entry on Miguel Barnet in the *Dictionary of Literary Biography: Latin American Fiction Writers,* vol. 11 (Luis 1994).

4. For the discussion of "belletrization" and "formal mimesis" see Glowinski 1987.

5. Hernán Vidal—who has done substantial work on testimonio—offers the following picture of Latin American literary criticism: "During the last few decades, these two modalities of development of Latin American literary criticism—the one technocratic and the other culture-oriented—have tended toward a frank enmity. One indication is the fact that the literary critical technocracy tends to congregate at the meetings of the Modern Language Association, while the culturalists gravitate toward the Latin American Studies Association" (1993, 116).

Marc Zimmerman Testimonio in Guatemala

Payeras, Rigoberta, and Beyond

A s several critics have recently argued, a consideration of Central American testimonial literature is important in the study of the region's recent years of crisis. Clearly literary and social considerations are necessarily intertwined in *testimonio*; and the form has great value in revealing the "hidden secrets of popular tradition in relation to questions of resistance," as well as in providing access to situations and modes of thought unknown or poorly understood by officially sanctioned culture (Rodriguez 1982, 85–86). In this light, testimonio is not only a form of representation of popular ideologies and cultural modes; it is also a means of popular-democratic cultural practices closely bound with the same forces that produce political and military insurgency.

Of course there have been varying perspectives on testimonio's origins, referentiality, and functionality. For George Yúdice (1985b), testimonio signals a popular struggle initially conducted within the frame of Cuban and then more generally Latin American literary discourse against the force of "bourgeois" boom literature and Western postmodernism. Although not questioning the political value or resonance of testimonial discourse, Hugo Achugar (1989) seeks to moderate the romantic effusions of leftist champions of testimonio who have seen it as a virtually unmediated voice of a revolutionary tending social subject constructed as "the people," arguing that testimonio is inevitably constituted with the intervention of and for the lettered.

Within the frame of these two perspectives, I would join with John Beverley (1987, 1989), in proposing that contemporary testimonio signals a transformation of literary production that may well symptomize at least those forces tending toward an overall transformation in national social formations or even (at the extreme) modes of production. It is, then, a form that takes its place in the struggle for the middle sectors so often crucial in supporting and opposing revolutionary struggles. It may help constitute a new national narrative or deconstruct limited and excluding national constructs.

Whatever we decide testimonial discourse might be or mean in the overall scheme of things, our concern here must be to portray the emergence and role of testimonio in Guatemala. As a major locus for the testing of testimonio's origins and functionality, few countries would seem more appropriate. For Guatemala is one of the places where, even long before the institutionalization of the form in Cuba, testimonio as such had developed and served as a prime mode for expressing the critical problems and situations of various marginalized and subaltern sectors whose active presence would be central to any serious national transformation.

In this context, it may be further argued that testimonio by the 1980s becomes the symptomatic site for the effort to merge exploited Indian and *ladino,* elite and popular, male and female, Marxist and religious, urban and rural sectors in a movement that is ultimately far more broadly based, multiple, and potentially more forceful than any prior phase of political opposition and resistance in Guatemalan history. Nevertheless, to this it must be added that with respect to the religious dimension, Guatemalan testimonio may point to the growing emergence of Protestantism as a dimension of the counterinsurgency that has threatened the very revolutionary and liberationist perspective among popular sectors.

Most discussions of Guatemalan testimonio have focused on Mario Payeras's *Días de la selva* (1980) and, above all, on Rigoberta Menchú's famous book (1983), but this essay will also look at other works emerging in Guatemala's recent history.

The Early Testimonial Tradition in Guatemala

Beyond the chronicles of the Quichés and Cakchicels at the time of the Conquest and the countless ethnographic accounts over the years, modern testimonio in Guatemala had its first major stirrings in fictional and autobiographical prose (Wyld Ospina, Arévalo Martínez, Asturias, Cardoza y Aragón, Monteforte Toledo, etcetera) dealing with the dictatorships of Manuel Estrada Cabrera and Jorge Ubico; and it had its early apogee with the accounts of the intervention of 1954, the U.S. and military manueverings, and the aftermath involving exile and imprisonment for so many national leaders.

If fictional and nonfictional portrayals of dictatorship are starting points for the importance of testimonial tendencies in modern canonic Guatemalan prose, certainly many documentaries and portrayals of Guatemalan history appeared throughout the century, especially in the 1940s and on to the present. However far removed they may finally be from that specific combination of attributes that correspond to any normative definition of testimonio, many of these treatments do contain at least some of the elements that are essential to the constitution of the genre; they stand as the immediate discursive context for the reception, if not always the production, of specifically testimonial texts. This is especially so with respect to memoirs and historical analyses emanating from military, laboral, and political circles.

Above all the works produced over the Ubico years, the most important in terms of testimonio is that of the dramatist/ideologue Manuel Galich, *Del pánico al ataque* ([1949] 1985). One of the outstanding student leaders against the Ubico regime, Galich became a major figure of the Reform period before he was forced into exile in 1954. Dealing with the efforts to bring down Ubico, this volume seems somehow to be halfway between testimonio and historical essay. At times the persona of the author and his participator-observer status seem to get lost in his efforts at broader contextualization. But the testimonial passages and moments are classic instances of the genre, as Galich shows how the revival of student rebellion spread to other sectors and signaled "the end of the panic" or terror prevalent under the dictatorship and "the beginning of the attack" against Ubico's power.

Perhaps the most fully testimonial text of the Intervention and the years that follow is *Guaridas infernales* by Rubén Barreda Avila (1960). Barreda had supported Jacobo Arbenz and was arrested, tortured, and imprisoned by the government of Carlos Castillo Armas. Clearly before the emergence of Cuban testimonio, Barreda published his book depicting the 1,096 days he spent in his "prison purgatory." Standing as an indictment of the regime, the volume was a clandestine text used throughout the 1960s as a kind of primer for new cadres; it is a bridge work, then, between the literature of the Reform period and the documentary and testimonial-oriented literature that would characterize subsequent phases of Guatemalan history.

Other testimonio-tending documents emerged throughout the 1960s and 1970s. However, the first full-blown guerrilla testimonio to emerge in Guatemala as a successor to work appearing and promoted in Cuba (and at the same time expressive of the initial phases of what will be an autochthonous national crisis) is Mario Payeras's impressive book, *Días de la selva* (1980).

Mario Payeras and the Emergence of Guerrilla Testimonio in Guatemala

By the early 1970s, with the foco-style guerrilla movements of the 1960s all but obliterated, the surviving members of Fuerzas Armadas Rebeldes (the Rebel Armed Forces, or FAR), the key guerrilla foco group, spawned two additional organizations, Organización del Pueblo en Armas (Organization of the People in Arms, or ORPA), and the Ejército Guerillero de los Pobres (Guerrilla Army of the Poor, or EGP), both of which were inspired by Che Guevara's example and rhetoric and worked primarily in the western highlands with Indians and poor ladinos. The question in Guatemala was the very future of militant left opposition, and this was tied to whether there were bases for developing a rural campaign and in fact joining ladino left concerns with the problems posed by the indigenous population.

Relating to an existing guerrilla testimonial tradition, Payeras (1980) tells how sixteen members of the EGP crossed the border from Mexico and began to reinitiate armed struggle. Already known as a prose stylist, Payeras was one of the EGP's founding members, and his book portrays the difficulties of the guerrilla renewal, in which the effort to survive subjects revolutionary strategy to the test of everyday life.

The volume tells of the first miserable days in the jungle when politics take a backseat to the rain, insects, and hunger. Then Payeras describes initial contacts with the villagers, the problems of overcoming Indian suspicions, of undoing the mistakes of the previous guerrilla groups, of getting involved in the life in the mountains, of coming to understand the Indians, of maintaining and expanding contacts, and of undertaking the initial military actions. Moments of physical and emotional courage, of optimism and pessimism, of courageous loyalty and tragic betrayal haunt this short and evocative text.

The question of rebirth posed by Payeras is what it takes to extend the revolutionary base and in fact redefine the revolutionary subject in ways that would make opposition viable. This theme is at the center of much "guerrilla testimonio": the formation and full emergence of revolutionary commitment under the most grueling circumstances during a key transition in the revolutionary orientation. However, these matters surface through a literary structure that, as Juan Duchesne demonstrates (1986), parallels and is modeled on, but is also distanced from, the narrative strategies and revolutionary orientation of Che Guevara. Indeed, Payeras's book may be said to constitute an intervention in the debates over Guatemalan revolutionary theory and practice by rewriting Che's texts.

In his introduction, Payeras notes that the ideas he and his compañeros had about "transforming the world" were corrected and enriched by practice; and it is his hope that his book builds on (but also diverges from) past experience and serves as a point of reference for future revolutionaries. However, the key dimensions and parameters crucial for this text are not fully "delivered." Payeras himself insists on this, describing his text as one constructed in function of "gaps," pointing to a "lack of balance" in treatment, which may well hurl readers toward the gaps. "The few anecdotes included here can only begin to give a sense of the wealth of meaning these early experiences had for us." But he justifies his writing the book as is, seeing his "narrative" as "tales" constituting a "historical testimony," which give an inevitably partial picture that can only be rounded out collectively. "In the meantime," he adds, "it was important to set down something of what we had lived through: time moves on and memories seem to be made for forgetting."

So the book is a construct against forgetfulness, and, as George Black insists (in Payeras 1983), an effort to obliterate the effects of disproven revolutionary orientations, by developing a new approach toward Indian and peasant mass participation through "popular revolutionary war." Such a war might take years to unfold, and those who enter the jungle do so to "build a network of peasant support" for the long struggle. But what we have in the first episodes of the five years portrayed is a struggle against disease and poverty. Only the vision of the future, and a sense of human endeavor as "implanting seeds," can suggest any viability to the action described.

Indeed, Duchesne points to the lack of action in the text and notes how it tends toward a cyclical and accumulative construction. The main preoccupation is not progressive action along a lineal time continuum carried out by active agents whose contribution to the action can be broken down into segments. We have instead a series of spatial, lyrical, and even psychological emphases. The text "describes" and "characterizes," as opposed to "narrates." It is, in effect, too soon for much action, it is a time for exploring, understanding, surveying. Matters are spatial, events tend to be anecdotes that better help define the space, the jungle, and the actual or potential actors. Thus, in human terms, the first question is apprenticeship in the jungle, a place seen as a "sad world" (Duchesne 1986, 109).

Duchesne sees the conceit of seeding as basic to the structure and particular narrative time of the text, at the conjuncture between primitive society and early civilization, between jungle and early implantation (Duchesne 1986, 108). The guerrillero's way to victory is through a descent into the jungle, a return to roots, a meeting and knowing of America and her indigenous peoples. In effect, we are dealing with the latest variation of a constant Latin American pattern or trope, that of José Rivera's *La voragine* (1944) or Alejo Carpentier's *Pasos perdidos* (1968): a return to origins to begin once again. Only here the Dantesque journey cutting "through jungle vegetation with machetes" is one of "shaping and living out political decisions essential to revolutionary change in Guatemala." As Duchesne observes, "The protagonists cross a sociogeographical space fragmented in an unevenly developed history, in search for a zone of vital reinauguration. The guerrilla column crosses the jungle painfully discovering symbolic ruins of Mayan civilization devoured by the vegetation" (Duchesne 1986, 111–12).

In the process of initiation and revitalization, of jungle walks and political work, with little action on the grand scale, the narrative is nevertheless epic in character, as the protagonists are subjected to great tests of their capabilities of resistance, adaptation, and transcendence. Above all, the narrative articulates the growth of collectivity among the guerrilleros, who must find their new sense of shared identity among themselves and with the people before they can actualize the qualities required for revolutionary action. Only as the guerrilleros learn through their initiation are they able to develop their own project, and attempt to teach the Quiché peoples their message of revolutionary defiance and struggle.

In sum, the days in the jungle constitute an initial school for the guerrilleros, as they attempt to learn from those they hope to work with and teach. The revolutionary strategy is a learning experience, which is transmitted to the readers of the text. The textual strategy, then, is to present an image of the days in the jungle that is so convincing that the readers mimetically share the initiation and thus corroborate its importance, to the point that they feel a lived solidarity that is productive for future stages of struggle. This procedure requires that, in the tight economy of this very concise book, there is a slight excess of detail aimed at producing "what Paul Ricoeur calls 'the referential pretension' of every narrative, regardless if the world referred to is real or not" (Duchesne 1986, 113).

As the crucial figures of the jungle journey and seed planting make evident, metaphoric and imagistic suggestiveness is one of the most striking qualities of Payeras's narrative, and perhaps the most crucial way in which he structures his referential world. Sometimes there is a sense of strain in the search for fitting equations. But the strain stems from the text's primary motivations and the difficulties they entail— primarily, questions of locus and relatedness: the intent by the guerrilleros to find a proper place to start their new work and find ways to link all the elements required for the struggle. "The EGP placed its greatest emphasis on the Northwest highland," George Black informs us, "convinced that only through the combined resolution of class conflict and ethnic demands could the Guatemalan revolution acquire its special stamp" (in Payeras 1983, 12–13).

Most of the members of the EGP were Marxists, but, Payeras shows, many of them felt they should incorporate religious dimensions in their orientation to be in touch with the Christian perspective that many of the people followed. Nevertheless, macro-ideology is not the key issue, but rather lived experience, lived language, and their value in the linking process. The primary way to foster revolution would be through shared experience as a form of Freirian pedagogy, such as sharing the guerrillero's education into the world of the jungle and the Indian peasant, or sharing the Indian's education into the world of revolutionary perspective.

What is required is a creative synchretism bringing together the more defiant Mayan representatives with the ladino left. Just as we have a catalogue of the literature the revolutionaries read (Marx, Che, Castro, Sandino, and García Márquez), so we have intense depictions of the milieu and its hardships: the diet of corn flour, rice, salt, sugar, oil, and meat, the water supply from rivers and stagnant puddles—so that the guerrilleros became subject to intestinal worms, diarrhea, malaria, hepatitis. Just as we have portrayals of ladino and indigenous guerrilleros (including representatives from Kekchi, Achi, Cakchikel, Quiché, Mam groups, etcetera), and the struggle to win more people and groups to the guerrilla side, so too we have Payeras's descriptions of the huge jungle parrots, the macaws, the quetzales.

Granted, the linkage between guerrillas and jungle is not always positive or complete. A requisite for the pattern of awakening is to portray not only successes but painful failures, and indeed, the book closes on one of those remarkable but terrible stories that are a constant part of modern guerrilla narratives: the story of the guerrillero who weakens under torture and betrays the movement—the one who does not succeed in the tests required by the harsh school of guerrilla life. So the last chapter, "Fonseca," tells of an exemplary militant who talks after being captured and tortured and thus precipitates innumerable reprisals and killings carried out against the guerrilleros, their Indian collaborators, and even innocent Indian villagers. "This man is only partially redeemed . . . by his acceptance of his responsibility and his expression of commitment as he faces death" (Duchesne 1986, 115).

Fonseca's story is indeed a memorable tragedy-in-miniature within the overall testimonial epic. As the last instance of action in Payeras's book, Fonseca's execution by his former compañeros points to the symbolic pattern to be found in this tragedy and its relation to the book as a whole: "At the moment of his execution, one of the women guerrillas could not hold back her tears. He told her not to weep because his death would keep others from making the same mistakes. At that moment the entire guerrilla unit felt a knot in their throats. In his grave were placed the thirty-two centavos his sisters had sent from his village to accompany him in death" (Payeras 1983, 93).

In death, Fonseca moves us beyond his individual plight to that of the guerrilla unit, the collectivity. At once Christ and Judas, Fonseca ultimately sacrifices himself so that others will not follow his negative example. And his example is such that it not only brings the guerrilleros together but links them to the Christianized Mayans—again, the linkage that many guerrillos themselves view as essential to their country's revolutionary struggle. The linkage is expressed in Payeras's last comments, triggered—in a brilliantly keyed example of testimonial effect and function—by the guerrilleros' listening to a tape recording Fonseca has made about his betrayal and his decision to surrender:

> Listening to Fonseca's tape, we thought about what it means to be a revolutionary. We recalled a faraway bridge back in the highlands where we had once gone to pick up supplies. It was an immensely long and slender tree trunk laid across a dizzying torrent. The endless rain and the turbulent current drenched the trunk, making it glassy-smooth and slippery. We had to cross over twice: to pick up supplies and bring them back—a hundred pounds on our backs. . . . Whoever hesitated at midpoint would become paralyzed, unable to go back or forward. The secret was to cross slowly but without hesitation. We could not have imagined such perils on that night, five years earlier, when we had . . . [begun] our days in the jungle. (Payeras 1983, 94)

Rigoberta Menchú

Its literary value to one side, Payeras's text has some special significance because it gives expression to a process that was extending and deepening in Guatemala during the years subsequent to those he narrates. The period from the late 1970s to the early 1980s is a time of crisis, in which Guatemala's military-backed land-development projects clash with indigenous interests, thereby producing a situation in which at least certain Indian sectors organize and begin working with the militant religious and political groups and, further, in which the army reacts in such a way that confrontations, killings, torture, and massacres become part of a generalized social experience. Writing about this period and the events leading up to it, Carol Smith and Jeff Boyer[1] observe:

> Learning from the mistakes of the early FAR, ORPA and the EGP attached themselves to grassroots protest movements, especially . . . Catholic Action groups and the . . . peasant-worker union, CUC [Comité de Unidad Campesina]. CUC was an independent organization of rural campesinos . . . protest[ing] the lower-than-subsistence wages and . . . life-threatening, working

conditions faced by . . . workers on Guatemala's . . . plantations. CUC's mobiliz-
ing efforts . . . led to an unprecedented farmworker strike in 1980. . . .
Beginning in 1978, in response to a peasant protest over land in Panzós and
stepping up in 1980 after the successful CUC strike, the Guatemalan military
began a new phase of counterinsurgency, directing their efforts against the
entire Indian population of the western highlands, especially those living in
zones where some form of nontraditional popular organization, often religious,
had developed. Immediately after military control of the highlands was se-
cured, the remaining Indian peasants in the "insurgent areas" . . . were herded
into "model villages" or development poles along the major roads. Between
1982 and 1984, most male Indians in the highlands were organized by the
military into civil patrols—i.e., conscripted for unpaid militia service [aimed
at ferreting out the guerrillas and their supporters]. (Smith and Boyer 1987,
210–11)

W. George Lovell adds:

An estimated one million Indians . . . fled or were displaced from their homes
between 1981 and 1985 as a result of counterinsurgency. . . . Some sought
refuge in the forest and mountains surrounding their gutted communities,
where they wandered for months in search of food and shelter. Others drifted to
the squatter settlements of Guatemala City. . . . Still others . . . moved into the
guerrilla fold, took up arms, and are now fighting back. At least one hundred
thousand Maya fled across the border west and north into Mexico . . . [and even
into] the U.S. and Canada. For native men left behind, demonstrating political
correctness may involve regular service in one of the civil defense patrols set up
by the Guatemalan army to help police in the countryside. (Lovell 1988, 47)

Although many explanations have been given for this crisis, there is
no doubt that the quintessential written expressions of the crisis are the
countless testimonials to various events and processes in the period, by
Indian and often women representatives. And there is also no doubt
that, of all the testimonios, none is richer and more complete than that
of Rigoberta Menchú.

Compiled and introduced by Venezuelan anthropologist Elisabeth
Burgos-Debray (Regis Debray's ex-wife), this work presents Rigoberta
narrating the crisis of a traditional Indian family and community networks in the late 1970s and the parallel transformation of the narrator
into an activist and organizer on behalf of her community. Rigoberta

Menchú speaks through her narrative directly of the pain of her people and their modes of internalization and resistance; of the corn-centered culture of the villages of the Guatemalan altiplano; her family's struggle to keep and survive off of its minifundio; the rites of birth, marriage, and death; the death of siblings from malnutrition; the oppressive experience of seasonal work on the coastal cotton plantations; migration to the city to seek work as a maid; machismo and problems of women's oppression in both ladino and Indian cultures; the efforts to build self-defense organizations and the responding massacres of the army; the emergence of the CUC, the major mass organization of Indian-ladino peasant solidarity; the torture and murder of one of her brothers and her mother by the soldiers; her own exile. Her personal history ties her to most of the major events of the Indian resistance movement: Panzós, Cajul, the occupation of the Spanish Embassy (in which her father was killed), the creation of the CUC and the 1980 strike and the march on Guatemala City, the counterinsurgency campaigns of the early 1980s.

Clearly, the question of Rigoberta's representativity becomes a major key to grasping the implications of her text. There is the question of whether she represents more than herself, more than her family, a sector of her group, the Guatemala Mayans, and so on. Then there is the question of her story's referentiality, its "truth content"—how the impression of veracity is achieved, and whether that impression can be confirmed. Rigoberta convinces, and she does this, however, despite her own efforts to raise the possibility of ambiguity, half-truth, and outright error. But if the text goes "beyond ideology," then what are the determinants of Rigoberta's perspective and what kind of truth might we find in her telling?

First, we have the problem that on the one hand she wants to tell her story to win sympathy to her people's cause, but on the other hand she is afraid to tell the whole truth, because her people know from experience the way others have used what they could find out about them. Second, we have the problem of the fact that she tells her story to a Paris-trained anthropologist and that this anthropologist clearly affects the text, ordering the material according to her own sense of priorities, framing the chapters and determining the questions she asks. We have the problem of Rigoberta's own motivations, as a politically minded cadre who has been trained to see reality in a certain way and to seek certain outcomes for her people. Then, too, we may question the way she sees her culture, about the relation between what she claims are Mayan beliefs and what they may authentically be, even in their transformation through time. And we have also the linguistic question—the use of Spanish by one whose real language is Quiché. These and other matters of representation clearly have absorbed the critics with every aspect of her text, starting with the title of her book and its by now almost classic opening lines.

As John Beverley notes, Rigoberta's role as a community activist explains why this opening passage is perhaps more explicit than other testimonios. The narrative voice has a metonymic function that is a latent aspect of its narrative convention, by which each individual testimony evokes an absent polyphony of other voices, lives, and experiences. The testimonial form affirms the speaking subject by addressing the reader in the form of an "I" that demands attention. We are meant to hear the testimonial voice as that of a real rather than fictional person, as the mark of a desire not to be silenced or defeated, to impose oneself on an institution like literature from the stance of the excluded or the marginal. What we have is an individual decentered by a collective textual mode (Beverley 1987, 161–62).

This matter of voice in testimonio is perhaps the key to the question of representation—specifically, testimonio as the written transmission of voice. To be sure, whatever doubts have been raised about details of Rigoberta's story, they have failed to shake its foundations: the atrocities, the losses in the context of events that many people know of from a wide variety of printed and taped accounts. What is most convincing of all is Rigoberta's even tone, as she speaks to Burgos-Debray out of a condition that would be absolutely traumatic and silencing for most of us. Indeed, at one point in her story, Rigoberta tells of a sixteen-year-old girl, the daughter, like herself, of a union organizer, who had been handed over to the military by a frightened priest, only to be raped repeatedly and rescued when she was already out of her mind (see Menchú 1984, 235). This tells us something about how testimonios come to be distorted by psychic stress and torment, just as it speaks to the crucial nature of many testimonios and their continuing weight in spite of such distortion—their absolute necessity as verbal representation, spurred on by the death or forced silencing, by the actual or subjective exile, of many who might have given varying, but ultimately confirming, versions of what somehow must be said.

Further, what is crucial about this testimonio is shown to be fully embedded in what Rigoberta at least understands to be the deepest reaches of her cultural heritage. So, in a telling passage, Rigoberta says that, first, when a member of the group is about to die, everyone becomes attentive to what he has to say and recommend: "We say that a person, on his deathbed, makes an inventory of his life, and his mind passes over all the places he has lived. . . . [Then] the death ceremony is performed in the house of the dead person. Everyone comes. . . . There's also a sort of ceremony. . . . Everyone recounts something about him. The family speaks, and if he hasn't any family, the village representative speaks because he is like his family. We talk about him and recount the things he did during his life, but we don't only praise him—we can criticize him too. We spend the whole night talking about the dead person, about his life, remembering him" (Menchú 1984, 202).

The act of testimonio for Rigoberta is a culminating life ceremony, as embedded in the life of the community, just as her "I" is embedded and absolutely tied to a "we." Her testimonio is like that of one who is going to die, one uttered as a last will and testament to a ceremony-respecting community; her testimony is also one that speaks of those who died, which consecrates the community's past errors and achievements, past failures and successes in function of the present and future. The testimonio is a sacred, ceremonial act in which the ultimate relations between body and soul, perceived identity and *nahual,* individual and community, humankind and nature are affirmed in a ritual of representation and transformation. The testimonio is also a mode that precedes Catholic confession as an attribute of Mayan culture. But it is a mode that then reemerges with the force of the return of the repressed, at a time of Catholic transformation, as a reaction to the sacred but socially damning silence of the confessional priests and their church and finally to the politically co-opting modes of Protestant testifying, a reaction that simultaneously reaffirms a mode that is both Mayan and Catholic, sacred and yet fully social.

If such is the case, then who better to deal with Rigoberta's story, to carry her oral voice into print culture than an anthropologist like Burgos-Debray? Because of the orientation of this narrator, the text achieves the order in which it is published. So, after Rigoberta declares her representativity, there follows a series of chapters on her family, birth ceremonies, and so on, which establish the cultural and historical context that specify what interconnected dimensions she in fact represents. The book's anthropological framing calls the role of mediation to the forefront of critical concern. For, as Beverley notes, the contradictions of gender, race, class, and age that may be at the heart of the narrative are reproduced, especially because the narrator usually requires an interlocutor with a different background to elicit the oral account and give it written form (Beverley 1987, 164).

Burgos-Debray's preface, describing the relationship she developed with Rigoberta in the course of advancing her testimonial project, "constitutes a sort of testimonio about the production of a testimonio." One of their problems was that Menchú had to speak to Burgos-Debray in Spanish, the language of the oppressor ladinos, which she just had learned very imperfectly. Indeed, the conflict in Guatemala between Spanish and the indigenous languages is one of the themes of Rigoberta's story. Consequently, Burgos-Debray had to decide what to correct and what not to correct in Rigoberta's speech. One could draw comparisons to the familiar dialectics of master and slave or colonizer and colonized, whereby Burgos-Debray manipulates or exploits the material Menchú provides her; but Menchú is also exploiting her interlocutor so that her story achieves its political task of reaching an international audience. Moreover, editorial power does not belong to Burgos-Debray alone. Menchú, worrying that her account could be used against herself or her people, notes that there are certain things she will not speak of. Indeed, although Burgos-Debray retains final responsibility in selecting and shaping the narrative, the individual narrative units are wholly composed by Menchú. The narrator-compiler relation represents the possible union of a radicalized intelligentsia and the poor; it points to a sense of sisterhood and mutuality in the struggle with a common oppressive system (Beverley 1987, 164–66).

Crucial to delving into the questions of representation are Rigoberta's Mayan views on human/natural relations and, as a special instance, the *nahual*; and then, her views on the interaction between tradition and change as fundamental to group identity. The fact is, we cannot understand what Rigoberta and her story represent if we do not understand the relation between her words and her social being and the relation between herself and the world. These relations are spelled out very early in our text as Rigoberta speaks of birth ceremonies and commemorations and all that is involved and evoked in them.

The child is progressively initiated into the history of the group, the sacred ancestors, the meaning of maize, its preparation and consumption, the value and necessity of ceremony and ritual, a veritable oral/ body code involving invocations of Indian heroes, and explanations of the primacy of oral, as opposed to written, traditions in expressing suffering and perseverance, which are essential for the preservation of the group. In this context, the child learns that the universe consists of earth, water, sun, and man (Menchú 1984, 11). What is striking about this assertion is that in most cosmologies, humankind is seen as composed of, but also external to, four elements, which are said to be basic to everything in the universe. This view enables humankind to manipulate what is essentially external; it is the basis of the subject/object split that has been the particular mark of the West, in its development of instrumental logic; it is, according to many, the basis of Western achievement, but also the basis of Western alienation and exploitation.

On the other hand, Mayan cosmology as presented by Rigoberta sees humankind as necessarily internal to other dimensions of nature. Human and other elements interpenetrate in a kind of pantheistic ecological whole, which patterns of conquest, colonialism, and more modern forms of domination have damaged, rechanneled, but never fully obliterated, at least from the Mayan mind. Humans being part of the natural world, says Rigoberta, means that there is one world that they and animals share and that their lives are parallel (Menchú 1984, 19).

Of course, the crucial dimension of Rigoberta's text is how residual aspects of Mayan culture and their subsequent overlays link with contemporary Guatemalan left thought in a dynamic future-oriented synchretism. Among the terms of human/natural relations, as well as the question of identity, representation, and change, no matter is more important and complex in this regard than Rigoberta's comments on her nahual.

According to Rigoberta, "everyone is born with a nahual. The nahual is like a shadow, his protective spirit who will go through life with him. The nahual is the representative of the earth, the animal world, the sun and water." That is, the nahual expresses one's direct tie to the rest of the world; it is also "our double, something very important to us" (Menchú 1984, 19). Most intriguingly, after establishing the importance of the nahual to one's identity, Rigoberta then indicates that the Mayas don't tell children what their nahuals are until they are grown. While a nahual is usually an animal, it can be a tree or several animals; in addition, a child's Mayan name may mean one animal or another, which may or may not be the person's nahual.

Finally, of course, Rigoberta says she is not at liberty to reveal specific things about the nahual because it is one of the secrets that her people keep hidden in order to protect their identity and culture. In effect, our narrator, who says her name is Rigoberta, has another name and identity that she will not reveal to us. Although she wishes to tell us much, she will not tell us all; and we are faced with the problem of trying to figure out what the whole truth might be and if it might alter what truth we do receive. Indeed, if the nahual is the true expression of one's identity, and if keeping secrets is crucial to the very future Rigoberta seeks by telling the story of her people, then our whole sense of truth becomes undermined and problematized, and indeed there is nothing we can know with certainty.

George Yúdice has drawn out the relation between religious and political aspects of Rigoberta's narrative and linked them to the question of representation in postmodern versus subaltern texts. "Representation for Rigoberta," he argues, "is quite different from European . . . norms . . . [and] the nahual represents the absence of domination through instrumental rationality." He continues, "It is something akin to the representativity of Jesus in early Christian lore, whose significance . . . lies in . . . Christ's embodiment of love. This is . . . the sense in which her community fuses Christianity with its own rituals in a syncretic body of practices for survival. . . . Their first contacts with Christianity have been through the . . . orthodox Catholicism of Acción Católica, which . . . only made it easier for the . . . large landowners to exploit them. . . . Thus, the Indians came to distrust those priests who, like other ladino[s], . . . reject[ed] Indian customs" (Yúdice 1985b, 10–11). For Rigoberta and her people, religion is "a product of a dialogical land, [which] . . . provides material sustenance [and] embod[ies the] *Dios Mundo* (earth god), cannot be owned or exploited instrumentally. The child undergoes certain rites to purify his hands so that he [or she] may never rob (i.e., take from the community, the social body) nor 'abuse nature' (i.e., the natural body). . . . The Indian analysis of existential and social strife, then, begins with the condemnation of private or state ownership of the land" (Yúdice 1985b, 12).

Indians turn to "primitive" Christianity in their effort to maintain an integrated social harmony. When they believe this harmony to be threatened by instrumental reason and exploitation, they call on both God and nature and use Catholicism's sacred texts as "popular weapons" for vindication. Seeking texts that can *represent* them, they turn to the examples of Judith, David, and most significantly, Christ, who died so that his people might live. In other words, "the oppressed are represented in Christ's embodiment of the practice of their suffering and their collective survival. . . . In embracing Christ as the symbol of revolutionary consciousness-conscience, [Rigoberta's] community also embraces him as the most important of a panoply of 'popular weapons,' which include both Christianity and Marxism" (Yúdice 1985b, 12).

Yúdice's perceptive analysis brings forward the sacred dimension of Rigoberta's political thought; it confirms and deepens our contention about the communal and ceremonial nature of her testimonio and enables us to see it as part of a shamanistic process whereby the group's broken relation with a sacred space is to be restored. Yet, Yúdice perhaps overidentifies with Rigoberta and loses critical perspective by accepting Rigoberta's basically affirming view of her own culture as she understands it.

First, it would be important to consider the degree to which Rigoberta's views, before and after their politicization, correspond to original or transformative modes of Mayan thought as understood by authorities on the subject. Second, we should note that idyllic Mayan land relations aside, the Quiché groups have had a horrendous problem with land use, and particularly vis-à-vis their wood-burning procedures. The theory of ancient Mayan decline, immigration, and wards based on an inefficient land use is not generally questioned. But the fact is that present use has been a problem in Guatemala and has led to severe enmities between Mayan refugees in Chiapas, Mexico, and the population native to that area. This matter may be read between the lines in Rigoberta's text; and with some understanding it emerges as a central concern or contradiction, which feeds back to the entire question of representation in Rigoberta's story. Thus, for example, Rigoberta tells us that village problems began with the establishment of INAFOR, an institution entrusted with the care of trees and forests in Guatemala. It is when their requirements for tree cutting could not be met by many of the peasants that the big problems with land division in the altiplano began (Menchú 1984, 158).

Clearly, new schemes for land development joined with government manipulations, extreme Mayan poverty, and the growing national population to precipitate a crisis on many levels throughout the Quiché area and the country. Mayan practices that were considered traditional and satisfactory in earlier stages of development now posed ecological problems, threatening land-use projects throughout an extensive area. At least one aspect of the Mayan resistance, and their search for change, is founded on a desire to maintain what they consider to be their fundamental traditions, including the role of testimonial and ceremonial. Although the major problems of land use are those caused by Guatemala's new entrepreneurs in their search for oil and minerals, the case of wood burning is just one indication of the difficulties all ladinos concerned with national development (whether capitalist or socialist) might have with indigenous rights and values.

Apparently the only solution pursued by the ruling powers in Guatemala was manipulation and force, leading to resistance and then reprisal. But the question remains how would an "enlightened" capitalist, indeed "democratic," regime deal with this problem, and how would an "enlightened" socialist regime work out a solution? This problem emerges with regard also to the alienations and enmities among Indian groups, their understandable but ultimately debilitating distrust of all non-Indian, ladino values, the male-centered values and attitudes of the Quichés, and also the problem of Indian drinking, matters (and especially the latter) underplayed or perhaps not adequately focused in Rigoberta's testimonio. The very presence of these problems spells out how many transformations would be required before we could speak convincingly of harmonious relations between humans and nature.

Once these questions are raised, are we on the verge of discounting the entire frame of this testimonio? This is, of course, not the intent here; rather, it is to point to some of the survival strategies implicit in the overall cultural apparatus of this text. What is involved in all of the strategies noted is a process of selective and creative change at a moment of conjunctural crisis and profound danger of spiritual and physical annihilation. Although Rigoberta underplays such problems as her people's sexism and chemical dependence, and the conservative goals of some of her fellow Quichés, we know that her doing so is not due to her lack of critical perspective, but rather because the time in which she lives, during the developmentalist crisis of Guatemala and the uprising of the Mayas, leads her to choose a complex path involving a process of selective acculturation. That is, she must choose which aspects of her culture to preserve; which to modify, transform, and reject; which to stress at one moment, and which to stress at the next. By her life and narrative choices, she and her text come to embody this process. So she tells us:

The community decided no one must discover our secrets now. . . . We prepared our signals . . . [which] were to be all the everyday things we use, all natural things. I remember that we performed a ceremony before beginning our self-defense measures . . . where we asked the lord of the natural world, our one God, to help us and give us permission to use his creations of nature to defend ourselves with. (Menchú 1984, 125)

We broke with many of our cultural procedures by doing this but we knew it was the way to save ourselves. (128)

We need to be on the constant lookout for new techniques. (130)

Clearly, to maintain the group's identity, they have to transform it. And here they must avail themselves of what Burgos-Debray defines as "disassociative acculturation": an attempt to restore the past by using techniques drawn from the culture that one wishes to reject (Burgos-Debray in Menchú 1984, xvii). As Barbara Harlow notes, Rigoberta's "political struggle already enjoins rigorous personal demands," requiring her to renounce marriage and motherhood. Harlow also points out that "just as her gender role undergoes important alterations, so too is her ethnic and linguistic identity reshaped through her political activities" (Harlow 1987, 119). Thus, Rigoberta draws on Christianity and on Spanish to find some "signals" that will end Mayan isolation and help them in their struggle. Thus, too, she goes to a ladino school and accepts help from the ladino left, because she realizes that her people cannot survive on their own.

Indeed, Rigoberta tries to forge all dimensions of the conquerors' culture into weapons that may be used to fight them for the sake of older anti-instrumental Mayan belief and ritual patterns. As a daughter of one of the leaders, and as one whose discourse is mediated not only by Burgos-Debray but also by her own virtually unrepresented contacts with the ladino left, she is far from typical of her group, but may be said to represent the extreme of potential consciousness of the Mayas of the 1980s—the extreme juncture of past tradition with the pressing realities of the historical conjuncture. If she has decided to give up her own traditional feminine role as wife and mother, to devote her life full-time to making revolution, she has done so knowing that people's gender relations and drinking patterns must be altered, but never assuming that these things may happen overnight.

Rigoberta knows that her people must change considerably to survive but she knows to be selective in what modifications and transformations she believes can be promoted at a given time. She knows the pain of her people and their modes of internalization. She has lived the oppressive and at times killing experiences of seasonal work on the coastal fincas, the horrendous massacres in Indian villages, the campaigns and then deaths of her father, mother, and brother. Her personal experience has tied her to most of the major events and atrocities of Guatemala's Indian uprising. Nevertheless, there is finally something playful in Menchú's strategies of resistance, something joyful in this story fraught with pain. She recounts that her father once told her: "Don't be afraid. Because this is our life, and if we didn't feel this pain, perhaps our life would be different, perhaps we wouldn't think of it as life. This is our life: we must suffer it but we must also enjoy it" (Menchú 1984, 193). It is by internalizing all she has experienced and learned, that Rigoberta comes to embody and represent revolutionary possibility and hope in her country.

Other Testimonios of the Early 1980s

Several other testimonial-style books published between 1981 and 1985 portray varying aspects of the Guatemalan crisis. But no works could seem more opposite in tone and orientation from Rigoberta Menchú's view of the late 1970s and early 1980s than the diaries of Ignacio Bizarro Ujpán (presented by anthropologist James D. Sexton), *Son of Tecún Umán* (1981) and *Campesino* (1985). These books cover the years of Ignacio's life from 1972 to 1983—that is, from the time of *Días de la selva* through the entire period described in Rigoberta's narrative—the intense years of Indian uprising and military reprisals. Like Payeras and

Rigoberta, Ignacio writes of the developing guerrilla movement and Indian-military relations. Both he and Rigoberta give accounts of infant mortality, tortures and deaths of priests, the role of the Catholic religion in the villages, accounts of the fincas, of sicknesses, and so on. But whereas Rigoberta only mentions alcohol consumption in passing and clearly underplays the alcohol problems of her parents and her people, Ignacio devotes pages to detailing his bouts of drinking and his efforts to overcome his alcoholism. Although Rigoberta describes land takeovers, and Indians fighting and organizing against the government, Ignacio goes into occasional outbursts about subversion. And, of course, Rigoberta is a partisan of social change and radical Indian-ladino alliances for the sake of a Mayan and human future, but Ignacio seems to be for Indian assimilation into a reformed, but ultimately progress-oriented, capitalist, and ladino-dominated, system.

Finally, whereas Rigoberta's testimonio is conceived as a particular instance of collective experience, Ignacio's, for all Sexton's efforts to see him as "representative" of a people, seems to best represent the more individualized, ladinoized Indians integrated in relatively privileged ways into the national system. On the other hand, of course, he may also represent the nonrevolutionary, antitraditional consciousness developing among and perhaps even beginning to dominate among Indians in the years following the presidency of Efraín Ríos Montt. To put this in terms of some older Marxist categories, if Rigoberta represents the "potential consciousness" of Guatemalan Indians, Ignacio may well represent their "real consciousness." And the real may be their future for some time to come: with his drift from Catholic, land-centered, Indian values, Ignacio may well be telling us where many of the Indians may be going in the near future.

The Testimonios of 1987

Three testimonios appearing in 1987 express the more recent stages of counterinsurgency, and of urban struggle, as they begin to answer some of the questions raised by the prior years of conflict.

In his testimonio, *Tiempo de sudor y lucha* (1987), militant labor leader and worker Miguel Ángel Albizures writes about the struggle of the Guatemalan workers of the Coca-Cola Bottling Company. According to Rodolfo Robles, who writes the introduction to Albizures's book, the author has lived through the major events of his union; and his book is of great importance, because there is little literature about the history of the workers' movement in Guatemala and because the way Albizures portrays the Coca-Cola strike makes his work symptomatic of the overall movement.

Without doubt, Albizures's effort has the virtue of placing his union's struggle in a historical span extending from the 1944 Revolution to the key moments of union action and governmental repression up to 1985. But the text may well seem too much like a labor history to qualify as a testimonio. There is too much formal historical narrative, with all the rhetoric of the partisan. There are too many details of a technical nature, too many dates and events without much detail. Nevertheless, considerable interest may be sparked for readers who notice how this story of urban ladino workers chronicles the famous events in the countryside, including the tragedy at the Spanish Embassy, where Rigoberta Menchú's father was killed. In effect, this narrative crisscrosses many of the events described in other well-known testimonios; it provides another dimension of the national crisis by focusing on workers' struggles, but also the linkage of these struggles to those of rural workers. Further, it merges testimonial motifs and moments with labor history and labor exhortation to create a virtual hybrid genre that also seeks to transcend and then unite categories. Although there is much that is prosaic and objectivist in the book, there are also moments that are personal, lyrical, satirical, sharp—stylistic turns that for a second may remind readers of the most famous Central American testimonies, such as Roque Dalton's *Miguel Mármol* (1987).

True, we wish there would be more—more personal materials, more effective syncretization with other social sectors, and so on. But this work reminds us of the interconnections of field and town, Mayan peasant and mestizo factory or office worker, in a Guatemala more and more intimately tied to the world economy. And so, even in its limited way, this hybrid text points to the kinds of unities hoped for and dreamed of in prior stages of Guatemalan resistance that would be required if there is to be any ultimate success.

Written during the Ríos Montt years, but dealing with events during "the fifth year" of the EGP's war against the military, Mario Payeras's second testimonio, *El trueno en la ciudad* (1987) presents another finely written text filled with powerful images and tropes, which go far toward dramatizing the errors of EGP guerrillas, first in the countryside and then in the city, that led to a deteriorating situation: the death of many peasants, of many comrades and allies, a decline of revolutionary support, and ultimately the break of the writer and some of his comrades with the EGP national directorate. Payeras portrays how he and other EGP members came out of the mountains to develop a program of urban struggle with a completely mistaken understanding of the power of the military and the limits to popular support for the guerrilla movement, and how these matters should have affected revolutionary strategy and action. The role of the volume is polemical, to criticize the left, to stir debate among Guatemalan revolutionaries so that they understand and do not repeat their errors. But a key point of Payeras's volume is its testimony to the sophistication of the undercover and other methods employed by the Guatemalan army in its intelligence operations. It thus corroborates the image we have received by our indigenous narrators and verifies the inner logic of Guatemalan testimonio: the terribly dire difficulties of a terribly dire struggle.

Finally, there is Victor Montejo's *Testimony* (1987), a book that has appeared only in English and that, although *written* by a poor but educated "middle sector" Mayan, nevertheless captures much of the spirit and urgency of Rigoberta Menchú's story in accounting the atrocity Montejo witnessed in the Quiché area. Montejo's book co-opts the entire genre with its title, but ironically, it is not a testimonio according to all the categories suggested by the specialists in the matter. However, there is little doubt of its documentary value and power. "Few have written firsthand with greater effect than . . . Montejo," writes W. George Lovell. "His *Testimony* is a moving account of how counterinsurgency affected his life, and those of many others in the small Cuchumatán community where he once taught school" (Lovell 1988, 57).

Dedicated to those Guatemalans that fell in the years of the holocaust, this slender volume is Montejo's firsthand account of a military attack on the village of Tzalalá in the northwest of Huehuetenango Department, which he witnessed as a primary school teacher in the town. The book presents a detailed portrait of the conflict between the townspeople and the army. As in other parts of the country, the army has "drafted" countless young men to serve in the "civil defense patrol," aimed at isolating and exposing revolutionaries and their sympathizers. Now, as hopes begin to fade for successful insurrection, the narrative depicts how the civil patrol of Tzalalá mistakes an army detachment dressed in olive fatigues for guerrillas and how this highly symbolic question of mistaken identities unleashes military hatreds toward the Mayan population, to the point that they terrorize, imprison, and execute many people.

Readers might find *Testimony* somehow undeveloped in comparison with Rigoberta Menchú's story. But this narrative confirms several cultural and historical matters projected in Rigoberta's narration. Thus, Montejo makes much of the marimba and of the *nixtamal* (the mixture used to make tortillas, or the adobe used to make homes), as basic dimensions of Mayan ceremony. Women are shown cooking, cleaning, washing their clothes in the river, bearing and taking care of children, usually with no help from their husbands—although they must help in the *milpa* at harvest time.

More profoundly, perhaps, Montejo partakes of Rigoberta's feeling for the sacred land, nature, and time—in contradistinction to the sacrilegious attitudes of the military. So when the army is about to carry out an unjust execution of five men, he writes, "The five condemned men . . . gazed toward the horizon as though to bid farewell to the hills that had nurtured them. The campesino feels he is part of nature. He spends all his life bound to it like a bud or an unseverable and timeless offshoot" (V. Montejo 1987, 57). Elsewhere, he exhibits an attitude toward conservative religion and its ties to Ríos Montt and the military that places him at odds with Ignacio and in harmony with Rigoberta. So, he writes: "I had read in a newspaper the astute Ríos Montt proclamation: 'I belong to a religious congregation in which we give thanks to God, keep faith with the word of God and practice the word of God.' I smiled inwardly. What cynicism. I had never thought the coup that overthrew Lucas García would in any way improve conditions in the country. So long as the army officers remain in power the situation remains the same" (55).

Above all, this story joins Rigoberta's account in confirming the hatred toward the Mayas on the part of the officers and the emergent role of the military not merely as a prop to Guatemala's old, conservative oligarchy but as a relatively autonomous power ready to foist its vision on others. "The military doctrine had undermined the foundation of an indigenous culture causing the Indian to act against his own will and best interests and destroying what is most sacred in his Ancient Mayan legacy: love and respect for one's own neighbor, which retranslates into a policy of mutual support" (V. Montejo 1987, 63). As Michael Richards corroborates in his remarkable interviews (1986), the military views itself as the only force able to bring civilization to the neglected, benighted Indians of Guatemala through their civilian patrol and "development pole" low-intensity warfare policies. Ominously, in his closing remarks, Montejo spells out a pattern that was to be all too pervasive during the months to come: "With the rise to power of Efraín Ríos Montt, all remaining human rights were abolished, and the army became the sole arbiter over the lives of the Guatemalans. As the situation deteriorated day by day, I became convinced that I had to protect my life somewhere else" (V. Montejo 1987, 113).

Still Other Recent Perspectives and Texts

As a new period of attempted restructuration has developed in Guatemala during the years of the Vinicio Cerezo presidency, specialists have attempted to look back at the previous period, to understand more fully the reasons for the patterns of insurgency and counterinsurgency and, again, for the apparent frustration of the revolutionary tide. Most of the theories emphasize objective matters such as the crises of agro-export economies and their repressive apparatuses, and so on. But in the context of such perspectives, ideological and cultural matters play key roles.

In this regard, it would be valuable to turn toward still more recent testimonial texts dealing with the plight of rural and urban sectors. The material is indeed abundant, but it exists mainly in the holdings of the Guatemalan Church in Exile located in Nicaragua, and in the hundreds of largely untranscribed (and not readily accessible) tapes made by researchers in the areas under siege in the early to mid-1980s and housed in the basement archives of the Instituto Folklórico de la Universidad de San Carlos as neutral ethnographic materials. Lacking such documentation, we turn to two texts that are not themselves testimonios, but which reproduce, draw on, summarize, and embody a large amount of testimonial material.

First, an account by anthropologist Sheldon Annis (1987), who interviewed and observed Indian peasant communities in the highlands of midwestern Guatemala, argues that Indian resistance to the government and the military was largely checked during the Ríos Montt period not only because of the "low intensity warfare" military tactics, but also because of the success of Ríos Montt's religious campaign in spreading fundamentalist Protestantism in what also has constituted a period of massive cultural and ideological conversion among a war-traumatized Indian population.

Skillfully combining economic and cultural strands in his analysis, Annis argues that most of the Indians, far from being followers of a new liberation theology synchretically joined to their pre-Christian practices and beliefs, are quickly becoming Protestant supporters of the regime. With this they leave Catholicism behind, and their new religion breaks down their prior allegiance to their plots of land (*milpas*) for growing corn and beans. Thus, deeply and quickly, their colonial construct of Indian identity is eroded and they begin to become ladinos, tending petty entrepreneurs (producers and merchants for the tourist trade), and agricultural workers, with a stake in the government's anti-guerrilla and modernization campaigns.

In studying these matters, "anthropologists may be the scholars best able to document and interpret the present conjuncture in Guatemala because few others know as well as they do the rural areas where the new revolutionary movement and subsequent counterinsurgency campaigns were most intense," argue Carol Smith and Jeff Boyer (1987, 212). They further indicate that a recent book, Robert Carmack's *Harvest of Violence* (1988), "takes a major step in this direction by providing portraits of several Indian communities. . . . [It was] written by anthropologists who did field work in the 1970s and who discovered through visits or personal contacts what happened to their [the Indians] field sites in the 1980s." Carmack's book contains many remarkable accounts of Indian resistance and atrocities in the crisis period. Again we turn to Annis's account, entitled "Story from a Peaceful Town," where he reconstructs a terrible tragedy in the early 1980s, based on many testimonial accounts, of a takeover of Indian lands, of their resistance to the police, and their slaughter, and concludes that a slow dying is taking place:

Cows are once again grazing on small, wired-off microplots. . . . Yet the farmers are renters rather than owners. . . . Those Indians . . . foolish enough to believe they too had rights . . . have been put in their place. They are, brutally, once again the indios whom they were bred . . . to be. . . . They have been reintegrated into their historic role. Today religion thrives. Work continues in the field and at the loom. But there are no community organizations, no leaders, and no vocabulary of protest. The town once again produces, waits, and seemingly expects nothing. (Annis, in Carmack 1988, 173, with an extrapolation from 172)[2]

What Annis says has great importance with respect to the situation of many Guatemalan Indian areas, as well as the question of testimonio and even narrative in relation to present circumstances. At one point, he tells us of a friend who is a novelist and who had read the above account. This friend supposedly said: "It could not be fiction; there are too many deaths. The plot is too thin to support that many people dying." It is a story only in reality (Carmack 1988, 172). And yet when he turns to the question of the survivors' present relation to their own story, he notes that "the people . . . have not mythified themselves or heroized their resistance. . . . To tell me what had happened [at the time of the Panzós massacre and the burning of the Spanish Embassy], an old friend took me to a hillside far above the town. . . . In his precise recounting of the facts, he does not revel in the towns' symbolic victories but says only that he and his neighbors fell victim to temporary madness" (in Carmack 1988, 173).

In spite of the importance of Annis's views and the overall pessimism for revolutionary transformation in Guatemala (in light of military control and reorganization of most Indian centers and the democratic reform veneer highlighted by the Cerezo government), we should question if Annis's emphasis on Protestant conversion does not exaggerate a tendency into a fixed characteristic and, given the history of Guatemala's poor, if Protestantism won't also be turned one day against the masters. We should not assume either that control can be eternal, or that timid reforms can resolve the basic conflicts on the country. No matter what transformations may be attempted in Guatemala, global and national economic patterns imply no ready solution to Guatemalan problems within the framework of capitalist modernization; and that modernization process may stir future stages of resistance. Already there are signs that the trauma of the early 1980s may be diminishing, as the people continue to face newer modes of oppression. So, as Richard Adams writes, in the concluding chapter of Carmack's volume:

People do pick up their lives and go on, families will re-form around survivors, and eventually the conscious fear will be repressed to some degree so that society can function. . . . It is unpredictable . . . just how the guerrilla activity will continue. . . . One cannot ignore what may be harvested from this decade of violence. What will be the future thoughts of the thousands of children, whose numbers will probably exceed 100,000 before the present era ends, growing up with the knowledge that their fathers or families were unreasonably killed by the army? What of the growing channels of information about different ways of doing things that are now coming in from refugees? . . . And, finally, what is the political future of a population that first learned about democratic participation in the revolutionary decade of 1944–54, only to have it snatched away by a CIA-backed coup, and to have been brought by frustration to active revolution, only to have it result in the slaughter of 1975–85? (Carmack 1988, 290–91)

From the early sacred Quiché text *Popol Vuh* to 1954, from 1954 to the present, and especially since the guerrillas initiated their struggles in the Guatemalan jungles, testimonio has been a dominant expressive form and literary trend or current used to articulate the most profound dimensions of Guatemalan life. As such, testimonio has served to express and project structural transformations among different groups. It has pointed to the causes of resistance, and also to the constraints inherent to the patterns of resistance activated at given stages of the development of key sectors. In this regard, we should remember how, in many instances, the testimonios of Guatemala have served as cadre literature, as models to emulate, as warnings to keep in mind, and so on; thus, they have not only expressed patterns but generated them. On the whole we may wonder in what ways the emergence of any new Guatemalan testimonios may not only tell us more about why the 1980s failed to generate a fully revolutionary movement, but also about when and on what bases future (and perhaps very different) phases and modes of resistance might begin.

Notes

1.   This and other quotations from this source are reproduced with permission from the *Annual Review of Anthropology,* Vol. 16, © 1987 by Annual Reviews Inc.

2.   From *Harvest of Violence: The Maya Indians and the Guatemalan Crisis,* edited by Robert M. Carmack. Copyright © 1988 by the University of Oklahoma Press. Used here by permission.

Doris Sommer *No Secrets*

The language-game of reporting can be given such a turn that a report
is not meant to inform the hearer about its subject matter but about the
person making the report.
—Ludwig Wittgenstein

Rigoberta Menchú's secrets astonished me when I read her testimonial over ten years ago. Secrets seemed then, as they do now,
the most noteworthy and instructive feature of her book, however one
judges the validity of the information or the authenticity of the informant. Why should she make so much of keeping secrets, I won-
dered, secrets that don't have any apparent military or strategic value?
The book, after all, is a public denunciation of murderous Indian removal politics in Guatemala, an exposé in an ethnographic frame. Yet
throughout, Rigoberta claims that she purposely withholds cultural
information. Is she a witness to abuse as an authentic victim, or is she
being coy on the witness stand? The difference is significant, even if we
discover that the alternatives are irreducibly tangled: either she is a
vulnerable vehicle for truth beyond her control, revealing information
that compromises and infuriates the government; or she is exercising
control over apparently irrelevant information, perhaps to produce her
own strategic version of truth.

In what follows, a reference to Nietzsche will help to negotiate the
distance between telling and troping, between relevant and irrelevant
data. Then, lessons from Enrique Dussel, Paul Ricoeur, and the shades
of church-affiliated victims of Guatemalan death squads can remind us
that bearing witness has been a sacred responsibility throughout Christianity, a responsibility that is related both etymologically and historically to martyrdom. I will suggest that Rigoberta glosses those lessons
in her performance of ethnically responsible survival. Her techniques
include maintaining the secrets that keep readers from knowing her too

well. One conclusion to be drawn is that productive alliances respect cultural distances among members. Like the rhetorical figure of metonymy, alliance is a relationship of contiguity, not of metaphoric identification. To shorten the distance between writer and readers would invite identifications that might suggest a redundancy of positions. Rigoberta is too smart to prepare her own removal, in the logic of metaphoric evaporations of difference. Embattled Indians generally know that reductions are dangerous.

Sympathy and Surveillance

But first we might notice that the audible protests of silence are, cf course, responses to anthropologist Elisabeth Burgos-Debray's line of questioning. If she were not asking what we must take to be impertinent questions, the Quiché informant would logically have no reason to refuse answers. From the introduction to *Me llamo Rigoberta Menchú* (1983), we know that the testimonial is being mediated at several levels by Burgos-Debray, who records, edits, and arranges the information, so that knowledge in this text announces its partiality. The book, in other words, does not presume any immediacy between the narrating "I" and the readerly "you." Nor does Rigoberta proffer intimacy when she claims authorship for the interviews that remain catalogued under the interrogator's name (Brittin and Dworkin 1993, 214). Yet some readers have preferred the illusion of immediacy, deriving perhaps from certain (autobiographical?) habits of reading that project a real and knowable person onto the persona we are hearing, despite being told that the recorded voice is synthesized and processed, and despite the repeated reminders that our access is limited. Could the ardent interest, and our best intentions toward the informant, amount to construing the text as a kind of artless "confession," like the ones that characterized surveillance techniques of nineteenth-century colonizers? Maybe empathy for an informant is a good feeling that covers over a controlling disposition, what Derrida calls "an inquisitorial insistence, an order, a petition . . . To demand the narrative of the other, to extort it from him like a secretless secret" (Derrida 1979, 87). The possibility should give us pause. Natives who remained incalculable, because they refused to tell secrets, obviously frustrated colonial state control (Bhabha 1994, 99).

Rigoberta might have guessed at the aggressively passive ruse, while her sentimental readers would miss the point. She too manages to frustrate unabashed demands for calculable confessions. One such frustration is recorded in Dinesh D'Souza's tirade against making her testimonial part of a required curriculum at Stanford University. He would surely have preferred scientific information about genuine Guatemalan Indians, stable objects of investigation; instead he gets a protean subject of multiple discourses in Indian disguise (D'Souza 1991, 71–73). Some of us, no doubt, would dismiss his inquisitorial demand for knowable essences—but my concern here is that the demand lingers in what passes for sentimental interest and solidarity. Sympathetic readers can be as reluctant as is D'Souza to doubt the sincerity of a life story; they are reluctant, as well, to question their own motives for requiring intimate truth, even when they know that the life in their hands is a mediated text.

"What draws the reader to the novel," in Walter Benjamin's scornful observation, "is the hope of warming his shivering life with a death he reads about" (Benjamin 1969, 101). But novels seem unobliging today, given the sheer intellectual difficulty of important Latin American fiction since the "boom" of the 1960s and 1970s. Testimonials promise more warmth. In a strong case for the genre's distinctiveness, John Beverley argues that *testimonio* is poised *against* literature: that its collective denunciatory tone distinguishes testimony from the personal development narrative of standard autobiography; and that it tends to erase the tracks of an elitist author who is mediating the narrative. This allows for a "fraternal or sororal" complicity between narrator and reader, in other words, a tighter bond of intimacy than is possible in manipulative and evasive narrative fiction (Beverley 1993a, 77, and generally chapters 4 and 5). I have already argued that the projections of presence and truth are less than generous here (Sommer 1991). Empathy is hardly an ethical feeling, despite the enthusiasm among some political activists, including some first-world feminists, for identifying with Others (see, for example, Cornell 1995, 97). In effect, the projections of intimacy allow for an unproblematized appropriation that shortens the stretch between writer and reader, disregarding the text's rhetorical (decidedly literary) performance of keeping us at a politically safe distance. To close in on her might be to threaten her authority and leadership.

The very fact that I am able to call self-critical attention to our culture-bound appetites is a sign that I have been reading Rigoberta. When I began, her forthright refusals to satisfy my interest woke me to the possibility that the interest was being cultivated in order to produce the rebuff. Concerns about the text's authenticity—that is, transparency—seemed beside the point, as I began to appreciate its evident manipulations. Perhaps the informant was being more active and strategic than our essentialist notions of authenticity have allowed. The possibility triggered memories of other books that had refused intimacy, perhaps more subtly, so that their distancing tropes came into focus only then, as corollaries to Rigoberta's lesson. The unyielding tropes add up to a rhetoric of particularism that cautions privileged readers against easy appropriations of Otherness into manageable universal categories. Among those rhetorical moves, I remembered El Inca Garcilaso's introductory *Advertencias* (warnings) about the difficulties of the Peruvian language, Manzano's refusal to detail the humiliating scenes of slavery, "Jesusa Palancares" 's gruff dismissal of her interlocutor, and Toni Morrison's distinction between love and the demand for intimate confession in *Beloved* (see Sommer 1993). There were white authors, too, who theatricalized their incompetence to narrate colored lives across social asymmetries and cultural barriers, for example, Villaverde's *Cecila Valdés* (1882) and Cortázar's "The Pursuer" (1959); later, Vargas Llosa's *The Storyteller* (1987) would fit into this cluster of texts I consider in a forthcoming book, called "Proceed with Caution: A Rhetoric of Particularism."

I also remembered Edward Said at a public lecture when he interrupted a question. A sincere colleague was asking about ways to cure the blindness Said had denounced in *Orientalism*. "How should we achieve a better understanding of the Arab world? How we can avoid the mistakes, get closer to the truth, and . . . " Said stopped him to ask why Westerners suppose that the "Orient" wants to be understood correctly. Why did we assume that our interest in the "Orient" was reciprocated? Did we imagine that the desire was mutual, or that we were irresistible? Could we consider, along with the dangerous spiral of knowledge and power decried in his book, the possibility that our interest was not returned? This possibility of unrequited interest is one lesson to be learned from the kind of textual resistance Rigoberta performs.

Learning to listen to subalterns is an ethical and political imperative. One lesson can come from postcolonial historians, such as Ranajit Guha, who manages to read a "discourse" of insurgency out of texts meant to silence it; another can derive from a general postmodern wariness of "hermeneutic circularity," in George Steiner's words (Steiner 1975, 355). Old interpretive habits have a way of violating the messages moved from one social and cultural context to another, while interpreters are loathe to acknowledge their incompetence to account for remainders left out of asymmetrical translations (let us say in the transaction between a Quiché informant and European-language interrogators). The problems raised by presumptive, masterful understanding are both epistemological and ethical, problems that ring familiar now that postmodern skepticism has lowered the volume on masterly discourses in order to hear some competing, even incommensurate, voices.

Obviously, the kind of dissonance or admission of readerly "incompetence" that I can advocate to displace uncritical sentimentality or surveillance is not the kind that Allan Bloom and others have lamented as a failure of education. Incompetence for me is a modest-making goal. It is the goal of respecting the distances and the refusals that some texts have been broadcasting to our still deaf ears. Respect is a strange, perhaps premodern rather than postmodern, reading requirement for those of us who inhabit carefree, or careless, languages of criticism. We are trained in a more aggressive approach that explores, interprets, freely associates, understands, empathizes, assimilates.

It is an approach that some particularist narrators try to intercept. One such narrator is Rigoberta Menchú, whose secrets can help to cordon off curious and controlling readers from the vulnerable objects of their attention. Menchú will repeat with Villaverde's contraband dealer in slaves, "Not everything is meant to be said" (Villaverde 1971, 112). But her discretion is more subtle than his, since it is entirely possible that she is hiding very little. Perhaps, as I suggested, Menchú's audible silences and her wordy refusals to talk are calculated, not to cut short our curiosity, but to incite it, so that we feel the frustration.

Staged Standoffs

What I find so noteworthy about the testimonial is that Rigoberta's refusals remain on the page after the editing is done. The refusals say, in effect, this document is a screen, in the double sense that Henri Lefebvre (1988, 78) uses the term: something that shows and that also covers up. From the beginning, the narrator tells us very clearly that she is not going to tell: "Indians have been very careful not to disclose any details of their communities" (Menchú 1984, 9; 1983, 42). They are largely "public" secrets, known to the Quichés and kept from us in a gesture of self-preservation. "They are told that the Spaniards dishonoured our ancestors' finest sons, . . . And it is to honour these humble people that we must keep our secrets. And no-one except we Indians must know" (Menchú 1984, 13; 1983, 50. See also, in English, 1984, 17, 20, 59, 67, 69, 84, 125, 170, 188; in Spanish, 1983, 55, 60, 118, 131, 133, 155, 212, 275, 299). By some editorial or joint decision, the very last words of the testimonial are, "I'm still keeping secret what I think no-one should know. Not even anthropologists or intellectuals, no matter how many books they have, can find out all our secrets" (Menchú 1984, 247; 1983, 377).

Readers generally have noticed the inevitable interference of the ethnographer in these transcriptions. And they have been predictably critical or disappointed at the loss of immediacy, perhaps with a resentment born of an ardor that chafes at insulating frames covering explosive life stories. Most disturbing to many readers is probably Burgos-Debray's introduction, where she presumes to have shared intimacy and solidarity with Rigoberta as they shared nostalgic plates of black beans in Paris. Almost unremarked, however, but far more remarkable for being unanticipated, are the repeated and deliberate signs of asymmetry throughout Rigoberta's testimony. Either the informant, the scribe, or both were determined to keep a series of admonitions in the published text. Uncooperative gestures may be typical of ethnographic interrogations, but they are generally deleted from the scientific reports as insignificant "noise." Here, however, scientific curiosity turns out to be impertinent, a conclusion we draw from the refusal to respond. Are we being warned that curiosity may be an impulse to warm our cold bodies with the fuel of passionate and violated lives? Ironically, in the backhanded logic of metaleptic effects, our curiosity—the cause of Rigoberta's resistance—is a product of her performance. I wonder if she staged even more questions than she was asked, so that she could perform more refusals. Without refusing our putative interest often enough for us to notice, she could hardly have exercised the uncooperative control that turns a potentially humiliating scene of interrogation into an opportunity for self-authorization.

Nevertheless, the almost 400 pages of the original book are full of information. About herself, her community, traditional practices, the armed struggle, strategic decisions. Therefore, a reader may wonder why her final statement insists, for a last and conclusive time, that we "cannot know" her secrets. Why is so much attention being called to our insufficiency as readers? Does it mean that the knowledge is impossible or that it is forbidden? Is she saying that we are *incapable* of knowing, or that we *ought* not to know? My line of questioning is not entirely original, of course. It echoes the quandary that Nietzsche posed in a now famous posthumous work about the nature of language. If I repeat his dilemma here it is to highlight a particular textual strategy in Rigoberta's testimonial, to notice it and to respect its results.

Nietzsche begins his consideration of the possible truth value of language, including philosophical language that makes claims to truth, by wondering what our general criteria for validity are. The first, he says, is the identity principle. "We are unable to affirm and to deny one and the same thing," but he adds immediately, "this is a subjective empirical law, not the expression of any 'necessity' but only an inability. . . . The proposition therefore contains no criterion of truth, but an imperative concerning that which should count as true" (quoted in de Man 1979, 119–20). In other words, the identity principle, which at least from Aristotle on has been the ground for logical claims to truth, merely *presupposes* that A equals A as an ethical restriction; it is a necessary beginning, a fiction that constructs a ground for systematic philosophical thinking. If the claims of philosophy are based on a fiction, there evidently can be no categorical difference between one kind of writing and another, between logic and literature. It is rather a difference of degree in self-consciousness. In literature, tropes are obviously constructed and fictional, while non-literary texts presume their tropes to be true. Yet language, Nietzsche argues, cannot absolutely affirm anything, without acknowledging that any affirmation is based on a collective lie. He concludes from this exposition that the difference between truth and fiction, philosophy and literature, constatives and performatives, philosophical persuasion and literary troping, is finally undecidable.

How then are we to take Rigoberta's protestations of silence as she continues to talk? Are there really many secrets that she is not divulging, in which case her restraint would be true and real? Or is she performing a kind of rhetorical, fictional seduction in which she lets the fringe of a hidden text show in order to tease us into thinking that the fabric must be extraordinarily complicated and beautiful, even though there may not be much more than fringe to show? If we happen not to be anthropologists, how passionately interested does she imagine the reader to be in her ancestral secrets? Yet her narrative makes this very assumption, and therefore piques a curiosity that may not have preexisted her resistance. That is why it may be useful to notice that the refusal is performative; as I said, it constructs metaleptically the apparent cause of the refusal: our craving to know. Before she denies us the satisfaction of learning her secrets we may not be aware of any desire to grasp them. Another way of posing the alternatives is to ask whether she is withholding her secrets because we are so different and would understand them only imperfectly, or whether we should not know them for ethical reasons, because our knowledge would lead to power over her community.

Rigoberta continues to publicly perform this kind of silence, almost like a leitmotif. At an address delivered at the Political Forum of Harvard University, in April of 1994, she opened with some literally incomprehensible words. It was an incantatory flow pronounced between smiling lips under friendly eyes, words that a student asked her to translate during the question period. "No," was her polite response, "I cannot translate them." They were a formal and formulaic greeting in Quiché, she said, and they would lose their poetic quality in a different rendering. This speech act was not hostile, as I said; but it was an ethical reminder of difference that located meaning elsewhere, beyond translation, in the very foreignness of words.

As in the case of Nietzsche's meditation on the nature of rhetoric in general, the choice between ethics and epistemology is undecidable. Because even if her own explicit rationale is the nonempirical, ethical rationale (claiming that we should not know the secrets because of the particular power attached to the stories we tell about ourselves) she suggests another reason. It is the degree of our foreignness, our cultural difference, that would make her secrets incomprehensible to the outsider. We could never know them as she does, because we would inevitably force her secrets into our framework. "Theologians have come and observed us," for example, "and have drawn a false impression of the Indian world" (Menchú 1984, 9 [translation altered]; 1983, 42).

Guatemalan Indians have a long history of being read in such a manner by outsiders who speak European languages. From the sixteenth century to the present, the Maya have been "Surviving Conquest," as a recent demographic analysis puts it. If some readers perceive a certain ahistorical inflection in Rigoberta's sense that the Spanish conquest is an event of the recent past, George Lovell might corroborate her sense of continuity in this new period of cultural genocide. "Viewed in historical perspective, it is disconcerting to think how much the twentieth century resembles the sixteenth, for the parallels between cycles of conquest hundreds of years apart are striking. Model villages are designed to serve similar purposes as colonial *congregaciones*—to function as the institutional means by which one culture seeks to reshape the ways and conventions of another, to operate as authoritarian mechanisms of resettlement, indoctrination, and control" (Lovell 1988, 47; see also Manz 1988). The less comprehension in/by Spanish, the better; it is the language that the enemy uses to conquer differences. For an Indian, to learn Spanish can amount to passing over to the other side, to the *ladinos,* which simply means "Latin" or Spanish speakers. "My father used to call them 'ladinized Indians,' . . . because they act like *ladinos,* bad *ladinos*" (Menchú 1984, 24; 1983, 66).

Double Duty

All the theologians could not have been equally insensitive, however. Rigoberta, after all, became a Christian catechist devoted to the socially engaged spirit of liberation theology; and she continued to believe in a God who inspires political commitment, even after marxist comrades objected. Those objections surely underlined her determination to keep an autonomous distance from allies. Testimony itself, the very kind of juridically oriented narrative that she produces for us to read, is a Christian's obligation, as Paul Ricoeur reminds us. He explains that from the moment God appeared directly to human beings, testimony has implied an investment of absolute value in historical, contingent events (Ricoeur 1980, 119). The Old Testament prophets had prepared the connection, with their divine intuitions of God's will. But it was with the New Testament, whereby eternal truth irrupted into human history, that the juridical act of bearing witness obliged even average people to confront a defensive and punitive world (Ricoeur 1980, 134). "When the test of conviction becomes the price of life, the witness changes his name; he is called a martyr. . . . *Martus* in Greek means witness" (Ricoeur 1980, 129).

The root word also grounds Enrique Dussel's project to Latin Americanize ethical philosophy by way of lessons from theology of liberation: "He who opens himself to the Other, is with him, and testifies to him. And that means *martys*; he who 'testifies' to the other is a martyr. Because, before murdering the Other, totality will assassinate the one who denounced its sin against Otherness" (Dussel and Guillot 1975, 29). One limitation of European, basically Levinasian, ethics, he objects, is that absolute and awe-inspiring Otherness leaves the philosopher paralyzed, too stunned and too cautious to do anything useful (8–9). Another limitation is that in order to face Otherness, ethics turns its back to a long tradition of subject-centered ontology that has ravaged difference by reducing it to more of the same. For Levinas, in other words, to identify the Self *as* the subject of history would be self-serving. But, Dussel argues, if an inhospitable First World has always had its back turned to oneself, the discovery of Otherness at home is nothing less than liberating (38). A Latin American ethics needs to be actively committed, not cautiously self-effacing. As a corollary, or rather as a precondition for activity, it needs to refocus the Levinasian asymmetry from this side of the relationship between colonial centers and colonized peripheries.

Gayatri Spivak used to quip that if the subaltern could speak, she would be something else (Spivak 1990, 158). But more recently and more reflectively in collaboration with subaltern historians, Spivak has appreciated the "subject-effects" of subaltern eloquence (Spivak 1988, 12). It is the eloquence of what might be called a genre of "speech-acts," which inverts the relationship between tenor and vehicle (just as Self and Other change places from the center to the sidelines) and recognizes the acts of organized resistance as a narrative speech. For Dussel, too, violence is the language of a "subaltern" committed philosophy. Liberation means reconstituting the alterity of the Other in a fallen world where Cain already has murdered Abel (Dussel and Guillot 1975, 27), a violated and violent world. "If there is no reply to domination, nothing happens; but if a reply is made, the war begins" (Dussel and Guillot 1975, 18). At the end of his essay, in a climax after which words are insufficient, he repeats, "The war begins" (43).

From the comments of Ricoeur and Dussel, it would seem that a commitment to absolute imperatives requires physical self-sacrifice, that the discourse of subalternity is written in blood and in the statistics of martyrdom. On the other hand, sacrificial responsibility somehow can be finessed. Maybe an immobilized posture of awe before so much responsibility can keep philosophy out of the fray; or maybe a purely rhetorical self-defense can slip off the martyr's mantle that witnessing would dress on its vehicles. In terms of Rigoberta's personal comportment, to recall the apparently incommensurable difference between vulnerable testimony and coy control, either she accepts the traditional Christian robe, or she designs disguises.

But Ricoeur confounds the polarity by adding another, mediating, term: it is the incorrigibly compromising term of our fallible human languages. Charged with a communicative duty imposed by absolute truth, language cannot avoid humanizing, not to say debasing, the message by interpreting it. There is no help for it; even sacred testimony passes through the contingency of interpretation. So, Ricoeur concludes, the only possible philosophy of testimony is a hermeneutics, an interpretation (1980, 143). Testimony is hermeneutical in a double sense: it both gives a content to be interpreted, and it calls for an interpretation; it narrates facts, and it confesses a faith during the juridical moments that link history to eternity (Ricoeur 1980, 142).

Rigoberta apparently appreciates the double duty of testifying: the message of liberation pulls in one (ideal) direction, and the (earthly) medium of political persuasion pulls in another. To confuse the two would be worse than simply foolish. It might be disastrous to mistake unconditional demands for justice with what she evidently perceives as the sentimental interest of interrogators and readers. Their offers of solidarity may not pause to distinguish doing good from feeling good. The double challenge for this Christian leader, as new and as beleaguered as Christ's first witnesses, is to serve truth in ways that make a difference in the world. Testimony to that truth and coyness about how to convey it turn out to be voices in counterpoint. If we cannot hear the complexity, perhaps the inability is simply that, as Nietzsche would remind us, rather than a sign that contradictions cannot exist.

"J'accuse" rings loudly throughout the text, between the provocative, and protective, pauses of information flow. The pauses work in two directions, because it seems quite clear that Rigoberta's secrets are doubly strategic. They stop avid readers in their appropriative tracks, tracks that threaten to overstep the narrator's authority by assuming that the textual terrain is unobstructed and accessible to their mastery. Also, and more subtly, the secrets serve to whet anemic appetites by producing intrigue that can turn into productive, collaborative, political desire. If her secrets are so important, they must be interesting, no?

Strategic Losses

One paradox that Rigoberta must negotiate in her politics of cultural preservation is the possibility of becoming the enemy because she needs Spanish as the national lingua franca in a country of twenty-two ethnic groups. It is the only language that can make her an effective leader of the CUC (Comité de Unidad Campesina), a heterogeneous coalition of peasants and workers. Her father warns that with a formal education, "you'll forget about our common heritage" (Menchú 1984, 89; 1983, 162). That is one reason he and other community elders resisted learning Spanish. They recognize that Indian identity is a fragile cultural-linguistic construction, not an indelibly "racial" given. It is no wonder, for example, that the Quiché marriage ceremony includes the couple's promise to raise children as Indians. "After that they ask forgiveness from their parents and for help with bringing up their children as Indians, remembering their traditions, and throughout trouble, sadness and hunger remaining Indians" (Menchú 1984, 67 [translation altered]; 1983, 131). The danger, in other words, is as much assimilation as it is aggression. Whether the ladinos are welcoming or murderous, they bring cultural extinction. And that fear of mixing racial and linguistic categories is either the cause, or the effect, of a general prohibition against stirring up differences in Quiché ritual life: "Bread is very meaningful for the Indian, because of the fact that it was mixed with egg, flour with egg. In the past, our ancestors grew wheat. Then the Spaniards came and mixed it with egg. It was a mixture, no longer what our ancestors ate. It was White Man's food, and white men are like their bread, they are not wholesome. . . . We must not mix our customs with those of the whites" (Menchú 1984, 71; 1983, 137). From this we can sense how perfectly possible it is, and (personally) tragic for Rigoberta, to stop being an "Indian," because her political work depends on mixing and transgressing categories, on violating the ethnic boundaries that safeguard secrets. In the CUC, and at forums such as the United Nations, she constructs herself in Spanish; that is, she reads herself in a homogenizing code. Rigoberta attributes her political doubts, for example, to the fact that she has strayed from the community. "I was very ashamed at being so confused, when so many of my village understood so much better than I. But their ideas were very pure because they had never been outside *their* community" (Menchú 1984, 121; 1983, 207). The third-person possessive that I italicize here is one measure of her alienation. Nevertheless, we can note a hint of Rigoberta's "deconstructed" practice, in which the traditional categorical rigidity is simultaneously revered and sacrificed. For the price of the destabilizing distance from her community she earns some political clarity. "Indianist to my fingertips, I defended everything to do with my ancestors. But I understood this incorrectly, because we only understand ourselves in conversation with others . . . Ladinos . . . with us, the Indians" (Menchú 1984, 166 [translation altered]; 1983, 269).

Ser *and* Estar, *Autobiographical Essence and Testimonial Tropes*

I pose the question of rhetorical strategy, about whether Rigoberta is persuading or troping, in order to read appropriately and responsibly this text that ceaselessly calls attention to its difference from the reader and to the danger of overstepping cultural barriers. Personally, I prefer to think that her secrets are more "literary" than "real." Let me explain why. Reading her refusal of absolute intimacy as a deliberate textual strategy, whether or not much data come between the producer and consumer of this text, makes the gesture more self-conscious and repeatable than it would be if she merely remained silent on particular issues. The gesture precisely is not silence but a rather flamboyant refusal of information. Calling attention to an unknowable subtext is a profound lesson, because it hopes to secure Rigoberta's cultural identity, of course, but also because it is an imitable trope. Not that a reader should want to compete with Rigoberta's text, but that she or he might well want to learn from it how to coordinate intense political engagement, even at national and international levels, with a defense of difference. The calculated result of Rigoberta's gesture for sympathetic readers, paradoxically, is to exclude us from her circle of intimates. In fact, any way we read her, we are either intellectually or ethically unfit for Rigoberta's secrets, so that our interpretation does not vary the effect of reading. Either way, it produces a particular kind of distance akin to respect. So simple a lesson and so fundamental: it is to modestly acknowledge that difference exists. This is hardly a paralyzing admission, as Sacvan Bercovitch has so intelligently argued for rethinking the field of American studies. Recognizing our limitations is "enabling," because such an act has a double valence: acknowledging what we cannot know *and* what we can (Bercovitch 1993, 5). This defends us from any illusion of complete or stable knowledge, and therefore from the desire to replace one apparently limited speaker for another more totalizing one.

Finally, the undecidability of how to read Rigoberta is rather academic, because in both cases she is evidently performing a defensive move in the midst of her seduction. Her testimonial is an invitation to a tête-à-tête, not to a heart-to-heart. This should not necessarily be a disappointment; putting heads together is precisely what members of her community do every time they meet to discuss plans for a wedding or tactics for confronting the government. The respectful distance that we learn from Rigoberta's textual seduction is an extension of the same kind of respect for secrets learned repeatedly inside her own community. "The thing is that Indians have secrets and it's not always a good thing for children to know them. Or not so much that it's not a good thing but because it's not necessary. . . . We respect the different levels in the community" (Menchú 1984, 84; 1983, 155). Perhaps, then, our difference from that community is one of degree; maybe we are not so much outsiders as marginals, allies in a possible coalition rather than members. We are not excluded from her world, but kept at arm's length.

Still, this is surprising in a first-person autobiographical narrative, because we expect self-writing to be personally revealing, more intimate and confessional than coy. Now, clearly, I can register surprise only because I am presupposing (the first step in any deduction, as Nietzsche reminds us) that I am reading an autobiography. What is even more mechanical, perhaps, is my assumption that autobiography is a genre that blushes with a confessional glow. Yet, as Sylvia Molloy points out, this is a relatively recent expectation, "supported by the introspective streak found in certain autobiographical writings since the nineteenth century" (Molloy 1991, 3).

To suggest how Rigoberta's text may not quite fit the genre in either its early or late forms, perhaps it will help to historicize the desire for writing the self. Since Georges Gusdorf published "Conditions and Limits of Autobiography" in 1956, and especially since James Olney's publication (1980), students of autobiography have had to consider its originally parochial and then imperializing nature. "It would seem that autobiography is not to be found outside of our cultural area; one would say that it expresses a concern peculiar to Western *man,* a concern that has been of good use in *his* systematic conquest of the universe and that *he* has communicated to *men* of other cultures" (Gusdorf 1980, 29; my italics to show his complicity in the exclusion). Not surprisingly, the autobiography is a latecomer to Western literature, associated with humanism's focus on "the singularity of each individual life." "Throughout most of human history, the individual does not oppose himself to all others; he does not feel himself to exist outside of others, and still less against others, but very much with others in an interdependent existence that asserts its rhythms everywhere in the community." Even if the genre began with Saint Augustine "at the moment when the Christian contribution was grafted onto classical traditions" (Gusdorf 1980, 29), autobiographies became really popular during the Renaissance and Reformation, when self-made men became the rage.

Part of their charm for the reader, no doubt, is their contagious self-aggrandizement. Autobiographers write themselves precisely because they are convinced of their singularity, a conviction that spills over the page, so that readers of a relentless "I" can fantasize that the pronoun refers to him or her. It is an imperious metaphorization of the Other, after the initial metonymic relationship between the reader and the autobiography she or he takes in hand. "The autobiographical moment happens as an alignment between the two subjects involved in the process of reading in which they determine each other by mutual reflexive substitution" (de Man 1984, 921). We become the Cellini or Franklin figure who is conquering the world by dint of sheer talent and hard work. This is how Domingo Faustino Sarmiento (1931, 161; my translation) read his Franklin. "I felt that I was Franklin; And why not? I was very poor, like he was, studious like him, and trying as hard as I could to follow his footsteps, I could one day be as accomplished as he . . . making a place for myself in American letters and politics." And even if the text resists identification with the reader, insisting that the heights or depths of his or her experience are beyond us, we are free and maybe even fueled by the insistence on individuality to conjure up our own particular "I" (as Sylvia Molloy suggested to me) to be the subject of a new autobiography. A particular kind of textual resistance is the claim that women autobiographers typically make about their difference from other women (readers) in order to speak through what they consider to be more differentiated, male personae, as Nancy Miller (1988) has shown for France. Or, as Elaine Marks puts it, women's autobiographies proclaim that "I am my own heroine" (Marks 1975, 1). Of course, some autobiographers assume that they represent others, and that the reader is ideally among them. (See Leduc 1964, who begins, "Mon cas n'est pas unique"; and Leiris 1948–76.)

Perhaps the most salient rhetorical difference between autobiography and the women's testimonials that concern me here is the implied and often explicitly "plural subject" of testimony. Instead of an inimitable person, Rigoberta is a representative, not different from her community but different from us. She opens by disclaiming her particularity: "The important thing is that what has happened to me has happened to many other people too" (Menchú 1984, 1; 1983, 30). This sounds almost like a quote from another testimonial, written six years earlier by a representative of the Comité de Amas de Casa in a Bolivian mining town. Domitila Barrios begins *Si me permiten hablar* (1977) like this: "I don't want anyone at any moment to interpret the story I'm about to tell as something that is only personal. . . . What happened to me could have happened to hundreds of people in my country" (Barrios de Chungara 1978, 15). And Claribel Alegría's testimonial montage of the already-martyred heroine in *No me agarran viva* (They Won't Get Me Alive) starts with this prologue: "Eugenia, exemplary model of self-denial, sacrifice and revolutionary heroism, is a typical case rather than an exception of so many Salvadoran women who have dedicated their efforts and even their lives to the struggle for their people's liberation" (Alegría and Flakoll 1983, 9; my translation). Alegría experiments with a multiple mirror image that constructs her testimonial subject; instead of one narrator who assembles her community by extension, here a community of narrators reconstructs the life of a single revolutionary.

The testimonial "I" in these books neither presumes nor even invites us to identify with it. We are too foreign, and there is no pretense here of universal or essential human experience. That is why, at the end of a long narrative in which Rigoberta has told us so much, she reminds us that she has set limits that we must respect. The claim that she is representative helps to explain why, like autobiographers, she uses a singular pronoun, "I," not "we." That is, at the same time that she refuses intimacy with the reader—since intimacy invites identification and perhaps our imperializing substitution of her as the protagonist of the story—she also takes care not to substitute her community in a totalizing gesture. Instead, her singularity achieves its identity as an extension of the collective. The singular represents the plural, not because it replaces or subsumes the group, but because the speaker is a distinguishable part of the whole. In rhetorical terms, whose political consequences should be evident by now, there is a fundamental difference here between the *metaphor* of autobiography and heroic narrative in general, which assumes an identity-by-substitution, whereby one (superior) signifier replaces another (I substitutes for we, leader for follower, Christ for the faithful), and *metonymy,* a lateral move of identification-through-relationship, which acknowledges the possible differences among "us" as components of a centerless whole. This is where we can come in as readers, invited to be (*estar*) with the speaker rather than to be (*ser*) her.

The phenomenon of a collective subject of the testimonial, then, is hardly the result of a personal style on the part of the writer who testifies. Rather, it is a translation of a hegemonic autobiographical pose into a colonized language that does not equate identity with individuality. It is thus a reminder that life continues at the margins of Western discourse, and continues to disturb and to challenge it. This relative autonomy, however, may be on the eve of capitulation because, as Gusdorf further observes, the very fact that a first-person singular is marshaled to narrate a plural history is a symptom of Western penetration. "When Gandhi tells his own story, he is using Western means to defend the East" (Gusdorf 1980, 29). At the same time, though, testimonials also point beyond the dialectic of resistance and capitulation. They are models of experimental syncretism that represent a "return of the repressed" (Rosenblatt 1980, 169) in both traditional and Westernizing discourses. What has been generally "repressed" in standard auto-biographical writing is the degree to which the singular "I" depends on a complicated pronominal system. It nurtures an illusion of singularity, assuming it can stand *in* for others, whereas testimonies stand *up* among them.

Arguably, the tradition of Latin American autobiography had antic-ipated Rigoberta and Domitila's identification with a cultural group outside of which the text would be misread. The tradition assumes that the autobiographer is continuous with his or her community, as op-posed to assuming the radical individualism that we associate with, say, some European writers of the genre. Sarmiento, as Molloy points out, creates intimacy and complicity with the Argentine, ideal reader, as a result of excluding others: "The Spanish American 'I' (if one dare gener-alize in this fashion) seems to rely more than other 'I's—to rely in a nearly ontological manner—on a sort of national recognition. Represen-tativeness and identity are closely linked in Spanish American self-writing. Sarmiento dedicates the book [*Recuerdos de provincia*] that will show him as the true son of the new republic 'to my compatriots only'—those who will truly understand him and give him being" (Molloy 1991, 151). Even Victoria Ocampo, who knows she is especially priv-ileged, understands her specialness in terms of her family's prominence in national history, that is, in a context she has in common with her readers (Molloy 1991, 166). From them, Sarmiento and Ocampo claim to have no secrets.

Halting Readers

But for Rigoberta there are literally no ideal readers. The notion is a contradiction here. Those who ideally understand Rigoberta, members of her own Quiché community, are not readers at all, neither in Spanish nor in English. Instead, their communal life depends on resisting Span-ish language education, because it invariably substituted particular cultural practices associated with survival for an equalizing, annihilat-ing modernity. Her father's warnings haunt her and us: "I remember my father telling us: 'My children, don't aspire to go to school, because schools take our customs away from us' " (Menchú 1984, 169; 1983,

274); "'if I put you in a school, they'll make you forget your class, they'll turn you into a ladino'" (Menchú 1984, 190; 1983, 301). In other words, Rigoberta resists identification with other women in a very different way from Miller's French autobiographers. She resists us, her European(ized) readers, and claims at the same time that her individuality is irrelevant. If we are to be readers at all, we enter into a peculiar kind of pact, not the "autobiographical pact" of sincerity between writer and reader that Philippe Lejeune (1971; 1973; 1975) used to believe in, but one in which we agree to respect Rigoberta's terms. This means agreeing to forfeit the rush of metaphoric identification described by Paul de Man.

Nevertheless, and despite the interesting variations that this testimonial presents, it and others are undeniably autobiographical. Are they not? They are life histories narrated in a first-person voice that stress development and continuity. In fact, the full title of Rigoberta's book is *Me llamo Rigoberta Menchú y así me nació la conciencia.* A regular nonfictional bildungsroman! I say this in order to register a doubt about the genre of this text, as well as my impression that generic labels are meaningful here. I can simultaneously try to frame testimonials inside the perhaps more general category of autobiography *and* emphasize their departure. I should confess that I chose particular books to raise this issue; they fit somewhere at the seam of testimonials themselves, related, as it were, metonymically, but not as typical or substitutable exemplars of the heroic genre. When women in Latin America enter politics as an extension of the domestic realm and narrate their life stories to journalists or anthropologists (who have sought out these sometimes illiterate informants as representatives of particular historical struggles), we need not consider the results to fall into the familiar category of autobiography, or even the heroic testimonial norm of male informants.

My second quandary, therefore, is about what kind of text I have in hand. Do I continue to think about testimonials as a subgenre of the autobiography, and so to take their strategic coyness as a permissible departure from the familiar genre; or does the departure constitute a generic and political difference? Evidently this presents another moment of tension between *can* and *should*. At what political and aesthetic price might I favor one generic category rather than highlight the nagging lack of fit? Does the difference boil down to an ethical imperative?

Should I defend the difference as an extension of Rigoberta's own cultural self-defense, even in the face of an apparent overlap with a familiar form? Again, the question finally may be undecidable outside of tactical concerns. Some readers will prefer to project themselves in familiarly heroic autobiographical terms through this apparently available text; and others will take note of its warnings against appropriation.

One feature that continually reminds us of Rigoberta's guarded distance is her peculiar Spanish, studied for only three years before she testifies. The sometimes discordant language is a reminder of the difficult negotiations that constitute her life and story; it is also a measure of respect for the informant's voice, a feature of recent experiments in coauthored ethnography with bicultural informants (see, for example, Bernard and Salinas 1989, and Diskin 1995). Minor language errors keep stopping our reading of Rigoberta, while the flavor of translation consistently distracts us toward a foreign code. Just to give one stunning feature, the figural assumptions embedded in Spanish seem to be lost on her. This allows her own Quiché associations to disturb what would otherwise be a rather closed and less promising code. In Spanish, as in many Western languages, the word earth is regularly metaphorized as woman; that is, woman is substituted by the land, which is the prize of struggle between men as well as their material for (re)production. On the other hand, man is metonymized as her husband; his agency and power are extended through the figure. From this follows a scheme of associations, including the passive and irrational female contrasted by the active, reasoning male. This opposition has generated a populist rhetoric in Spanish America that functions left, right, and center of the political spectrum. The most bitter enemies will agree that the people's goal is to preserve or repossess the beloved land from a usurper (Sommer 1983). Rigoberta would surely sympathize, but first she would know who the people are and how they relate to the land; her gender lines are quite different: "The earth gives food and the woman gives life. Because of this closeness the woman must keep this respect for the earth as a secret of her own. The relationship between the mother and the earth is like the relationship between husband and wife. There is a constant dialogue between the earth and the woman. This feeling is born in women because of the responsibilities they have, which men do not have" (Menchú 1984, 220; 1983, 342).

Paradoxically, in this rhetorical tug-of-war, pulling backward from the "modernizing" Western codes to the indigenous ones may be going forward. The daughters' subversion sometimes brings back the forgotten egalitarian assumptions of the community's "Law" and promises to replace the phallocentric European "Law of the Father" with that of the Indian parents. I am thinking specifically about Rigoberta Menchú's use of the *Popol Vuh,* the cosmogony and "paideia" of the Guatemalan Indians. It is not exactly an epic, according to translator Munro S. Edmonson: "Although it belongs to a heroic (or near-heroic) type of literature, it is not the story of a hero: it is (and says it is) the story of a people, and the text is bracketed by the opening and closing lines declaring and affirming that intent" (Edmonson 1971, xiv). Rigoberta's frequent references to this sacred pre-Hispanic tradition is probably typical. To read early Spanish translations of the "Book of Counsel" one would think that patriarchy was at least as fundamental to the ancient Guatemalans as it has been in the West. In fact, Edmonson seems to miss his own point about the nonhierarchical and communal nature of this tradition when he reports that, "traditional Quiché life revolves around a patriarchal, patrilineal, and patrilocal family" (xv–xvi). His translation, nonetheless, gives a clue to the opportunities for lateral moves the book offered Rigoberta because along with the "somber" or sacred feeling of responsibility, it describes an egalitarianism in gender that Western monotheism finds heretical. That equality was lost in older translations, in which the term *father* achieved the broad meaning of parent through a synecdochal evaporation of the whole. This recuperation of the female into the male may have been prepared by the Spanish language, in which the plural of father, *padres,* means parents. Or it may be a more general habit in the West since the monotheistic editors of the Old Testament tipped the balance of the first version of human creation, "male and female he created them," to the myth of Adam's original loneliness, which made him help to engender Eve. Whatever his interpretation, Edmonson's translation of the Quiché cosmogony provides the term *engenderers,* male and female, to replace the *fathers* of earlier translators. " . . . it was told / By the Former / And Shaper, / The Mother / and Father / Of Life / And Mankind / . . . Children of the Mother of Light / Sons of the Father of Light" (8). With insistent repetition, the females precede the males: "They produced daughters; / They produced sons" (24).

The gender equality extends to communal organization, as Rigoberta tells us in her recently acquired Spanish, a hierarchical language whose insistence on gender and number concordance means that it can barely accommodate the system she describes. "In our community there is an elected representative, someone who is highly respected. He's not a king but someone whom the community looks up to like a father. In our village, my father and mother were the representatives. Well, then the whole community becomes the children of the woman who's elected. So, a mother, on her first day of pregnancy goes with her husband to tell these elected leaders that she's going to have a child, because the child will not only belong to them but to the whole community, and must follow as far as he can our ancestors' traditions" (Menchú 1984, 7; 1983, 39). Evidently Rigoberta loses power from having to use a language borrowed from the oppressive ladinos. The loss is common to all colonized peoples, as María Lugones reminds us when she defines the racial and class exclusivity of existing feminist theory. "We and you do not talk the same language. When we talk to you we use your language. We try to use it to communicate our world of experience. But since your language and your theories are inadequate in expressing our experiences, we only succeed in communicating our experience of exclusion" (Lugones and Spelman 1983, 575)." Without minimizing the importance of this complaint, I think there is another equally valid if less apparent consequence of borrowing the politically dominant language: that is, the transformative process of borrowing. Rigoberta's Spanish is qualitatively different from that of the ladinos who taught it to her. And her testimony makes the peculiar nonstandard Spanish into a public medium of change that (makes) appeals to us.

Beyond revealing the traces and scars of translation, as well as the liberating tropes that come from code switching, the book retains an unmistakable oral quality through the edited and polished version that reaches us. As a device, the orality helps to account for the testimonial's construction of a collective self. Unlike the private and even lonely moment of autobiographical writing, testimonies are public events. To make a stylistic distinction, we might say that while the autobiography strains to produce a personal and distinctive *style* as part of the individuation process, the testimonial strives to preserve or to renew an interpersonal *rhetoric* (see Jameson 1976). That rhetoric does not need to postulate an interchangeable "I" of the ideal reader, as the autobiography does. Instead, it addresses a flesh-and-blood person, the interviewer, who asks questions and avidly records answers. The narrative, therefore, sometimes shifts into the second person. The interlocutor and by extension each reader is addressed by the narrator's immediate appeal to "you." This appeal is not only consistent with existing cultural assumptions about the community being the fundamental social unit; but it has political implications that go beyond, perhaps to corrupt, the cultural coherence that the narrators seek to defend. When the narrator talks about her*self* to *you,* she implies both the existing relationship to other representative selves in the community and the potential relationships that extend her community through the text. She calls us in, interpellates us as readers who identify with the narrator's project and, by extension, with the political community to which she belongs. The appeal does not produce only admiration for the ego-ideal, of the type we might feel for an autobiographer who impresses us precisely with her difference from other women, nor the consequent yearning to be (like) her and so to deny her and our distinctiveness. Rather, the testimonial produces complicity. Precisely because the reader cannot identify with the writer enough to imagine taking her place, the map of possible identifications through the text spreads out laterally. Once the subject of the testimonial is understood as the community made up of a variety of roles, the reader is called in to fill one of them. A lesson to be learned from reading these narratives may be that our habit of identifying with a single subject of the narration (implicitly substituting her) simply repeats a Western, logocentric limitation, a vicious circle in which only one center can exist. If we find it difficult to entertain the idea of several simultaneous points of activity, several simultaneous and valid roles, the testimonials help to remind us that politics is not necessarily a top-down heroic venture (see Laclau and Mouffe 1985).

Conscious of working in a translated, borrowed language, testimonials do not have to be reminded of the arbitrary nature of the sign. They live the irony of those linguistic dis-encounters. From their marginal position vis-à-vis existing discourses, they may typically adopt features of several, not because they are unaware of the contradictions between being a mother, a worker, a Catholic, a communist, an indigenist, and a nationalist, but precisely because they understand that none of the codes implied by these categories is sufficient to their revolutionary situation. Rigoberta Menchú's community, for example, will adapt the story of

Moses, a model of spiritual and political leadership, for a theology of liberation. Enrique Dussel singles him out, too, as an active, ethical listener, silent enough to hear the Other's call (Dussel and Guillot 1975, 21), and as a human subject, particular enough to be called by name. No abstract universal subject of totalizing Greek ontology, Moses is a concrete, historical, and potentially free agent (Dussel and Guillot 1975, 24). But even this deontologized difference falls short of Rigoberta's gloss, a more radical departure from Western paradigms of personal heroism. Her adjustment of his particular name to a cacophonous but promising plural is a sign that privileging the lone figure of Moses, ideal for metaphoric identifications, misses the dynamic metonymy of collective liberation. "We compared the Moses of those days with ourselves, the *Moseses* of today" (Menchú 1984, 131; my emphasis; 1983, 221).

As for feminism, it is not an independent goal, but the by-product of class or ethnic struggles that some might consider inimical to women's issues. Her priorities remind the reader of Domitila Barrios's reluctant feminism. This Bolivian miner's wife resists identifying herself with gender struggles. "Our position is not like the feminists' position. We think our liberation consists primarily in our country being freed forever from the yoke of imperialism and we want a worker like us to be in power" (Barrios de Chungara 1978, 41). But her political practice, as a woman who should have left politics to men, was necessarily and aggressively feminist. For this woman who identifies herself primarily as a housewife, since the first struggle was to get out of the house, gender relations are her first target (36). The trick is not to identify the correct discourse (Marxism, or feminism, or nationalism, or ethnic survival) and to defend it with dogmatic heroism, but to combine, recombine, and continue to adjust the constellation of discourses in ways that will respond to a changeable reality. This flexibility or eclecticism is doubtless why, despite Havana's initial promotion, women's testimonials outside Cuba tend to be written just beyond the constraints of party lines, or any lines. "I want to emphasize that, because it seems there are people who say that they made me, their party made me. I don't owe my consciousness and my preparation to anything but the cries, the suffering, and the experiences of the people. I want to say that we have a lot to learn from the parties, but we shouldn't expect everything from them. Our development must come from our own clarity and awareness" (163).

Alliances, Metonymies

Rigoberta's community is equally cautious about being limited by rigid institutions. Instead, it tends to be syncretic, as in the worker-peasant alliance of the CUC, and to be selective, as, for example, with its adoption of Catholicism. "In this way we adjusted the Catholic religion, . . . As I said, it's just another way of expressing ourselves. It's not the only, immutable way, but one way of keeping our ancestors' lore alive" (Menchú 1984, 81 [translation altered]; 1983, 150). Not surprisingly, the conservative nuns and priests of Acción Católica were sure this was heresy. "They say, 'You have too much trust in your elected leaders.' " Why, Rigoberta muses, do they fail to get the point? "But the village elects them *because* they trust them, don't they?" (1984, 9; 1983, 42). "Nevertheless" she adds, careful to keep opportunities open, some missionaries who came to the area as anticommunists learned a new political language: "they understood that the people weren't communists but hungry, . . . And they joined our people's struggle too" (1984, 134; 1983, 225). The codes are always plural, in varying alliances. "The whole truth is not found in the Bible, but neither is the whole truth in Marxism, . . . We have to defend ourselves against our enemy but, as Christians, we must also defend our faith within the revolutionary process" (1984, 246; 1983, 376). Her multiple unorthodoxies constitute what poststructuralists might call an exercise in de-centering language, sending the apparently stable structures of Western thought into an endless flux in which signifiers are simply destabilized, not abandoned.

Some academic readers of testimonials have fixed on only part of their language lesson, the part that insists on the reality of reference. Therefore, they tend easily to agree that the signified determines the signifier. To worry about the instability of the signifier and the need to reinvent language as part of political struggle would seem treacherous to them; it would tend, so the argument goes, to reinforce the system of oppression by doubting the efficacy of that or any other system. The response is consequently to affirm the power of the existing order, in order to affirm the efficaciousness of struggle against it. What is lost here, evidently, is first, the irony that can help to wither the apparent stability of the ruling structure, and second, the testimonials' playful—in the most serious sense of that term—distance from any preestablished coherence. That distance creates the space for what Mikhail Bakhtin (1980) calls *heteroglossia,* the (battle)field of discourse where revolutions are forged from conflict, not dictated. In terms of contemporary, neo-Gramscian political theory, what is lost is a strategy for establishing a socialist hegemony based on coalitions as opposed to the insistence on a Leninist, party-centered politics.

In *Hegemony and Socialist Strategy: Towards a Radical Democratic Politics,* Ernesto Laclau and Chantal Mouffe theorize about this promise in a thoughtful post-Marxian analysis. The book is fundamentally a critique of the essentializing habits of Marxism, especially in its orthodox, Leninist varieties. Political complexity and the opportunities for change, they point out, cannot be addressed if the terms of the discourse are rigid. Logically, the result of conceptual rigidity is the perpetuation of a repressive political language rather than the promotion of change. In a fixed system, particular words (such as the *working class*) can be substituted for others (such as the *proletariat,* the *people,* the *masses,* the *vanguard*), or in the least case considered to be "equivalent" for others and so describe a very limited scope of operative differences and interactivity. "We, thus, see that the logic of equivalence is a logic of the simplification of political space, while the logic of difference is a logic of its expansion and increasing complexity" (Laclau and Mouffe 1985, 130). Along with their critique of words such as *class* and *contradiction,* Laclau and Mouffe also dislodge the political "subject" from a vocabulary of essences. The subject, like other signs, is internally fissured, available simultaneously for different contexts, including workers' groups, feminist movements, ecological activism, and so on. In their appropriation of the rhetorical moves learned from deconstruction, they go so far as to contrast the unproductive habits of *metaphoric* substitution in party politics with the more promising *metonymic* or lateral moves of coalitional politics. "[A]ll discourse of fixation becomes metaphorical: literality is, in actual fact, the first of metaphors" (111). By contrast, "we could say that hegemony is basically metonymical: its effects always emerge from a surplus of meaning which results from an operation of displacement. (For example, a trade union or a religious organization may take on organizational functions in a community, which go beyond the traditional practices ascribed to them, and which are combated and resisted by opposing forces)" (141).

Curiously disappointing, though, is the way reified categories smuggle themselves in as soon as their analysis is de-centered from the industrialized West. When Laclau and Mouffe refer to the "periphery," well after the middle of the book, an aporia is evident between their theoretical sophistication and their political sympathies. For some reason, after *class* and *subject* are withered away as stable signs, equally "fictional" terms such as the *Third World* or the *people* remain:

It would appear that an important differential characteristic may be established between advanced industrial societies and the periphery of the capitalist world: in the former, the proliferation of points of antagonism permits the multiplication of democratic struggles, but these struggles, given their diversity, do not tend to constitute a "people," that is, to enter into equivalence with one another and to divide the political space into two antagonistic fields. On the contrary, in the countries of the Third World, imperialist exploitation and the predominance of brutal and centralized forms of domination tend from the beginning to endow the popular struggle with a centre, with a single and clearly defined enemy. Here the division of the political space into two fields is more reduced. We shall use the term *popular subject position* to refer to the position that is constituted on the basis of dividing the political space into two antagonistic camps; and *democratic subject position* to refer to the locus of a clearly delimited antagonism which does not divide society in that way. (Laclau and Mouffe 1985, 131)

This double standard is as baffling as it is disturbing. (On p. 148, note 40, Laclau retracts one point from his 1980 article, about contradiction necessarily leading to antagonism. But he still defends his more controversial and uncritical support of populism in this book.) Why, we may wonder, are not Rigoberta's peasant organization or Domitila's Housewives Committee as constructive of "democratic" subject positions as are the examples given here? Why are they not as valuable in theorizing a fissured political sign available for metonymic, or hegemonic, politics? Certainly a trade union or a religious organization can be as humble and local as are the Latin American movements. And if the popular Catholic Church, with its theology of liberation and base communities, is brought to bear, the Latin American space seems far more promising indeed. Why, then, are its struggles imagined as unitary, as if they were a matter of replacing one masterful signifier for another? In fact, we learn from first-person testimonies that those struggles are as multiple and flexible as any in the so-called First World, often combining feminist, class, ethnic, and national desiderata. One advantage of reading the "First" from the "Third" World is to notice that what Laclau and Mouffe call "contradictions" (Laclau and Mouffe 1985, 124) become glaringly visible without necessarily becoming antagonisms, just as the authors point out. No one ideological code is assumed to be sufficient or ultimately defensible for either Rigoberta or Domitila; instead they inherit a plurality of codes that intersect and produce a flexible and fissured political subject. If Laclau and Mouffe miss the point, it may be because their skepticism about narrative, which they assume to be necessarily teleological, has steered them clear of these testimonials. The result is a reifying distance from the Latin American subject, a distance that seems more patronizing than respectful; it liberally allows for theoretical permissiveness rather than exciting any curiosity to learn from subjects they can consider as Others.

But to read women's testimonials, curiously, is to mitigate the tension between First World "self" and Third World "other." I do not mean this as a license to deny the differences, but as a suggestion that the testimonial subject may be a model for respectful, nontotalizing politics. There is no good reason for filling in the distance that testimonials safeguard through secrets with either veiled theoretical disdain or sentimental identification. Instead, that distance can be read as a lesson in the condition of possibility for coalitional politics. It is similar to learning that respect is the condition of possibility for the kind of love that takes care not to simply appropriate its object.

Note

I would like to thank Luis Cifuentes, Bradley Epps, Antonio Benítez-Rojo, Amrita Basu, and Jonathan Flatley for their encouragement.

PART

Santiago Colás *What's Wrong with Representation?*

Testimonio *and Democratic Culture*

In a recently published essay, the respected Latin Americanist and cultural theorist George Yúdice writes that Rigoberta Menchú "is not an elite speaking for or representing the 'people'" and that her *testimonio,* entitled *I, Rigoberta Menchú,* "is not at all about representation or about deconstructing representation by the violence to the marginal." "Instead," Yúdice concludes, "it is a practice, a part of the struggle for hegemony" (Yúdice 1991a, 29; also this volume, 000). In another recently published essay, Yúdice states the position more simply: testimonio operates "más allá de la representación"—"beyond representation" (Yúdice 1991b, 8). These essays provoked for me the question that forms the title of this essay: What's wrong with representation? To address it, I want first to sketch briefly a history, focused on the notion of "representation," of the critical reception of the testimonio. I will then return to Yúdice's arguments, and finally, I will offer some speculative suggestions regarding some of the larger implications of the testimonio for democratic culture in Latin America.

In what has been called both a "manifesto" (Beverley and Zimmerman 1990, 207n. 1) and a "poetics" (González Echevarría 1985, 119) of the genre, Miguel Barnet, writing in 1969, championed the testimonio as a foundational, revolutionary alternative to the creole elite literature of Latin America. Whereas the latter viewed the region as though through a foreign lens, from the outside, the testimonio speaks with a native voice. Whereas literature betrayed the alienating and oppressive differences of class, race, and imperialism, the testimonio seeks to establish identities: between protagonist and collective, between researcher and protagonist—and consequently, between reader, researcher, protagonist, and collective, between present subject and objective history, and between the written and the living, spoken language.

By contrast, Roberto González Echevarría—in the first of a series of "De Manian" deconstructions of the testimonio (González Echevarría

1980, 6)—challenges the testimonio's self-constituting extraliterary positioning. In the case of Barnet's own testimonio, González Echevarría argues that the protagonist is, by his own account, isolated from the Cuban people and therefore singularly unrepresentative. As Barnet sought a window through which to bypass the mediating structures of writing and reach the collective consciousness, he found instead a mirror that reflected (his own) narrative as a symptom of distance and mediation. Nevertheless, González Echevarría values the testimonio precisely for this reversal: the native—as in the *crónicas de la conquista,* the chronicles of conquest—in the very process of being written, turns the tools of writing back on the colonizer and shows his "need of the native . . . to be as great as the need he thought the native had of him" (González Echevarría 1985, 123). In this sense, González Echevarría also champions the testimonio, even as it may function as a foundational writing, but in precisely the opposite sense discussed by Barnet. This opposition may be easier to see as I turn specifically to the question of representation.

Representation takes on antithetical meanings in the positions of Barnet and González Echevarría. For Barnet, representation implies transparency, an open door offering access to the represented, while for González Echevarría, representation entails self-referentiality, offering up only the specular image of itself. Thus, to say that, for Barnet, Esteban represents the collective, is to say that he is the collective. The process of representation establishes a relationship of identity between representative and represented. Extending that relationship of identity, the testimonio itself, as a representation of Esteban's life and consciousness, simultaneously represents, makes present, the collective. In that sense, the representation effaces itself and its own conditions of possibility, namely, the distance or gap between representative, or representation (as object or process), and represented.

By contrast, for González Echevarría, every instance of representation, every occasion for it, marks nothing more strongly than the distance between the two terms, and, more specifically, the insuperability of that distance. Every representation ultimately refers to itself in that it speaks of its own inability to efface itself by closing the gap between itself and that "other," which it is supposed to make present, to represent. Thus, for González Echevarría, Esteban does not represent the collective, not only because he does not do many of the things that the collective did, but especially because he does something that the collective does not do: namely, appear as a protagonist/narrator in a testimonio. In other words, the protagonist of a testimonio can never be—de facto for González Echevarría—representative of the collective. And if this is so, then the entire (anti-)representational project of the testimonio must collapse in on itself. For if Esteban is more representative of Barnet than of the collective, then his narration does not serve as a "link" (Barnet's word) to the collective, but rather to Barnet and the entire world of writing and literature that *he* represents. Without the relationship of identity between narrator/protagonist and collective, all the other relationships of identity and immediacy in the form necessarily collapse.

To put this opposition in another way—which not unproblematically borrows from the lexicon of European literary history—Barnet articulates a realist view of representation and González Echevarría a modernist one (Eysteinsson 1990, 192). Fredric Jameson, in revisiting the Brecht-Lukács debate, has historicized the realism-modernism debate for European literary history and situated both positions as symbolic solutions to historically specific experiences of daily life under capitalism. Jameson's intervention opens up the space of what Jonathan Arac has called "postmodern literary studies." "Current advanced theory," Arac writes, "crosses these lines [between "an antirepresentational antihumanism" and "humanist defenders of representation"]: it is antihumanist, but it acknowledges—critically— our enmeshment in representation" (Arac 1987, 295).

But if Jameson's account thus suggests the possibility of a postmodern mode of thinking representation, alternative to those offered by either realism or modernism, the question for us is whether postmodernity offers us an alternative position beyond the mutually exclusive and antagonistic stances of Barnet and González Echevarría—a Cuban revolutionary and a Cuban expatriate, respectively. One of the obstacles to the formation of such a position, interestingly enough, is that both the realist (in obvious ways for Barnet) and modernist (Cortázar's "revolution in literature"; even the anti-Castro González Echevarría's claim that "his" deconstructive testimonio functions as the genuine revolutionary literature) modes of representation associated themselves with the Cuban Revolution.

The question of postmodernism in this case reveals a more concrete political dimension. For if realism and modernism both cast their lot with the revolution, then my question also implicitly asks, Must revolution remain the paradigm for progressive social change? This question itself acquires a special urgency today as that revolutionary project undergoes its most harrowing attacks to date. This urgency, at the very least, dictates that an exploration of the postmodernity-postrevolutionary question with respect to representation be taken more seriously, that it be measured not in relation to a received field of possibilities, but rather in relation to the concrete forms of sociocultural practice, including the testimonio, in the region today, even, or especially, if those seem to challenge that existing field of possibilities.

George Yúdice has made precisely such an inquiry in his numerous studies of *I, Rigoberta Menchú*. Yúdice, also known for extensive work on the question of postmodernism and Latin America, argues that this testimonio goes "beyond representation," skirting the false dichotomies of realism and modernism. Yúdice argues, for example, against Barnet's realist testimonio, that there is no preconstituted collective identity or consciousness that the testimonio could represent transparently. Rather, the testimonio itself serves as a fundamental component in the practice of constituting such an identity and consciousness. The testimonio is more a cause, than an effect, of group identity. Rather than opposing, like Barnet, some "super-realist," near-scientific testimonio to literature on the grounds of its superior representational capacities, Yúdice argues that testimonio works from within literature to subvert it, not because "the 'people' have taken expression into their hands," but because it challenges the concept of the aesthetic in which the institution of literature is grounded, and again, not by aestheticizing life, but by making an "effort to recognize and valorize the aesthetics of life practices themselves" (Yúdice 1991a, 21; also this volume, 49). The difference between these two involves the role of the artist, which is eclipsed in the testimonio. Similarly, Yúdice establishes the testimonio as a counterhegemonic incursion of the popular in the hitherto exclusive sphere of high literature as embodied in the "boom"—itself reduced to the cultivation of "self-referentiality, simulation, and poststructuralist écriture" (26; also this volume, 54).

Yúdice takes on González Echevarría's modernist (and poststructural) view of representation by carefully situating the testimonio within postmodernity—given that it rejects master narratives and attends to marginality—but as antagonistic to " 'hegemonic' postmodern [read: poststructuralist] texts" (Yúdice 1991a, 21; also this volume, 49). He argues that marginality in the discourses of deconstruction "do[es] not provide the marginalized elements with their own specificity outside of hegemonic discourse; they exist as the hidden fuel with which that discourse reproduces itself." Deconstruction does *not* "vindicate or emancipate the marginalized elements," but only shows (off) how dominant culture represses the marginal and unwittingly reproduces that repression. Hegemonic discourses cannot establish the positivity of the marginal (its existence as anything other than the repressed, absent, or excluded term on which the dominant discourse is founded) because "they operate according to a logic of representation and displacement that posits the very definition of literature at the (dis)juncture of the two" (22; also this volume, 50).

That is, literature in general, and modernist representation specifically, emerges from the unrepresentability of the other. It is the experience of the limit of itself. This is absolute otherness; what, by definition, cannot be in the text. But postmodernism's recognition that the aesthetic is grounded on a violence done to the marginal does not translate into a real concern for violence done to the marginal person. The marginal cannot be the locus of counterhegemonic subjectivity precisely because it is the oppression of the marginal that "excites"—that motivates—the written representations of postmodernism. Instead, Yúdice considers that because the Indian community sees itself as at one with materiality (ground, earth, and body), then representation is not "born of the exclusion of the 'limiting otherness' " as it is in poststructuralism and postmodernism.

I welcome Yúdice's attempt to advance the discussion of representation, and admire his critiques of the earlier positions, but what about his claim that the testimonio operates from a field "beyond representation"? Consider Yúdice's account of testimonio as an internal challenge to literature on the basis of the eclipse of the artist and the valorizing of the aesthetics of life practices. Here, a desire for immediacy, for an erasure of the distance that bears with it representation, is smuggled in. The artist (outsider, by definition separated from life and the people), a "vocationally dedicated artist," is devalued in favor of an "agent" of the community. But the status of this agent is more ambiguous than is admitted here. For the agent, while undoubtedly inside the community (whatever that might mean since the community is constituted only in the process of that agent's narration), has as the conditions of possibility of his or her speech in the testimonio his or her simultaneous exteriority with respect to that community. In short, this agent is not identical to the other members of the community, precisely because he or she has chosen to speak.

While this objection in no way compromises Yúdice's central claim that the testimonio, as a form/process, subverts the hegemonic category "literature," it does simultaneously reveal and block his desire to repress the testimonio's representational nature. Similarly, when Yúdice castigates the self-referential boom for not having represented, as the content of its novels, the social processes of the 1960s, a realist representation once again implicitly appears at the core of the testimonio's value.

Now consider the points of Yúdice's opposition of the testimonio to that "hegemonic postmodernism" whose poststructuralist representational values actually bear close affinities with the modernist views of González Echevarría. Regarding his valorization of the Indian community's materialism, Yúdice restricts the meaning of "other" to that materiality, sensuous being, or body fetishized in poststructuralism. Because the Indians—unlike postmodernists—do not view their "groundedness" as a limiting otherness, it is implied that they have no "other," or at least, that representation could not spring from the gap between consciousness and materiality. But what if we conceive of their "other" as desire? Does not the testimonio—as practice *and* representation—spring precisely from desire: the desire for dignity and humanity; or even from an awareness of the artificial, material—precisely and tragically bodily— limits that an oppressive state and oligarchy have sought to place on the fulfillment of that desire?

Perhaps it is true that the representational ceremonies of the Indians do not spring from instrumental reason, but rather from a harmony and union with materiality; but it seems equally true that the testimonio— as a new form of Indian representation, *self*-representation, even collective self-representation—does spring from the destruction of that harmony, the division cleaved between an Indian's self-consciousness as human and the inhuman material conditions of his or her life. To this extent, the opposition constructed, along an axis of representation, between testimonio on the one hand and boom, poststructuralist, or other kinds of literary representation on the other, begins to blur.

Yúdice argues, moreover, that the *nahual*—which is his emblem for the Indian mode of representation—"more than a representation, is a means for establishing solidarity" (Yúdice 1991a, 27; also this volume, 56). This implies, first, that a representation in and of itself cannot establish solidarity, recalling Barnet's opposition between alienating literary representations and identity-forming testimonios; but also, second, that solidarity can somehow—perhaps, even, can only—be established without representation.

This, even in the cases of the nahual, or of the testimonio, is demonstrably untrue. The nahual's capacity to serve as a "means for establishing solidarity" is actually a function of its iterability, its repeatability beyond its original site of production—of its capacity to be made present again. It establishes solidarity exactly because it can be represented in, say, the Quiché oral tradition, a testimonio, or even a critical essay like Yúdice's. Indeed, the same could be said of the oral narrative that primarily makes up the testimonio itself. Without its representative aspects, both its depiction of a collective life experience and its repeatability, without these, it would fail to establish solidarity beyond that existing between the narrator/protagonist and her interlocutor.

Finally, consider Yúdice's conclusion, with which I began this essay: "[Menchú] is not an elite speaking for or representing the 'people.' Her discourse is not at all about representation [what I have called Barnet's realism] or about deconstructing representation by the violence to the marginal [what I have called González Echevarría's modernism]. Instead, it is a practice, a part of the struggle for hegemony" (Yúdice 1991a, 29; also this volume, 57). First, by contrasting Menchú to "an elite," Yúdice creates the false impression that since she is not an elite (though she is certainly not "just like" all the rest of the people, since all the rest of the "people" do not know Spanish, are not organizers, are not as self-conscious about their tradition and its relationship to struggle, and, most importantly, are not *testimonialistas*), she must not be "speaking for or representing the 'people.'" But of course, one could be not elite and still adopt a representative position—indeed, Menchú highly values this quality in her father, as numerous references to it indicate (Menchú 1984, 107, 109, 115, 188). Second, Yúdice collapses the differences between two distinct contents with respect to representation: the fact that "Her discourse is not at all about . . . deconstructing representation by the violence to the marginal" is rhetorically equated with Yúdice's claim that it is "not at all about representation" period.

Yet, the deconstruction of representation, while clearly purchased at the expense of the marginal in the cases of Didion and Kristeva, need not necessarily repress the marginal. And beyond this, we also have seen that if Menchú's discourse is not about doing violence to the marginal (though, it might also be said, perhaps scandalously, that her text also could not exist without that prior violence done to the marginal), it is certainly very much of and about representation. The two characteristics by which Menchú's testimonio is *negatively* defined—first, that it is an elitist text speaking for or representing the people; second, that it is about representation or about deconstructing representation by violence to the marginal—these two features of discourse are opposed to "practice, a part of the struggle for hegemony." Is this to say that discourses about representation are not part of the struggle for hegemony? Are not practices?

To sum up, we might say that Yúdice's notion of a "practical aesthetics" is admirable, desirable, and surely essential to a transformative politics. However, it need not be opposed to other forms of writing or cultural production, which are thereby relegated to the elitist or postmodernist categories of an exclusively oppressive high culture; moreover, this "practical aesthetics" need not rest on the false, indeed impossible (at least for any society where desires go unmet, which is to say for any hitherto existing society), claim to go "beyond representation." "Representation," as Gayatri Spivak has written in an essay aimed, like Yúdice's, at poststructuralism's colonizing fetish of the "other" or the marginal, "has not withered away" (Spivak 1988, 308).

As I already have mentioned, Yúdice's essay thus provoked for me the question: What's wrong with representation? Why does the construction of the testimonio as radical political object require its placement "beyond representation"? And Spivak's statement, recalling Lenin's notoriously unfulfilled forecast for the withering of the state under communism, and thereby evoking the intersection between aesthetic and political representation, suggests a possible answer. If Yúdice preserves, on a very subtle level, the desire to escape representation, it may be because of what representation has implied in Latin America.

Consider just two of the social practices in which representation functions centrally: literature and democratic politics. Both have operated historically as practices of exclusion. If representation, as I have argued above, always presupposes a distance, then in Latin America, literary representations and representative democracy always seem to extend the distance under the illusion of narrowing it (Sommer 1993). This illusion of immediacy also may explain why Yúdice is not content with the realist position that constructs representation as immediacy and identity. Such an illusion never has been realized concretely in Latin America, despite the euphoric hopes raised by the Cuban Revolution.

In that case, Yúdice is left with no alternative—if he wishes to assert both the novelty and the radicalness of the testimonio—other than to reject representation altogether. But is this really the case? And is it really possible, for that matter? Here, I believe we can seek assistance from postmodernist theory, but only provided we challenge, following Andreas Huyssen, the homogenizing equation of postmodernism with a certain poststructuralism (the many forms of this having been reductively caricatured to a kind of playful, Barthesian *écriture*).

The Argentine political theorist Ernesto Laclau, for instance, writes that "representation cannot simply be the transmission belt of a will that has already been constituted, but must involve the construction of something new" (Laclau 1990, 38). Laclau rehearses Yúdice's argument about the testimonio as identity-forming practice, but—rather than opposing this to representation—he makes clear that it is effective as such only because it *is*, precisely, a representation. Laclau continues:

> There is thus a double process: on the one hand, to exist as such, a representation cannot operate completely behind the back of the person represented; and on the other, to be a representation at all requires the articulation of something new which is not just provided by the identity of what is being represented. . . . [a]bsolute representation, the total transparency between the representative and the represented, means the extinction of the relationship of representation. If the representative and represented constitute the same and single will, the 're-' of representation disappears since the same will is present in two different places. Representation can therefore only exist to the extent that the transparency entailed by the concept is never achieved; and that a permanent dislocation exists between the representative and the represented. (38)

For representation to exist, and we have seen how the efficacy of the testimonio's project depends on the operation of representation, Menchú cannot be identical to the oppressed of Guatemala, and the testimonio can be identical neither to her spoken testimony nor to the experiences of identity-formation that it relates.

Thus, it is not necessary that representation be abandoned in order for the testimonio to function as community-forming practice. On the contrary, it is essential that representation (in Laclau's "translucent" or "impure" postmodern sense, and not in the realist "transparent" or modernist "self-reflexive" sense) be operative for the testimonio as practice to fulfill itself. The resistance value of the testimonio as cultural practice and artifact, far from resting on either the absolute identity between a people, their representative, the interlocutor, and the foreign sympathizer, seems rather to derive from the tension generated by the disjuncture between these different subjects. It is not the testimonio's uncontaminated positing of some pure, truthful, native history that makes it so powerful, but rather its subversion of such a project.

This may or may not run counter to the testimonialistas' own beliefs or intentions regarding their project. In the case of Rigoberta Menchú, the Guatemalan Indian woman and testimonialista who recently won the Nobel Peace Prize, her migration into ever-widening circles outside her native culture—first she learns Spanish, then she learns to read, then she travels to France, and so on—would suggest a recognition of the fact that only the mutability of its form, as determined by different contexts, ensures the testimonio's continued viability as a form of cultural resistance.

Indeed, confirmation of this notion comes, surprisingly and perhaps unfortunately, from the neoconservative cultural observer Dinesh D'Souza, for *I, Rigoberta Menchú* figures prominently in his harangue on curriculum revision at Stanford University (D'Souza 1991, 71–73). What bothers him so much—and it is the intensity of his irritation that I take as an index of the efficacy of this testimonio—is not that she tells a different version of Guatemalan history. Rather, it is that she both presents the appearance of being a "genuine" Guatemalan Indian and frustrates our expectations with regard to the proper contents of such an identity. She tricks us by being a Euro–North American Marxist and feminist in Indian's clothing. Not the stability of her identity, nor the fixed truth of her discourse, but the protean character of these confounds D'Souza and lends her work such "dangerous" power.

Given that the history of both literature and representative democracy in Latin America has been a history of exclusive practices of oppression against broad sectors of the population, the challenges testimonio poses both to representational narratives and to representational politics are significant. As our own nation's newspapers and newsweeklies are happy to inform us, Latin America seems to be emerging from its most recent cycle of revolution and counterrevolutionary repression to embrace U.S.-style democracy and the free market. If, as many progressive political theorists in Latin America recently have argued, revolution and right-wing dictatorship are both, though with opposite social valences, radically antirepresentational political practices (Habel 1991; Loveman and Davies 1989), then the delegitimation of those alternatives seems to imply a return to representation. Certainly, the obsequious posture of the new governments in Latin America has been that of the resumption of the temporarily interrupted project of duplicating U.S. social institutions in Latin America. Latin America, like a rebellious, prodigal child, is now congratulated for having returned to its senses and abandoned attempts to think and act in a new way. Against this general celebration of representation as usual, Nancy Fraser has called for a "critique of actually existing democracy," a project whose urgency is dictated, as she points out, by the fact that " 'liberal democracy' is being touted as the *non plus ultra* of social systems for countries that are emerging from Soviet-style state socialism, Latin American military dictatorship, and Southern African regimes of racial domination" (Fraser 1990, 56).

In the context of testimonio, the very existence of Yúdice's testimonio, together with a wave of intellectual investigation into democracy by Norbert Lechner, Benjamin Arditi, Carlos Altamirano, José Nun, and others—often departing from a consideration of the relevance of postmodernity to Latin America (Colás 1996)—as well as the development of new social movements, all stand as question marks, inscribing a contestatory, oppositional discourse that seeks to reoccupy and redefine—not escape or flee—the terrain of representation. In this sense, what is at stake in constructing the function of representation in the testimonio may be nothing less than reestablishing the parameters of democracy's function within Latin American society at large and of suggesting, perhaps, that representation—at least in the impure, postmodern sense of the term sketched in above—need not be an alienating marker of the distance to be traversed in the struggle for emancipation, but rather the ineluctable form that all emancipatory practices must take.

Fredric Jameson **On Literary and Cultural**

Import-Substitution in the Third World

The Case of the Testimonio

I f one cannot solve contradictions, at least they can be used against each other in productive ways: the contradictions of your contradictions do not necessarily turn out to be your friends, but they modify the rules of the game just as surely as time does itself, when it causes the problems, like Alice's flamingos, to rear up and take on an unexpected shape. This is what seems to have happened to the classic question of the Old and the New on either side of that divide, in First and Third Worlds alike: on the one side, progress and Western science, as opposed to superstition and stuffy traditionalism; on the other, the anguish of imported values that seemed—in industry and warfare, and in medicine—to have practical results, as opposed to the traditional ones that seemed to promise that elusive thing called identity. But now perhaps the First World is older than the Third; maybe progress itself is one of those stuffy traditional values we need to get rid of, while identity is as fresh as DNA and as exciting as the latest model word processor or theoretical concept. What is certain is that something has happened to the dualisms themselves, which were always, in the modern period, the occasion for a brilliant new worldview, while in the postmodern they offer at best the material for the mental gymnastics of the sophism and the paradox, in that returning to the archaic vocation of the first or primal one of all these dualisms, in the mythic opposition between identity and Difference itself. But this is so only when the struggle between the ideas of Old and New has been deserted by the third term of political praxis or the collective project.

The first meager shelf of "Third World classics," an archaeological canon of non-Western novels as those might be laboriously searched out and assembled, in English translations some forty years ago, by patient librarians or adventuresome planners of humanities or great-books courses (generally junior faculty without tenure), consisted almost exclusively of bildungsromane from the immediate postwar period: Camara Laye's *L'enfant noir* of 1953 (oddly translated as *The Dark Child*) is both iterative and singulative, characteristic of all that was to follow and itself something like the precursor text, which solved the formal problem of narrating the colonial experience by setting it in the perspective of childhood and organizing it around the efforts of the protagonist to acquire an education (that is to say, as we shall see shortly, to escape that experience altogether).

That the novel of "formation," the education novel, was somehow a formal solution of historical significance[1] can be demonstrated by the frequency in which it appears in a range of different cultures, and at once becomes exportable to the West. I think, for example, of the equivalent filmic breakthrough, Satyajit Ray's *Pather Panchali* (1955), itself derived from a now classic 1929 Bengali bildungsroman by Bibhutibushan Banerjee. What the new narrative format seems to do is to pry the nascent text away from the social substance of the family itself, and allow the novel—as the registration of the new and the unique—to come into being as though for the first time. This is also sometimes known as the emergence of subjectivity or individualism, a way of speaking and thinking that has its obvious and immediate orientalist overtones and consequences—replaying a whole myth of the teeming masses of the East and the free personalities of the Greco-Judaic West—but which may be equally immediately defamiliarized, if not demystified, by narrative analysis. Subjectivity, indeed, is a mythic concept if there ever was one; but that the emergence of a certain kind of storytelling documents the existence of the kind of social life in which those stories can be found—that, as a tautology, is surely an irrefutable position.

Something is here also implied about the family, as an institution about which "individualistic" stories of that kind cannot be told, except in the hapless efforts of its various members to free themselves from it. History, in such family material, is the external element in which the ship threatens to founder, in which, with war or inflation, or challenges to traditional value and authority, the time of its reproduction is menaced, requiring its defenders to sally forth into what cannot yet be called a "public sphere" in the Western ideological sense (Arendt, Sennett, Habermas), but what is certainly a male, public realm dramatically separated off from a female, private one. Mahfouz's novels (and Egyptian films and literature generally) have seemed to offer the strongest images of this virtually Hegelian opposition between the chthonic substance of the family and the public realm of history and business;[2] what is even more interesting about them is the formal or narrative problem they thereby act out before our very eyes—how to wrest the novelistic (in some henceforth Western sense) from this archaic family or clan material.

What must be added is that the bildungsroman in that sense is also the beginning of the Western novel as such, if we substitute the Lazarillo de Tormes for the Quijote as the formal ancestor and if we take the European eighteenth century as its paradigmatic moment. This then seems to reconfirm the offensive developmental or teleological view of a universalist history, in which the most unrelated societies scattered in time and space all dutifully come around in the end to repeating the basic stages, and working their way up out of this or that precapitalism into their individualistic bildungsroman moment, while waiting for multinational consecration later on. People have been unnecessarily unkind to this view of history, in my opinion, perhaps because they take it to be boasting on the part of the "Westerners" who advance it; but from a Marxist perspective (or even a Weberian one) there is nothing particularly Western about an industrial capitalism and rationalization that lies in wait for social formations like their own doom. Only those who believe exclusively in power can think otherwise; but they can obviously never be refuted in their own terms. The line between power and industrial revolution is an uncertain one, which becomes clearer when, for the account in terms of industrialization, that of capitalism and commodification (in which machine production is included) is substituted: at that point the possibility for something like a capitalist system to emerge in this national/religious area rather than this other one comes to be seen not positively but negatively, as the breakdown process of a certain structure; its precondition is the weakness of the structure in question, the absence of this or that fundamental feature, which might have kept the older structure intact, capable of reproducing itself, and thus of becoming "nonadvanced." This is the spirit in which we are told that only certain feudalisms have it in them to enable the emergence of capitalist organizations in the course of their own disintegration: but presumably no one believes that the achievement of feudalism is a matter of any particular national, racial, or religious pride or superiority.[3]

Still, the age no longer seems to like to tell itself these temporal narratives or stories, which can certainly be substituted by more complicated and postmodern spatial ones, in which only the present exists. What the past then hands down is a certain technology, whose formation, function, or purpose has been forgotten: like an inexplicable meteorite, it interacts synchronically with its new context. Such technologies can be ideological, as Benedict Anderson (1983) has shown for the trappings of nationalism itself, which, once invented, can be transferred to the most unlikely settings; they can be political or institutional, matters of state power, as with the Leninist vanguard party or the single-party, proto-Stalinist industrializing state. Can they also be psychic? Can neurotic styles be exported? Is the mimesis of various forms of subjectivity conceivable? Surely, as I've already suggested, it becomes impossible to tell the difference between the alleged first appearance of a certain kind of hitherto foreign "mentalité" and the practices whereby that structure of feeling is sustained, conjured up, or produced in the first place. But that fashions, very much including the practices of daily life, can be thought of in terms of import and export, no one is better placed to understand than the subjects of late capitalism, even if we have not gone very far in the theoretical exploration of this very peculiar phenomenon we assume in advance to be covered by classic descriptions of the market.

Cultural forms, however, are surely among the more obvious commodities transferred by caravan or fax machine, which it may also be desirable to look at in more complicated ways. We do not, for example, have the old idea of "influence" around any longer to explain such transfers: after the "end" or "death" of the subject, it made no sense in terms of the individual relationship between one writer's style and another's, and it may therefore be presumed to make even less sense when it is a question of the adoption of other countries' forms or indeed of cultural imperialism itself.

Meanwhile, the coming of the media age has made it clear in retrospect that everything hitherto thought to be literary or classical was in reality itself a primitive stage in the development of the media. Just as in technological history the first forms of the media are the Roman road or the automobile, so also classical odes or even novels themselves are now to be rethought as structures that foreshadow television, if I may put it that way.

But the case for grasping literary forms as media probably needs to be absolutized, and driven back into language itself, which the postvernacular imperial powers have always wanted to think of as some transparent, natural media, free from the taint of ideology or mechanical infrastructure. But not merely the whole range of current Third World debates, but also the history of the various European vernaculars at the moment of their own renaissances and inscriptions, suggests that the matter of language—far from offering the classical version of a neutral technology—is very much politically connoted, an ideological issue and a crucial component of most revolutionary struggles. In the bourgeois period, the role of language in social revolution is of course masked as pedagogy; but the great literacy campaigns, from the positivist imposition of lay education in France in the late nineteenth century, to the great socialist mass movements to eradicate illiteracy in the Soviet Union, China, and Cuba in our own century, have all been central revolutionary projects. But Ngugi wa Thiong'o's decision, as a political intellectual, to write in the vernacular is only a contemporary replay of the central preoccupation of the May Fourth movement in China—first of all, the great student political and revolutionary movements in the twentieth century, whose demonstrations are the forebear and the model for May '68 in the West—with the production of a written literature that breaks with the canons of dead or classical tradition (Ngugi wa Thiong'o 1986). Indeed, if the media revolution has been able to teach and deconceal the materiality of literary form, perhaps the obligation to include language revolution in discussions of Third World literature will also have a positive effect on the habits of First World intellectuals.

Two very different contradictions, these: the disgrace of the pseudo-concept of "influence" and the discovery of the mediality of literature. Yet, perhaps this solves that: and the old moral problem of the shamefulness of submitting to influence from the West (by writing new Western-style novels for example, or using the vernacular like they do) becomes transformed and displaced when it is thought of as the import of a new technology—which is to say, not merely the object, like an automobile you bought in Europe and have shipped back, but also a production process. To have to watch American television programs all day long may well be culturally and politically disgraceful for a Third World nation (or even a Second or First World one), but to set up your own automobile factory or your own film studio is surely not. The naturalist novel, from Maupassant on, but particularly in the canonical form given it by Zola, was one of the most successful cultural exports in modern history and one of France's most signal commercial and technological successes. It may say something about local levels of production when a national reading public has to depend year-in year-out on the arrival of such shipments (which it may well read in French); but the attempt to start up your own local factory for naturalist novels is surely an admirable piece of initiative and entrepreneurship about which the principal question the current world system (quite different from the previous one, around the turn of the century) raises for it is whether it is still possible at all to begin with, or whether small-scale cultural entrepreneurs are not, like all the other kinds, squeezed out by corporate forms of production and distribution.

This is the way it seems fruitful to look at the old political debates about "advanced" literary technologies, in particular those associated with a then Western modernism: the now tiresome matters of stream of consciousness or symbolism, formalisms or aestheticisms, nonfigurative painting, non- or post-tonal music: there is an optical illusion at work here where a kind of production that is anticommercial and anticapitalist at home and in Europe becomes simply the sign and emblem, as it were the logo, of European domination abroad (which in some sense it surely also is).[4]

Postmodernism globally is probably the moment when such debates lose their meaning, because the social and historical meaning invested in the technique or formal innovation is lost through generalization and universal dissemination. Just as the modernist techniques, in a later stage of capitalism, turned into the basic equipment for commodity and fashion production, so now, when formal iconoclasm and representational subversion have lost their historic value as a cultural politics in the metropolis, they become a relatively neutral technology that can be developed everywhere around the globe without political consequences: save in those touching anachronisms, as when a Solzhenitsyn suggests that his political co-religionaries abandon the abomination of the internal combustion engine and go back to the old-fashioned village: a situation in which the scandals of artistic modernism would also presumably recover some of their initial freshness. Otherwise, everywhere else (outside of Vermont), modern and postmodern technologies are taken for granted, producing an odd convergence effect between First World postmodernisms (in a narrower aesthetic and formal sense) and the rich new production of a whole range of Third World countries, which are not merely often technically a match for European and North American high cultures, but often, as with the Latin American boom, or the Caribbean and subcontinental diasporas in Great Britain, path-breaking and pathsetting for those in the first place. This kind of convergence then offers a practical as well as a theoretical rebuke to the tradition of Left cultural criticism that thought it was possible to give ideological marks exclusively on the basis of formal analysis; but it also raises disquieting questions in its own right, most notably the old fears of unconscious co-optation, in a situation in which nobody quite knows what subversion is anymore, but everyone has had some experience of being co-opted.

As for the old mistrust of Western modernisms in the political Second and Third Worlds, however, it also receives an unexpected solution in the new conjuncture, as I was surprised to learn in a conversation with the distinguished Beijing novelist, Deng You-Mei (whose novella "Snuff Bottles," about the late imperial period, is known in English in the West [Deng You-Mei 1985]). After confessing his lack of interest in Western high modernism—a point in which he already seemed to "converge" with Western postmodernists—and before proposing the idea of a return to traditional Chinese storytelling—a decidedly narrative and antipoetic, antidescriptive discourse organized in strings of episodes, without any great commitment to psychology or point of view—Deng You-Mei added this, which is of interest to us here: "As far as that goes, I'm not interested in realism either, which is fully as Western a form and mode of discourse as the modernist ones." He did not add the words "technology" and "import substitution," but the lesson is unmistakable, and valid for debates raging in other parts of the world, such as those in Africa that oppose political realists and activists to modernists of the type of Wole Soyinka.[5] The postmodern lesson is, in other words, the postdualistic one, that a repudiation of the modern does not commit you to realism as the only other logically available category and position. The remark also, in its qualifier, warns us not to fetishize the matter of storytelling itself, as some postmodern enthusiasts have seemed to do (probably including myself).[6] It is of traditional Chinese storytelling that it is a question here, not of that of the nineteenth-century European novel. The description makes me think of those Boroo myths to which Lévi-Strauss prophetically delivered the key—but if it is to that aesthetic that we are all somehow supposed to return, then the point of convergence can only be the eclipse of the subject, the end of "point of view" and individualism alike.

On the new synchronic perspective, then, the past itself short-circuits its own lessons by way of constitutive discontinuities with a present that is formed by it on condition of ignoring it altogether. Such seems, for example, to be the case with the other face of Western literary and cultural technology in the older late-modernist period: for the Ray films mentioned earlier not only deploy the technology of the bildungs-roman, they can also be seen to connote a very different technological position and ideology to the degree to which we remember Ray's indebtedness (like that of so many other non-Western filmmakers of his generation) to Italian neorealism. Neorealism can be said to be a set of techniques and aesthetic values, which finally includes a whole politics within itself, or at least a social ideology, and in particular a populism expressed, for the Italians themselves, through a neo-Christian worker-ism still close enough to the Communist Party to allow interesting cohabitations and ambiguous ideological messages, and in that respect a kind of late flowering of the Popular Front period Italy was unable to have. This populism then authorized a set of aesthetic positions against stars and against traditional narratives and fixed scenarios, and must have been attractive for the non-European filmmakers not only because of its financial economy but also because of the premium placed on the new realities of the great industrial city that had not yet found their processing, as raw material, in official film itself. Neorealism can thus be grasped as projecting its own unique forms of excitement and enthusiasm (quite inconsistent with the stereotypes of aesthetic realism imposed by the modernist tradition), which are essentially those of production itself, of the deconcealment of new and hitherto unexpressed, uncodified, and generally urban realities, and of a general resistance to reification and an old-clothes spirit that repudiates convention and established form or codified narrative in the name of improvisation and discovery. It is a spirit that will be renewed in cinema verité, and in a variety of other forms, all the way to contemporary (postmodern) independent film, but whose ideological program was worked out into a new kind of political aesthetic by the Cubans, in their notion of "imperfect cinema": here a final step is taken and the economic privations that, a necessity in the immediately postwar Europe but also in the underdeveloped situation of the colonized or immediately postcolonial world, seemed to determine the new form now become its reason for being in a different sense. As developed by Julio Garcia Espinosa (1982) and others, technical "imperfection," with all its obvious material and economic causes, must also be grasped, not only as a lack, but also as a positive choice and a refusal of that technical gloss and perfection characteristic of Hollywood and thus of North American cultural imperialism. It is a remarkable example of the making over of necessity into a virtue: now global struggle is inscribed in the form itself, and the technical imperfections of Third World film can also stand for a repudiation of all the myths of efficiency and productivity, of modernization and "advanced" industrial plant, associated with American empire and inseparable from the styles and glossy surfaces of North American consumerism, very much including the commodity consumption of fantasies and dreams. Here then, as with the roughly contemporaneous French New Wave, with their handheld cameras and their aesthetic of the home movie, a moment emerges, in which, for a time, form was in itself a political issue, although it was that in a uniquely self-referential way, which tried to include the external context within itself.

Whether any of this still obtains, after video technology, and in a situation in which Third World film production has reached a remarkable level of technical perfection that does seem at least relatively independent of the question of whether money is available to finance any productions this year—that is all part of the matter of a putative convergence between First World (or postmodern) and Third World (or postcolonial) cultures referred to earlier. It also raises the more immediate issue of what the linguistic or literary equivalents of "imperfect cinema" might be; and it is to this that a brief discussion of the testimonial novel (or *testimonio*) may have some contribution to make.

The testimonial novel clearly has its First World analogies—in the development of oral history, for example—but has formal specificities that are blurred when we overstress its value as a mere historical document or record, but which are sharpened when we juxtapose it with that other high literary form with which it seems to have a certain dialectical relationship, namely, the autobiography—that is, the quintessential form in which the so-called centered subject has been constructed in the

West, and a form that since Rousseau has had incalculable impact on the development of the novel as well.[7]

The crucial zone here will then be that of childhood, which comes to take on a disproportionate role in autobiographical reflection in a two-fold way: first, as the space of the formation of the personality or ego, of the emergence of the "subject" in that charged poststructural sense; and second, as the occasion for the deployment of the theme and the experience of memory as a privileged relationship to time itself. We need to try to see both of these features as artificial and historical developments; we need initially to rid ourselves of the feeling that both are somehow profoundly natural and eternally human (particularly since that sense of the obvious natural importance of childhood and memory is itself an effect generated, produced, and perpetuated by the historical form of the autobiography and its related and accompanying novelistic equivalents). After all, the emergence in the last years of family and childhood histories—sparked in part by Philippe Aries's *Centuries of Childhood*—far from demonstrating our new and even greater interest and obsession today with the phenomenon of childhood, is on the contrary predicated on the sense that "childhood" as such is a fairly recent and historical phenomenon; that earlier periods and other societies utterly lacked our own "autobiographical" sense of the uniqueness of childhood experience and of the "child" itself.

Meanwhile, the theme of memory and temporality can also be seen as a relatively recent one, for in our culture it is above all strongly linked to high modernism proper (where it is surely a cliché to murmur the names of Proust and Mann, of Rilke and T. S. Eliot); yet our very distance today from the modernist paradigm ought to make it possible for us to understand this theme also in a historical way, to "estrange" it (in Brecht's sense) and to see it, not as a feature of eternal human experience, but as a social phenomenon (and even a social institution) bound in time to a certain historical situation, which may no longer be our own.

So autobiography constructs the personal subject and the illusion of a personal, a subjective, a private identity, by way of two illicit operations. First, it retroactively reads an allegorical meaning back into the past of childhood, which is now seen as the place in which my present ego was formed and developed; and I call this operation illicit because—like some forms of historiography—it presumes that the present (still then a future) was already there when the events of this past took place. The canonical joke about this retrospective illusion, this projection of the present back into a past, for which that present was as yet utterly undreamed of, turns on the paradox of the birth date: Diderot was born in 1713. But of course, at that date, there was as yet no "Diderot" in our sense, no "author of *Le Neveu de Rameau,*" no director of the Encyclopédie. So what is really meant is something a little more bizarre: in 1713 the "future" Denis Diderot was born. This is a thought mode most exquisitely parodied by that character of Raymond Roussel, who claimed to have seen, in a small provincial museum, under glass, "the skull of Voltaire as a child." As for the theme of memory and deep temporality, its obligatory pathos, and the elegiac tone with which it is always invoked and deployed, alert us sufficiently to an ideological component and impulse, and to the will, here, to construct a specific vision of human nature, which carries with it just such melancholy and contemplative effects. Both of these operations are, one would think, crippling for a human praxis oriented toward the future, and also for a literature organized around events, stories, or adventures, rather than around subjectivities and what might be called essences of the personality or of personal identity.

Both operations are also prolonged in a certain form of the novel, which has often been taken as the dominant one in the modern development of the genre, namely the bildungsroman, or the novel of development, which has already been mentioned above. So let me prolong my technological metaphor for these literary forms: they are, I want to argue, machines for producing subjectivity, machines designed to construct "centered subjects." They are components in a bourgeois cultural revolution, whereby people whose experience of social fragmentation and atomization—in the destruction of precapitalist collectives, peasant villages and communes, extended manors—is now endowed with a new cultural meaning, transmitted, among other things, by the new novelistic and autobiographical forms. This nameless experience of social isolation is now given the name of bourgeois subjectivity, of the personality or the ego: the emergence of this last can now mask the loss of collective belonging. Meanwhile, if Europe suffered this massive experience of fragmentation and modernization at that earlier moment, in which among other things the bildungsroman and the autobiography make their appearance, the Third World can be said to be experiencing it now, in this century, and in many places in a very recent period indeed.

This explains some convergences between the formal histories of the two areas. I have dwelt at some length on the bildungsroman or education novel as the very epitome of an ideologically charged technical apparatus or technological innovation (which can then be exported from the West in all directions). It now seems to me useful to describe briefly and very provisionally the pattern these things take in Third World culture—provided it is understood that this is not yet even a theory, but rather a hypothesis designed to provoke a variety of reactions and to gather new materials, which may either confirm it or render it uninteresting.

One's impression, however, remains that many Third World cultures begin, or at any rate know a significant renewal, with the bildungsroman form itself, and more specifically with the childhood-formation story. I have already mentioned Camara Laye's book, often stereotypically described as the inaugural text of neo-African prose: all of the features attributed to autobiography are present here—the history of the construction of the ego, as well as the pathos of memory and time—with the additional specification, not always evident in the Western version of these things, that the personality thus in the process of formation is a professionally and socially very special kind of personality, namely, that of the intellectual.

Insofar as in the Western tradition this autobiographical paradigm tends to be read back into a general metaphysics of human nature, we have here already a feature of Third World culture that may be helpful to us in demystifying our own social illusions. For the Third World text cannot but specify the restricted social status of the ego or personality or "centered subject" who comes into being in these works: and to reread them as the formation of an intellectual already situates them socially in a way we have lost the habit of doing. Let me give a few more examples of this first moment. I have already mentioned the childhood-experience paradigm in *Pather Panchali,* novel and film alike, which can thus also then be seen as an analogous moment in contemporary Bengali culture. In Chicano literature, to open up a rather different area of what may still largely be called Third World culture, the inaugural texts—I am thinking, for example, of Anaya's *Bless Me, Ultima*—are largely childhood narratives of the same type, while Quebec literature (for a time another Third World culture) knows its First World–wide diffusion with that other variant of the childhood narrative, which is Marie-Claire Blasis's *Season in the Life of Emmanuel*. Books like these then clearly formed the core of that older canon of Third World classics I referred to; and I put it this way to underscore the fact that this moment is past, and that these elegiac evocations of childhood are no longer on the cultural agenda. What it is then interesting to ask is not merely what replaces them, but also what happens to the then still dominant category of the psychic subject, of the ego and subjectivity and introspection. (I should also add that it is only against this background that we can see the formal originality of another key Third World novel [often included in list and dating from the same general period in the 1950s], namely, George Lamming's *In the Castle of My Skin:* for it seems to me clear that Lamming's novel is rather to be seen as a deconstruction of that older form than as a replication of it. The complexity of Lamming's book, in our context, is better grasped as an attempt to strike out from the nostalgic materials of the childhood story toward a new kind of form in which collective and relatively more impersonal—I will shortly call them anonymous—narratives can be registered.)

My hypothesis then is this: that the moment of the childhood novel—the attempt to construct a Western-style bourgeois subjectivity, including "personal identity" and the temporality of memory—breaks down and gives way to two distinct and antithetical strategies: the one openly Westernizing, if I may put it that way, the other archaic (but also postmodern in its way). Here again, Chicano literature—positioned between two worlds—offers some useful and paradigmatic examples. The recent, widely acclaimed, but also heatedly debated autobiographical book by Richard Rodriguez, *Hunger of Memory,* may then serve as a textbook example of the fate of autobiography when prolonged in a Third World context, since it is avowedly integrationist or assimilationist (for that reason drawing the wrath of various radicals and cultural nationalists), and also offers a rather painful example of the exercise of pathos in the expression of social isolation and the fetishization of childhood plenitude and its loss. As with the earlier Third World works I mentioned, however, Rodriguez's story of the formation of a bourgeois subject is also necessarily the story of the plight of the alienated intellectual as such—in this case, I am tempted to say, the colonial rather than the postcolonial intellectual.

But if this account has any validity, it would seem at least logically to follow that any postmodern Third World literature that displaced this tradition ought to be characterized, at least initially, by the absence of these two features—by depersonalization or the return of anonymity on the one hand, and by spatialization rather than temporality on the other. Both these things do seem to me in fact to have something significant to do with the testimonio as such, provided anonymity is understood as designating what the poststructuralists envisage as some new "decentered subject," or what political people celebrate as genuine democracy or plebeianization, a social world without special privileges, including that very peculiar form of special privilege and private property that is the old bourgeois ego or "personal identity." This is then a good anonymity that I have in mind; but it will still be misleading to the degree that the word suggests namelessness, facelessness, the indistinction of the mass, the empty representativity of the sociological case or example. In one of the most important contemporary works on autobiography, Philippe Lejeune (1975) links the form to the linguistic peculiarity of the proper name as such: but the anonymity I mean, the anonymity of that counterautobiography, which is among other things the testimonial novel, is then in that sense not the loss of a name, but— quite paradoxically—the multiplication of proper names. "The Autobiography of Esteban Montejo," by Miguel Barnet (Barnet 1973), "The Life of Rigoberta Menchú," by Elisabeth Burgos-Debray (Menchú 1984)—these second appended names are not merely those of editors or collators, indeed we have as yet no appropriate categories for rethinking their specific work, which may better be seen in analogy to the creativity of the translator.[8]

Or we may wish to return to the fundamental meaning Bakhtin gave to his concept of dialogue and polyphony—the using of the speech of someone else in a situation that both dispels "authorship" of the old centered-subject private-property type and institutes some new collective space between named subjects and individual human beings. Add to this Rigoberta Menchú's insistence on the nature of what she herself calls her testimony: "I'd like to stress that it is not only my life, it's also the testimony of my people. . . . The important thing is that what has happened to me has happened to many other people too: My story is the story of all poor Guatemalans. My personal experience is the reality of a whole people" (Menchú 1984). Anonymity here means not the loss of personal identity, of the proper name, but the multiplication of those things; not the faceless sociological average or sample or least common denominator, but the association of one individual with a host of other names and other concrete individuals. This is a concept, then, that is both literary (having to do with the nature of a certain kind of narrative discourse and its basic category of the character, or more particularly the protagonist—the hero or heroine) and also a social concept insofar as it offers what I think is a new conception of collectivity and collective life—very different from the threatening mobs and faceless masses of First World fantasy—and specific to the culture and experience of the Third World itself.

Yet such depersonalization, in at least some of its aspects, character- izes First World postmodernism as well: the rhetoric of postmodernism includes a certain populist program (however you eventually decide to evaluate that), and very specifically repudiates the old myths of the high modernist demiurges or geniuses, with their elite visionary or prophetic roles and their gestures of the master around whom a small avant-garde group assembles. More than that, particularly in the arts most open to technological reproduction, the very notion of a personal style has dis- appeared, to the point at which the assembler of collages or installa- tions—whose "art work" may be, like that of Hans Haacke, "merely" a juxtaposition of ads and images, texts and historical background—may therefore no longer seem very much like the older kind of artist who was still supposed to include some component of "personal expression." The radicalism of the First World political postmodernists, who appropriate the texts and intertexts of an image and media society, may not look very much like the radicalism of Third World political culture, but I think it is important to stress at the least the intersection of both in this matter of the shedding of the dead skin of an older subjectivity or psyche, and the breaking through to some new form of anonymity, an anonymity that is not something you lapse back into but rather some- thing you have to conquer.

Let me now come at this from another angle, where First and Third World cultures can be more effectively distinguished: one of the other themes of contemporary poststructuralism (which is of postmodernism itself) is a whole rhetoric of desire, largely buttressed by certain con- temporary readings of Freud. It is on the face of it essentially an anar- chist and contestatory value, which posits a force of repressed or unconscious desire that can never be satisfied and that always erupts to unsettle the established order and to blur the lines and contours of the art of that established order. Leaving aside the relationship of this influential contemporary theme with a new awareness of the body in literature and theory and First World social life, and also with the intensities of the sex and violence pornography that increasingly marks First World culture and social experience, it does seem clear that desire—as a virtually metaphysical preoccupation—is also central to autobiography as a form, from St. Augustine to Rousseau (continuing to resonate down into titles like that of the book of Richard Rodriguez, alluded to earlier—*Hunger of Memory*). What it seems significant to observe is that desire—term and concept alike—is by no means as central in Freud himself as all this seems to imply; for our purposes, indeed, it is even more significant that the operative category—and the operative force— in the fundamental Freudian text, *The Interpretation of Dreams*, is not at all the glamorous and metaphysical notion of *desire*, but rather the far more humble everyday notion of the *wish* (Freud's great discovery was that all dreams are wish-fulfillments). This terminological shift rather effectively dramatizes the difference in style between the pathos of the bourgeois ego, in the throes of desire, and the more prosaic everyday business of wishes and wants. Desire, indeed, speaks the language of the sublime and of the great elite and aristocratic forms; wishes, on the other hand, are the fundamental narrative category of a very different literary tradition, the fairy tale, the oldest form of peasant storytelling.

From the fairy-tale dimension of peasant literature then emerges what is often called "magic realism"; but as far as the testimonio is concerned, I am inclined to see its laconic, behavioristic style as something like a zero degree of the wish, and to try to formulate its relationship to subjectivity now in a somewhat different way. In the testimonial, I think, experience moves back and forth between two great polarities or dialectical limits to the individual subject—one is collective or peasant ritual, always present in these testimonies. The other is history, in the sense of a brutal irruption, of catastrophe, of the history of the others, that breaks into the peasant community from the outside, and most specifically into peasant space as such.

It is thus ironic that Ricardo Pozas—in some ways the very founder of the genre, and in the genealogy of the form, Barnet's mentor—should obscure this dialectical movement by too great a sociological emphasis on typicality and sociological representativity; thus he tells us, in his preface to *Juan Pérez Jolete:* "Our example is typical, in that it characterizes the conduct of many of the men of his group (excepting for the participation in the armed movement of the Mexican Revolution, which was an accident of his life)" (1952, x–xi). In hindsight, the qualification seems utterly erroneous: the great testimonios are those in which a life is necessarily intersected by the convulsions of history—for Esteban Montejo, the wars of independence, for Rigoberta Menchú, the struggle for Guatemalan liberation. The two poles of ritual and History (in this special sense) are the shadows thrown by lives lived on the axis and the intersection between precapitalist village life and the convulsive new dynamics of capitalism, of money, exchange, commodity production (or what is in the West euphemistically called modernization). Indeed, what seems essential in the content of Third World literature generally is precisely this intersection—not the older village culture in and of itself, in some anthropological purity—not Camara Laye's *Black Child,* but Achebe's *Things Fall Apart*—the nightmarish moment in which the "modern" or the Western-capitalist and the archaic or the older village form coexist in vivid brutality as in the strobe-light flash of a flare or tracer bullet.

This is the point, indeed, at which to say something about ritual and religion itself in this literature, where, in my opinion, ritual—present in everything from René Maran's 1921 *Batouala,* allegedly the "first" African novel, and winner of that year's Prix Goncourt, to Kidlat Tahimik's film *The Perfumed Nightmare*—should be grasped as something like ritual-seen-by-the-Other, and where "religion" should be very much forced to retain its etymological sense as the external form and embodiment of collective identity as such. Indeed, the discussion of anonymity above lacked the complementary discussion of collective identity. I believe that it is and must always be subaltern,[9] and that in some deeper way religion in one form or another (from superstition to orientalist fantasies about the Islamic character) is always what is concealed behind "concepts" of other people's "ethnicity." But it is very difficult to do justice to the dialectic of otherness without a complexity that tends to be laborious and unreadable; it leaves its trace here in the very distinction between First and Third Worlds, something that leads on into a final qualification, namely, that this "anonymous" emphasis on wishes and wants ought not to be thought utterly lacking in recent First World cultural developments either.

Such categories are very much in evidence in oral history, for example; but other theoretical developments should also be stressed and juxtaposed—in particular, the reemergence of the notion of everyday life, of daily life or the quotidian, as that was pioneered by Henri Lefebvre and has opened up new and unexplored spaces in sociology (ethnomethodology), in history (the new historicism), and in literature (cultural studies). For everyday life is quintessentially the space of the modest daily wish, as well as of the equally omnipresent daily forces that frustrate wishes and prevent the fulfillment of wants and needs.

Those aspects of daily routine, of shopping or searching for food, of work or unemployment and seasonal migration, are also the spaces crisscrossed and swept, ravaged and convulsed, by a History that bears the faces that poor people see: the periodic cyclical or dynastic upheavals of the "great" that we write textbooks about, but that the peasantry learns through rumor, in hope and trepidation ("O vicissitudes of the epochs, you hope of the people!"):

> When the house of the great of this earth collapses
> Many smaller folk are crushed.
> Those who have no share in the fortune of the mighty
> Often share their misfortune. The runaway car
> Drags the seating oxen with it
> Into the abyss.[10]

These are the spaces through which Esteban Montejo confronts the whirlwind of the Cuban wars of independence; through which Rigoberta Menchú experiences the violence of the mercenaries and the movements back and forth across the land of the repressive armies of Guatemala. It is to be sure a very different perspective on history than the bombardier's-eye view of James Dickey's "The Firebombing," a quintessential First World meditation on contemporary war from the other side, or even from Michael Herr's canonical postmodern evocation of the American experience in Vietnam, *Dispatches.* Nonetheless, it seems to me that it is here in the passing of the older psychic subject, in the return to storytelling and a literature of wishes and of daily life, and in the experience of History "anonymously" rather than under the aegis of great men, great names, world-historical "heroes"—that the intersections as well as the radical differences between First World postmodernism and the cultures of the various Third Worlds can most fruitfully be explored.

Notes

1.   An earlier version of this essay was first presented at Dickinson College, Carlisle, Pa., in 1986 for the Morgan Lectures. But see Moretti 1987 for a reevaluation of the social meaning of this form.

2.   The reference is to the Antigone chapter—"The true spirit. The ethical order"—of Hegel's *Phenomenology of Spirit* (1977).

3.   This is in particular the position of Pierre-Philippe Rey; see Brewer 1980, 185–88.

4.   This kind of peculiar reversal from progressive to reactionary is dramatically registered in C. L. R. James's *The Black Jacobins* (1989), where the sansculotte movement—populist and radical in France during the Revolution itself—becomes the spearhead of racist and proslavery forces in Haiti.

5.   Documented in Georg M. Gugelberger's valuable collection, *Marxism and African Literature* (1986).

6.   Such as this, for example: "The Nobel Prize awarded to Claude Simon, one of the standard-bearers of the linguistic novel, coincides with the death of this form. . . . That novelists have finally decided to fight the mass media for the privilege of telling stories, that true literature is again going out on the street to load up on adventures, is all to the good. It's the only way possible for the vast reading public and real writing to meet. Which, of course, is just what they did in the 19th century, when the great novelists had no compunction about admitting that one of their main obligations was to entertain the reader." (Vargas Llosa 1986). It does not seem inappropriate to add that Vargas Llosa's own early work, in particular *La casa verde* and *Conversation in the Cathedral,* are no less formalist jigsaw puzzles than *Les corps conducteurs.*

7.   John Beverley, however, has suggested a formal affinity between the testimonio and the picaresque novel; here, as elsewhere, I have drawn on his *Del 'Lazarillo al sandinismo* (1987) (or see "The Margin at the Center: On *Testimonio,*" this volume).

8.   At this point, a waggish comrade whispers in my ear: *The Autobiography of Alice B. Toklas by Gertrude Stein;* yes, it is suggestive. Barnet is, of course, the most eminent practitioner of the form, if not its inventor; his own essays on the subject are of the greatest interest (see Barnet 1983).

9. I must explain elsewhere that I mean here something a little wider and more positive than Gramsci's original concept; something that owes an intellectual debt to Sartre's discussion of the "us-object" in *Being and Nothingness* (1966), and to his theory of the group in *The Critique of Dialectical Reason* (1976).

10. My translation of the song, "Wenn das Haus eines Grossen zusammenbricht," from Brecht's *The Caucasian Chalk-Circle;* the line included in the text is from another song from the same play, "O Blindheit der Grossen."

Alberto Moreiras The Aura of Testimonio

Testimonio and the Question of Literature

High literature has suffered a drastic loss of cultural capital in recent years.[1] Traditional literary preoccupations seem at times almost residual even in what one would assume to be among their most powerful strongholds, namely, major literature departments in U.S. universities. In retrospect, it is easy to say that the rise of theory contributed to the loss of prestige of literary endeavors; it is equally easy, however, and possibly more accurate, to believe that poststructuralist theory was, in fact, for a few years high literature's last hope for revival in the present sociocultural configuration. The situation may seem paradoxical in that this downturn of literary cultural capital is coincidental with the continued influence upon other disciplines of methodological and theoretical tools first developed in literature departments since the late 1970s.

The contestation of traditional cultural canons and the ongoing theorization of emerging transnational, translinguistic, and transmedial loci of enunciation do not exhaustively explain the seemingly radical reduction of the literary field. Whether literature will return to assert its long-held hegemony in the cultural sphere is an open question—although for some it already has been answered in the negative.[2] In any case, the pretensions of the cultured literary elite to keep dictating taste and imposing conditions for mostly national and/or individual self-understanding may well be considered outdated at the very least. In this sense, Neil Larsen's warning that it is not high literature that must be mourned, but rather only the modernist canon (and its tendency to imperialize and reduce to itself every other form of literary practice), is quite suggestive.[3]

In the case of Latin America, the exhaustion of the Boom/post-Boom literary models has not occurred merely because metropolitan postmodernity has erased the possibility of a convincing allegorization of the national (Boom), and therefore also of its deconstruction (post-Boom). Rather, the almost uncanny proliferation in recent years of postnational or non-national social movements in Latin America, and its concurrent imposition of changes in the cultural sphere, are probably a function of the decline of a way of conceiving sociopolitical and cultural praxis that had a lot to do with the Cold War and its attendant phenomena.[4]

Under Cold War conditions the Latin American national security state made politics turn around the issue of revolution, in the sense that it was understood as a national revolution.[5] Cultural workers of all shades in the political spectrum were forced to confront the revolutionary question, since that was, it was thought, what ultimately regulated their relationship to the state. The perception of culture was therefore heavily determined by national politics, although national politics was understood, according to individual political positions, through the prism of class and interclass alliances around the primary revolutionary possibility. Literary production came heavily and predominantly to figure as national/individual allegory in relation to the revolutionary configuration—a revolution that, for the cultural elite, was most significantly thought of in cultural and national, rather than in socialist and anticapitalist, terms.

But under current post–Cold War conditions identity politics seems to have replaced class politics as the best way to fight for the limited democratization that the third stage of capital is thought to be able to accommodate. Identity politics seems to have become the primary means for contesting the homogenizing apparatus that an increasing socioeconomic globalization is imposing in the cultural sphere.[6] And, of course, identity politics drastically questions the self-given credentials that the cultured elite had appropriated in terms of vertical representation of their mostly national, but sometimes continental, constituencies. From the point of view of identity politics, literary artifacts such as the Boom, and even the post-Boom, novel have little to offer, if and when they are not perceived in the first place as in themselves part of the cultural structure that is to be dismantled. The cultural dimension of identity politics is mostly committed to identitarian representations that no longer pass through revolution, or through national/individual allegorizations, and that are best, but not exhaustively, understood as resistance against the homogenizing pull of global postmodernity, even though necessarily mediated by power configurations at the national or intranational level.

All of the above presents a problem for the literary critic. As preservers of cultural capital, literary critics could comfortably justify their endeavors by remaining sheltered in the unquestioned assumption of literature's hegemony and its organic link with the self-understanding of the given national or multinational tradition and its projections for change and continuity. Those selfsame national traditions reach a historical breaking point all over Latin America in the ominous decades preceding the final collapse of the socialist block, especially in Southern Cone national security states, and in the Central American counterinsurgency regimes. When global conditions during and after the years of gestation of said collapse preempt the possibility of reconstituting those national traditions according to the old parameters, then Latin American literary writing loses cultural hegemony, and literary critics must start acknowledging the possibility that a belated death of (high) literature follows the dissolution of national grammars and the withdrawal of the communal gods. High literature is no longer effective, it would seem, in the fight against late-capitalist globalization: instead, other cultural possibilities must be investigated.

From the point of view of identity politics, literature may indeed appear as colonial discourse, because the literary demand can no longer be recognized, cannot even be heard in its compensatory, potentially preparatory tones.[7] For identity politics the literature of the Boom/post-Boom becomes no more than an obsolete melodrama where the forces in confrontation are only relevant for the sake of historical appreciation, but not for the history of the future. If it is true, as many critics have said, that the Latin American Boom novel occurs around the historical event of the Cuban Revolution and the continental hopes it elicited, the (assumed) end of revolutionary hopes closes a vast literary cycle in Latin America, which did not really start with the Cuban Revolution, but with Enlightenment hopes for social emancipation and the rise of the European novel.

It is often heard that *testimonio* is the most significant cultural production to have come out of Latin America in the eighties—although the beginnings of testimonio as a consciously cultivated discursive option date to the Cuban late sixties and early seventies.[8] The literary status of testimonio is a hotly debated issue. Sklodowska repeatedly has called into question the more or less naive, more or less ideological attempts at turning testimonio into a purely referential discursive act. Her discussion of testimonio's paratextual apparatus is a useful and necessary reminder that the literary, even in its merely aesthetic dimension, is in any case a constant and irreducible presence in the testimonial text (Sklodowska 1992, 7–53, 68–76, 93–101). Nevertheless, the cultural significance of testimonio includes an extraliterary dimension that is just as irreducible. Such extraliterary dimension is certainly tenuous, and perhaps it would be best defined in the negative, as a mere insistence upon the referential limits of the literary: thus, also as an insistence against the globalizing elements of the modernist literary apparatus, which is now perceived as not too different from the ideological state apparatus, if not in itself a part of it.

I am not suggesting that testimonio can exist outside the literary; only that the specificity of testimonio, and its particular position in the current cultural configuration, depend upon an extraliterary stance or moment, which we could also understand as a moment of arrest of all symbolization in a direct appeal to the non-exemplary, but still singular, pain beyond any possibility of representation.[9] Testimonio is testimonio because it suspends the literary at the very same time that it constitutes itself as a literary act: as literature, it is a liminal event opening onto a nonrepresentational, drastically indexical order of experience. In other words, the attraction of testimonio is not primarily its literary dimension—even though it remains true, of course, that the most successful testimonios are also those that have a better claim to literary eminence. Yet what can make the reading of testimonio an addictive experience, from the literary as well as from the political perspective, is the fact that testimonio always already incorporates an abandonment of the literary. Testimonio provides its reader with the possibility of entering what we might call a subdued sublime: the twilight region where the literary breaks off into something else, which is not so much the real as it is its unguarded possibility. This unguarded possibility of the real, which is arguably the very core of the testimonial experience, is also its preeminent political claim.

The significance of testimonio, even when used as a weapon against the traditionally literary, is more political than it is literary. In fact, as Yúdice has observed, the rise of testimonio criticism, which is an obvious gauge of the consecration of testimonio as one of the primary objects of critical reflection for the Latinamericanist literary left, cannot be understood without reference to the solidarity movement of the early 1980s.[10] At that time, a proliferation of civil wars in Central America, and the quasi-genocidal practices of the Central American military, made the dissemination of testimonial accounts one of the most important ways to express solidarity for those, generally outside Central America, in a position to do so. A similar point also could be made for the urgency of disseminating a different kind of testimonial account: namely, testimonials concerning torture and political murder in the Southern Cone. Beverley and Zimmerman, among others, also have emphasized the importance of the solidarity element not just in testimonio's dissemination, but even in its production:

Testimonio is not . . . a reenactment of the function of the colonial or neo-colonial "native informant," nor a form of liberal guilt. It suggests as an appropriate ethical and political response the possibility more of solidarity than of charity. . . . Testimonio in this sense has been extremely important in linking rural and urban contexts of struggle within a given country, and in maintaining and developing the practice of international human rights and solidarity movements in relation to particular struggles. (Beverley and Zimmerman 1990, 177)

The solidarity movement today almost has waned, but testimonio criticism has come to be an important academic activity in the context of Latin American literature and cultural studies departments. For many of us testimonio has become one of the main bridges between traditional literary concerns and a different, not necessarily more critical, but apparently more relevant way of articulating our reflection on Latin American cultural production under current conditions. If "testimonial literature is emerging as part of a global reordering of the social and economic contexts of power/difference within which 'literature' is produced and consumed" (Gugelberger and Kearney 1991, 6), then testimonio criticism must also react to that aspect of the cultural game. From this perspective, solidarity, although not in any case to be excluded, no longer can be the sole motivation for us to engage testimonio as its readers and disseminators.

It needs to be said that the contemporary attraction of testimonio for literary or postliterary reflection does not solely depend on the fact that testimonio does introduce suppressed and subaltern voices into disciplinary discourse; it does not solely depend on the welcome possibility of articulating, through disciplinary discourse, a political praxis of solidarity and coalition; and it does not solely depend on the intriguing promise of expanding disciplinary discourse onto cultural practices that seem to threaten as much as they revitalize discussions about what exactly constitutes literature.[11] Two other determinant factors account for the contemporary emblematic importance of testimonio criticism among the Latinamericanist left: the first is the fact that testimonio allows for a conceptualization that is not only useful but also necessary to Latin American identity politics, insofar as testimonio signals the discursive irruption of alternative, that is, nontraditional subjects of enunciation; and the second is the fact that testimonio allows the literary critical enterprise to break out of the collapse-of-high-literature impasse described above—indeed, perhaps even to recognize it as an impasse in the first place. In this second sense, epistemic constraints seem to take precedence over political articulation.[12]

Testimonio criticism differs from testimonio in a very special way, which is not parallel to the way in which traditional literary criticism differs from literary practice. If testimonio, in one form or another, can conceivably be affirmed to represent the cultural entry of Latin American identity politics into the transnational public sphere (regardless of the fact that its first practitioners would not have thought of it in this way), it is because the testimonial subjects are themselves immediately recognized as the voices around which new social movements must be articulated.[13] The voice that speaks in testimonio—I am referring to the testimonial voice, and not to the paratextual voice of the author or mediator—is metonymically representative of the group it speaks for. But this is not true for the critic of testimonio, who is at best—in this sense not unlike the paratextual voice of testimonio—in a metaphoric relation with the testimonial subject through an assumed and voluntaristically affirmed solidarity with it. There is thus a radical break between testimonio's subject and the enunciating subject of testimonio criticism that does not bear comparison with the merely positional distance between the literary author and its paraphrastic or exegetic critic.

Such a radical break or discontinuity has equally drastic epistemic implications. In virtue of the experiential distance between enunciator and receptor around which testimonio is essentially constructed, the enunciator of testimonio can paradoxically only become "one of us" insofar as she signals herself to be primarily an other. Solidarity is precisely the emotional apparatus that enables our metaphoric identification with the other, and a double conversion of the other into us, and of us into the other. This conversion has a strong emotional-political character, an ethical character if you will, but I would claim that its epistemological status remains severely limited, and structurally so. Solidarity allows for political articulation, but cannot by or in itself provide for an epistemological leap into an-other knowledge, understood as a genuine knowledge of the other.

The basic consequence of this structural limitation is that the testimonial subject, in the hands of the Latinamericanist cultural critic, has a tendency to become epistemologically fetishized precisely through its (re)absorption into the literary system of representation. In other words, solidarity, which remains the essential summons of the testimonial text and that which radically distinguishes it from the literary text, is in perpetual risk of being turned into a rhetorical tropology. But there can be no poetics of solidarity when it is the function of solidarity to produce a break away from poetics. My point is that solidarity, although it can indeed be represented, is an affective phenomenon of a nonrepresentational order—as such, either it manifests itself as praxis or it is by definition nothing but the epigonal false consciousness of a Hegelian beautiful soul.

The disciplinary importance of testimonio for Latinamericanist criticism turns the risk of fetishizing testimonio, in a farcically ideological gesture of willed compensation for what may be perceived to be a domestic political stasis as well as a global disciplinary catastrophe, into a particularly urgent problem. Since Latinamericanist literary criticism, given high literature's loss of cultural capital, has come to need testimonio from the point of view of its own partial rearticulation as an epistemologically viable enterprise, testimonio has paradoxically and dangerously come to be the main source, or one of the main sources, for a Latinamericanist "aesthetic fix," to borrow a sentence that Yúdice uses in a different if related context, a sort of methadone in the absence of an effective literary critical practice. As an aesthetic fix, of course, testimonio does not produce solidarity, but only a poetics of solidarity of a fallen and derivative kind.

This "literary" question that I am attempting to develop in connection with testimonio has strong implications. Given power/knowledge constraints and the difficulties for any disciplinary knowledge to assert total lucidity over its object of study and the conditions that determine its constitution as such, what is ultimately at stake here is nothing less than whether the attraction of testimonio for the Latinamericanist critic is a function of Latinamericanism as an instrument of colonial domination or a function of Latinamericanism as an obstacle to colonial domination. This question goes well beyond the intentionality of the critic upon whom it falls, since colonial discourse, which is radically constitutive of Latinamericanism, although not its only ingredient, talks through and by means of power/knowledge constraints that are by definition beyond purely subjective control. If "the imperial power cannot represent itself to itself, cannot come to any authentic form of representational self-knowledge, unless it is able to include within that representation the represented realities of its own colonies" (Jameson 1993b, 59), it needs to be asked whether testimonio criticism might end up becoming, or is in constant danger of becoming, a tool for the imperial representational self-knowledge of which it was supposed to be the very opposite. Of course, only testimonio itself has handed over this question, in virtue of its tenuous abandonment of the literary, which has paradoxically enabled us to see, under a better light, the deep implications of literary discourse with power/knowledge effects.

What follows will focus on certain by now classic essays of testimonio criticism. They all position themselves to the left of the political spectrum, given their advocacy of solidarity with the oppressed. I am far from engaging them critically for that reason: on the contrary, I hope to be perceived as speaking from a sympathetic political perspective. My commentary, though, is not so much addressed to what those essays have to say or have said, as it is addressed to what the readers of those essays might be tempted to understand in them. The rest of this essay then pretends to anticipate, and perhaps peremptorily damage, critical developments that might tend to blindly emphasize those aspects of testimonio criticism that are most subject to question from a political perspective.

The danger is to fetishize testimonio as merely a new disciplinary, that is, aesthetic, literary, or cultural object—a redemptive one, insofar as it comes to save the literary critic from the doldrums of forced and repetitious disciplinary pieties. Of course, today's innovative perspectives will be tomorrow's disciplinary pieties—except that, insofar as testimonio criticism always has understood itself to be antidisciplinarian in origin and intent, its predictable disciplinary co-optation becomes doubly undesirable, and thus doubly, albeit perhaps melancholically, to be resisted.

If testimonio, as I argued above, signals the irruption of a new kind of Latin American politics into the transnational public sphere, and if it founds the possibility of a dismantling and rearticulation of the disciplinary literary-critical apparatus in what we may have to call, following Beverley, a postliterary sense, then it is incumbent upon testimonio criticism to follow the call of its object. This essay on testimonio metacritics only pretends to be a prolegomenon to that postliterary, or perhaps just postmodernist, disciplinary politics—and thus, in a way, a partial attempt to think through the implications of identity politics for those who, from a disciplinary perspective, have no relevant identity claim to make: those for whom an implication in disciplinary representational self-knowledge may have become, perhaps in spite of themselves, more powerful than any other form of belonging.

An Auratic Practice of the Postauratic

I would suggest that the ongoing reconfiguration of the Latin American literary field goes through a particularly powerful trope, which has not yet managed to transcend the discursive practice set forth in section 12 of Pablo Neruda's *Alturas de Macchu Picchu* (1946). The end of *Alturas* enacts a prosopopoeia of the dead, which is prefigured in section 6, when the poetic voice, after having climbed through "lost jungles" (sec. 6, 126) reaches Macchu Picchu.[14] The famous verse says, "Esta fue la morada, este es el sitio" (sec. 6, 137). The ruined, fallen dwelling is reconstituted and refigured as the new site of utterance, the primary if postoriginary region of attunement. As an empty dwelling, as a literal cenotaph, the sacred city can only set a voiceless ground, which therefore requires the prosopopoeiac positing of the dead as living, talking dead. In section 7, in the mention of "la rosa permanente, la morada" (sec. 7, 188), we find the beginning of the foundational trope that will bring posthumous, metonymic life to those who already have died: "una vida de piedra después de tantas vidas" (sec. 7, 197). The life of stone becomes the living stone, the site of interpellation that can only be constituted as such in the affirmation "el reino muerto vive todavía" (sec. 8, 259). Those living dead are the ones who must then accept the injunction of the poet, "Hablad por mis palabras y mi sangre" (sec. 12, 423). Such problematic resurrection of the dead, a tenuous tropology, is the historical foundation of the Latin American poetic site, understood as what we might call an auratic practice of the postauratic. It is also the historical foundation of the contemporary Latinamericanist critical site along the same lines.

Auratic practice here means the constitution of a self-legitimizing locus of enunciation through the simultaneous positing of two radically heterogeneous fields of experience—the experience of the dead and the experience of the living, my or our experience and theirs—and the possibility of a relational mediation between them through prosopopoeia. It is a practice of the postauratic because the relational mediation between the heterogeneous realms is no longer based on mimesis, but it is based precisely upon the impossibility of mimesis: a simulation, then, a repetition, whose moment of truth is the loss of truth itself, "Esta fue la morada, este es el sitio."[15] The poetic voice now only can perform in an intransitive sense, since the object to be performed is a lost, ruined object.

This auratic experience of the postauratic is based on what I will call the production of abjection. The abject in Neruda's poem is an unlivable zone, a zone of ruinous death without whose textual reproduction as such the possibility of the poem itself, and of the discursive practice that founds the poem, would not exist. Abjection would be, in the sense in which I am using the notion here, a certain originary and founding outcasting whose most concrete task is to produce empowerment, but whose most precise discursive result is the constitution, or if you want, the repetition of a realm of social unlivability. Judith Butler opens her book on the discursive limits of "sex" with the following definition: "The abject designates . . . those 'unlivable' and 'uninhabitable' zones of social life which are nevertheless densely populated by those who do not enjoy the status of the subject, but whose living under the sign of the 'unlivable' is required to circumscribe the domain of the subject" (1993, 3). But whose subject? In Neruda's case, it seems that we can confidently respond that it is the poetic subject who is seeking self-empowerment through prosopopoeiac activity. The mass of the dead, and in particular of the dead insofar as they were oppressed while alive, the slaves and peasants of Macchu Picchu whose memory survives in double abjection, constitute in Neruda's poem the very foundation of the self-enabling voice of the redemptive poet: a voice that is therefore constituted, even attuned, in the production or the reproduction of abjection.

Beverley thinks that testimonio in general, and *Me llamo Rigoberta Menchú* in particular, are textual configurations where a radically other model of self-legitimation is enacted. Beverley calls it a "horizontal" representation, since "the narrator . . . speaks for or in the name of a community or group, approximating in this way the symbolic function of the epic hero without at the same time assuming his hierarchical and patriarchal status" (Beverley 1993a, 74). For Beverley testimonio breaks the vertical form of representation, which is to be found in Neruda, in favor of "a fundamentally democratic and egalitarian form of narrative in the sense that it implies that *any* life so narrated can have a kind of representativity" (75; also Beverley and Zimmerman 1990, 175). At stake is what Beverley identifies as the erasure of the authorial function in testimonio, with the implied consequence that the reading experience calls for a different form of hermeneutics, a hermeneutics of solidarity. Beverley recognizes that the positional distance between the literary text and the literary critic is different from the radical break separating the testimonial subject and its reader. The testimonial subject, by virtue of its testimonio, makes a claim to the real in reference to which only solidarity or its withholding are possible. The notion of total representativity of the testimonial life, which in fact points to a kind of literary degree zero in the testimonial text, paradoxically organizes the extraliterary dimension of the testimonial experience: solidarity is not a literary response, but that which suspends the literary in the reader's response.[16]

But, beyond that, what happens when the unlivable zones produced in testimonio meet a critical reception that rearticulates them as privileged sites of until then subjugated knowledges? What happens when those abjected knowledges are reaffirmed as such in order to be posited as the foundation of a critical/political practice, which is then assumed to be new, or performed as new? Well, those abjected knowledges are then made to speak prosopopoeiacally, through the voice of its critical representation. Even though I agree with Beverley on the notion that testimonio itself as a discursive practice is substantially different from what I just called the auratic practice of the postauratic occurring in Neruda's foundational poem, I am not so sure that the appropriation of testimonio in critical discourse can in fact go beyond said auratic practice.[17] If I am correct, what happens when Latinamericanist criticism reads testimonio is that we, perhaps inevitably, regress to the prosopopoeiac position emblematized in section 12 of *Alturas de Macchu Picchu*: what is poignant about it, and should require some reflection, is that this critical return to Neruda's redemptive site is generally blind to itself, because the return to the site is produced in the very affirmation that claims to have overpassed it. As testimonio criticism grounds itself in the affirmation of the extraliterary dimension of the testimonial text, it unavoidably puts said extraliterary dimension at the service of a literary-critical performance that reabsorbs the extraliterary into the literary-representational system. You can't have a hermeneutics of solidarity without a poetics of solidarity to go with it.

The price of testimonio criticism's appropriation of testimonio may be that such an appropriation necessarily reabsorbs the testimonial subject into a system of prosopopoeiac (that is, literary, or if you will, tropological) representation. As I said earlier, however, there can be no poetics of solidarity when it is the function of solidarity to produce a break away from poetics.

If the attraction of testimonio, as a postliterary genre, depends upon the fact that in testimonio the literary breaks off into the unguarded possibility of the real, then testimonio's attraction is radically undermined when its postliterary character is elided into prosopopoeiac representation (since testimonio is now, and can only be after the critical intervention that so defines it, that which guarantees a reading following a critical poetics of solidarity with the subaltern). In prosopopoeiac representation solidarity turns into a production of abjection where the producing agency, testimonio criticism, retains an aura that has been literally sucked off the testimonial subject, now abjected.

It is as if testimonio criticism were forced to operate under the injunction of the literary: in principle and origin oriented by the extraliterary dimension of its object, testimonio criticism cannot be but a literary supplement, and a dangerous one, whose effect it is to tenuously repress and substitute for the extraliterary dimension of the testimonial text.[18] As a consequence of this turning of solidarity into a critical poetics, or a hermeneutics, of solidarity, testimonio criticism reauthorizes itself within the epistemological power/knowledge grid at the expense of that which it originally sought to authorize. Testimonio will then be institutionalized within a strict codification: the canonization of testimonio in the name of a poetics of solidarity is equivalent to its reliteraturization following preassigned tropological and rhetorical registers. Thus, in the hands of testimonio criticism, testimonio loses its extraliterary force, which now becomes merely the empowering mechanism for a recanonized reading strategy.

Restitution and the Secret

Rigoberta Menchú's word is founded on the continuous insistence on a secret that will not be revealed. The secret is foundational in Menchú's text to the extent that, as secret, and therefore as impassable limit, it produces "a constitutive outside to the subject, an abjected outside, which is, after all, 'inside' the subject as its own founding repudiation" (Butler 1993, 3). For Doris Sommer, this secret in Menchú's text is emblematic not so much of testimonial production as of the strong identity claim that testimonio makes: it is interesting to note that the testimonial claim in Sommer's interpretation is also a claim to identity, and that this identity should to a large extent determine the reader's counteridentity as reader, in the sense of establishing for her or him an ethical *non plus ultra:* Menchú's secret becomes the key for the development of the notion of a "proper and responsible reading," a reading respectful of a cultural difference that is presumed to be radically heterogeneous (see Sommer 1993, 419).[19]

Sommer's position should perhaps be compared to what Jorge Luis Borges tried to think in a short story called "El etnógrafo" (1969). The story tells us about Fred Murdock, a student at a large university in the North American Southwest who doesn't really know what to do with his life. He is a quiet and unassuming man. Having suggested to him that he should study indigenous languages, his professor, a rather old man, eventually asks him to go and do fieldwork in an Indian reservation, and perhaps try to find out what the shamans tell the initiate during a certain ceremony, try to get that secret, then come back, and write his dissertation. Murdock goes into the reservation and lives with the Indians, goes native, takes his experience seriously, does what the Indians do. One of the wise men asks him to remember his dreams, and he dreams of buffalo. Finally, one day, he is told the secret. Eventually he leaves the reservation and goes back to his university. He tells his old professor that he has the secret, but has decided not to write his dissertation after all.

Borges's story talks about a kind of difference that cannot be bridged or resolved. It would be something like absolute difference—a difference whose very recognition as such already implies a cover-up, since recognition disciplines it as difference and attempts to tame it. The story suggests that Western ethnoscience is but an attempt to erase said difference. Perhaps the proliferation of differences, in which ethnoscience seems to relish, is nothing but a cover-up of that absolute difference that cannot be expressed, cannot even be erased, but can only be contained. Borges's story raises then a set of questions, to which Sommer gives a particular answer: What should we do with the secret, once we know it is there? Should we keep away from it? Should we be ethical and proper and let whoever has it keep the secret?

Insofar as Rigoberta Menchú is talking to us as a testimonial subject, she seems to have no choice but to foreclose that which enables her to talk to us, that which had kept her from talking to us before her performative act became possible. She does not foreclose her people, but she forecloses the content of the secret, thereby opening a fold that becomes not only the site of identity, but precisely the site of abjected identity, as well as the site of a certain resistance to abjection. Menchú's secret in my opinion is at the same time the metonymic displacement of the necessary (re)production of abjection in Menchú's text, and its most proper cipher. After all, Menchú must produce or reproduce unlivability, in order to be persuasive as testimonio; on the other hand, however, Menchú's word is lucid enough to make of that necessary (re)production of abjection, which gives her a place to speak, the region for a counterclaim where abjection is reversed and passed on to the reader: as far as *we* are concerned, Menchú seems to say, our place will remain uninhabited by you, the truly abject ones. Going so far as to speak, in speaking to us, the very unsayability of what must remain unspoken is what makes Menchú's word an epistemologically privileged text in the tradition of Latin American testimonio. I would claim that the secret, in Menchú's text, stands for whatever cannot and should not be re-absorbed into the literary-representational system: the secret is the (se-cret) key to the real as unguarded possibility.

Once we as readers, however, accept the injunction to become ab-jected from Menchú's textual site, our relationship to the text is in one specific but crucial sense indistinguishable from the relationship en-acted by Neruda with the Macchu Picchu dead: a fissure opens, across which only prosopopoeia can take us. The border, that without which there would be no outcasting, and therefore no abjection, then once again must be understood as a limit to the expansion of knowledge as a war machine: a limit to be overcome by a further expansion, or else a limit to be defended and protected from conquest, which is what I understand to be Sommer's position.

Sommer's essay, perhaps the most careful reading of *Me llamo Rigo-berta Menchú* yet produced, together with Gareth Williams's "Trans-lation and Mourning: The Cultural Challenge of Latin American Tes-timonial Autobiography" (1993), goes a long way toward recognizing and absorbing the radical break that separates the testimonial subject and the enunciating subject of testimonio criticism. By recognizing the break as such, and by positing the necessity of respecting it, Sommer moves away from a poetics of solidarity insofar as her solidarity is pre-cisely enunciated in an alliance against any possibility of a prosopo-poeiac representation. And yet, it seems to me that the danger of fetish-ization (and therefore of tropological reabsorption) has not totally been conjured away by Sommer's rigorous effort.

Sommer's essay is framed as a disciplinary attack on the discipline, and particularly on disciplinary reading. According to her, disciplinary reading traditionally has understood itself as appropriating, with a kind of appropriation that would reproduce stereotypical male sexuality:

Difficulty is a challenge, an opportunity to struggle and to win, to overcome resistance, uncover the codes, to get on top of it, to put one's finger on the mechanisms that produce pleasure and pain, and then to call it ours. We take up an unyielding book to conquer it and then to feel grand, enriched by the appropriation and confident that our cunning is equal to the textual tease that had, after all, planned its own submission as the ultimate climax of reading. Books want to be understood, don't they, even when they are coy and evasive? (Sommer 1993, 407)

I will not attempt to contest Sommer's implication that macho sexuality is a good model of disciplinary reading competency as traditionally understood. What I am interested in is rather her contention that a resistance in the text could under some circumstances signal what she calls "a genuine epistemological impasse" (409). If a text claims indeed that the reader is incompetent to penetrate its deepest layers, that is, if the text claims that it gives itself off as its own secret, then the impasse is in place, Sommer would argue, and this impasse traces an impassable disciplinary limit.[20]

Out of a sense of respect for the disciplinary object, Sommer is willing to concede that a disciplinary limit, that is, a resistance to reading, should be recognized and accepted as such under some circumstances. Recognition and acceptance here, far from expressing a disciplinary failure, are on the contrary enabling gestures, gestures that enable us to transcend "our still deaf ears" (Sommer 1993, 408). In those gestures, Sommer implies, we can address a demand for restitution that had up to now gone unheard. But it is not that restitution makes itself felt as a new demand; rather, we are finally able to radicalize restitution, insofar as we have already seemingly rejected the paradigm of object-appropriation, which was and has always been a false paradigm, just as stereotypical male sexuality has always already misunderstood the real. Restitution, over against appropriation of the object, is the moment of truth in disciplinary practice. In fact, I believe that to be the underlying proposition of Borges's story: Fred Murdock opts for silence, and it is an active silence that impugns the very possibility of disciplinary appropriation. Murdock opts for restitution.

Radicalizing restitution may be another name for the action that was described above as the entry into the unguarded possibility of the real. For Sommer, Rigoberta Menchú's testimonio has an irreducible extraliterary dimension that is constituted in the enunciation of the textual secret as impassable literary limit. It would then seem that Sommer has accomplished a reading that, by renouncing a poetics of solidarity as the only way to keep solidarity as such, and by refusing to engage in prosopopoeiac representation, succeeds in making an antidisciplinary gesture that would take testimonio criticism beyond the auratic and into the postauratic; that is, into the possibility of a postliterary disciplinary politics.

Enrico Mario Santí, in an article entitled "Latinamericanism and

Restitution," without in my opinion turning against the idea that restitution is to be revealed as the moment of truth of disciplinary practice, lucidly calls our attention to the built-in possibilities for self-duping that restitution as truth entails. For Santí, "restitution is supplementary in character—in compensating for a previous lack, it exceeds rather than simply restores the original" (Santí 1992, 89). What we can call restitutional excess at the foundation of the discipline, or at the foundation of disciplinary practice today, is what I would now like to interrogate.

The excess in restitution, as Santí says, is not avoidable, but belongs in the very structure of disciplinary restitution. Restitutional excess is the other side of the fact that a discipline constitutes itself by means of a foundational restitution in which the disciplinary object is first brought to light. That the object should be brought to light by means of a restitution already implies the previous existence of a system of symbolic exchange. Within this system, the act of restitution restores anew the disciplinary object, but in so doing makes it a disciplinary object, that is, an object loaded from the start with an epistemological burden that exceeds it. As an example, let me remind you of the situation that I mentioned earlier regarding a hermeneutics of solidarity: a text that summons us to solidarity with previously unheard voices appears, and the text is then made to function as exemplary for a new cultural-political critical practice. We see here at the same time a critical act of object restitution and its other side, that is, a disciplinary act whereby an excess with respect to restitution announces itself and burdens the object of restitution.

Thus, the epistemological grid that first makes the disciplinary object possible as such, that is, as disciplinary object, at the same time conceals the object and constitutes it in partial loss. It constitutes it as a partially lost object, thereby assuring itself that the demand for restitution will continue to make itself heard. Restitution carries within itself its own need for excess, its own need to exceed itself, so that it can, in a sense, survive itself, and therefore guarantee the survival of the discipline. Without restitutional excess no metacritics of testimonio would be possible: but then also, testimonio criticism would not have been able to constitute itself over against traditional literary criticism.

Restitutional excess is a destabilizing mechanism at the very heart of disciplinary constitution: it is as such the site where disciplinary politics are essentially played out. Restitutional excess can be used in at least two radically opposed senses: on the one hand, restitutional excess can organize the site for theoretical reflection, that is, it can be the region where disciplinary restitution seeks to interrogate itself (as, for instance, in metacritical practice); but restitutional excess can also choose to negate itself as such, it can look for its own point of closure in an attempt to come to the end of itself. I define spectacular redemption as a particular form of disciplinary practice whose overt or hidden premise places the theoretical end of the discipline it enacts in the horizon of accomplished restitution. Spectacular redemption is a paradoxical form of disciplinary practice in that its completion would tendentially mean the end of the discipline. In other words, if the ultimate goal of the discipline is the redemption of the object, so that the object can go back to being fully itself, with no remainder, if the discipline plays itself out in the wager for the self-identity of its object of study, then that self-identity, once accomplished, would void the need for reflection, would abolish the discipline as such.

But of course the discipline cannot be abolished by its object, insofar as it is the discipline that first creates the demand for the self-identity of the disciplinary object. An epistemologically impossible predicament ensues, which seems to me the danger of radicalizing Sommer's position, which is also Murdock's position. Because Murdock's silence, once articulated as such, as silence, can do nothing but serve (by furthering) the ends of disciplinary practice.

Both Beverley and Sommer have made brilliant contributions to our understanding of the possibilities of testimonial discourse for a rethinking of the status of Latin American literature and Latinamericanist literary criticism in contemporary times. What I am trying to do is not primarily aimed at revealing any possible rhetorical blindness of identificatory, restitutional practices, and thus its potentially dangerous political effects. It seems to me that the properly political task is to find, in the tenuous borders of subjective self-grounding, "a critical resource in the struggle to rearticulate the very terms of symbolic legitimacy and intelligibility" (Butler 1993, 3). In Rigoberta's use of the secret we understand precisely that struggle for the legitimation of her ability to speak, for its very intelligibility as a thoroughly political, thoroughly historicized locus of enunciation in the context of colonial and anticolonial practices. I think that both Beverley and Sommer have broken the ground for that understanding. Within the realm of questioning they themselves have opened, however, there is room for a further questioning: namely, whether in their critical practice, the critical practice that they have enacted in their analyses of the Menchú text, they are still residually engaging in what I earlier called an auratic practice of the postauratic, and therefore whether they are residually, but significantly, caught up in a certain representational strategy, which they themselves claim to have overcome: in other words, whether their concern for restitution passes over into spectacular redemption.

Auratic practice is that which consists of producing a self-legitimizing locus of enunciation through the simultaneous positing of two radically heterogeneous fields of experience. In *Alturas de Macchu Picchu* the dead and the living are the poles of heterogeneity. The aura is produced at the expense of what in translation becomes represented as the silent pole, which the expressive pole vampirizes, as it were, in ventriloquy. "Yo vengo a hablar por vuestra boca muerta" (sec. 12, 406) is thus not coincidentally coupled with the injunction to "hablad por mis palabras y mi sangre." The second expression only becomes sayable after the dead have been endowed with the voice of the living through prosopopoeia. Prosopopoeia refers to a mask through which one's own voice is projected onto another, where that other is always suffering from a certain inability to speak. The relational mediation is then always unequal and hierarchical, even at its most redemptive.

It is a practice of the postauratic because it turns away from mimesis, or in other words, it pronounces the impossibility of mimesis. I understand mimesis in the Aristotelian and Benjaminian sense, as a repetition of truth, where the repeating term follows the lead of that which is to be repeated. Neruda's representational strategy understands itself as emanating from the ruins and ashes themselves, and finds authorization in the loss of the object of representation, to which it brings purely symbolic restitution, but always of a supplementary character.

For both Beverley and Sommer, and they are here themselves emblematic of an inevitability within the epistemological field, the legitimation of their critical practice takes place in the (re)production of abjected objects. Beverley must assume an epistemological privilege, which is not in a mimetic but in a supplementary relationship with its object, even as he chooses to model his own critical practice upon the discursive production of the Latin American poor and disenfranchised: he does have the choice, which shakes the possibility of mimesis and makes it become a simulatory tactic, no matter how deeply felt, called solidarity. But in order for us to articulate solidarity from an alternative region of experience we must engage in a prosopopoeiac mediation: we must incorporate the abject, for only the abject, which lives in the unlivable, requires solidarity.

Sommer is more explicitly forceful in her rejection of mimesis, which she understands as an appropriative apparatus. Her model of resistant texts and incompetent readers opens onto a fissure that is not to be crossed if we are to follow the injunction of the texts themselves for us to develop, to use a phrase by Emmanuel Levinas that Sommer herself quotes, "a non-allergic relation to alterity" (Sommer 1993, 423).[21] Sommer would protect the border that resistant texts trace, for that border is itself the mark of a resistance to the mimetic apparatus, in which an unassailable and nonmimetizable textual truth lies:

> Perhaps they withhold secrets because we are so different and would understand them only imperfectly. Or should we not know them for ethical reasons, because our knowledge would lead to a preempting power? Like Nietzsche's meditation on the nature of rhetoric in general, the difference between cannot and should not is undecidable. Because even if Rigoberta's own explicit rationale is the nonempirical, ethical reason about keeping powerful information from outsiders, she suggests another constraint. It is the degree of our foreignness, our cultural difference that would make her secrets incomprehensible to the outsider. (Sommer 1993, 417)

Mimesis is not possible, or otherwise not ethical. Sommer's wonderfully complex text may be reading mine, in the sense that my comment already may be anticipated in it. However, let me risk the statement that to discover the truth of the text in the text's refusal to give up its truth is to bring the (re)production of abjection to a culminating, extreme point, which may indeed indicate the need for what Sommer calls "a paradigm shift" (426): the true epistemological impasse that Sommer's text presents is set forth in the question "If our training assumes that learning is a progression, that it is always learning something, how does interpretive reticence make sense?" (427). Well, perhaps it doesn't, if interpretive reticence comes to represent the site of a new interpretive paradigm, for reticence speaks too, and not unlike prosopopoeia.

A tenuous fetishization thus insinuates itself into Sommer's reading. Testimonio becomes the privileged site for the critical affirmation of an interpretive reticence in which radicalized restitution finds its own excess and passes over into criticism's self-redemption. Criticism is thus able to refigure its own aura at the expense of textual reticence and precisely in virtue of its relationship with it. In Sommer's essay there is no prosopopoeiac chatter: but silence, identical to itself, and therefore in itself its own end, has here been made to speak, and thus also tropologized as that which is beyond the "impassable" limit.

The Aesthetic Fix

In yet another text centrally and in fact foundationally concerned with the analysis of the chiasmic relationship between *Alturas de Macchu Picchu* and *Me llamo Rigoberta Menchú,* George Yúdice makes of resistance to abjection the paradigmatic site for an understanding of the cultural politics of testimonio, and by extension of Latin American postmodernity. For Yúdice, abjection is "hegemonic postmodernism's privileged aesthetic principle" (Yúdice 1991a, 23; also this volume, 51), whereas nonhegemonic postmodernity—that is, the Latin American one—announces an alternative aesthetics of solidarity, which becomes the foundation of a new political practice for the Latinamericanist intellectual. Yúdice seems in this in total agreement with both Beverley and Sommer. Perhaps Sommer has expressed more concisely than the others the fundamental thrust of this variety of postmodern politics: "The strategically demure posture allows us to imagine, I want to speculate, a politics of coalition among differently constituted positionalities, rather than the identity or interchangeability of subjects as the basis for equality. And a political vision adventurous enough to imagine differences, yet modest enough to respect them, may be the most significant challenge posed by learning to read resistance" (Sommer 1993, 421).

Resistance is for Yúdice a strategy of survival. He understands abjection as the fetishization of otherness, which is what resistant texts would make it impossible for their readers to develop. The call to complicity, solidarity, and coalition in these readings would tendentiously or logically preempt the possibility of the abjection experience, which comes to be seen as the "aesthetic fix" (Yúdice 1991a, 25; also this volume, 50) of hegemonic postmodernity's dealings with alterity.

Yúdice might be thinking of a critical resistance to abjection as the only way to avoid the impossible reconstitution of solidarity into a poetics of solidarity. A resistance to abjection, in my reading, is for him precisely a recognition of the extraliterary dimension of the testimonial text, which is what properly summons us to solidarity. Yúdice is in that sense, I would argue, not so much disagreeing with Julia Kristeva's elaboration of the abject as "the violence of mourning for an object that has always already been lost" (quoted in Yúdice 1991a, 23; see also Yúdice 1992a, 217), where that lost object is constitutive of the subject's own subjectivity, as he is asking for the displacement of the production of abjection toward nontestimonial texts. If for Kristeva the contemporary subject comes to terms with its own need for abjection in art and literature, that is, in the aesthetic experience as it is hegemonically understood, then Yúdice is saying that testimonio, in view of its extra-aesthetic, extraliterary moment, should be considered a discursive space totally without the purview of abjection. In other words, for Yúdice it is the extraliterary dimension of testimonio that preeminently makes testimonio a site in resistance to abjection. Abjection should come to serve as an "aesthetic fix" only where the fetishization of otherness is structurally entitled to take place, that is, in the literary, in the aesthetic: thus, not in testimonio, if it is true that, as I have been arguing, testimonio's truth is essentially extraliterary.

I am in full agreement with Yúdice's position as here interpreted. If my understanding of abjection is correct, however, even the most committed and solidaristic of Latinamericanists cannot escape it: Latinamericanist discourse, it can be said, needs abjection to constitute itself, for only the (re)production of abjection can draw the perpetually receding border along which the negotiations between the subjects and the objects of Latinamericanism either align themselves or are aligned. For Latinamericanism there seems to be no way to avoid putting itself in the position of the dangerous "literary" supplement vis-à-vis the claim of the object. Within Latinamericanism, restitutional excess is always tropologized at the service of the self-legitimation that Kristeva posits as the function of literature and art in secularized times. In Yúdice the self-legitimating event also can be read against the grain of his own writing, as in Beverley and Sommer, at the moment in which he claims that testimonio provides for a resistance to abjection, a resistance that is in itself constitutive of an aesthetics of solidarity in which an alternative, nonhegemonic postmodernity is born. But an aesthetics of solidarity is a break away from solidarity, insofar as it takes the radical summons of solidarity into an alien realm, the realm of the aesthetic. Again, I am not suggesting that this unwanted diversion is easy to avoid, or even at all avoidable: just that it happens.

If abjection is indeed a fetishization of otherness, as Yúdice says, then the abjection of abjection becomes a counterfetish that partakes of the essence of the fetish just as fully as non-A is always implied in A. One does not have to embrace abjection: but rejecting it, reducing abjection itself to an abject position, is an insufficiently critical gesture whose most direct consequence is that it returns us to an auratic practice of the postauratic that does not dare look at itself in the face. In the abjection of abjection, we miss the opportunity to understand the nature of the relational mediation between readers and texts as always already conditioned by a rupture, a fissure, a border alongside which the force of disciplinary epistemology creates radically unequal determinations.

The issue is then whether it is structurally possible for testimonio criticism, indeed for Latinamericanism, to avoid falling into Yúdice's notion of the "aesthetic fix." The aesthetic fix is here understood to be the reabsorption of the extraliterary dimension of testimonio into the disciplinary system of representation: a system that, as we have seen, cannot dispense with the production of abjection insofar as it needs to abject the other in order to speak about it. The best testimonio criticism—and the essays analyzed here are quite obviously among the best and most influential—always has understood itself to be an antidisciplinary gesture, where a newly conceptualized practice of solidarity was trusted upon to preempt the very possibility of vertical representation on which the production of abjection rests. But the game of attempting to avoid vertical representation has proved to be exceedingly complex, insofar as it must be played from a disciplinary perspective.

The question I am posing, and which I cannot adequately answer in this essay, does not circumscribe its field of questioning to testimonio criticism. If testimonio as we understand it today is a primary form of cultural manifestation for a wide variety of social movements whose politics are politics of identity, then the question ultimately affects all the disciplinary possibilities of dealing with the identitarian claims of social movements. To formulate it again: it remains to be decided whether it is possible for Latinamericanism to avoid reifying extraliterary experience into mere tropes for a systemic representational poetics. In other words: is it possible for academic criticism to deal with the cultural-discursive production of nonliterary subjects from a perspective other than the one subsumed under the terms "auratic practice of the postauratic"? And if so, how?

It would seem that an auratic practice under Latinamericanist power/knowledge conditions (and all Latinamericanist practices are necessarily auratic) is still and always on the side of the epistemological subordination of the represented, and can then only with extreme difficulty avoid the charge of exerting itself in the interests of colonial or neocolonial domination. This is so even when the auratic practice seeks accomplished restitution in a practice of spectacular redemption. Spectacular redemption, that is, the auratic call for the absolute self-identity of the object of study, which will presumably put an end to disciplinary necessity by making it redundant, is always made from within disciplinary constraints: for spectacular redemption is only the shamefaced, embarrassed other side of disciplinary power/knowledge, working in spite of itself to give the discipline further legitimacy, providing it with an alibi, blind to the fact that the discipline speaks through us, always and everywhere, no matter what we say and what we do not say.

I will finish with two partial references: the first, to Neil Larsen's introduction to *Reading North by South,* which is probably also the first lucidly sustained metacritical analysis to have appeared on Latinamericanist discourse on testimonio.[22] As it happens, Larsen also concentrates on the essays by Beverley, Sommer, and Yúdice that have been the main focus of my commentary. Larsen's perspective on those essays, although different from mine, will nevertheless enable me to come back to the question of literature with which I began.

Larsen duly notes that a "significant revision" in the way the (Latinamericanist) North has sought to authorize itself for reading Latin American texts has been underway for a number of years (Larsen 1995, 3). After proposing the term "canonical decolonization" to refer to the previous moment, that is, to the moment in which Latinamericanism was avidly reading Boom novels and seeking to incorporate Latin American culture into the supposedly universal modernist paradigm (9), Larsen suggests that the recent "counter-canonical development, notwithstanding what appears to be its status as a 'paradigm shift,' indicates not the *supersession* of the older, boom-fixated mode of readerly self-authorization but rather its *crisis*" (7–8). In fact, Larsen says, "the elevation, or *counter-canonization* of the testimonial as post-literary, post-representational, and the like, effectively exempts the reader-as-theorist from questioning his or her own dogmatically modernist preconceptions regarding the nature of the 'literary' itself" (10).

What is at stake for Larsen, as he tells us later in the text, is to open the way for a vindication of an antimodernist, realist literature. He therefore needs to do away with testimonio criticism's insistence on the death of (high) literature, as well as with the notion that the extraliterary dimension of testimonio is somehow connected with a better possibility than the one obtaining in realism for a full restitution of the object of representation. This is Larsen's significant conclusion:

> It is not only the general crisis of radical political consciousness in the North that foregrounds the peculiar idolatry of testimonial theory, but the fact that this consciousness could only project itself as universal, i.e., as historically integral with the South, in an aesthetic and cultural plane. The act of "discovering" in the testimonial both an "end of literature" [Beverley] and a cultural frontier of pure, unrepresentable, and unreadable "difference" [Sommer] discloses, by the very *conjuncture* of these two antipodes, modernism as the still dominant framework of assumptions. To read the testimonial in this way is to read into it not only the northern radical's own ideologically ambiguous relationship to imperialism, but what almost seems a nostalgia for this ambiguity itself—as if, merely by conjuring away a *false* universal (modernism, or the "literary"), one would thereby be able to produce a *true* particular. (Larsen 1995, 18)

I do think that Beverley, Sommer, and Yúdice would have no major problems accepting Larsen's diagnosis in these respects. First, modernism, as the hegemonic literary-cultural paradigm, is indeed the framework of assumptions from which and out of which an alternative must be devised. And modernism did indeed impose a particular brand of aesthetic utopianism on the Latinamericanist left which must now be shed, upon having been revealed as insufficient or catastrophic.

Within that context, Beverley, Sommer, and Yúdice underwrite testimonio criticism's attempts at doing without the "aesthetic fix," at renouncing a cultural politics based upon the hegemony of modernist aesthetic claims, and at claiming the "true" particularity of the testimonial subject's recourse to the unguarded possibility of the extraliterary real. These attempts may undoubtedly still be swamped, as I hope to have shown, in "epistemic murk," to use Michael Taussig's apt expression.[23] Nevertheless, insofar as they constitute rigorous if unfinished attempts at breaking away from the "auratic practice of the postauratic," which always has organized and seemingly has circumscribed the field of the Latinamericanist literary representation of the hegemonically oppressed, they do not seem open to challenge, or at least immediately vanquished, from a perspective intent on salvaging the representational possibilities of literary realism in postliterary times.

It is acceptable for Larsen to criticize unwanted remnants of "a modernist discourse of aesthetic utopianism" (Larsen 1995, 17) in contemporary critical practice, but, insofar as Larsen's project contemplates the possibility of "a genuinely realistic portrayal of contemporary life in Latin America" (20), the question to Larsen would be whether he can in fact argue for the possibility of a present or future realism that would not be an auratic practice under the terms defined. If so, it would be the first such realism indeed—since realism, by tendentially assuming the transparency of its own discourse as one free of ideological presuppositions (it is not ideology but truth that guides the realist hand, by definition), always has fully identified itself with the auratic extreme.[24] The question may not be just for Larsen, since the very possibility of a renewal of the literary stands or falls with it; and with it also, the possibility of an emancipatory cultural politics that could proceed outside and beyond the mournful confines of identitarian lamentations, commemorations, and ultimately dubious secrets, guarded or unguarded, in the real.

We seem to be caught in a predicament: either we renounce, from the perspective of radical solidarity with the subaltern, the representational pretensions of high literature, and thus the traditional presumption of the aesthetic, to mediate the movement for general social emancipation; or we renounce such a renunciation by reaffirming the possibility of an aesthetic practice (and reflection) with a legitimate claim to the expression of social truth. In the first case, we run the risk of fetishizing subaltern production, of blindly reaestheticizing it as the perceptual ground for a reconfiguration of critical practice that will always be excessive with respect to its object; in the second case, we are seemingly forced to state an essentialist epistemology conversant with the truth of the world and in full control of its own conditions of production.

My final reference will be to Nelly Richard's notion of the "hyper-literary," developed in the context of an interpretation of Diamela Eltit's *El padre mío* (1989). In *El padre mío,* which transcribes the testimonial ramblings of a Chilean schizophrenic vagrant, the resources of testimonio seem to be turned against themselves. The extraliterary dimension of testimonial production is here also constituted by the indexical reference to the singularity of a pain beyond any possibility of representation: except that *El padre mío* refuses to be read, as much as it refuses to read itself, as an identitarian construction. The testimonial subject, as Richard says, here projects himself "as an image lacking all interiority and profundity," to complicate "the idea of testimonio as a vector of social consciousness and of an identitarian formation . . . rooted in ethos-sharing" (Richard 1994, 4). For Richard, the erratic singularity of el padre's voice configures a hyper-literary space where testimonio exceeds its condition as a "document" of social reality, and as a "monument" of Latinamericanist representation (9).

If that is so, is *El padre mío* the site of a restitutional excess strong enough to ceaselessly undo Latinamericanism's aura, and yet weak enough to allow for its conceptualization as a merely aberrant, all-too-abject exemplary instance? How do we read it, as literature, beyond literature?

Notes

1.   I am borrowing the notion of cultural capital from John Guillory, although it was first developed by Pierre Bourdieu. My use here, as it relates to the way literature is taught and reflected upon primarily in the U.S. university, depends on the following: "Literary works must be seen rather as the vectors of ideological notions which do not inhere in the works themselves but in the context of their institutional presentation, or more simply, in the way in which they are taught" (Guillory 1993, ix).

2.   To mention in this connection two of the primary interlocutors of this essay, see John Beverley, "¿Postliteratura? Sujeto subalterno e impasse de las humanidades" (1993b), and more generally his book *Against Literature* (1993a), which partially includes the article previously mentioned. Beverley's position

is not totally "against literature," in spite of his title. He finishes both the article and the first chapter of the book with the words: "it is not a matter of liquidating the subject [i.e., literature] (in spite of its own anxious fantasies), nor of curing it once and for all, but simply of reforming it on new bases so as to make it somewhat more capable of solidarity and love" (Beverley 1993a, 22; 1993b, 24). George Yúdice goes beyond literature to encompass all artistic production: "If art was once thought to be a privileged actor in the struggle for civil society, I am afraid that this struggle now takes place in other terrains" (Yúdice 1993, 555).

3. For Larsen the current crisis concerns literary modernism, and never in any case literature as a whole. Indeed, his current project involves "an uncompromising rejection of modernism and a concomitant advocacy of realism" in an attempt to answer the question "what are the constituents of and the historical conditions of possibility for realism in an imperialized world, especially on its southern and Latin American flanks?" (Larsen 1995, 19).

4. See Arturo Escobar and Sonia Alvarez (1992b) for an important collection of essays on Latin American social movements, as well as some significant attempts to understand their recent global proliferation and their Latin American specificity. See in particular the "Introduction" by Escobar and Alvarez (1992a), and the multiauthored essay by Fernando Calderón, Alejandro Piscitelli, and José Luis Reyna (1992), and by Escobar (1992).

5. On "national security" see Chomsky 1985; Rial 1986; Loveman and Davies 1989, esp. 163; and Weschler 1990, 111–23, among other possible sources.

6. See Mato 1993. Mato understands the "irrupción y creciente importancia política y cultural de nuevas organizaciones de base y movimientos políticos y sociales organizados en torno a identidades locales, étnicas, de clase social, de género, generacionales, y otras" (218) as a direct response to globalization in contemporary times. See also Yúdice 1992a, 7 passim.

7. The notion of literature as colonial discourse in the case of Latin America has been presented by Beverley: "Latin American literature [is endowed] with an ambiguous cultural role and legacy: literature (or, less anachronistically, *letras*) is a colonial institution, one of the basic institutions of Spanish colonial rule in the Americas; yet it is also one of the institutions crucial to the development of an autonomous creole and then 'national' (although perhaps not popular-democratic) culture. [Contemporary literature] still bears the traces of this paradox" (Beverley 1993a, 2). See also Rama 1984.

8. See, for instance, Achugar 1989, 279–81. Elzbieta Sklodowska quotes Angel Rama's declaration that he was the one who recommended to *Casa de las Américas* a new category for testimonio for their literary contest in January 1969 (Sklodowska 1992, 56). John Beverley and Marc Zimmerman argue that in the mid-1960s the popularity of ethnographic life-stories such as those by Oscar Lewis and Ricardo Pozas and of more directly political testimonial

accounts, such as, in Cuba, the ones inspired by Ernesto Che Guevara's *Episodios de la guerra revolucionaria cubana,* was in fact responsible for the canonization of the genre only a few years later (Beverley and Zimmerman 1990, 173–74). Yúdice emphasizes the sense of cultural-literary belligerence against the mostly liberal supporters of boom-like literature attached to these institutional beginnings of testimonio (Yúdice 1991a, 26; also this volume). In fact, however, boom literature was destined to occupy hegemonic ground all through the next decade and a half. In the early to mid-1980s a certain exhaustion with boom and post-boom fiction came together with the solidarity movement and the general horror in the face of repression in Argentina and of Central American civil wars and government atrocities in the early 1980s to assure a widespread popularity to testimonio. About the genealogy of testimonio in general, all critical opinions have been shown to be partial, and therefore partially misguided, by Sklodowska (1992, 55–68).

9.   The extraliterary aspect of testimonio has been expressly emphasized by Beverley and Zimmerman (1990): "In principle, testimonio appears . . . as an extraliterary or even antiliterary form of discourse" (178); "[testimonio] functions in a zone of indeterminacy between" antiliterature and "a new, postfictional form of literature, with significant cultural and ideological repercussions" (179). In contrast, Sklodowska concludes that "el testimonio mediato guarda tan estrecho parentesco con la novela que puede considerarse como una de las actualizaciones ('género histórico') de la novela concebida como 'género teórico'" (Sklodowska 1992, 97).

10.   It was suggested by Yúdice and discussed during the panel on "Testimonio y abyección," Latin American Studies Association Meeting, Atlanta, March 1994.

11.   See Achugar (1992) for a sharp discussion of the elemental importance of those three features in the academic institutionalization of testimonio.

12.   Beverley and Zimmerman (1990) state: "literature has been a means of national and popular mobilization in the Central American revolutionary process, but that process also elaborates or points to forms of cultural democratization that will necessarily question or displace the role of literature as a hegemonic cultural institution" (207). I don't think that the Central American revolutionary process causes a hegemonic shift concerning literature's cultural capital; rather, a shift in literature's cultural capital creates the ideological framework for that argument.

13.   Testimonio is generally regarded to have reached full maturity as a genre in connection with revolutionary struggle in Central America in particular. For Antonio Vera León, Latin American testimonio models itself "sobre el proyecto revolucionario de poner a los productores en control de los medios de producción como el modo de erradicar la dominación y la represión producida por la modernidad capitalista" (Vera León 1992, 184). See, however, Gareth

Williams (1993) for a response to Vera León and a highly persuasive conceptualization of testimonio as an identity-producing discourse on the basis of radical loss: "[In testimonio] the discursive reconfiguration of personal and collective experience . . . is ultimately facilitated by a movement of mourning in which loss of original selfhood is fought against and reconciled to itself by its absorption and translation into the very basis of cultural resistance and survival" (G. Williams 1993, 97). I am indebted to Williams for the notion that testimonio is a primary cultural manifestation of identity politics—indeed, for an understanding of the production of identity on the basis of an introjecting resistance to, as well as assimilation of, original loss. For Williams discourses of identity in contemporary Latin American testimonio must be understood as phenomena of mourning, and of its peculiar dialectics of lamentation and commemoration. In reference to Rigoberta Menchú, for instance, Williams writes: "the reconfiguration of one's life through discourse becomes equatable with a process of mourning in which the incorporation and assimilation into the self of painful severance—from one's cultural laws, one's past, one's language, from the body of a tortured and murdered mother and brother, from a father killed in the act of resisting—is a remembrance of loss which, nevertheless, is also seen to permit a new process of becoming" (G. Williams 1993, 94). I am arguing that the identity-politics dimension of testimonio grows immensely during the 1980s and 1990s, and that such identitarian dimension is dominant today in testimonio's cultural capital. In fact, leaving aside considerations of literary quality or formal interest, the overwhelming presence of *Me llamo Rigoberta Menchú* in discussions of testimonio seems to me to be directly related to the identitarian, and not to the social-revolutionary dimension in testimonio's cultural capital. See also, in reference to the connection between testimonio and identity politics, Yúdice (1992a, 208, 213, 223)—"estos textos enfocan las maneras en que diversos grupos oprimidos . . . practican su identidad no sólo como resistencia a la opresión sino también como cultura afirmativa, como estética práctica" (213); and Marín (1991, 53, 55, 59, 65). For a different and intriguing take on the issue (insofar as testimonio's general capability to induce solidarity at the service of the social emancipation of the subaltern is quite radically called into question), see Zimmerman (1992). But Zimmerman is in my interpretation still supporting the general notion that testimonio articulates, or even primarily articulates, identity-dimensions of people's lives.

14. Actually, it should be spelled "Macchu Pichu." See Santí (1961) for a sharp interpretation of Neruda's orthographic addition. According to Santí, "la letra suplemental no [es] una mera errata: se trata de la marca de un punto de mira a la vez exterior e interior al ser americano y desde el cual se delata la mirada mediatizada del cronista, su interpretación deliberada y escandalosamente occidental" (90).

15. See Gugino (1991, 195–209), for an interpretation of Neruda's dwelling ("morada") as "the turning in need to a without, a *chora* that is at the same time a site of potential participation" anticipating or seeking "a possible encounter" (195). Although my reading of Neruda's gesture toward that encounter does not follow Gugino's reading, I don't regard mine as incompatible with his: Neruda's "morada" is overdetermined. Let me also suggest the possibility of reading Neruda's famous verse through G. W. F. Hegel's appropriation of the Greek proverb *Idou Rodos, idou kai to pedema* ("Here is the rose, dance here") in his *Introduction to the Philosophy of Right* (1970, 26).

16. This notion of "total representativity" is equated by Fredric Jameson to testimonio's drive toward "the multiplication of proper names" (Jameson 1993a, 26; also this volume, 186), and the implied notion that testimonial anonymity "means not the loss of personal identity, of the proper name, but the multiplication of those things" (Jameson 1993a, 27; also this volume, 185). Jameson goes on to talk about testimonio as expressive of a "zero degree of the wish," since for him, in testimonio's subjective positioning, "experience moves back and forth between two great polarities or dialectical limits to the individual subject—one is the collective or peasant ritual, always present in these testimonies. The other is history, in the sense of a brutal irruption, of catastrophe, of the history of the others, that breaks into the peasant community from the outside, and most specifically into peasant space as such" (Jameson 1993a, 207; also this volume, 187).

17. However, it needs to be constantly kept in mind that by testimonio, no matter how much we choose to emphasize in our reading the voice of the testimonial subject, we also generally mean a text in which an act of transcription has taken place. Vera León's splendid essay on the testimonial transcription settles the fact that the testimonial text is, always already, "el espacio en el que el transcriptor construye su autoridad" (Vera León 1992, 191). Vera León's conclusion points to the unsettling fact that testimonio itself, in its canonical examples, is never free of contamination from the sort of critical practice, based on the production of abjection, that I am here calling "auratic practice of the postauratic": "En el proceso testimonial la vida del 'otro' no es simplemente el referente real aludido por el texto . . . De ahí que el texto testimonial pueda leerse como el lugar de tensiones irresueltas . . . donde se negocia un relato que documenta la vida del 'otro' así como las formas de contarla, que también son formas de imaginarla y de apropiarla para la escritura" (195). "Hacer hablar" is in several important senses at the genealogical foundation of what I imagine to be my own contribution to testimonio metacritics.

18. I am appropriating, as well as referring to, Jacques Derrida's notion of the "dangerous" supplement, developed in his analysis of Rousseau's references to masturbation. See Derrida (1976, 141–64).

19. For a similar notion of the operativity of the secret in Menchú's text, but a

different interpretation of how the secret was textually intended, see G. Williams (1993, 95–97).

20. "Announcing limited access is the point, not whether or not some information is really withheld. Resistance does not necessarily signal a genuine epistemological impasse; it is enough that the impasse is claimed in this ethico-aesthetic strategy to position the reader within limits" (Sommer 1993, 409). Even though resistance does not *necessarily* signal an epistemological impasse, the implication of Sommer's analysis throughout her essay is that resistance in the subaltern text in fact creates that impasse for the reader: whether or not the impasse exists becomes undecidable, and the undecidability is itself a part of the impasse.

21. "Resistant Texts and Incompetent Readers" is the title of the essay Sommer published in *Latin American Literary Review,* which is a partial version of the longer article I am referring to.

22. A metacritical analysis on some aspects of testimonio production and interpretation is also offered by Robert Carr, although from a different perspective and thus lacking in the Latinamericanist specificity that Larsen develops. Carr's project is "to map the contexts and implications of First World intellectuals occupied with Third World texts" (Carr 1992, 91).

23. Epistemic murk in the sense in which Taussig uses the expression can be briefly described as the engagement of fictitious realities whose allegorical as well as literal effect is "a betrayal of Indian realities for the confirmation of colonial fantasies" (Taussig 1987, 123). I am not suggesting that testimonio criticism willfully produces epistemic murk: rather that epistemic murk is the disciplinary medium of Latinamericanism, since Christopher Columbus.

24. Although it probably has nothing to do with what Larsen has in mind when he talks about realism, I cannot pass this opportunity to cite a Latinamericanist disciplinary text that paradoxically seems to go a long way toward ridding itself of auratic practices by almost paroxysmally intensifying them to their extreme: Ruth Behar's *Translated Woman* (1993). It is a strange sort of text, in that it is an ethnobiography-cum-testimonio where the traditional mediator figure at times becomes the testimonial subject herself. It is a maddening text: it problematizes the authorial position because it takes to an extreme the irreducible conflict between political desire and epistemic constraints; it pretends to translate without ignoring the fact that translation shows the original to be dead, that it in fact kills the original; it allegorizes the relationship between anthropologist and subject as that between a wetback and her coyote, maybe even the worst kind of coyote; it calls itself redemptive ethnography knowing full well that there is no redemption actually happening anywhere; it denounces its own *malinchismo;* it purports to go beyond the self/other division without actually bothering the self/other division. *Translated Woman,* as a Latinamericanist text, has some claim to go beyond Latin-

americanism, to come close to a region of writing without disciplinary entitlement, without permission. It problematizes the notion that the Latin American testimonial/ethnographic subject is the ground of disciplinary thought, at the same time that it challenges the reader to move beyond disciplinary thought, toward a raw encounter with its imaginary basis, or its basis in the imaginary.

Gareth Williams **The Fantasies**

of Cultural Exchange in Latin American

Subaltern Studies

Ideology . . . is not just a matter of what I think about a situation; it is
somehow inscribed in that situation itself. It is no good me reminding
myself that I am opposed to racism as I sit down on a park bench
marked 'Whites Only'; by the act of sitting on it, I have supported and
perpetuated racist ideology. The ideology, so to speak, is in the bench,
not in my head.—Terry Eagleton

The recent publication in *boundary 2* of the Latin American Subaltern Studies Group's "Founding Statement" is the culminating
point in identity/solidarity-based Latinamericanism's project of redefining current disciplinary configurations, and rethinking the effective
conditions of contemporary paradigm shifts. The apparent collapse of
any social system other than capitalism, together with the increasing
transnationalization of contemporary forms of metropolitan knowledge
production—Euro–North American technological resources, ideas, and
cultural representations—have led to what could be considered a crisis
in the traditional disciplinary processes of self-legitimation within Latinamericanism. This crisis consequently has produced the demand for
active engagement in redefining the symbolic authority by which we
can effectively mediate, rather than dominate or monopolize, contemporary discourses of cultural exchange between "Third World" cultural
production and the "First World" institutional sites of theorization and
appropriation.

It is from within the contemporary processes of shifting disciplinary
paradigms that the collective work of the Latin American Subaltern
Studies Group emerges, and significantly contributes to the ongoing
debates on the validity of current disciplinary practice within Latinamericanism.[1] This, of course, is a field of debate that the group fully
recognizes, and whose challenges they locate at the center of their intellectual venture: "The redefinition of Latin American political and cul-

tural space in recent years has . . . impelled scholars of the region to revise established and previously functional epistemologies in the social sciences and humanities. The general trend toward democratization prioritizes in particular the re-examination of the concepts of pluralistic societies and the conditions of subalternity within these societies" (Beverley and Oviedo 1993, 110–11).

Thus the "Founding Statement" of the Latin American Subaltern Studies Group should be read as a collective call for new forms of conceptualization and intellectual intervention, an attempt to actively engage U.S. identity/solidarity-based forms of Latinamericanism in a debate born from the need to renegotiate what we could consider to be the "I/Other dichotomy in the re-representation of 'other' cultures" (Hitchcock 1993–94, 11) within U.S.-based Latinamericanism. Ultimately what is at stake in the group's call for disciplinary self-interrogation is our ability to engage in discourses of exchange between Latin American popular cultural production and U.S. practices of theorization that establish a transcultural politics of coalition with the subaltern, rather than one of annihilation or neocolonialism.[2]

A fundamental component in the project of disciplinary revision and redefinition of the hegemonic paradigms by which colonial and postcolonial social structures have been traditionally construed, is the disciplinary *positionality* assigned to the subaltern in academic modes of re-representation. We could say that the subaltern either protagonizes or falls victim to the conditions of exchange that mediate both its social existence and its increasing presence in radical institutional critiques in the First World. Thus, the institutional mechanics of the constitution of the "Other" engenders the need to identify and counter exploitative modes of conceptualization by reflecting upon the underlying politics of transcultural academic intervention, and consequently tracing the problematic lines of domination and subordination that inhabit the borderlands of radical critique and neocolonial assimilation.[3] Obviously, as Latin American cultural studies become increasingly implicated in the redefinition of transcultural processes and strategies of exchange and intervention with the Latin American subaltern, it is almost inevitable that at some point or another we address the ways in which subaltern cultural production can be chronicled *alongside,* rather than *beneath* the strategies of intellectual production that render re-representation possible in the first place. It would seem that, in order to do this, identity/solidarity-based Latinamericanism would have to directly question, as Peter Hitchcock does below, contemporary processes of academic engagement in order to counteract discourses of collusion and complicity with contemporary global discourses of domination and subjection; as Hitchcock asks, "[W]hat strategies might obtain to disable the continued reproduction of the logic of Western cultural critique that fosters the 'othering' of the so-called 'Third World Subject'? Does the rise of cultural studies in the American academy foreshadow the dissolution of the Subjected Other or the next round of a neo-colonialist project that advocates 'know thy global neighbors' the better to exploit them. . . . How do theories and theoreticians resist the 'inevitability' that 'thinking global' is the next chapter in the Western will-to-hegemony?" (Hitchcock 1993–94, 11).[4]

Of course, these problematic issues lie at the heart of identity/solidarity-based Latinamericanism's ability to engage the subaltern object of analysis in an effective practice of cultural exchange without succumbing to the very discursive elaboration of subaltern subjugation that is inevitably produced in the establishment of colonialist forms of academic appropriation and incorporation. As such, the preeminent question raised by the "Founding Statement" of the Latin American Subaltern Studies Group is how to re-represent the subaltern in U.S.-based Latinamericanism without yielding under the burden of fetishistic or exploitative forms of discursive practice. This must surely lead us to actively reflect on the problematics of establishing an effectively "democratic" or "horizontal" transnational cultural politics between First World intellectual and Third World subaltern, in such a way as to question the positional implications of the subaltern's increasing presence in this country as a Latinamericanist growth industry, in which money and institutional resources are thrown at academic research, and in which Latin American subaltern cultural production becomes increasingly intertwined in the labor of U.S. institutions of information dissemination and knowledge construction. To what extent, then, can we reevaluate and redefine the heterogeneous positionalities of the I/Other dichotomy that underlies the postmodern conjunctural siting of Latin American subaltern cultural production within the academic networks of the United States?[5]

My purpose in this essay is to contribute to the ongoing debate surrounding the current paradigm shifts and disciplinary configurations within identity/solidarity-based Latinamericanism, and to do so by calling attention to the problematic gaps and fissures that underlie the discipline's contemporary treatment of exchange between Latin American subaltern cultural production and the discipline's sites of intervention. This is not to say that, by attending to discursive "gaps" and "fissures" in contemporary strategies of cultural exchange, my own interest is to establish a position that is exterior to or "against" that of Latin American subaltern studies, nor, I might add, is it to engage in what Nancy Scheper-Hughes calls an obsessive and self-reflexive hermeneutics in which the self, and not the other, becomes the subject of academic inquiry (Scheper-Hughes 1993, 28). Rather, I position myself very much within the critical trajectory that has been developed by Latin American subaltern studies over the last fifteen years, and which has led to the increasing delegitimation and displacement of the "boom aesthetic" and its criticism within contemporary disciplinary configurations and debates.[6] Nevertheless, in the interests of establishing what Scheper-Hughes might call a "good enough" Latin American subaltern studies—that is, a practice "envisioned as a great Bakhtinian banquet where everyone can find a place at the table and a share in the feasting" (Scheper-Hughes 1993, 30)—I think it necessary that we examine the ways in which Latin American subaltern studies attends to the problem of positioning within its strategies of critical intervention with the object of study. Thus, what is at stake in my analysis, as it is in the work of the Latin American Subaltern Studies Group and, indeed, as it is in the corpus of criticism on testimonio that has emerged in the last decade or so in the United States, is not only how to represent the Latin American subaltern, but equally how to represent ourselves—our own positionality at the disciplinary banquet table—within metropolitan processes of Latin American subaltern re-representation.[7]

In my opinion, given the increasing production of knowledge on the subaltern in U.S. academic networks, critical reliance upon a modernist faith in the validity of discrete, inherently oppositional positionalities—in which the perceived authenticity of each site of enunciation can be located as the essential Cartesian origin from which oppositional identities and knowledges emerge—reflects a conceptual matrix grounded in and fully reliant upon the establishment of mutually exclusionary fields of cultural and theoretical production. Thus, I shall postulate that the challenge for future reexaminations of the conditions of cultural exchange between Latin American subaltern and U.S. metropolitan sites of theorization—for a "good enough" Latin American subaltern studies, in other words—lies in the specific strategic dilemmas that emerge from the ideological implications of a disciplinary practice that automatically positions the subaltern as "peripheral" to our theoretical site of "centrality." This, in turn, will lead us into the realm of what I call "disciplinary fantasy" and "Latinamericanist enjoyment," and the relationship that these discursive agents hold to the imposition of normative forms of critical practice and institutional appropriation such as those of the aforementioned center-periphery dyad. At this point I should qualify my analysis by adding that within the contemporary processes of intellectual representation, it is becoming increasingly evident that a problematic paradox lies at the heart of identity/solidarity-based Latinamericanism's ability to engage in nonexploitational critical relations between Third World cultural production and the First World institutional sites of theorization and appropriation. As such, an epistemological impasse is easily reached in the discursive practicality and disciplinary agency of a Latinamericanist who, while perhaps acting in full solidarity with his or her object of study, nevertheless masks a particular form of exploitation within the labor of discursive elaboration itself. Obviously, the materialization of exploitation within the makeup of the effective social activity of solidarity-based Latinamericanism—even when cultural liberation is an explicit goal—implies the need for us to further scrutinize the ways in which Latinamericanist desire structures and exercises itself in its conjunctural engagement with the Latin American subaltern. Indeed, I would even hazard to say that, in many of its present guises, the contemporary constitution of the subaltern as an object of knowledge masks the repression of an underlying mode of discursive agency that inherently conflicts with and perhaps even contradicts the specific goal of the project of solidarity formation at hand. One consequence of this is that U.S.-based Latinamericanists working to establish active ties of solidarity with their objects of analysis—a transnational politics of coalition or horizontality between Latin American subaltern and First World academic production, let's say—run the risk of doing so at the expense of succumbing to fetishistic modes of intellectual labor, or of implementing an implicitly vertical political matrix in their project of horizontalist solidarity formation. Thus, in the institutionalized discourses of U.S. identity/solidarity-based Latinamericanism, it seems that it is becoming increasingly difficult to ignore the power of an underlying mode of disciplinary agency in which heterogeneity, cultural difference, and collective liberation from metropolitan forms of conceptualization are actively advocated, yet are done so through the implementation of totalizing and normative strategies of disciplinary appropriation.

Indeed, it appears that this problematic logic of internal antagonism is inscribed into the I/Other dichotomy that underlies the very production of Rigoberta Menchú's testimonio itself. For example, when Elisabeth Burgos-Debray declares in her prologue to *Me llamo Rigoberta Menchú* that "ella [Rigoberta] me permitió el descubrimiento de mi otro yo. Gracias a ella mi yo americano ya no es una 'inquietante rareza'" (Menchú 1983, 21), Rigoberta is positioned as the object of "centrist" desire by means of which the metropolitan restitutor embarks upon a transatlantic journey of self-restitution to "America," and to the uncanny "strangeness" of her American identity. It is precisely at this point, in what appears to be its perverse enjoyment of Rigoberta's discourse of subalternity and obligatory silence, and equally of its own processes of self-restoration and restitution, that it becomes increasingly difficult to ignore the ways in which advocacy of a respectful, nontotalizing politics of coalition between subjects actively positioned as center and periphery—as absolute self-identity and radical difference—can carry the signature of horizontality's "Other scene"; namely, neocolonial verticality. It appears that we have stumbled upon what could be considered a constitutive fantasy space in which the liberating gesture of Latinamericanism toward the subaltern subject depends for its very existence and completion upon an internal discursive breakdown heterogeneous to the ideological field that it establishes. In turn, the misrecognition of the internally antagonistic agency of Latinamericanist fantasy seems to be the positive condition upon which Latinamericanism can enjoy its self-legitimizing strategies of intervention. In other words, if Burgos-Debray were to recognize the constitutive fantasy that governs her positioning of Rigoberta, as well as the implications of her own explicit self-positionality within the processes of cultural exchange, then this knowledge would undermine the Latinamericanists' enjoyment of her own self-restituting positionality. Fantasy and the enjoyment of that contradictory space, then, appear to be two highly problematic agents for the successful practice of identity/ solidarity-based Latinamericanism.[8]

Obviously, with the increasing presence in U.S. academic networks of subaltern knowledge formations and Third World theoretical practices, the limits of possibility for an effective theorization of subaltern "resistance," for example, are becoming increasingly difficult to conceptualize, and this is so precisely at the very moment in which testimonio, to cite just one example of such subaltern knowledge formations, is increasingly incorporated into U.S. academic and institutional networks, and in which many forms of U.S.-based Latinamericanism call for a transnational politics of resistance to hegemonic discourses of domination. Of course, equally difficult to conceptualize in this ill-defined frontier space of cultural appropriation and what could perhaps be thought of as resistant counterappropriation, are the limits of agency enacted between the First World critic and re-representations of subjugated forms of knowledge.

With the growing presence over approximately the last fifteen years of subaltern cultural production such as testimonio in U.S. Latinamericanist critical practices, boundaries between "inside" and "outside"— for example, between U.S. institutions and people working within their confines, and Latin American subaltern politics—have become far less discrete than they might ever have seemed. This is so not just because Rigoberta Menchú, for example, indirectly brings the Maya-Quiché to the United States in her testimonio (mediated of course by the ghostly presence of Elisabeth Burgos-Debray), but because the institutional interests of transnational capitalism inevitably impact in one way or another on any critical discourse on Rigoberta Menchú that emerges from the U.S. academy.

As a result of the apparently increasing sites of conjuncture between subaltern cultural production and our own critical practices, desire for delimited categories or discretely oppositional global, transcultural, or transnational positionalities is rendered ambivalent, and ultimately undermined, by simultaneous appropriations between heterogeneous sites of enunciation that inevitably question the value of such categories as . inside and outside.

Latin American subaltern studies marks one area of identity/ solidarity-based Latinamericanism in which a systematic center-periphery dyad has been particularly prevalent, even though it can be thought of as a normative, universalizing allegory of systematic inclusion and exclusion. What I propose, then, is a symptomatic reading of identity/solidarity-based Latinamericanism's contemporary strategies of engagement with the subaltern subject: a reexamination of academic processes of objectification and "otherization" that addresses the specific agency of normative positioning (center-periphery thinking), of disciplinary fantasy, and of Latinamericanist enjoyment of the subaltern. My analysis will focus primarily on the founding concepts and strategies of the Latin American Subaltern Studies Group, precisely because their presence and the drive of their collective venture represents the defining accomplishment of the numerous contributions to intellectual debate that have been instigated by identity/solidarity-based Latinamericanism over the last fifteen years.

The declared purpose of the Latin American Subaltern Studies Group is to call for "new ways of thinking and acting politically" given the post–Cold War displacement of revolutionary projects, the contemporary processes of redemocratization in Latin America, and the advent of new transnational economic arrangements between competing trading blocs (Latin American Subaltern Studies Group 1993, 110). Fundamental to the success of the project's ability to engage politically with subaltern objects of analysis is the recognition that "elite historiography" has systematically failed to represent the subaltern as historical agent (118). The group's goal, then, is to embark on what could be considered a redemptive project of recuperating the figure of the subaltern as historical agent, and of re-presenting that agency that has remained until now unrepresented. Thus, by recognizing historically constituted metropolitan constructions of subalternity, and of subaltern agency in given social formations, the group proposes to restore disciplinary presence to the traditionally absented object of elite historiography by systematically considering the practices of elite intellectuals as historically constituted neocolonial forms of appropriation and objectification, grounded in inevitable blindness to nonscriptural subaltern forms of cultural production and representation. The purpose of the group, then, is to actively combat the exploitative forms of conceptualization, appropriation, and incorporation that inevitably silence the Latin American subaltern subject.

The group's project of nonexploitative subaltern restoration tends to problematize itself by actively positing the Latin American subaltern as a currently exterior and inaccessible site of academic pilgrimage, from those positioned as "center" to those located as margin or "periphery": "We need to access the vast (and mobile) array of the masses— peasants, proletarians, the informal and formal sectors, the sub- and under-employed, vendors, those outside or at the margin of the money economy, lumpens and ex-lumpens of all sorts, children, the growing numbers of the homeless. . . . Clearly, it is a question not only of new ways of *looking* at the subaltern . . . but also of building new relations between ourselves and those human contemporaries whom we posit as objects of study" (Latin American Subaltern Studies Group 1993, 121). Thus, in the interests of "building new relations" between a "them" to be "accessed," and a noncoincident "we" that needs to "access," the Latin American subaltern is implicitly located by the group—in the very elaboration of its discursive labor—as the exteriorized example and positional site of the historically obliterated subject. In this sense, their active conceptualization of the predicament of the Latin American subaltern is achieved through the positive maintenance of a center-periphery paradigm in which the periphery is accessed by the center, and converted as such into an object of contemporary counterhegemonic knowledge-production and theoretical practice. It could be said that identity/solidarity-based Latinamericanism's treatment of subaltern cultural production becomes inherently flawed by its apparent tendency to maintain conceptual boundaries between the peripheral places of production (Latin America) and the centralized places of theorization (North America). Moreover, this has been effected without sufficiently problematizing the means by which the two inevitably impact each other in the relatively new cultural topography of the U.S.-inspired project for globalized loose accumulation, and the international divisions of labor that this implies.

In much of its treatment of testimonio, for example, identity/solidarity-based Latinamericanism has maintained a conscious and apparently necessary disjuncture between "inside" and "outside" cultures by imposing upon Latin American subaltern production the exigencies of a modernist center-periphery binary. In this mechanism, testimonio comes to be a homogeneous and totalizing resistance to the metropolitan center and to metropolitan discourses of centrality.

Yet recurrence to a critical model grounded explicitly or implicitly in the center-periphery duality undermines is own efficacy since it inevitably establishes truth regimes that reveal as much about the imposition on the object of Latinamericanist intervention and knowledge-management, as they do about the effective properties of the object itself. The center-periphery dyad, in its very implementation and practice, must first pass through a foundational process by which it can assume the preexistence of inherently oppositional sites, and second, needs to integrate them into a harmonious, auratic, trans-social totality implicitly characterized by analytical integration, continuity, connectedness, and structural harmony.[9]

Of course, at this point, those who actively support its implementation will say that the center-periphery dyad is extremely valuable as a faithful explicative of the location of Latin America within contemporary configurations of global cultural politics. It is, after all, an abstraction or a universalization of a concrete situation. Nevertheless, by the very same token, in the very disciplinary *practice* of imposing the center-periphery binary upon testimonio, or any other mode of subaltern expression for that matter, the social realities of the subaltern—the concrete—come to count as being little more than a phenomenal form of that which is deemed as abstract or universal. In other words, the concrete cannot necessarily be thought through the abstract universalizations of a center-periphery model that is itself an allegorical abstraction. Every Latinamericanist knows that social realities—poverty, exploitation, colonialism—are concrete manifestations, yet in the disciplinary appropriation of those realities—in the institutionalized analysis of testimonio in the United States, for example—many of us act as if the concrete were only accessible to us through the universality of abstraction. In the effective elaboration of our social activity we render Latin American subalternity abstract—peripheral to the center in which we position ourselves—yet act as if within our appropriative practice we were not in fact allegorizing or fetishizing the concrete in such a way as to reify heterogeneity, in order to make it more representable or more controllable. In short, we act as if Latin American subalternity were not, in the very practice of cultural exchange, inevitably submitted to discursive commodification, as if the object actually realized itself as something other than exchange-value within the space occupied and delineated by U.S. institutional critical practices on Latin America.

Within the disciplinary production of knowledge, insistence on the methodological vehicle of the center-periphery model isolates the object, encoding its cultural paradigms within a specific position to be defined only as a single place within an objective set of global relations. These relations correspond to a belief—or a need to believe—in the singularity of, for example, cultural identities and collective practices, constructed around socially predefined differences. In the active implementation of center-periphery thinking, then, it very often becomes the act of positioning itself that defines the site of what the metropolitan critic may call resistance or ideological struggle. As such, in thinking Latin American subaltern modes of cultural production, the indigenous, women, and many examples of the testimonio genre can so easily come to be considered "resistant" to the imposition of hegemony simply because their constructed identities are viewed as remaining somehow beyond the limits of dominant ideology.

Thus, by systematically positioning Latin America as periphery, knowledge tends to come to the always already positioned disciplinary site of North America—the so-called center—not so much as a locus of engagement and struggle defining itself as an active source of meaning production, but rather as an implicit site of struggle always in relation to metropolis, the center. This of course positions and maintains the subaltern, or through a metonymic relation the "Third World," as the antagonistic outside of the "First," a space of exclusion and totalized difference always resisting the demands of the center's ideological projects of modernity and postmodernity. It also implicitly locates the radical agency of the periphery as a fundamental means by which the center can critique itself and define the parameters of its own institutional struggles. In this sense, identity/solidarity-based Latinamericanism's engagement with testimonio, for example, often may be seen to run the risk of becoming as much a critique of the moralizing rhetoric of the North American academy—a metropolitan lamentation on the sociopolitical and cultural challenges of modernity inflicted on peripheral societies—as it is an analysis of the Latin American social anatomy from which cultural narratives emerge.[10]

While we have generally proclaimed testimonio to be wholly oppositional to the postmodern logic of late capitalism, as well as to metropolitan discourses of ethnography and anthropology, our criticism of testimonio has maintained the dualism of center and periphery in order to privilege the peripheral as a totalizing subversion of the center. Of course, to some extent this reflects the foundations of a con-

tradictory utopian project in which metropolitan intellectuals value
testimonio as contestatory, yet do so by actively blanketing its local-
ized and heterogeneous production with the systematic application of a
center-periphery binary that, historically, is and has been so crucial to
the foundational self-legitimizing practices of Euro–North American
modernity in Latin America.

The repeated implementation of the center-periphery paradigm to
describe, explain, or even begin to think through Latin American subaltern cultural production, such as that of testimonio, is enacted by
Latinamericanism in terms of its exchange-value. In other words, Latin
America as periphery can be viewed as an expression of value, and more
specifically, of a value placed on the Latin American subaltern by a U.S.-
based critical discourse attempting to define and position the object of
study in the global cultural economy. Yet the center-periphery dyad
implies that without the center the social reality of the periphery would
cease to exist as such, and in the same way, without the periphery the
center could not define itself. Thus, it might be said that the sometimes
mechanical implementation of a center-periphery model—this constitution and imposition of transcultural radical "difference"—to explain
Latin American cultural production does not, in and of itself, reflect
anything more than an implicit conformity with the maintenance of
this "othering" allegory of social positionalities as a means of reductive
elucidation and wholesale appropriation.

Of course, a center-periphery dependent Latinamericanism runs the
risk of engaging in a seemingly homogeneous conceptualization of extremely complex social realities, almost a continuation and consolidation—rather than a redefinition or problematization—of the system of
thought that prevailed in the Cold War, and which eventually led to
what Aijaz Ahmad has called the "propensity to think of global divisions in monolithic terms" (Ahmad 1992, 310). Within this system of
thought, the use of the center-periphery model might allow U.S.-based
Latinamericanists to "access" moments of subaltern resistance, for example, but those counterhegemonic sites of historical agency can too
easily be linked to a moment of "authenticity" implicitly placed at the
mercy of the hegemonic incorporation of the margins by the center, a
process that virtually guarantees the systematic, though perhaps unin-
tentional, appropriation of all sites of subaltern expression by the U.S.-
based critic/institution.[11]

This conceptual logic is extremely problematic for the practice of identity/solidarity-based Latinamericanism since, in its very implementation, it seems to re-present the movements of neocolonial appropriation and the homogenizing strategies of domination indicative of a transnational capitalism that has so recently engineered the implementation of its new foreign policy, euphemistically named the North American Free Trade Agreement. Blind recourse to center-periphery models, to "us" accessing "them" in other words, might very often be seen to mark the underlying critical desire for a unified totality in difference, or perhaps even an implicit critical hyperconformity to the institutional logic of transnational capitalism masked as essentialist resistance.

By defining transnational cultural relations through the workings of an unreflexive center-periphery duality, gestures of solidarity and contestation involve an implicit essentialization of the very effective processes of cultural exchange by which subaltern cultural production can be declared as being the object of solidarity in the first place. The I/Other dichotomy—this conjunctural ground upon which testimonio narratives and U.S.-based Latinamericanism's interventions are constructed—is the result of a particular form of discursive labor. Within the elaboration of this activity, there is always an estranging abstraction at work in the processes of exchange between the subaltern object of analysis and its commodifying discourse, in which disciplinary knowledge-formation is always contestable precisely because, by definition, it is not and can never be the knowledge of the Other as the Other would know herself or himself (Hitchcock 1993–94, 16). "Otherness," then, marks the foundational grounding upon which the exchange of cultural capital between dominating and subordinate social structures is constructed. Moreover, I would add the following caution: that if the I/Other dichotomy that preconditions our strategies of engagement is negotiated by means of an intellectual social activity whose interest lies in locating the subaltern as a periphery to be accessed by its centered intellectual, then the object is inevitably obliged to succumb to a doubly essentializing exotopic position from which she will be dragged into the field of critical discourse by a secondary act of abstraction that inevitably names *itself* as the object's "Other scene": that is, the organizing support and guarantor of the center's discourses of knowledge appropriation and re-presentation.

In the practical implementation of center-periphery thinking, then, the primary foundational estrangements implicit in cultural exchange are rendered doubly alienating as the subaltern finds herself positioned as the epistemological means by which metropolitan institutions come to position *themselves,* and perhaps even define their *own* sites of struggle. The practice of thinking the subaltern as the peripheral site of pilgrimage both constitutes the subaltern as Other, and renders its own practice a project that is "also the asymmetrical obliteration of the trace of that Other in its precarious Subject-ivity" (Spivak 1988, 280). Such a practice of active subaltern "otherization"—one inevitable, the other less so—brings our desire for nonexploitative political practices of coalition between differently constituted transnational positionalities—the nonreflexive critical gesture of solidarity with the Latin American subaltern, in other words—to the brink of what could be called its own "dimension of fantasy"; that is, to the inevitable and unavoidable recognition of a symptomatic point of exception or epistemic breakdown that can be detected and that, moreover, functions as the internal negation of the very possibility of the horizontal politics of coalition that is being advocated. Fantasy occurs when this point of exception remains necessarily masked in order for the discourse to attain closure. In this sense, declaring oneself in unquestioning solidarity with the Latin American subaltern by means of the normative positioning of the center-periphery dyad marks a critical gesture that begins and ends in the content of its own declaration and demands, therefore, a leap into the realm of disciplinary fantasy in order to achieve solidarity with the necessarily inaccessible and silenced peripheral object.

Indeed, the capricious agency of epistemic breakdown and disciplinary fantasy that identity/solidarity-based Latinamericanism seems to invoke in its discourses of solidarity between a center and its peripheries is foregrounded in the Latin American Subaltern Studies Group's further elaboration of its founding concepts and strategies. Quite simply the group is calling for the future death of "elite" intellectual practices, and this as a means of restoring presence to the non-elite. The underlying paradox, of course, is that in order to embark upon their proposed project of reinaugurating the peripheral subject's sovereignty—and this by declaring themselves in opposition to the "elite" symbolic networks of the intelligentsia and its characteristic hegemonic intellectual practices—they have to do so by diverting their attention away from the scriptural, yet do so exclusively in and from writing. This paradox first comes to light in their quoting the work of Ranajit Guha as being of primary importance for their own counter-hegemonic reading of subaltern agency: "Reading this [official, 'elite'] historiography 'in reverse' . . . to recover the cultural and political specificity of peasant insurrections has, for Guha, two components: identifying the logic of the distortions in the representation of the subaltern in official or elite culture; and uncovering the social semiotics of the strategies and cultural practices of peasant insurgencies themselves" (Latin American Subaltern Studies Group 1993, 111).

Having said this, however, in the Latin American Subaltern Studies project the process of critical self-representation and self-interrogation implicit in Guha's first component—namely, the necessary identification and deconstruction of the logics of symbolic "distortions in the representation of the subaltern in official or elite culture"—is apparently bypassed when they somewhat paradoxically, yet consciously, declare their support for Guha's work and simultaneously their aversion to the self-interrogating positionality of metropolitan historiography, apparently because it is viewed as being a disabling rather than an enabling site of reflection: "retaining a focus on the intelligentsia and on its characteristic intellectual practices—centered on the cultivation of writing, science, and the like—leaves us in the space of historiographic prejudice and 'not-seeing' . . . where Said and Retamar envision a *new type of intellectual* as the protagonist of decolonization, the, admittedly paradoxical, intent of Subaltern Studies is precisely to displace the centrality of intellectuals and intellectual 'culture' in social history" (Latin American Subaltern Studies Group 1993, 120).

In this sense, the group appears to be actively working toward its own self-protagonized demise by erasing the "I" in the I/Other dichotomy that underlies and preconditions the existence of exchange between subaltern cultural production and U.S. Latinamericanism's theoretical appropriation. It would appear, then, that this critical self-positional antipositionality, this ideological self-debasement above and beyond the deconstruction of the social activity of First World intellectual interventions, implies an essentialist utopian politics that, by actively abstaining from strategies of self-representation in order to render the historically invisible visible or give voice to the voiceless, refuses to take into account the ideological ground of intellectual appropriation that makes that re-representation of the subaltern possible in the first place.

By effectively *stepping over* metropolitan institutional forms of knowledge production and "directly" accessing the Latin American subaltern (since it is considered that "retaining the focus on the cultivation of writing, science, and the like—leaves us in the space of historiographic prejudice and 'not seeing' " [Latin American Subaltern Studies Group 1993, 120]), the group appears to unmask an underlying desire to not have to attend to the mechanics of representation that precondition all cultural exchange. Rather, it would seem, their proposed re-presentations of the subaltern are the result of an underlying desire to represent themselves as transparent non-agents (as no longer subject to the mechanics of "the centrality of intellectuals and intellectual 'culture' in social history" [120]). The group effectively rejects intellectual centrality, yet actively occupies a center from which to access the periphery. Hence, the group's desire to sidestep the production of the knowledge of social relations between subaltern cultural production and its academic sites and modes of appropriation—that is to say, their collective desired erasure of self-representation by obliterating the signifiers that they nevertheless have to implement in order to erase—seems to rely on a form of labor power in which the intellectual presides over the object through an act of positional disavowal in which he or she refuses to address intellectual positionality in the engagement of the subaltern.[12]

The practical and strategic dilemma raised by the Latin American Subaltern Studies Group's declared disavowal of the mechanics of self-representation in transcultural processes of exchange and appropriation between center and periphery is that it actually represents a labor power that is staged in order to represent the value of the centered intellectual as the agent of power, even though that power is exercised in the interests of disclaiming the exercise of power itself. Thus, in their explicit project it is only by assuming unto themselves the exigencies of self-sacrifice—the active erasure of the "I" in the I/Other dichotomy—that the subaltern can be recognized and restored to a position as central historical agent. Curiously, this desire to engender collective intellectual aphanisis in order to invoke subaltern restoration obliges us to acknowledge the problematic presence of a basic contradiction between the content of the group's enunciation and the group's site of enunciation, in such a way that it is only through their practice and existence as a group that the subaltern can be restituted, and it is equally only through their practice and their demise that the subaltern can be restituted. Here, it would seem, we are on the brink of an auratic critical space protagonized by a performative or "spectacular" mode of redemptive discourse whose prerequisite for successful elaboration involves misrecognizing or overlooking the agency of its own constitutive dimension of fantasy.[13]

Indeed, we glimpse what could be considered to be a constitutive moment of symptomatic fantasy when, toward the end of the Latin American Subaltern Studies Group's statement, and having already declared that "we need to access the vast (and mobile) array of the masses— peasants, proletarians, the informal and formal sectors, the sub- and under-employed, vendors, those outside or at the margin of the money economy, lumpens and ex-lumpens of all sorts, children, the growing numbers of the homeless" (Latin American Subaltern Studies Group 1993, 121), the group then concludes its statement with the following observation: "Clearly, it is a question not only of new ways of *looking* at the subaltern . . . but also of building new relations between ourselves and those human contemporaries whom we posit as objects of study. Rigoberta Menchú's injunction at the end of her famous testimonio is perhaps relevant in this regard: 'I'm still keeping secret what I think no-one should know. Not even anthropologists or intellectuals, no matter how many books they have, can find out all our secrets" (121).

At this point, we finally discern in what way the Latin American Subaltern Studies Group's counterdiscourse of subaltern presence-formation seems to demand a necessary assumption of prohibition and self-exclusion onto the U.S.-based Latinamericanist. In the interests of "building new relations" between "us" and "them," they desire to access the "vast array of the masses," yet recognize that they may be masses who don't necessarily see the benefits of being "accessed." In this sense, the success of the project's agency paradoxically lies and depends upon the recognition of its own operative impasse. They desire to displace hierarchy-producing intellectual endeavor by means of accessing subalterns who reject their gesture of horizontality because, like Rigoberta, they fully recognize and defend themselves against the inevitable hierarchies built into the production of transnational objects of knowledge and transcultural exchanges of value. In short, by rejecting the accessing of metropolitan Latinamericanists working toward subaltern acknowledgment, and simultaneously toward their own demise, it appears that the subaltern would give the Latin American Subaltern Studies Group what it desires; namely, an exotopic space of epistemic breakdown and disciplinary fantasy from which it can actively engage in the enjoyment of its own exclusion and "otherization," together with the opportunity to act out its spectacular (non)agency in its processes of cultural exchange.

It would seem, then, that we have entered the uncertain realm of disciplinary fantasy, of a critical practice that seems to carry within itself, as its very ground of possibility, the very impossibility of its grounding in possibility. Moreover, the critical space of metropolitan self-exclusion that the group advocates and hopes to enjoy, this collective act of self-sacrifice elicited in order to renounce the practices of exploitative or dominant ideological forms (and this as a means of accessing the periphery and restoring to the Latin American subaltern the possibility of a representation of historical agency), is a problematic positionality since it could be considered to be a stratagem of occultation itself, that conceals a disciplinary unwillingness to *fully* sacrifice itself and willfully enter the realm of *absolute* self-exclusion by renouncing the very gesture of self-sacrifice itself. The ultimate self-sacrifice, of course, as Žižek points out (Žižek 1993b, 213), would be to sacrifice self-sacrifice itself, since this act would impede the self-elevation of the Latinamericanist intelligentsia.[14] But perhaps Latinamericanist enjoyment of the spectacular gesture of self-aphanisis and the dimension of disciplinary fantasy that this act presupposes, could be seen to impede such a gesture of absolute solidarity with the subaltern.

Thus, while the group claims the authority of the subaltern in their analyses and explicitly rejects modes of critical practice that implement and embody centrist forms of self-positioning in relation to the subaltern, it appears that they do so by positioning themselves in relation to the subaltern in terms of their own destitution. Yet, once again, this could be seen to be a problematic site from which to engage the subaltern since guaranteeing their own destitution—their own self-induced exclusion or peripherality—negotiates the space from which subaltern restitution may prevail. In this way, in negotiating subaltern restitution through self-destitution—perhaps what could be thought of in terms of the spectacular performance of "affirmative self-exclusion"—

the Latin American Subaltern Studies Group still exercises a considerable margin of control over the social meanings of their *own* positionality over the subaltern. Latinamericanist enjoyment of subaltern restitution through self-destitution paradoxically maintains the centralized site of the intellectual in the processes of restoring the subaltern to historical agency. Indeed, in this internally antagonistic logic, which could be said to be similar to that of Elisabeth Burgos-Debray's already cited gesture of self-restitution ("ella me permitió el descubrimiento de mi otro yo. Gracias a ella mi yo americano ya no es una 'inquietante rareza'" [Menchú 1983, 21]), self-destitution appears to restore the agency of restitution to the site of the metropolitan restitutor, and implicitly elevates the positionality of the center over those peripheral subjects whose historical marginality is supposedly being combated.

At this point, it is necessary to broaden the debate by briefly signaling the problematic disciplinary implications to be found in what I take to be a somewhat extreme, yet perhaps emblematic example of identity/solidarity-based Latinamericanism's incursions into the problematic realm of disciplinary fantasy, enjoyment, and the relationship that these two agents maintain with normative strategies of appropriation such as those exemplified by an unreflexive center-periphery dyad. Thus, I will consider a particular example of metropolitan critical practice that both embodies and unmasks the symptomatic agency of Latinamericanist disciplinary fantasy, as well as the constitutive näiveté that seems to have grounded much of our treatment of subaltern cultural production such as that of the testimonio. What follows, then, exemplifies the problematics raised by a Latinamericanist politics of location that fails to address self-positionality in contemporary processes of cultural exchange. As we will see, when discourses of exchange actively overlook the deconstruction of what Peter Hitchcock calls "the centered subjectivity of the academy" (Hitchcock 1993–94, 19), they remain blind to the processes of reification that precondition cultural exchange, and the theoretical appropriations of the subaltern by U.S.-based Latinamericanists.

In *Against Literature* John Beverley quotes a U.S. academic who has incorporated *I, Rigoberta Menchú* into a world literature course. Following are the reasons for this critic's act of inclusion: "[*I, Rigoberta Menchú*] is one of the most moving books I have ever read. It is the kind of book I feel I must pass on, that I must urge fellow teachers to use in their classes. . . . My students were immediately sympathetic to Menchú's story and were anxious to know more, to involve themselves. They asked questions about culture and history, about their own position in the world, and about the purposes and methods of education. Many saw in the society of the Guatemalan Indian attractive features they found lacking in their own lives, strong family relationships, community solidarity, an intimate relationship with nature, commitment to others and to one's beliefs" (quoted in Beverley 1993a, 91). Rigoberta Menchú and the Maya-Quiché are viewed as an expression of value: that of carrying the load of a single social, global function; becoming the means by which the First World can reflect upon itself and define its own areas of struggle and political engagement. The Latin American subaltern becomes everything the United States lacks and craves in order for it to think itself.

Without a doubt, this passage represents a symptomatic materialization in critical discourse of a network of social relations established between cultures positioned as center and periphery, as inside and outside. It can equally be read as the making explicit of the active misrecognition required to engage in and enjoy the agency of a disciplinary fantasy masked in essentialist sympathy for the Latin American subaltern. As a result of the interactions of a normative center-periphery ("us" and "them") positioning, coupled with the agency of fantasy required to misrecognize the workings of such neocolonialist incorporation, and the subsequent enjoyment of that misrecognition, the Latin American subaltern becomes an expression of value in which counterdiscourse is domesticated and even provides the epistemological means by which metropolitan capitalist institutions and their discourses of knowledge (in this case the "multicultural classroom") define *themselves* and their *own* particular needs. Rigoberta Menchú is obliged to become little more than an unsuspecting participant in the transference of discursive property rights, victim of a relation of cultural exchange between an "otherized" "outside" (Rigoberta and the Maya-Quiché) that, nevertheless, permits an "inside" (U.S. networks of knowledge accumulation) to define the parameters of its own dilemmas and institutional struggles, even when "voice" as a positional site of resistance is articulated within that transcultural exchange.

Moreover, a relationship of self-authoring enjoyment appears to establish itself with the cultural "Other" as Menchú is rendered the exotopic object of U.S. sympathetic re-presentation, recognition, "respect," and assimilation. First World enjoyment of the Maya-Quiché is guaranteed, then, through the metropolitan production of otherness, and by the subsequent introjection into critical discourse of that by-product of neocolonial cultural exchange and commodification. Indeed, the movement of apprehension and domestication implicit in the repressive establishment of "shared values" or concerns (what Spivak calls the "ferocious standardizing of benevolence" [Spivak 1988, 294]) between a culture of domination and its subjugated objects tends to repress historical social inequities and neocolonial cultural paradigms, systematically expelling them from discourse in such a way as to render the subordination of colonization doubly so in U.S. liberal discourses of "sympathy" and "respect."[15]

Latin American subaltern expression faces the threat of becoming systematically domesticated by an implicit essentializing faith in the authenticity of discrete transcultural positionalities—the center-periphery binary—and this permits the U.S.-based theorist *to locate* resistant "authenticity," yet to do so by guaranteeing its incorporation into U.S.-based canonizing and capitalizing institutions and their discourses of knowledge accumulation.

Testimonio counterdiscourse, for example, is symptomatically "otherized" in its exchange with U.S. capitalist culture, and unquestioning inclusion—the active misrecognition of exploitative processes of intellectual objectification—can become, as in this particular example, almost a means of reminding the dominant classes of what it was necessary to lose in order to attain their position of transnational dominance ("strong family relationships, community solidarity, an intimate relationship with nature, commitment to others and to one's beliefs" [as quoted in Beverley 1993a, 91]). Indeed, it is precisely in the misrecognition of interior political matrices of verticality, and in the recognition of having lost something on the long, hard road to hegemony, that the perversity of U.S. enjoyment of the subaltern constructs itself: thus, in the fantasy-based elaboration of enjoyment, a negatively signed colonial history of subaltern loss and systematic exploitation is transformed into a "positive" reminder to the hegemonic of their own possible myth of origins.[16]

In disciplinary interventions with the Latin American subaltern that misrecognize, overlook, or sidestep their effective preconditions of cultural exchange and processes of objectification, the subaltern undergoes the risk of being positioned as the appropriated object— the outside—upon which institutional discourse—the inside—is constructed in the United States. In its treatment of the subaltern, much of identity/solidarity-based Latinamericanism has chosen to overlook or sidestep the ideological mechanics of its institutional appropriative practices and processes of symbolization that precondition the strategic production of knowledge. As a result, purely sociological analyses of testimonio, for example, tend to remain necessarily blind to their own elaborative practices of appropriative performance, while the subalterns' "proper" place becomes prearranged in the effectivity of essentialized exchange processes between Latin American subaltern cultures and U.S. capitalist institutions. The obscene place of subaltern truth— that of social inequity, exploitation, oppression, abjection—becomes inevitably reenacted in the unreflexive theater of Latinamericanist sociological performance.

But a discipline no longer blind to the institutional neocolonial conditions of its own strategies of production—perhaps a practice reminiscent of what Gayatri Spivak calls "a knowledgeable Eurocentrism, rather than this kind of naive Eurocentrism" (Spivak 1993a, 55–56)— can mark the parameters of a self-cognizant space of philosophical reflection in which the very recognition of the neocolonial implications of transnational cultural politics must lead to our problematization of Latinamericanist intellectual labor. In my opinion, the threefold challenge for such reflection would be to engage in the conceptualization of a critical space beyond the implementation of discrete, modernity-based sites of enunciation, in which the perceived authenticity and exclusivity of positionalities invariably secures discursive hegemony for the already hegemonic (the center-periphery duality, for example), and to attend to the problematic underlying agency of Latinamericanist fantasy and enjoyment in contemporary processes of disciplinary objectification. Such an analysis of our processes of "otherization" would necessarily address our strategies of appropriation and reification by engaging in a Latinamericanist politics of positionality that would "deconstruct the centered subjectivity of the academy in order to understand the objectification involved in the 'appreciation' of another culture" (Hitchcock 1993–94, 19). This, of course, differs from the founding concepts and strategies of the Latin American Subaltern Studies

Group, whose access to the historical protagonism of the subaltern (and to its own inevitable epistemic impasses) appears to be guaranteed by means of the paradoxical movement of self-erasure and the overstepping of what they view as the blindness of "retaining a focus on the intelligentsia and on its characteristic intellectual practices" (Latin American Subaltern Studies Group 1993, 120). In contrast to this position, the analysis of Latin American subaltern studies as a social endeavor itself that is *deeply* and unavoidably implicated in transnational constructions of knowledge and identity—an analysis of the means by which we render subaltern cultures objects of institutionalized knowledge in the United States—would inevitably question the parameters of Latinamericanist identity/solidarity politics as we have come to know them. Indeed, this proposed politics of positionality in identity/solidarity-based Latinamericanism might even open a self-reflexive critical space of partial redemption or liberation—or a "good enough" subaltern studies—in which Latin American subaltern cultural production might be spared the exigencies of neocolonial appropriation and incorporation that it has been obliged to assume in what appear to be the fantasy-based mediations of contemporary Latinamericanism.

Notes

1. For the genealogy of the group's existence and an explanation of the emergence of the "subaltern" as a concept within the disciplinary field of Latin American Studies, see the section of the "Founding Statement" entitled "The Subaltern in Latin American Studies" (Latin American Subaltern Studies Group 1993, 111–16).

2. For an analysis of the challenges inherent to cultural studies' ability to think social agency in relation to processes of identity-formation, together with the field's ability to combat logics of incorporation in contemporary processes of cultural exchange, see Hitchcock 1993–94.

3. For an analysis of the role of the Western intellectual and of the ideology of representation within contemporary processes of exchange between Third World cultural production and the metropolitan sites of theorization, see Spivak 1988.

4. In his recently published book, *Against Literature*, John Beverley expresses similar concerns regarding the increasing presence of testimonio in the U.S. academic marketplace. Beverley obviously has reservations as to the epistemological efficacy both of his own treatment of testimonio, and possibly of *all*

treatment of the genre to this date. Thus, he asks what are doubtlessly some of the most important and, as yet, curiously unasked questions concerning this particular form of cultural production, including its canonization in the U.S. practice of Latinamericanism and its increasing presence in U.S. academic networks as a new form of cultural capital. In the first of his two essays dedicated to this problematic ("The Margin at the Center: On *Testimonio*"; in this volume), Beverley asks the following question: "How much of a favor do we do testimonio by positing, as I do here, that it is a new form of literary narrative or by making it an alternative reading to the canon, as in [the] case of the Stanford general education requirement?" (Beverley 1993a, 85–86; also this volume, 39). In his second essay on testimonio, written after the electoral defeat of the Sandinistas in 1990 ("Second Thoughts on Testimonio"), Beverley proposes the following dilemma: "Is testimonio . . . simply a new chapter in an old history of the literary 'relations' between dominant and exploited classes and groups, metropolis and colony, center and periphery, First and Third Worlds. Is it yet another version of a subaltern subject who gives us now—in addition to the surplus value her exploitation in the new circuits of global capital produces—something we desire perhaps even more in these times of the political economy of the sign: her 'truth,' a truth that is, as stated at the start of *I, Rigoberta Menchú*, 'the reality of a whole paper'?" (Beverley 1991, 89). These, of course, are questions that are crying out to be answered since they are crucial to Latinamericanist knowledge formation.

5. It goes without saying that in contemporary Latinamericanism, testimonio, for example, has become a resource to be mined, almost a new frontier of institutionalized intellectual endeavor. To mine, of course, implies gains, losses, appropriation, exploitation, introjection, and consumption. And this, precisely, marks the socialized space—or rather the trans-social or transnational space—of an exchange-value of the object that, in the transcultural exchange that preconditions interpretative appropriation, can potentially kill it, yet might do so in the name of solidarity or of providing voice to a previously voiceless identity. Although testimonio has been hailed by the Latinamericanist Left as a more effective form of popular cultural production and "resistance" to hegemonic cultural forms, Fredric Jameson, in "On Literary and Cultural Import-Substitution in the Third World: The Case of the Testimonio" (1993a; in this volume), warns us as to the possible presence of Latin American cultural production, including testimonio, as a co-opted object of the metropolitan project of late capitalism, and of its homogenizing processes of transnationalized dissemination. While Jameson's direct reference in the referred passage is to the presence of the Latin American boom novels in the metropolis as a problematic postmodern site of convergence between First and Third Worlds, without a doubt the same warning for the effective practice of leftist cultural critique functions for the contemporary treatment and dis-

semination of testimonio, since transnational postmodern sites of convergence offer "a practical as well as a theoretical rebuke to the tradition of Left cultural criticism that thought it was possible to give ideological marks exclusively on the basis of formal analysis; but it also raises disquieting questions in its own right, most notably the old fears of unconscious co-option, in a situation in which nobody quite knows what subversion is anymore, but everyone has had some experience of being co-opted" (Jameson 1993a, 18; also this volume, 178).

6.   Of course, this essay could have addressed the corpus of critical work on Latin American testimonio exclusively. However, the recent publication of the founding precepts and strategies of the Latin American Subaltern Studies Group represents, in my opinion, a concise statement of the political goals and critical aspirations of those critics who have been most responsible over the last decade or so for the increasing presence and analysis of subaltern forms of cultural production—such as testimonio—in U.S. academic networks. Thus, one cannot analyze Latin American testimonio without addressing the critical positions reflected in the group's "Founding Statement," and one certainly cannot address the thinking of the Latin American Subaltern Studies Group without recourse to the corpus of criticism on testimonio. It is, after all, a corpus that has established U.S. identity/solidarity-based Latinamericanism as the fundamental protagonist in contemporary disciplinary debates.

7.   Meta-analyses of the contributions made by testimonio criticism, and of the problematic issues that they raise for U.S.-based Latinamericanism's interventions into the field of subaltern studies, are to be found in Neil Larsen's introductory chapter to his *Reading North by South: On Latin American Literature, Culture, and Politics* (1995), and in Alberto Moreiras's essay, "The Aura of Testimonio" (this volume). Also see the introductory pages to Scheper-Hughes's book, *Death without Weeping: The Violence of Everyday Life in Brazil* (1993, 1–30). In this work, the author characterizes a "good enough" ethnography as a discipline that recognizes and actively engages in analysis of its own epistemological limits, and does so in order to establish a practice that is "open-ended and that allows for multiple readings and alternative conclusions" (30). As such, she consciously presents her own practice as one that has "tried to keep the cuts and sutures of the research process openly visible and suppress the urge to smooth over the bumps with a lathe. This hopefully good-enough ethnography is presented as close to the bone as it was experienced, hairline fractures and all" (30).

8.   What I advance as the symptomatic agency of Latinamericanist fantasy has its origin in Slavoj Žižek's critique of ideological fantasy in *The Sublime Object of Ideology* (1992). For the concept of enjoyment as discursive and social agent, see Žižek 1993b, 165–237.

9.   Center-periphery positionalities correspond to what Moreiras terms "the

auratic practice of the postauratic," a foundational self-legitimating site of contemporary Latinamericanist practice that results from the "positing of two radically heterogeneous fields of experience . . . my or our experience and theirs," and which becomes postauratic "because the relational mediation between the heterogeneous realms is no longer based on mimesis, but is based precisely upon the impossibility of mimesis: a simulation, then, a repetition, whose moment of truth is the loss of truth itself" (author's manuscript). This auratic practice of the postauratic, this foundational practice of self-legitimation enacted between a center positing a periphery as the absolute auratic "other" of the center, equally conditions the conceptual terrain of Neil Larsen's treatment of the ways in which the North posits the South as the silent and silenced pole that nevertheless enables the North to think and reauthorize itself (Larsen 1995). Moreover, it could also be said that it corresponds to the positional production of absolute difference or "otherness" (what Moreiras terms "the production of abjection"), that nevertheless is introjected into the body of the center. It therefore marks an intellectual project that actively constitutes the colonial subject as Other, and consequently incorporates that Other in a self-authorizing epistemic violence that runs the risk of belonging "to the exploiters' side of the international division of labor" (Spivak 1988, 280).

10.   This form of conceptualization, of course, is intimately linked to the maintenance of the self-legitimating authority by which the North has historically read the South. As Neil Larsen indicates, "in directing its attention elsewhere, the North necessarily concedes something about its own sense of identity and authority, its own position on the 'hermeneutic map.' The question of the *object*'s legitimacy—why read *this* and not something else?—cannot finally be detached from the question of *self*-legitimation: what, at the outset, authorizes or justifies the subject as the reader/writer of this object? Thus, in reading 'North by South,' the North, concurrently, re-reads itself" (Larsen 1995, 2–3).

11.   In *In Theory* Ahmad warns against homogeneous modes through which to think the complexities of contemporary global realities, noting in particular that "the capitalist world today is not divided into monolithic oppositions: . . . Rather, its chief characteristics in the present phase are (1) that it is a hierarchically structured global system in which locations of particular countries are determined, in the final analysis, by the strengths and/or weaknesses of their economies; and (2) the system itself is undergoing a new phase of vast global restructuring. . . . The position that any given country occupies in the hierarchical structure of global capitalism is determined by a host of . . . factors [differences in demography, sociohistorical formation, economic scale, levels of accumulation, modes of articulation]. In other words, the tendential law of global accumulation functions not towards greater homogenization or sim-

ilarity of location in zones of backward capitalism, but towards greater differentiation among its various national units" (Ahmad 1992, 311–13). Obviously, the implementation of an implicit or explicit deproblematized and totalizing center-periphery dyad in the appropriation of Latin American subaltern cultural production immediately tends toward the oversimplistic misrecognition of the heterogeneous character of the contemporary global cultural economy.

12. Interestingly, in "Can the Subaltern Speak?" Spivak engages in a critique of Foucault and Deleuze that seems to be strikingly similar to the self-positional transparency—or antipositionality—proposed by the Latin American Subaltern Studies Group: "In the Foucault-Deleuze conversation, the issue seems to be that there is no representation, no signifier (Is it to be presumed that the signifier has already been dispatched? There is, then, no sign-structure operating experience, and thus might one lay semiotics to rest?); theory is a relay of practice (thus laying problems of theoretical practice to rest) and the oppressed can know and speak for themselves. . . . Further, the intellectuals . . . become transparent in the relay race, for they merely report on the nonrepresented subject and analyze . . . the workings of (the unnamed Subject irreducibly presupposed by) power and desire. The produced 'transparency' marks the place of 'interest'; it is maintained by vehement denegation: 'Now this role of referee, judge, and universal witness is one which I *absolutely refuse* to adopt' " (Spivak 1988, 279–80). Of course, what Spivak views as an act of "vehement denegation" and that I have chosen to call an underlying act of "positional disavowal" in the group's proposed restoration of sovereignty to the peripheral subject must inevitably lead us to question the essentialist power that is exercised by the group in order to stage itself as a proposed utopian non-agent in the dynamics of cultural exchange. Indeed, to what extent can it be said that the process of positional disavowal by which the intellectual labors to position itself in transparency in order to access the subaltern, actually labors in favor of the subaltern? For Spivak, there is no doubt that "this S/subject, curiously sewn together into a transparency by denegations, belongs to the exploiters' side of the international division of labor" (280).

13. For Moreiras, "spectacular redemption" is "a particular form of disciplinary practice whose overt or hidden premise places the theoretical end of the discipline it enacts in the horizon of accomplished restitution. Spectacular redemption is a paradoxical form of disciplinary practice in that its completion would tendentially mean the end of the discipline. In other words, if the ultimate goal of the discipline is the redemption of the object, so that the object can go back to being fully itself, with no remainder, if the discipline plays itself out in the wager for the self-identity of its object of study, then that self-identity, once accomplished, would void the need for reflection, would abolish the discipline as such. But of course, the discipline cannot be abolished

by its object, insofar as it is the discipline that first creates the demand for the self-identity of the disciplinary object . . . spectacular redemption is only the shamefaced, embarrassed other side of disciplinary power/knowledge, working in spite of itself to give the discipline further legitimacy, providing it with an alibi, blind to the fact that the discipline speaks through us, always and everywhere, no matter what we say and what we do not say" (author's manuscript). Obviously, it is not difficult to see that Latinamericanism's disciplinary discourses of subaltern "spectacular redemption"—of a foundational performative non-agency—presuppose the existence of a dimension of Latinamericanist fantasy the explication of which allows us to detect a symptomatic point of internal negation of the possibilities of subaltern redemption and restitution that are being advocated.

14.   Latinamericanism's treatment of Rigoberta's secrets, it seems, follows a similar logic of desired self-erasure and Latinamericanist enjoyment. Rigoberta Menchú's testimonial self-grounding in the exotopic silence of ancestral secrets—this self-obliteration that equally posits her readers in the hermeneutic space of exclusion—reflects a privileged site of metropolitan solidarity formation within the corpus of the genre since, paraphrasing John Beverley in *Against Literature,* it is almost as if she and her silence gave us something, now, that we desire: that is to say, her truth and that of her community; the truth of exclusion. I would add that the exclusion that her silence produces and that she obliges us to assume in the hermeneutic process of her testimonio also provides us with the means of incorporating ourselves into a space of fantasy by which we can simultaneously advocate radical difference and cultural inaccessibility between positionalities, and yet practice the construction of an illusory co-presence between heterogeneous enunciative positions grounded in co-exclusion. It is precisely in this sense that Rigoberta Menchú's strategic silences allow the disciplinary discourses of U.S.-based Latinamericanism to effectively enjoy the effects of their own symptomatic processes of exotopic "otherization," and from this space of enjoyment, and as a result of it, engage in its discourses and gestures of solidarity formation with the radically "other" subaltern. Of course, the implicit perversion of this enjoyment lies in the fact that Rigoberta's necessary self-exclusion from certain realms of discourse is a mechanism of self-defense, whereas the performative renunciation of exploitative reading practices between First and Third World subjects ultimately permits the metropolitan critic to maintain and enjoy the self-elevated site of the intellectual in the very advocacy of the impossibility of the hermeneutic process.

15.   In the always provocative words of Guillermo Gómez-Peña: "Like the United Colors of Benetton ads, a utopian discourse of sameness helps to erase all unpleasant stories. The message becomes a refried colonial idea: if we merely hold hands and dance the mambo together, we can effectively abolish

ideology, sexual and cultural politics, and class differences" (Gómez-Peña 1993, 57).

16. This same perverse logic, it must be said, is shared by the recent "boom" in Hollywood ethno-products such as *Dances with Wolves, The Last of the Mohicans, Geronimo: An American Legend,* and *The Broken Chain,* all of which in one way or another seem to share the same underlying fantasy scenario: they invariably express "respect" for the indigenous "way of life"; again, for subaltern "strong family relationships, community solidarity, an intimate relationship with nature," and so on, yet simultaneously naturalize the inevitability of Euro–North American expansionism, of indigenous subjugation to processes of modernity, cultural appropriation, displacement, and demise. Paraphrasing Žižek, these appropriations of the subaltern into networks of U.S. cultural imagery-production belie a certain underlying fantasy scenario that, on the one hand, provides the hegemonic with a myth of the origins of a national heritage, yet, on the other hand, posits the subaltern as an ideological fossil created retroactively by ruling ideologies in order to divert attention away from contemporary antagonisms in their own processes of transnational domination and appropriation (Žižek 1993b, 232).

Javier Sanjinés C   *Beyond Testimonial Discourse*

New Popular Trends in Bolivia

R ecent studies speculate about the future aesthetic and ideological significance of testimonial discourse. In an issue of *Revista de crítica literaria latinoamericana,* John Beverley observes that just as we have seen a decrease in the importance of the "escritores del boom latinoamericano," we now witness the uncertain condition of testimonial narrative. He further suggests that new forms of communication may be surpassing the effectiveness of testimonial discourse (Beverley 1992, 7–18). I believe that these observations apply well to Bolivia, where the essence of *testimonio* is being challenged very significantly by new popular movements.

Talk shows and interactive television are forms of electronic reproduction that the new Bolivian social actors, born out of the retrenchment of the political Left, use in order to interpellate, to appeal to the dispossessed and the marginal sectors of society. These new forms of communication step outside established political mechanisms, abandon the traditional forms of representative democracy, and question the role that the political parties play in society. I am particularly interested in the analysis of those theatrics and dramaturgical actions that conceal the conservative aims of a rising *cholo* bourgeoisie, and challenge the political effectiveness of the seigneurial groups in power. I will argue that these new actions do not rely on authentic dialogue, but on a strategic discourse of power that distorts communication.

This essay is divided into three parts: in the first part, I consider Domitila Barrios de Chungara's well-known "*Si me permiten hablar . . .*" (1977) in discussing the importance of testimonio not only as an act of communication, but also as an act of political participation; in the second part, I demonstrate that the retrenchment of the Left has affected the dialogue essential to testimonial discourse. The case of the *relocalizados,* unemployed miners of the once powerful working class, helps us to understand the repression of consciousness and the disruption of communication. Finally, the third part explores the ways in which the new popular movements are modifying the social and political spectrum of society. *Palenquismo* and *maxismo* are linked to the rise of neoliberalism as the two most important tendencies of this emerging *cholo* bourgeoisie. Both tendencies manipulate the patronal festivals of the cities in order to enhance their social power. The result, I argue, negates the type of communicative action that is essential to testimonio.

Domitila's Modus Operandi

An important aspect of testimonio is its internal connection to a liberating communicative action that is conceptualized and organized around the system of language. *"Si me permiten hablar . . . ,"* Domitila Barrios de Chungara's testimony of her struggle for survival in the Bolivian mines, participates in the belief that language is tied to practice and action. In her work it is clear that only through verbal communication can people achieve a meaningful world in which they participate as intelligible and moral members. In a world that hinders this communication, and in which people do not listen to one another, there may be decision, force, or brute politics, but there can be no social or political consensus.

As an act of communication, Domitila's text also touches the corporeal, the human body, in the political struggle for survival. When Domitila speaks of hunger strikes, she is not evoking a passive, "anorexic" experience, but giving an added importance to undernourishment. In Domitila's narration, hunger strikes become an integral part of a poetics of nonviolence that makes use of the human body in order to construct solidarity. This is again a new experience of communicative action, free from ideological distortions, one which makes expressive use of corporeal materiality, and celebrates life by showing that undernourishment can morally and spiritually defy those who are responsible for the fragmentation of society. Domitila reveals that hunger strikes transform ethical and personal concerns into public and collective actions. They are a public demonstration of individual and social resistance: "Yo me declaré en huelga de hambre. Ya no comía para vengar la muerte de mis hijos" (Barrios de Chungara 1977, 141).

"Si me permiten hablar . . ." enriches the experience of liberation movements. It is an oral narrative that inaugurates a true popular com-

munication, free from the ideological distortions that are inherent to
military dictatorship or to bureaucratic authoritarianism. Domitila's
testimony wishes to participate in the construction of a "proletarian
sphere"—a transgression of the public and private spheres of bourgeois
culture—so as to instill the deep understanding and alliance of a unified
popular front. However, her efforts to establish such a utopia, like the
attempts of other progressive forces of the Left, were thwarted by the
political and economic reforms that modified the whole spectrum of
Bolivian society.

The neoliberal reforms of the second half of the 1980s have been able
to break away from more than thirty years of "revolutionary nationalism" and are superseded by a free-market logic that addresses the modernization of the economy and the enhancement of private enterprise.
While it is clear that these neoliberal administrations have had real
success in stabilizing the economy since 1985, it is also true that the
new policies have incurred tremendous social costs. Driven by a decline
in real wages and a sharp upturn in unemployment, the standard of living has deteriorated among the lower classes and the dependent middle
classes. In addition, the almost exclusive attempt to link the economy
to the strategic pursuit of interests has resulted in the decentralization
of state enterprises and sell-offs to private investors. Most important
was the reorganization of the state mining corporation (COMIBOL)
created by the revolutionary regime in 1952 and the firing of the mine
workers. Not coincidentally, the program to restructure COMIBOL has
severely weakened the mine workers' federation (FSTMB), the central
organization of Bolivian workers (COB), and, in effect, the entire labor
Left. Due to massive firings in the state mining corporation, the FSTMB
has been stripped of power to become nothing more than a committee
for the unemployed. The discussion of the *relocalizados* will help us
understand why these actions also have affected the class consciousness
of the working force.

"I Expel Myself": The Crucifixion of the Relocalizados

In May of 1987, one hundred and twenty unemployed miners and their
families, commonly referred to as *relocalizados,* pitched tents in the
Alto region that surrounds the La Paz international airport. Two years

later, in April 1989, twenty of approximately three hundred *relocalizados* who occupied the grounds of the University of La Paz decided to crucify themselves on the gates and flagpoles of the university, torturing their bodies to reinforce their economic demands ("Nosotros no hemos venido a pedir limosna sino justicia en la nivelación de nuestras liquidaciones," they declared to the press).

When the unemployed mine workers "crucify" themselves on the gates and flagpoles of the university, their bodies no longer symbolize the solidarity and the vivifying possibility of the working class, but, quite to the contrary, a neurotic defense that freezes the patterns of communication. There is thus a repression of the symbolic, wherein the human body regresses into the imaginary, to employ the Lacanian metaphor of the preverbal in which we are confronted with the loss of signification. Both ridiculous and terrible, this crucifixion shocks consciousness and rationality because it becomes a form of corporeal waste and refuse.

The crucifixion, just like the repression of language, is now the abject and grotesque representation of the working class. Hence the displacement to a situation that is no longer vivifying and enriching, but replaced with the suicidal: "un lanzarse al vacío por lo aburrido de la vida," as these *relocalizados* also told to the press. What we see here is the neurotic deformation of personality, a contradictory and empty enactment of the Christian symbol.

Having lost its redemptive force, the crucifixion cannot be taken here as a symbol of revolutionary consciousness, nor can it be seen as one of the most important panoplies of "popular weapons" that provide a point of departure for a radical questioning of the marginal and of the oppressed. To the contrary, the *relocalizados* reduce the act of communication and the practice of liberation to suicide, an illusory form of vengeance in which the aggressor suffers little or no punishment at all. It is then easily understandable that the same political forces involved in the distortion of communication may also be ready to meet, demagogically and in times of political campaigning, the economic demands of the unemployed.

Although highly culturally variable, it appears that all cultures have some corporeal processes that are degraded. The rural indigenous cultures of the Andes, repressed for centuries by the dominant urban sectors of Spanish ancestry, always have been the uncomfortable "other," undecidable inside and outside the social body. They are part of this nonrational "otherness" that haunts, like the *relocalizados,* the urban system and its order. But these indigenous cultures go far beyond abjection to create a different, redemptive, and vivifying form of the grotesque in the "jubilant" and "ecstatic" way in which marginality invades the city.

The Margins in the Center: The Cholo Bourgeoisie

Temporarily undefined, marginals are beyond the normative social structure. This liberates them from urban obligations and places them in a close connection with the nonsocial or asocial powers of life and death. The "antistructural" nature of marginality appears in specific festivals, particularly in the *Fiesta del Señor del Gran Poder,* without doubt the most important and complex representation of the growing power of the new sectors of society in the city of La Paz.

The *Fiesta del Señor del Gran Poder* (The Festival of Our Lord of Great Power) has attained great popular signification in the past fifteen years. It has grown beyond the limits of specific neighborhoods and counties, to become the patron festival of the city, thus seizing power through ritual. It is interesting to note that in the cult of Our Lord of Great Power, the original image showed three faces, an old way of representing the Holy Trinity. The two lateral images, later prohibited by the Church because they were "horrendous and distorted," portraying Satan and the Devil, are remembered by the collective memory not as terrible or horrendous, but rather as "grotescas y jubilosas" (Albó 1986).

Particularly interesting is the fact that the grotesque is not perceived as regressive and alienating; on the contrary, it has now deep connections with the sociological notion of "ecstasy" (Berger 1990).[1] Here sociology refers not to some abnormal heightening of consciousness in a mystic sense, but rather, quite literally, to the act of standing or stepping outside (literally, *ekstasis*) the taken-for-granted routines of society. Ecstasy is more likely to take place in the passage from rural to urban cultures, among groups that are marginal to society than among those at its center, as it is more likely in groups that are insecure in their social position.

Applied to the festival of El Gran Poder, the concept of ecstasy indicates the situation of the migrating peasantry with no definitive macrovision of society. What is interesting about these marginals is that they often look to their group of origin, the so-called inferior group, for community values, and to the more prestigious group—the *mestizo* or *cholo* bourgeoisie—as their reference group for higher status. The cholo bourgeoisie, on the other hand, reinforces its social prestige in the festivals of El Gran Poder or *Virgen de Urcupiña* (Our Lady of Urcupiña), through kinship structure and *compadrazgo*. In this way, this new bourgeoisie gives the migrating peasantry, the pauperized urban middle classes, and the informal sectors of the economy a triumphant image—grotesque and jubilant, I may add—of success.

As we have seen, the festival of El Gran Poder gives expression to the ambivalent and problematic situation of the city of La Paz: it is a ritual not only of the marginal peasantry but also of the emergent *cholo* bourgeoisie. By combining local traditions with the power of money, these groups are modifying the social and political spectrum of society. Though difficult to define, these new social forces are forming a new identity that is rooted in a free-market economy that looks to Miami— the market of computers and other smuggled electronic goods is actually named *miamicito*—as the new "promised land." High culture must now surrender to "cerveza and chicha" (beer and beer maize) culture, and the upper classes participate with the *cholaje* in the opening of the popular festivals; the *cholos* want to be *señores* and the peasants struggle to be entrepreneurs.

So confusing is this society of clashing groups that local political sociology has decided to label it *ch'enko,*"[2] an Aymara word for "mess." Indeed, the informal sectors have captured the city, co-opting its economy and culture. Just as it happens in El Gran Poder, the economic power of the *empresarios de tez morena* (dark skinned entrepreneurs) interpellates the marginals in everyday life by reinforcing the status quo, and making arguable and debatable the emancipatory construction of society that was once envisioned by testimonial discourse.

Once peripheral and now ready to occupy the center of society, the *cholo* bourgeoisie is the unwanted product of the Revolution of 1952. If this major event did not create a national bourgeoisie of "its own," it was also unable to destroy both the seigneurial mental structure and the strong oligarchical constitution of Bolivian society. Recent studies of political sociology tend to argue that the main achievement of this revolution may have been the unsolicited promotion of the *cholaje* to the status of bourgeoisie, overstepping the barrier of seigneuralism (Mayorga 1991, 24).

Until recently, this new entrepreneurial class did not have any political representation nor did it partake in the economic decision making. It could be said that although the *cholaje* achieved the level of an economic bourgeoisie, the oligarchical sectors of society—both in the Right and in the Left—managed to keep it away from the center. That has been the ideological function of *nacionalismo revolucionario,* marking this social group as "premodern."

Furthermore, it would be too simplistic to place the *cholo* bourgeoisie within capitalism and forget its complexity, its cultural *ch'enko.* Behind this category lies the clashing combination of economic, ethnic, and cultural factors that make it impossible to treat *cholaje* in a linear way. In economic terms, for example, this new bourgeoisie shows a modality of accumulation of capital that is quite different from that of the seigneurial bourgeoisie. Indeed, this new sector was not born under the protection of the state; it reinvests its capital gains within Bolivia, and does not privilege high consumption, but spends in ritual ceremonies and festivals such as *ch'allas,* baptisms, marriages, and *presteríos.*

Two new political parties represent the *cholo* bourgeoisie: on the one hand, *Conciencia de Patria* (Consciousness of Fatherland) and *palenquismo,* named after its leader, "el compadre" Palenque; on the other, *Unión Cívica Solidaridad* (Civic and Solidarity Union) and *maxismo,* named after its leader, the beer entrepreneur Max Fernández.

Labeling the two political programs *maxismo* and *palenquismo* could give the somewhat erroneous indication that both parties intend to put *populismo* back on stage. Just like the other sociological definitions— even the opposition bourgeois/proletariat simplifies things to the point of distortion—*populismo* would be a vague description of the rising movements. Indeed, Conciencia de Patria (CONDEPA) and Unión Cívica Solidaridad (UCS) have grown without any state intervention, meaning that there was no welfare state to back them up. Besides, they seem at ease with free-market policies and accept the challenges of social and economic Darwinism. Clearly, they are new right tendencies that interpellate marginality and subalternity through microgroup politics. These policies, I argue, cannot promote the liberating communicative action sought by testimonial narrative precisely because they reinforce the egocentric aims of the *cholo* bourgeoisie within the free-market economy.

Palenquismo *and Talk Show Democracy*

The 1970s, entrapped by military authoritarianism, allowed very few possibilities for public expression and participation. Nevertheless, mass media, controlled as it was by the state, developed popular radio and television programs that were to grow into true public spheres.[3] It is precisely through these programs that Carlos Palenque became one of the most interesting figures in Bolivia to combine mass media and politics.

Affectionately known as *el compadre,* Palenque is a good example of how politics has acquired the nature of a spectacle. By a form of communication increasingly based on emotionally charged images rather than on rational discourse, *el compadre* reaches the marginal and informal sectors of society in order to fill the vacuum that trade unions and political parties left over the years. The task that Palenque consciously undertakes is to place radio and television talk shows as new mediating public spheres between the state and marginality. Though the immediate purpose is well intentioned, demanding that justice be done to those sectors of society that otherwise would remain unrepresented, the underlying aim of securing political power at all costs distorts the original intent. What *el compadre* does is put into practice a shrewd, manipulative scheme: how to benefit from these increasingly important informal sectors of society.

CONDEPA opens to the public the possibilities of a talk show democracy that mixes politics with social action; demagoguery with spectacle and entertainment. Combining tragedy with melodrama, arousing and heightening the senses of his audience, Palenque attains great popular attraction. His talk shows could be considered a public rite of hospitality for migrant peasants, servants, unemployed, smugglers, vendors, and all types of "déclassés" and parvenus. Carefully prepared, the set reproduces a model of humanity that is clearly found in rural communities: affective warmth, close-knit kinships, egalitarian tendencies. As could be expected, these elements are opposed to the fragmented hierarchies of urban structure. What we finally have is a miseen-scène, a dramaturgical action of that very sociological ecstasy this paper touched before—this time intentionally provoked to attract those who need to escape day-to-day urban obligations.

By reinforcing the Aymara values in the marginals of urban society, Palenque seeks to rebuild that lost "we" through the family as the metaphor of society. Thus his program *La tribuna libre del pueblo* (The free platform of the people) portrays the family as the privileged metaphor of social cohesion with which Palenque wishes to decolonize the seigneurial order. In the talk show, this metaphor can also function as a rite. Indeed, Carlos Palenque leads the show as the father, the *compadre*. Since the audience is selected and presumably coached, the host's personality is dominant and determines a well-defined structure of authority. The show is, therefore, ideologically charged and creates an illusion of reciprocal response and intersubjectivity. In fact, Palenque does not debate or inform; he is not interested in a balance of viewpoints but in a serial of accusations. In this sense, his talk show is not cognitive but therapeutic, with the orchestration more inconsequential than argumentative.

Palenque, the *compadre,* is followed by his wife, the *comadre* Mónica, who not only shares his mission but has functions of her own: she helps interpret the necessities of the lower groups of society and is always next to the *compadre.* She adds an important element of symbolic power to the events of the talk show: the male and female complementarity of the rural areas, where couples, rather than individuals, must always fill the ritual posts.

If *comadre* Mónica represents the maternal side of the metaphor, the talk show has another *comadre,* Remedios Loza, the typical *chola* who embodies the vigorous, rising bourgeoisie. Through popular vote—she is now a senator of the Republic—*comadre* Remedios is a powerful figure of how far the popular sectors can go. Finally, the *compadre* Paco represents the lower strata of the middle class, and his job is to link the talk show to that social group.

As in the family, the women in Palenque's talk show play a significant role: they politicize the private sphere, turning it over to the public sphere; they also humanize the space, holding progressive linkages between rural communities and the urban structure. Thus, they are crucial in staging the dramatic ecstasy with which CONDEPA and Palenque have been so successful in attaining political and social power.

Not Marxismo *but* Maxismo

Like CONDEPA, Unión Cívica Solidaridad is the other political formation to challenge the traditionally dominant oligarchical structure of
society. Through CONDEPA, Max Fernández, the beer baron who uses
the network created by his brewery to promote the new political party,
comes from "below" to represent both *cholos* and *indios*. Born in poverty
and orphaned at an early age, Fernández (often called "don Max") rose
from being a beer distributor to buying a controlling interest in the
Bolivian National Brewery for a reported eight million dollars (Farah
1992). So sure is Max Fernández of his political future and of the social
groups he represents, that in a recent interview he made it clear that he
would not forgive the circles that once shunned him because of his social
standing and racial background. He told of how General Banzer, the
authoritarian leader of the 1970s, once pulled a pistol on him and
threatened to kill him for a remark he made. Fernández calmly replied,
"Go ahead. You only have six bullets," implying that his feline instincts
and the social forces he embodies needed a seventh bullet to be destroyed (there is a popular belief that says that "cats have seven lives").
   It is interesting to note that Unión Cívica Solidaridad uses the
brewery and the ritual festivals to promote the *maxista* discourse. Not
only does the beer distribution network expedite his political campaigning; it also reinforces ritual drinking and libations that are at the
center of all festivals. Nevertheless, it should also be pointed out that
maxismo is the same representational discourse that guides liberalism
and the unlimited possibilities of a free market.[4] In other words, underlying *maxismo* is the belief that freeing people from governmental obstacles will give the economy back to the market, which alone can create
jobs, prosperity, and a nation in progress. As the basic spokesman of his
policies—his parity is a one-man structure—Fernández believes that
actions speak louder than words, and that Bolivia needs more business-
men and fewer politicians.
   Maxismo does not encourage dialogue. On the contrary, the "I" of the
enunciation is projected to the audience as a representation of the self.
In other words, it is the "cogito" that represents the "other" and manipulates his/her consciousness. Deeply at odds with the communicative
and moralizing functions of testimonios like Domitila's "*Si me permiten
hablar . . . ,*" Fernández, who is running second in most opinion polls, a

few points behind the mainstream Nationalist Revolutionary Movement, often speaks of himself in the third person. His *asistencialismo,* meaning that instead of attracting backers with ideological appeals, Max Fernández buys support through thousands of projects, makes him a combination of Ross Perot and Santa Claus. He indicates that his hard work has allowed him to fund three thousand projects in recent years, and while he would not estimate their total value, his collaborators say it is tens of millions of dollars.

Debate about Fernández centers on his role in Bolivia's fragile democracy, channeling popular discontent within the system. His modus operandi most certainly distorts communication because it combines flexible tactics with strategies of uncertainty. Just like Ross Perot, Fernández fails to give a thorough explanation of his political program. With conscious ideological ambiguity, he translates strategic uncertainty into tactical flexibility, thus occupying many social spaces but no political or ideological "center."

Finally, it should be emphasized that the new popular trend introduced by Max Fernández negates even more clearly than *palenquismo* the possibilities of communicative action; indeed, the solidarity that Fernández inscribes in the initials of his party only reproduces a personality that should be imitated by others. Without authentic dialogue, the efficacy of testimonial narratives seems to be left behind in the transitional moment of social change that marked the downfall of military authoritarianism. As we have seen, the new popular movements under neoliberal democracy replace the function of testimonials with strategic discourses of power that challenge the dominant groups of society not from the verticality of the state but from the very concreteness of everyday life.

Notes

1.   The notion of ecstasy opens new perspectives in the study of the grotesque. The two most vigorous and original thinkers on the subject, Wolfgang Kayser and Mikhail Bakhtin disagree about the nature of the grotesque and the center of their disagreement is the opposition of its comic and fearsome sides. Both Kayser and Bakhtin commit the same essential error: mistaking the part for the whole. The discussion of the grotesque should be headed for areas that

include both the serious and the comic. I believe that the notion of ecstasy opens up a new area of research: the ecstatic and jubilant grotesque. Bolivian narrative offers a splendid case study with the works of Jaime Saenz, particularly with his novel *Felipe Delgado.*

2. Notion that Carlos Toranzo Roca explores in his introduction to Fernando Mayorga (Mayorga 1991).

3. A good theoretical approach to this problematic is Carpignano, Andersen, Aronowitz, and Difazio 1990.

4. The notion of representational discourse is explained in Yúdice 1992a.

John Beverley   The Real Thing

in memory of Kurt Cobain

However unfeasible and inefficient it may sound, I see no way to avoid insisting that there has to be a simultaneous other focus: not merely who am I? but who is the other woman? How am I naming her? How does she name me?—Gayatri Spivak (1987, 150)

This is an essay on Rigoberta Menchú and what she means, or does, for us. The title involves a perhaps overelaborate conceit, which may be forgiven someone who has spent a large part of his academic career studying the poetry of Góngora. It refers, on the one hand, to the phrase "the real thing" in American English (as in the advertising slogan "Coke is the real thing," which of course means something quite different if the reference is to the drug rather than to the soft drink) and, on the other, to Lacan's notion of the Real as the order of "that which resists symbolization absolutely."

What may be less familiar is the peculiar sense Lacan, in his seminar on *The Ethics of Psychoanalysis* (1992), gave the capitalized form of the word Thing, following on the Freudian term *das Ding*. For Lacan, *das Ding,* which he distinguishes from the German *Sache*—thing as "a product of industry and of human action as governed by language" in the sense of a created or linguistically elaborated object (*Wort*)—designates a traumatic otherness that cannot be represented or incorporated by the subject in language: the negative, in a sense, of the reassuring image the mirror or specular other—the face or presence of the parent—gives back to confirm "orthopedically" the subject's either yet unformed or perpetually fading sense of itself in the mirror stage. The Thing is where the reality principle itself, in its connection to the pleasure principle and the regulatory function of the superego, founders.[1]

In a recent essay on *The Crying Game,* Slavoj Žižek elaborates the concept apropos Lacan's concern with the representation of the Lady in the discourse of courtly love as a tyrant "submitting her subjects to senseless, outrageous, impossible, arbitrary, capricious ordeals." In such representations, Žižek writes, "The Lady is thus as far as possible from any kind of purified spirituality." Rather,

she functions as an inhuman partner in the precise sense of a radical Otherness which is wholly incommensurable with our needs and desires; as such she is simultaneously a kind of automaton, a machine which randomly utters meaningless demands. This coincidence of radical, inscrutable Otherness and pure machine is what confers on the Lady her uncanny, monstrous character—the Lady is the Other which is not our 'fellow-creature,' i.e. with whom no relation of empathy is possible. . . . The idealization of the Lady, her elevation to a spiritual, ethereal Ideal, is therefore to be conceived as a strictly secondary phenomenon, a narcissistic projection whose function is to render invisible her traumatic, intolerable dimension. . . . Deprived of every real substance, the Lady functions as a mirror onto which the subject projects his narcissistic ideal. (Žižek 1993a, 96)[2]

The Lady in question, then? Our Rigoberta? Why does it seem so natural, in our discourse about Rigoberta Menchú, to speak of her as Rigoberta? The use of the first name is appropriate, on the one hand, to address a friend, or, on the other, to address the subaltern. Is it that we are addressing Rigoberta Menchú as a friend in the work we do on her *testimonio*? We would not say with such ease, for example, Paul, for Paul de Man, or Fred, for Fredric Jameson, unless we wanted to signify a personal relationship with them. Jameson himself (who continues to speak of Rigoberta, however) has noted that while testimonio involves the displacement of the "master subject" of modernist narrative, it does so paradoxically via the insistence on the first-person voice and proper name of the testimonial narrator.[3] The Spanish title of the testimonio, *Me llamo Rigoberta Menchú, y así me nació la conciencia*—My name is Rigoberta Menchú, and this is how my consciousness was formed— underlines the point, and also manages to avoid the essentializing implications of the subtitle for the English version, *An Indian Woman in Guatemala*.

In her interview with Alice Brittin and Kenya Dworkin some years ago, which I will come back to several times here, Menchú herself insisted on her right to appear as the coauthor of *I, Rigoberta Menchú*: "Lo que si efectivamente es un vacío en el libro es el derecho de autor . . . Porque la autoría del libro, efectivamente, debío ser más precisa, compartida, ¿verdad?" (What is in fact an absence in the book is the author's rights . . . Because the authorship of the book, in fact, should have been more correctly indicated, shared, no?) (Brittin and Dworkin 1993, 214). Menchú is referring to the fact that Elisabeth Burgos, the Venezuelan anthropologist (and, not incidentally, the former wife of Regis Debray) who acted as her interlocutor in the conversations in Paris that produced the testimonio, appears in most editions of the book as its author.

In deference then to political correctness, not to say politeness or respect for a person I have met only formally, I always try to say or write Rigoberta Menchú or Menchú, therefore, but I have to keep reminding myself on this score. My inclination, like yours, is to say Rigoberta—our Rigoberta—and I have to constantly censor this impulse. But of course, in another sense I would like to address Rigoberta Menchú as a friend, a *compañera,* in the way we used to say Fidel or Che: that is, someone who is in the same party or movement.

What is at stake in the question of how to address Menchú is the status of the testimonial narrator as a subject in her own right, rather than as someone who exists *for us.* Jameson's point about the depthless or decentered character of the postmodernist narrator suggests the question, Do testimonial narrators such as Rigoberta Menchú have an unconscious, and would a psychoanalytic reading of their narratives be useful? The answer on both scores, it seems to me, should be yes. Without doing violence to the story, one could easily read at least one strand of *I, Rigoberta Menchú* as an Oedipal bildungsroman built around the working-through of an Electra complex: an initial rejection of the Mother and motherhood in favor of an Athena-like identification with the Father, Vicente, the *campesino* organizer;[4] but then also an authority struggle with the Father, who does not want his daughter to leave home and become educated; then the death of the Father at the hands of the repressive apparatus of the state, which leads to a possibility of identification with the Mother, now seen as an organizer in her own right, someone who controls the subversive arts of subaltern speech and rumor; then the death of the Mother, again at the hands of the state; finally, in the act of narrating the testimonio itself, the emergence of Menchú as a full speaking subject, an organizer and leader in her own right.

As in the case of Richard Rodriguez's *Hunger of Memory*, but with very different outcomes in terms of a sense of community, identity, and politics, *I, Rigoberta Menchú* not only narrates but also embodies in its own textual aporias the tensions involved in this almost paradigmatic "coming of age" sequence, which marks the transition (or, perhaps more correctly, the oscillation) between the orders of the Imaginary and the Symbolic, local gemeinschaft and national or transnational gesellschaft, oral and print culture (Menchú telling her story orally and its textualization by Elisabeth Burgos), ethnographic narrative and "literature." Where for Rodriguez, Spanish is the "maternal" language of the private sphere that has to be rejected in order to gain full access to the authority of the Symbolic order represented by English, so that *Hunger of Memory* is among other things a celebration of English writing programs and a critique of bilingualism, by contrast it is Menchú's contradictory and shifting relationship to her Mother, who represents the authority of oral culture and Mayan languages, as much as any specifically "political" experience, that is at the core of her own process of *concientización* as well as her ability to authorize herself as a narrator.[5]

At the (apparent) cost of relativizing the political-ethical claim *I, Rigoberta Menchú* makes on its readers, what such a psychoanalytic reading would do is foreground its "complexity" as a text, the fact that its analysis is interminable, that it resists simply being the mirror that reflects back our narcissistic assumptions about what it should be. Despite all the misunderstandings her essay has provoked, this was surely Gayatri Spivak's point in answering the question "Can the Subaltern Speak?" paradoxically in the negative. By doing this, she was trying to suggest how the good faith of the "committed" ethnographer or solidarity activist who "allows" or enables the subaltern to speak the trace of the colonial construction of an Other who is available to speak to us— with whom we *can* speak (that is, feel comfortable speaking with)— neutralizes the force of the reality of difference (and antagonism).

In his essay in this collection, Alberto Moreiras has suggested, following on Edward Said's *Orientalism*, the idea of a "Latinamericanism" as an institutionally located discursive formation involved with constructing forms of representation and of power—colonial or otherwise— *over* others. As in the case of Orientalism, Moreiras argues, Latinamericanism requires a "native" informant or interlocutor to authorize itself. He asks, in this respect, if in effect Rigoberta Menchú is not that, if the personal assumptions we bring to reading a testimonio are also those by which Latinamericanism seeks to define and appropriate its Other, and if, therefore, the promotion of testimonio undertaken by critics such as George Yúdice, Doris Sommer, or myself is not "still residually, but significantly, caught up in a certain representational strategy which they themselves claim to have overcome."[6]

I believe Elzbieta Sklodowska has in mind something similar when she claims that, despite its appeal to the authority of an actual subaltern voice, testimonio does not in fact represent "a genuine and spontaneous reaction of a 'multiform-popular subject' in conditions of postcoloniality, but rather continues to be a discourse of elites committed to the cause of democratization."[7] The appeal to authenticity and victimization in the critical validation of testimonio stops the semiotic play of the text, she seems to imply, fixing the subject in a unidirectional gaze that deprives it of its reality.[8]

At the same time, the deconstructive appeal to the "many-leveled, unfixable intricacy and openness of a work of literature" (Spivak 1987, 95), which I think captures Sklodowska's position on testimonio, itself has to be suspect, given that this "openness" happens in literature only in a structural relation in which literature itself is one of the social practices that generate the difference that is registered as subalternity in the testimonial text. The limit of deconstruction in relation to testimonio is that it produces (or reveals) a textual unfixity or indeterminacy that not only misrepresents—in the sense both of "speaking for" and "speaking about"[9]—but itself produces and reproduces as a reading "effect" the fixity of relations of power and exploitation in the real social "text." The danger is that by being admitted into the academic canon, as in the course on "Cultures, Ideas and Values" developed by Renato Rosaldo and Mary Louise Pratt to meet the undergraduate requirement in Western Civilization at Stanford University, Rigoberta Menchú becomes simply a Clintonesque variant of Richard Rodriguez, yet another subaltern reprocessed into the hegemony by Stanford, which specializes in that sort of thing (Rodriguez's narrative hinges on his experience as an undergraduate "scholarship boy" at Stanford).

Is testimonio, as Sklodowska and, by implication, Moreiras suggest, simply another chapter in the history of what Angel Rama (1984) called the "lettered city" (*ciudad letrada*) in Latin America: the assumption, tied directly to the class interests of the creole elites and their own forms of self-authorization, that literature and the literary intellectual are or could be adequate signifiers of the national? The question is relevant to the claim made by Dinesh D'Souza, in the public debate over the Stanford Western Culture curriculum, that *I, Rigoberta Menchú* is not good or great literature. D'Souza wrote, to be precise: "To celebrate the works of the oppressed, apart from the standard of merit by which other art and history and literature is judged, is to romanticize their suffering, to pretend that it is naturally creative, and to give it an esthetic status that is not shared or appreciated by those who actually endure the oppression" (D'Souza 1991, 87). To my mind, *I, Rigoberta Menchú* is the most interesting work of *literature* produced in Latin America in the last fifteen years; but I would rather have it be a provocation in the academy, a radical otherness, as D'Souza feels it to be, than something smoothly integrated into a curriculum for "multicultural" citizenship of an elite university. I would like—and this was also Pratt and Rosaldo's aim—students at Stanford, or for that matter at the University of Pittsburgh, where I teach (although the stakes in class terms are somewhat different, since Pittsburgh is a university for the middle class, not the elite), to feel uncomfortable rather than virtuous when they read a text like *I, Rigoberta Menchú*. I would like them to understand that almost by definition the subaltern, which will in some cases intersect with aspects of their own class or group identity, is not, and cannot be, adequately represented in literature or in the university, that the literature and the university are among the institutional practices that *create* and sustain subalternity.

I recognize that there are problems with such a stance, beginning with the fact that I myself have taught *I, Rigoberta Menchú* at, among other places, Stanford. I am not claiming, therefore, to have some specially privileged, "politically correct" stance on testimonio. In fact, I am beginning to think that my sense of testimonio as a kind of antiliterature[10] may well neglect the fact that the Althusserian idea of "theoretical antihumanism" on which it is based is passing, for all practical purposes, from leftist professors like myself to pragmatic administrators concerned with downsizing and adapting the traditional humanities curriculum to suit the emerging requirements of economic globalization, with its new emphasis on media, communications, and cybernetics. Menchú herself makes a point of defending in the interview with Brittin and Dworkin what she explicitly calls "humanism," seeing its destruction or attenuation as a cultural effect of capitalism: "No perder el humanismo porque ¿qué es lo que está dañando a mucha humanidad hoy por hoy? Que mucha gente ha perdido el humanismo" (Not to lose humanism because, what is it that's hurting a lot of people today? The fact that they've lost humanism) (Brittin and Dworkin 1993, 214).

By the same token, the question of literature and "great books," or what gets taught as such, is not one that is easily displaced. There is an important political and cultural point to be made, for example, by answering Saul Bellow's question (which I paraphrase), Who is the Tolstoy of the Zulus? The Proust of the Papuans? with the names Ousmane Sembène or Ngugi wa Thiong'o—who are entitled to ask in reply, What has Saul Bellow written lately anyway? I take it that something like this is what Edward Said had in mind in the concluding section of *Culture and Imperialism,* where he sees the great tradition of the European novel as being appropriated, assimilated, and transformed by non-European writers like Sembène and Ngugi in the process of decolonization. Angel Rama's notion of "narrative transculturation" in Latin American fiction pointed in a similar direction.

But where Said envisions a new type of intellectual capable of producing in literature what he calls "a new way of telling," which would embody a sense of subaltern agency, part of the force of the discussion of testimonio and ethnographic narrative we have been involved in over the last five or six years is precisely to displace the centrality of intellectuals and what they recognize as culture—including literature itself. Of course, Menchú is an intellectual, too, but Said has in mind more a postcolonial version of what Gramsci called a traditional intellectual, that is, someone who meets the standards of and carries the authority of high culture. By contrast, the concern with the question of subaltern agency in testimonio depends epistemologically on the strategy of what Ranajit Guha has called "writing in reverse," founded on the radical suspicion that intellectuals and writing practices are themselves complicit in maintaining relations of domination and subalternity.[11]

Along with my reservations about the idea of literary transculturation of the colonial or postcolonial subaltern *from above* (as Said and Rama suggest), I think it is also important to admit the counterpossibility of transculturation *from below:* in this case, for example, to worry less about how *we* appropriate Menchú, and to understand and appreciate more how she appropriates *us* for her purposes. This is a key theme in both *I, Rigoberta Menchú* (see, for example, the sections on how the Mayas use the Bible and Christianity, or why Menchú decides to learn Spanish) and in Menchú's interview with Brittin and Dworkin, where among other things she talks about the appropriation of modern science and technology by indigenous communities in the Americas.[12]

Sklodowska is right to point out that the voice in testimonio is a textual construct, a *differend* in Lyotard's sense of the term, and that we should beware of a metaphysics of presence perhaps even more here, where the convention of fictionality has been suspended, than in other areas. Since the Real is that which resists symbolization, it is also that which collapses the claim of any particular form of cultural expression to representational adequacy and value. As such, the Real is, like the subaltern itself, with which it is connected both conceptually and "really," not an ontological category but a relational one, historically, socially, and psychically specific. Just as there are different strokes for different folks, one might say there are different Reals for different Symbolics. As subjects our (non)access to the Real is necessarily through the Symbolic. Sartre asked in his book on anti-Semitism what it would take to make someone give up anti-Semitism, since the very structure of prejudice guarantees that the only empirical evidence it will allow to consciousness is that which always already confirms the prejudice. The answer is something like being trapped with the Other in an elevator that has broken down for several hours, that is, in a "limit-situation"— to use Sartre's own language—that involves an involuntary breakdown of ego-boundaries.

That would be an experience of the Real, as is, via the experience of the transference, psychoanalysis, which undoes the structure of neurosis or trauma. The picaresque novel in sixteenth-century Spain and Europe offered (the simulacrum of) an experience of the Real vis-à-vis the idealistic genre conventions of pastoral and chivalric novels. But a picaresque novel like the anonymous *Lazarillo de Tormes* (1554)—perhaps the first modern novel in European literature—isn't really "realistic": it is *too* sordid, too centered on elementary bodily processes and on the elaborate tricks the *picaro* has to play on his masters to get something to eat—more a kind of grotesque intertextual inversion of the genre conventions and devices of the novels of chivalry than a plausible representation of even the lower depths of the society of its day. Bakhtin made much the same sort of claim for the role of the "dual-tone" and comic debunking in his study of Rabelais.

On the other hand, the Real is not the same thing as the concept we are perhaps more comfortable using, the "reality effect," as it is used in Barthesian or Althusserian criticism. When Lazarillo is beaten or the blind man crashes against the stone post, they are experiencing the Real, not a reality effect. In that sense, and here perhaps Sklodowska and I might find common ground, the Real, at least in its effects, is not too different from what the Russian Formalists used to call *ostranenie* or defamiliarization. Perhaps intending the pun with the French *touché,* Lacan himself uses the Aristotelian category of *tuché* or "fortune" to describe the (sudden, fortuitous) "encounter with the Real," as he puts it: the knock on the door that interrupts our dream (either as outside the dream or as another reality *in* it), for example, or, more prosaically perhaps, the piece of gum or dog shit that sticks to the sole of our shoe resisting all attempts to dislodge it.[13]

Something of the experience of the body in pain or hunger or danger inheres in testimonio. That is certainly the sense of that extraordinary passage in *I, Rigoberta Menchú* where Menchú narrates the torture and execution of her brother in the town plaza of Chajul. At the climax of the massacre, she describes how the witnesses experience an almost involuntary shudder of revulsion and anger, which the soldiers sense and which puts them on their guard. Reading this passage, you also experience this revulsion—and possibility of defiance even in the face of the threat of death—through a mechanism of identification, just as you do at the most intense moments of *Schindler's List*—for example, when the women in the concentration camp, who have been congratulating each other on surviving the selection process, suddenly realize that their children have been rounded up in the meantime and are being taken to the gas chambers in trucks. These are instances of *tuché,* a place where the experience of the Real breaks through the repetitious passivity of witnessing imposed by the repression itself. By contrast, romanticizing victimization would in fact confirm the Christian narrative of suffering and redemption that underlies colonial or imperialist domination in the first place and that leads in practice more to a moralistic posture of guilty, benevolent paternalism than of effective solidarity, which presumes an equality between the parties involved.[14]

The narration of the death of Menchú's brother is, as it happens, precisely the passage in *I, Rigoberta Menchú* whose literal veracity the anthropologist David Stoll has contested, claiming on the basis of his own interviews in the area Menchú comes from (where he spent several years doing field research) that the torture and massacre of her brother happened in a different way, that Menchú could not have been an eyewitness to it, and that, therefore, her description is, in his words, "a literary invention." Stoll has not chosen to press this charge, and Menchú has categorically denied it (no one, in any case, questions the fact itself of the torture and murder of the brother by units of the Guatemalan army); but he has retained the implication that Menchú is not a reliable narrator, that her transformation into something like a secular saint of the struggles of Guatemalan indigenous communities is unwarranted.[15]

Let me attempt a reply to Stoll's and similar reservations[16] about the representativity of Menchú's account via an episode in Shoshana Felman and Dori Laub's book on testimonial representations of the Holocaust, which is connected to my mention of *Schindler's List* above. It has to do with the case of a woman survivor and the eyewitness account of the Auschwitz uprising she gave for the Video Archive for Holocaust Testimonies at Yale. At one point in her narrative the survivor recalls that in the course of the uprising, in her own words, "All of a sudden, we saw four chimneys going up in flames, exploding. The flames shot into the sky, people were running. It was unbelievable" (Felman and Laub 1992, 59). Months later, at a conference on the Holocaust that featured a viewing of the videotape of the woman's testimony, this sequence became the focus of a debate. Some historians of the Holocaust who saw the video of the woman's testimony pointed out that only *one* chimney had been destroyed in the uprising, and that the woman had not mentioned in her account the fact that the Polish underground had betrayed the uprising. Given that the narrator was wrong about these crucial details, they argued, it might be better to set aside her whole testimony, rather than potentially give credence to the revisionists, who want to deny the reality of the Holocaust altogether by questioning the reliability of the factual record.

Laub and Felman note that, on that occasion,

A psychoanalyst who had been one of the interviewers of the woman, profoundly disagreed. "The woman was testifying," he insisted, "not to the number of the chimneys blown up, but to something else more radical, more crucial: the reality of an unimaginable occurrence. One chimney blown up at Auschwitz was as incredible as four. The number mattered less than the fact of the occurrence. . . . The woman testified to an event that broke the all compelling frame of Auschwitz, where Jewish armed revolts just did not happen, and had no place. She testified to the breakage of a framework. That was historical truth." (Felman and Laub 1992, 60)

The psychoanalyst was Laub, who goes on to explain that

In the process of the testimony to a trauma, as in psychoanalytic practice, in effect, you often do not want to know anything except what the patient tells you, because what is important in the situation is the *discovery* of knowledge— its evolution, and its very *happening*. Knowledge in the testimony is, in other words, not simply a factual given that is reproduced and replicated by the testifier, but a genuine advent, an event in its own right. . . . [The woman] was testifying not simply to empirical historical facts, but to the very secret of survival and of resistance to extermination. The historians could not hear, I thought, the way in which her silence was itself part of the testimony, an essential part of the historical truth she was precisely bearing witness to. . . . This was her way of being, of surviving, of resisting. It is not merely her speech, but the very boundaries of silence which surround it, which attest, today as well as in the past, to this assertion of resistance. (62)

I have argued elsewhere that it would be yet another version of the "native informant" of classical anthropology to grant testimonial narrators like Rigoberta Menchú only the possibility of being witnesses, but not the power to create their own narrative authority and negotiate its conditions of truth and representativity. "This would be a way of saying that the subaltern can of course speak, but only through the institutionally sanctioned authority—itself dependent on and implicated in colonialism and imperialism—of the journalist or ethnographer, who alone has the power to decide what counts in the narrator's 'raw material' and to turn it into literature (or 'evidence')" (Beverley 1993a, 97).

It is not incidental that Stoll relates his doubts about the veracity of *I, Rigoberta Menchú* to an uneasiness with what he calls explicitly "postmodernist" anthropology: "What I want to say," he notes, "is that if our frame is the text, the narrative, or the voice instead of the society, culture, or political economy, it is easy to find someone to say what we want to hear" (Stoll 1990a, 11). But his own basis for questioning

Menchú's account are interviews years later with people from the village where the massacre occurred. That is, the only things he can put in the place of what he considers Menchú's inadequately representative testimony are other testimonies: other texts, narratives, versions, and voices.

We know something about the nature of this problem. There is not, outside of discourse, a level of social facticity that can guarantee the truth of this or that representation, given that what we call "society" itself is not an essence prior to representation but precisely the consequence of struggles to represent and over representation.[17] That is the deeper meaning of Walter Benjamin's aphorism "Even the dead are not safe": even the memory of the past is conjunctural, relative, perishable, dependent on practice. Testimonio is both an art and a strategy of subaltern memory.

Since Stoll raises the question of the authority of conventional anthropology against what is, for him, its corruption by the postmodern kind, let me say a few words about the relation of Menchú to Mayan tradition. In a sense, though it is founded on a notion of the authority of tradition, there is nothing particularly traditional about Menchú's narrative: this is not what makes it, as she claims, the expression of "toda la realidad de un pueblo" (the whole reality of a people), because there is nothing particularly ancestral or traditional about the community and way of life that her testimonio describes either. Nothing more "postmodern," nothing more traversed by the economic and cultural forces of transnational capitalism—nothing that Stoll or, for that matter, we can claim anyway—than the social, economic, and cultural contingencies Menchú and her family live and die in. Even the communal mountain *aldea,* or village, that the text evokes so compellingly, with its collective rituals and economic life that make it seem like an ancestral Mayan Gemeinschaft that has survived five hundred years of conquest more or less intact, turns out on closer inspection to be a recent settlement, founded by Menchú's father, Vicente, on unoccupied lands in the mountains in the wake of its inhabitants' dispossession by landowners from their previous places of residence, much as squatters from the countryside have created the great slums around Latin American cities, or returned refugees in Central America have tried to reconstruct their former communities.[18]

I do not mean by this to diminish the force of Menchú's insistent appeal to the authority of her ancestors or of tradition, but want simply to indicate that it is an appeal that is being activated *in the present,* that it is a response to the conditions of proletarianization and semiproletarianization, which subjects like Menchú and her family are experiencing in the context of the *same* processes of globalization that affect our own lives. In some ways, in fact, Latin American cultural studies theorists such as Néstor García Canclini or Carlos Monsiváis, or postmodernist performance artists like Gloria Anzaldúa or Guillermo Gómez-Peña, might be better guides to Menchú's world than anthropologists such as David Stoll or Elisabeth Burgos, who, whatever their differences about the truth-value of Menchú's narrative, assume they are authorized or authorize themselves to represent that world for us. We all remember, in particular, Burgos's description (which I'm sure she now bitterly regrets) of Menchú's Indian clothing ("She was wearing traditional costume, including a multicolored *huipil,*" and so on) in her preface to *I, Rigoberta Menchú,* and probably tend to see this as an example of the self-interested benevolence of the hegemonic intellectual toward the subaltern. But Menchú's outfit is not so much an index of her authenticity as a subaltern, which would confirm the ethical and epistemological virtue of the *bien pensant* intellectual in the First World—both as a field worker in the huge agro-export coastal plantations of Guatemala and as a maid in Guatemala City she had to learn how to dress very differently, as she tells us herself in her narrative. It speaks rather to a kind of "performative" transvestism on her part, her use of traditional Mayan women's dress as a cultural signifier to define her own identity and her allegiance to the community she is fighting for (I am told by the Guatemalan writer Arturo Arias, who has worked with her, that Menchú prefers blue jeans and T-shirts outside the public eye).

There is a question of agency here, as in the construction of the testimonial text itself, and as Menchú puts it in a phrase Brittin and Dworkin use as the title of their interview, "los indígenas no nos quedamos como bichos aislados, inmunes, desde hace 500 años. No, nosotros hemos sido protagonistas de la historia" (We Indians have not remained like strange, isolated beasts for five hundred years. No, we have also been protagonists of history) (Brittin and Dworkin 1993, 212).

The Real that *I, Rigoberta Menchú* forces us to encounter, in other words, is not only that of the subaltern as "represented" victim of history but also as agent of a transformative project that aspires to become hegemonic in its own right. For this project, testimonio is a means rather than an end in itself. As distinct from *Hunger of Memory,* becoming a writer, producing a literary text, cannot be the solution required by the "situation of urgency"—to use René Jara's phrase—that generates the telling of the testimonio in the first place, whether or not these things actually happen. Menchú is certainly aware that her testimonio can be an important tool in human rights and solidarity work that might have a positive effect on the genocidal conditions the text itself describes. But *her* interest in creating the text is not in the first place to have it become part of the canon of Western civilization, which in any case she distrusts deeply, so that it can become an object *for us,* in a sense, our means of getting the "whole truth"—"toda la realidad"—of her experience. It is rather to act tactically in a way that she hopes and expects will advance the interests of the community and social groups and classes her testimonio represents: "poor" Guatemalans. That is why *I, Rigoberta Menchú* can never be "great literature" in the sense that Dinesh D'Souza means this, because the response it elicits is something outside of the "field" of literature in its present form.[19]

The Real is supplementary in the Derridean sense, in that it indicates something that is in excess of the closure of representation. Asked by Brittin and Dworkin if she believes that her struggles will have an end, Menchú answers: "Yo si creo que la lucha no tiene fin. . . . Yo creo que la democracia no depende de una implantación de algo, sino que va a ser un proceso en desarrollo, se va a desenvolver a lo largo de la Historia" (I believe that the struggle does not have an end. . . . I believe that democracy does not depend on the implantation of something, but rather that it is a process in development, that it will unfold in the course of History) (Brittin and Dworkin 1993, 213). She sees her own text in similar terms as a conjunctural intervention that responded to a certain strategic urgency, now relativized by what was not or could not be included in it—the imperfect metonym of a different, potentially more inclusive, and complete text. It is not so much that she is bothered, as we have often imagined, by Elisabeth Burgos's editing of the original transcript. Except for wanting to be recognized as the author, she doesn't complain about this. Her concern is elsewhere:

Ahora, al leerlo, me da la impresíon que es una parte, que son fragmentos de la historia misma, ¿verdad? Tantas anécdotas que uno tiene en la vida, especial-mente la convivencia con los abuelos, con la familia, con la tierra, con muchas cosas. Son fragmentos los que tiene el libro y ójala que algun día pudieramos redocumentarlo para publicarlo, tal vez para nuestros nietos, posiblemente después de poner una serie de otras leyendas, testimonios, vivencias, creencias, oraciones, que aprendimos de chiquitos, porque el libro tiene una serie de limitaciones. (217)

(Reading it now, I have the impression that it's a part, that there are fragments of history itself, no? So many stories one comes across in life, in our experiences with the family, with the land, with so many things. What the book has are fragments and I hope that one day we could redo it, maybe for our grandchildren, maybe after putting in a series of other stories, testimonies, experiences, beliefs, prayers that we learned as children, because the book has a lot of limitations.)

Note that Menchú distinguishes in this passage between her text as *a* testimonio, in the sense of the book *I, Rigoberta Menchú* ("son fragmentos los que tiene el libro"), and *testimonios* in the plural as concrete acts or practices of witnessing and recounting in her own society, as in "una serie de otras leyendas, testimonios, vivencias, creencias, oraciones . . ." Testimonio is for Menchú, in other words, only *one*, highly specialized and conjunctural, part of a much larger testimonial practice in subaltern culture, which includes the arts of oral memory, storytelling, gossip, and rumor: precisely those she learns from her mother, whose own life she calls a "testimonio vivo," or living testimony.[20] It happens to be the part that *we* get to see via the intervention of an interlocutor who is in a position to make a printed text out of it, but this is not to say that it is not somehow connected to that larger testimonial practice and the intentionalities that underlie it, that it is simply a new way of constructing the subaltern in literature by or for intellectuals, as Sklodowska, in effect, argues.

It is useful to remember in this respect that the subaltern does not *want* to remain subaltern: it is not the intention of its cultural practices, particularly where these address an interlocutor from the hegemony, as in the case of *I, Rigoberta Menchú*, to simply signify its subalternity. This is perhaps the best way to confront the circumstance that frames this collection: the moment of testimonio is over. Not, so that I am not misunderstood on this point, testimonio as such: that will go on, just as testimonial forms have been present at the margins of Western literature ever since its constitution as a modern episteme in the sixteenth century. But testimonio's moment, the originality and urgency or—to recall Lacan's phrase—the "state of emergency" that drove our fascination and critical engagement with it, has undoubtedly passed, if only by the logic of aesthetic familiarization. Testimonio began as an adjunct to armed liberation struggle in Latin America and elsewhere in the Third World in the sixties. But its canonization was tied even more, perhaps, to the military, political, and economic force of counterrevolution in the years after 1973. It was the Real, the voice of the body in pain, of the disappeared, of the losers in the rush to marketize, that demystified the false utopian discourse of neoliberalism, its claims to have finally reconciled history and society. At the same time, testimonio relativized the more liberal or even progressive claim of the high-culture writers and artists of the boom to speak for the majority of Latin Americans. It marked a new site of discursive authority, which challenged the authority of the "great writer" to establish the reality principle of Latin American culture and development.

Testimonio was intimately linked to international solidarity networks in support of revolutionary movements or struggles around human rights, apartheid, democratization; but it was also a way of testing the contradictions and limits of revolutionary and reformist projects still structured in part around elite assumptions about the role of cultural vanguards. Detached from these contexts, it loses its special aesthetic and ideological power, and runs the risk of becoming a new form of *costumbrismo,* the Spanish term for "local-color" writing.

In his essay (included in this volume) on Domitila Barrios and her well-known testimonio about Bolivian mining communities, *Let Me Speak!,* Javier Sanjinés C in a sense is writing the epitaph for testimonio. Barrios had ended her narrative with the wish that the text of her story would find its way back into the mining communities it described, as a tool for consciousness-raising and struggle. That question, the way in which subaltern groups themselves appropriate and *use* testimonio, I have suggested here, has not been addressed adequately in the discussion on testimonio that has gone on among ourselves in the metropolitan academy. Sanjinés C, however, is concerned with a different problem altogether: the fact that these mining communities, like the gigantic steel works of my own city, have been significantly reduced in size or have ceased to exist altogether as the shifts of the global economy in the last twenty years have undermined the viability of the tin mining industry in Bolivia, and that new forms of proletarian and subproletarian life have begun to appear in their place.

His point is that testimonios like *Let Me Speak!* can no longer be considered an adequate representation of (again, as both "speaking for" and "speaking about") subalternity in relation to domination; that— along with much of the traditional left and trade union movement— they have become a nostalgia; that new forms of political imagination and organization are needed; that, as in everything else in life, we have to move on. While Menchú speaks of redoing *I, Rigoberta Menchú,* she also suggests in the interview with Brittin and Dworkin that simply returning to testimonio is now beside the point, for she has other things she needs or wants to do, which include writing conventionally literary poems in Spanish (the interview concludes with the text of one of these, "Patria abnegada"). In a way, that is as it should be, because it is not only *our* purposes that count in relation to testimonio.

Fredric Jameson speaks in his review article on the Routledge *Cultural Studies* reader of "the desire called Cultural Studies," describing that desire as "the project to constitute a 'historic bloc,' rather than theoretically, as the floor plan for a new discipline" (Jameson 1993c, 17). Could we ask similarly, What is left today of the desire called testimonio? There are many ways one could answer this question, but it might be enough to say simply, understanding that it has functioned politically as something like what Lacan meant by the Real, Chiapas.

Notes

1. "The *Ding* is not in the relationship—which is to some extent a calculated one insofar as it is explicable—that causes man to question his words as referring to things which they have moreover created. There is something different in *das Ding*. . . . If Freud speaks of the reality principle, it is in order to reveal to us that from a certain point of view it is always defeated; it only manages to affirm itself at the margin. And this is so by reason of a kind of pressure that . . . Freud calls not 'the vital needs'—as is often said in order to emphasize the secondary processes—but *die Not des Lebens* in the German text. An infinitely stronger phrase. Something that *wishes.* 'Need' and not 'needs.' Pressure, urgency. The state of *Not* is the state of emergency in life. . . . As soon as we try to articulate the reality principle so as to make it depend on the physical world to

which Freud's purpose seems to require us to relate it, it is clear that it functions, in fact, to isolate the subject from reality" (Lacan 1978, 46).

2. Žižek's remarks follow on Lacan's observation in the *Seminar* that the experience of the Mother as frustration by the subject, as in Kleinian theory, is an instance of the Thing.

3. "I always insist on a third possibility beyond the old bourgeois ego and the schizophrenic subject of our organization society today: a *collective subject*, decentered but not schizophrenic. It emerges in certain forms of storytelling that can be found in third-world literature, in testimonial literature, in gossip and rumors and things of this kind. . . . It is decentered since the stories you tell there as an individual subject don't belong to you; you don't control them in the way the master subject of modernism would. But you don't just suffer them in the schizophrenic isolation of the first-world subject of today" (Jameson, quoted in Stephanson 1987, 45). On this point, see also Jameson's essay in this collection.

4. "Figures like the goddess Athena—'father's daughters self-professedly uncontaminated by the womb'—are useful for establishing women's ideological self-debasement, which is to be distinguished from a deconstructive attitude toward the essentialist subject" (Spivak 1988, 308).

5. I return often to Walter Mignolo's observation about the Spanish practice of segregating the children of the Indian aristocracy from their families in order to teach them literacy and Christianity. The violence of such a practice, he writes, "is not located in the fact that the youngsters have been assembled and enclosed day and night. It comes, rather, from the interdiction of having conversations with their parents, particularly with their mothers. In a primarily oral society, in which virtually all knowledge is transmitted by means of conversation, the preservation of oral contact was contradictory with the effort to teach how to read and write. Forbidding conversations with the mother meant, basically, depriving the children of the living culture imbedded in the language and preserved and transmitted in speech" (Mignolo 1989, 67).

6. I quote from a draft version of Moreiras's essay he presented at the 1994 conference of the Latin American Studies Association in Atlanta. The revised version is included in this volume.

7. "No representa una reacción genuina y espontánea del 'sujeto-pueblo multiforme' frente a la condición postcolonial, sino que sigue siendo un discurso de las élites comprometidas a la causa de la democratización" (Sklodowska 1991, 113). The concept of "sujeto-pueblo multiforme" Sklodowska alludes to comes from the Chilean critic Jorge Narvaéz.

8. Fixes the testimonial narrator as a subject, that is, but also fixes us as subjects in what Althusser would have called a relation of double specularity created by an idealization or sublimation of her otherness, which in the end also isolates us from our own reality. It is useful to recall Menchú's own advice

that "Cada uno de nosostros tiene que conocer nuestra realidad y optar por los demás," which I translate loosely as "each of has to know our own reality, and then (be in a position to) express solidarity with others."

9. I refer here to Spivak's elaboration of the distinction between *vertreten* and *darstellen* in Marx in "Can the Subaltern Speak?" (1988).

10. See the chapters on testimonio in Beverley 1993a.

11. "[T]he historical phenomenon of [peasant] insurgency meets the eye for the first time as an image framed in the prose, hence the outlook, of counter-insurgency—an image caught in a distorting mirror. However, the distortion has a logic to it. That is the logic of opposition between the rebels and their enemies not only as parties engaged in active hostility on a particular occasion but as the mutually antagonistic elements of a semi-feudal society under colonial rule. The antagonism is rooted deeply enough in the material and spiritual conditions of their existence to reduce the difference between elite and subaltern perceptions of a binary pair. . . . Inscribed in elite discourse, it [the rebellion] had to be read as a writing in reverse. Since our access to rebel consciousness lay, so to say, through enemy country, we had to seize on the evidence of elite consciousness and force it to show us the way to its Other" (Guha 1983, 333).

12. "Yo creo que los indígenas debemos aprovechar y captar todos aquellos valores grandes de los descubrimientos de la ciencia y la tecnología. Hay grandes cosas que han alcanzado la ciencia y la tecnología y no podemos decir: 'los indígenas no vamos a ser parte de esto,' pues de hecho somos parte de ello" (Brittin and Dworkin 1993, 212). (I believe that Indians should take advantage of and assimilate all these great values offered by the discoveries of science and technology. Science and technology have accomplished great things and we can't say "we Indians aren't going to be a part of that," because in fact we are part of it.)

13. See Lacan's discussion in "Tuché and Automaton" (Lacan 1978, 53–66). René Jara has noted that "More than a translation of reality, testimonio is a *trace of the Real,* of that history which, as such, is unrepresentable" (Jara and Vidal 1986, 2–3).

14. This was, of course, the strategy of the antislave narrative produced by Latin American liberal elites or would-be elites in the nineteenth century. It is also a problem with *Schindler's List,* as the emerging critical discussion of the film has begun to register. The use of the Schindler story personalizes the Holocaust and brings it closer to the viewer: that was undoubtedly a brilliant stroke by Spielberg and it differentiates his film from a "modernist" treatment of the Holocaust such as Alain Resnais's *Night and Fog.* The price, however, is that the Jews (as a group) can be represented in the film only as victims, dependent on Schindler and the character played by Ben Kingsley, who allegorizes the role of the traditional Jewish leadership in the *Judenrat,* for their salvation.

A Zionist or communist representation would have critiqued the role of the *Judenrat* and stressed the possibility of Jewish self-organization from below and armed struggle against the Nazi system, instead of their reliance on the benevolence of both Jewish and non-Jewish capitalist-humanist elites. Even the representation of the Holocaust, in other words, is taken away in *Schindler's List* from the actual victims or participants; the film as a capitalist enterprise mirrors Schindler's business venture as the *necessary* vehicle for Jewish salvation. It is interesting to contrast Spielberg's strategy with the collective montage of direct testimonies by Holocaust survivors presented in the Holocaust Museum in Washington.

15. I quote from a manuscript copy that professor Stoll made available to me of the unpublished paper, "*I, Rigoberta Menchú* and Human Rights Reporting in Guatemala," he presented at the conference on " 'Political Correctness' and Cultural Studies" at the University of California Berkeley, 20 October 1990. Without noting the incident of the brother in particular, Stoll makes a similar claim about Menchú in Stoll 1990b (4–9, esp. 4–5). Stoll had been studying the process of evangelization of these communities by U.S.-sponsored fundamentalist Protestant sects, which began during the period described in *I, Rigoberta Menchú*, sometimes, particularly during the presidency of Efraín Ríos Montt, in direct connection with the counterinsurgency campaigns being mounted by the Guatemalan army in the highlands. It is not clear whether in questioning the validity of Menchú's testimonio Stoll's own position is that of an impartial observer, concerned with how the communities became trapped between the military and the guerrillas, or of someone who in one way or another identifies with or supports the evangelization process, in which case he would be predisposed to downplay Menchú because of her connection to Catholic base communities and the guerrillas, who were competing with the fundamentalists for support among these communities. In the same way (and, to my way of thinking at least, with similar political consequences), a social scientist involved with Buthelezi and the project of his Inkatha party might have questioned the claim of Nelson Mandela and the ANC to adequately represent black South Africans in general, for example.

16. See for example Marc Zimmerman's essay in this collection.

17. "Any statement of authority has no other guarantee than its very enunciation, and it is pointless for it to seek another signifier, which could not appear outside this locus in any way. Which is what I mean when I say that no metalanguage can be spoken, or, more aphoristically, that there is no Other of the Other. And when the Legislator (he who claims to lay down the Law) presents himself to fill the gap, he does so as an imposter" (Lacan 1977, 310–11).

18. See, for example, Beth and Steve Cagan's account of one such community in El Salvador (Cagan and Cagan 1991).

19. The *Nuevo Texto Crítico* interview confirms what sources close to Menchú

have noted previously: that the basic editing of the transcript was done not only by Elisabeth Burgos but also a team of Menchú's *compañeros* from the political organization she was associated with in Guatemala, including the writer Mario Payeras, working together with her in Mexico City after the sessions with Burgos in Paris. In a sense, *I, Rigoberta Menchú* is thus a text produced not only by a committee but by a central committee, with specific political goals in mind.

20.   Ranajit Guha offers a brilliant description of modes of oral discursive construction and transmission in peasant cultures in *Elementary Aspects* (1983). What is relevant to *I, Rigoberta Menchú* is that the mode of transmission is dependent on the highly socialized character of everyday community life, in which women play a key role.

Bibliography

Achugar, Hugo. 1989. "Notas sobre el discurso testimonial latinoamericano." In *La historia en la literatura iberoamericana,* edited by Raquel Chang-Rodríguez and Gabriella de Beer, 278–94. Hanover, N.H.: Ediciones del Norte.

———. 1992. "Historias paralelas / Historias ejemplares: La historia y la voz del otro." *Revista de crítica literaria latinoamericana* 36:49–71.

Aguirre, Mirta, Angel Augier, Roberto Fernández Retamar, and Onelio Jorge Cardoso. 1980. *Dice la paloma. Testimonio.* Havana: Letras Cubanas.

Ahmad, Aijaz. 1987. "Jameson's Rhetoric of Otherness and the 'National Allegory.'" *Social Text* 17:3–27.

———. 1992. "Three Worlds Theory: End of Debate." In *In Theory: Classes, Nations, Literatures,* 287–318. New York: Verso.

Albizures, Miguel Ángel. 1987. *Tiempo de sudor y lucha.* Mexico City: Práxis.

Albó, Xavier. 1986. *Los Señores del Gran Poder.* La Paz: Alenkar.

Alegría, Claribel, and Darwin J. Flakoll. 1983. *No me agarran viva: La mujer salvadoreña en lucha.* Mexico: Serie Popular Era.

———. 1989. *Ashes of Izalco.* Willimantic, Conn.: Curbstone Press.

Alencar, José de. [1857] 1960. *O Guarani.* Vol. 2 of *Obras Completas.* Rio de Janeiro: José Aguilar.

Alvarado, Elvia. 1987. *Don't Be Afraid, Gringo: A Honduran Woman Speaks from the Heart.* Translated and edited by Medea Benjamin. San Francisco: Institute for Food Development Policy.

Anaya, Rudolfo A. 1972. *Bless Me, Ultima.* Berkeley, Calif.: Quinto Sol.

Anderson, Benedict. 1983. *Imagined Communities: Reflections on the Origin and Spread of Nationalism.* London: Verso.

Anderson, Thomas. 1971. *Matanza: El Salvador's 1932 Communist Revolt.* Lincoln: University of Nebraska Press.

Annis, Sheldon. 1987. *God and Production in a Guatemalan Town.* Austin: University of Texas Press.

Arac, Jonathan. 1987. *Critical Genealogies: Historical Situations for Postmodern Literary Studies.* New York: Columbia University Press.

Argueta, Manlio. 1983. *One Day of Life.* Translated by Bill Brow. New York: Random House.

——. 1987. *Cuzcatlan: Where the Southern Sea Beats.* Translated by Bill Brow. New York: Random House.

Bakhtin, Mikhail M. 1980. *The Dialogical Imagination.* Translated by Michael Holquist and Caryl Emerson. Austin: Texas University Press.

Barnet, Miguel. 1969. "La novela-testimonio: socio-literatura," *Unión* 4 (October): 99–122.

——. 1973. *Esteban Montejo: The Autobiography of a Runaway Slave.* New York: Random House.

——. 1981. "The Documentary Novel." *Cuban Studies/Estudios Cubanos* 11, no. 1:19–32.

——. 1983. *La fuente viva.* Havana: Editorial Letras Cubanas.

——. 1984. *La vida real.* Madrid: Ediciones Alfaguara.

Barreda Avila, Rubén. 1960. *Guaridas infernales: Mi drama viviendo durante 1096 dias en las mazamoras penitenciarias, en el periodo en el que Carlos Castillos Armas detento poder y ultrajo la dignidad nacional.* Guatemala.

Barrios de Chungara, Domitila. 1977. *"Si me permiten hablar . . .": Testimonio de Domitila, una mujer de las minas de Bolivia.* Edited by Moema Viezzer. Mexico: Siglo XXI.

——. 1978. *Let Me Speak!* Edited by Moema Viezzer and translated by Victoria Ortiz. New York: Monthly Review Press.

Baudrillard, Jean. 1978. *Cultura y simulacro.* Barcelona: Kairos.

Behar, Ruth. 1993. *Translated Woman: Crossing the Border with Esperanza's Story.* Boston: Beacon.

Benjamin, Walter. 1969. *Illuminations.* Edited and with an introduction by Hannah Arendt and translated by Harry Zohn. New York: Schocken.

——. 1982. *Das Passagen-Werk.* Frankfurt: Suhrkamp.

Bercovitch, Sacvan. 1993. *The Rites of Assent: Transformations in the Symbolic Construction of America.* New York: Routledge.

Berger, Peter. 1990. "Sociological Perspectives—Society as Drama." In *Life as Theater,* edited by Dennis Brissett and Charles Edgley. New York: Aldine de Gruyter.

Bernard, H. Russel, and Jesús Salinas Pedraza. 1989. *Native Ethnography: A Mexican Indian Describes His Culture.* Newbury Park, Calif.: Sage.

Beverley, John. 1987. "Anatomia del testimonio." Chap. 7 in his *Del Lazarillo al sandinismo: Estudios sobre la función ideologica de la literatura española e hispanoamericana.* Minneapolis, Minn.: Prisma Institute.

——. 1989. "The Margin at the Center: On *Testimonio* (Testimonial Narrative)." *Modern Fiction Studies* 35, no. 1 (spring): 11–28.

——. 1991. "Through All Things Modern: Second Thoughts on Testimonio." *boundary 2* 18, no. 2 (summer): 1–21.

——. 1992. "Introducción." *Revista de crítica literaria latinoamericana* 36:7–18.

——. 1993a. *Against Literature.* Minneapolis: University of Minnesota Press.

——. 1993b. "¿Posliteratura? Sujeto subalterno e impasse de las humanidades." *Revista de la Casa de las Américas* (January–March): 13–24.

Beverley, John, and Hugo Achugar, eds. 1992. *La voz del otro: Testimonio,
subalternidad y verdad narrativa.* Special issue of *Revista de crítica literaria
latinoamericana,* no. 36.

Beverley, John, and José Oviedo, eds. 1993. *The Postmodernism Debate in Latin
America.* Special issue of *boundary 2,* 20, no. 3.

Beverley, John, and Marc Zimmerman. 1990. *Literature and Politics in the
Central American Revolutions.* Austin: University of Texas Press.

Bhabha, Homi K. 1994. *The Location of Culture.* London and New York: Routledge.

Bizarro Ujpán, Ignacio. 1981. *Son of Tecún Umán: A Mayan Indian Tells His Life
Story.* Translated and edited by James Sexton. Tucson: University of Arizona
Press.

Blasis, Marie-Claire. 1966. *A Season in the Life of Emmanuel.* Translated from the
French by Derek Coltman. New York: Farrar, Straus and Giroux.

Blest Gana, Alberto. [1862] 1977. *Martín Rivas.* Caracas: Biblioteca Aya-
cucho.

Borges, Jorge Luis. 1955. *Ficciones.* Buenos Aires: Emecé.

——. 1980. *Prosa completa.* 2 vols. Barcelona: Bruguera.

Boundas, Constantin V. 1993. *The Deleuze Reader.* New York: Columbia University Press.

Brecht, Bertolt. 1967. "Der kaukasische Kreidekreis." In *Gesammelte Werke.*
Vol. 5. Frankfurt am Main: Suhrkamp.

Brewer, Anthony. 1980. *Marxist Theories of Imperialism: A Critical Survey.* London and Boston: Routledge and Kegan Paul.

Brittin, Alice, and Kenya Dworkin. 1993. "Rigoberta Menchú: 'Los indígenas
no nos quedamos como bichos aislados, inmunes, desde hace 500 años. No,
nosotros hemos sido protagonistas de la historia.'" *Nuevo texto crítico* 6, no.
11:207–22.

——. 1995. "Close Encounters of the Third World Kind: Rigoberta Menchú
and Elisabeth Burgos' *Me llamo Rigoberta Menchú.*" *Latin American Perspectives* 22, no. 4 (fall): 100–114.

Brodzky, Bella, and Celeste Schenck. 1988. *Life/Lines: Theorizing Women's Autobiography.* Ithaca: Cornell University Press.

Bruner, Jerome. 1991. "The Narrative Construction of Reality." *Critical Inquiry* 18:1–21.

Burbach, Roger, and Orlando Nuñéz. 1987. *Fire in the Americas: Forging a
Revolutionary Agenda.* London: Verso.

Butler, Judith. 1993. *Bodies That Matter: On the Discursive Limits of "Sex."* New
York: Routledge.

Cabezas, Omar. 1983. *La montaña es algo más que una inmensa estepa verde.*
Managua: Editorial Nueva Nicaragua.

———. 1985. *Fire from the Mountain: The Making of a Sandinista.* Translated by Kathleen Weaver. New York: Crown Books.

Cagan, Beth, and Steve Cagan. 1991. *This Promised Land, El Salvador: The Refugee Community of Cotomoncagna and Their Return to Morazan.* New Brunswick: Rutgers University Press.

Calderón, Fernando, Alejandro Piscitelli, and José Luis Reyna. 1992. "Social Movements: Actors, Theories, Expectations." In Escobar and Alvarez, eds., 19–36.

Camara, Laye. 1953. *L'enfant noir, roman.* Paris: Plon.

Cardenal, Ernesto. 1978. *El evangelio en Solentiname.* Salamanca: Sígueme.

Carey-Webb, Allen. 1990. "Teaching Third World Auto/Biography: Testimonial Narrative in the Canon and the Classroom." *Oregon English* 12, no. 2 (fall): 7–10.

Carmack, Robert M., ed. 1988. *Harvest of Violence: The Maya Indians and the Guatemalan Crisis.* Norman: University of Oklahoma Press.

Carpentier, Alejo. 1968. *Los pasos perdidos.* Madrid: Ediciones Rialp.

Carpignano, Paolo, Robin Andersen, Stanley Aronowitz, and Wilhalm Difazio. 1990. "Chatter in the Age of Electronic Reproduction." *Social Text* 25/26:33–55

Carr, Robert. 1992. "Re-presentando el testimonio: Notas sobre el cruce divisorio Primer mundo / Tercer mundo." *Revista de crítica literaria latinoamericana* 36:73–94.

Casas, Nubya. 1981. "Novela-testimonio: Historia y literatura." Ph.D. diss., New York University.

Castro, Fidel. 1972. "Words to the Intellectuals." In *Radical Perspectives in the Arts,* edited by Lee Baxandall. Harmondsworth, England: Penguin.

Certeau, Michel de. 1984. *The Practice of Everyday Life.* Translated by Steven F. Randall. Berkeley: University of California Press.

Chomsky, Noam. 1985. "The Fifth Freedom." In *Turning the Tide: U.S. Intervention in Central America and the Struggle for Peace,* 43–84. Boston: South End.

Clifford, James. 1990. "Notes on (Field)notes." In *Fieldnotes: The Making of Anthropology,* edited by Roger Sanjek, 47–70. Ithaca: Cornell University Press.

Clifford, James, and George Marcus, eds. 1986. *Writing Culture.* Berkeley: University of California Press.

Cohen, Sande. 1993. *Academia and the Luster of Capital.* Minneapolis: University of Minnesota Press.

Colás, Santiago. 1996. "Impurity and the Cultures of Democracy in Latin America." In *The Postmodernism in Latin America,* edited by Claudia Ferman. Hamden, Conn.: Garland.

Cornell, Drucilla. 1995. "What is Ethical Feminism?" In *Feminist Contentions: A Philosophical Exchange,* edited by Seyla Benhabib, Judith Butler, Drucilla

Cornell, and Nancy Fraser, 75–106. Introduction by Linda Nicholson. (New York: Routledge). Originally published in *Der Streit um Differenz* (Frankfurt: Fischer Verlag, 1993).

Dalton, Roque. 1981. *Poetry and Militancy in Latin America.* Willimantic, Conn.: Curbstone Press.

———. 1983. *Miguel Mármol: Los sucesos de 1932 en El Salvador.* Havana: Casa de las Americas.

———. 1984. *Poems.* Translated by Richard Schaaf. Willimantic, Conn.: Curbstone Press.

———. 1987. *Miguel Mármol.* Translated by Kathleen Ross and Richard Schaaf. Willimantic, Conn.: Curbstone Press.

Davis, Lisa. 1986. "An Invitation to Understanding among Poor Women of the Americas: *The Color Purple* and *Hasta no verte, Jesús mío.*" In *Reinventing the Americas,* edited by Bell Gale Chevigny and Gari Laguardi, 224–41. Comparative Studies of Literature of the United States and Spanish America. New York: Cambridge University Press.

Deleuze, Gilles, and Félix Guattari. 1986. *Nomadology: The War Machine.* New York: Columbia University Press.

———. 1991. *A Thousand Plateaus.* Minneapolis: University of Minnesota Press.

de Man, Paul. 1979. *Allegories of Reading.* New Haven: Yale University Press.

———. 1984. "Autobiography as De-facement." In *The Rhetoric of Romanticism,* 67–82. New York: Columbia University Press.

Deng You-Mei. 1985. "Snuff Bottles." *Chinese Literature* (autumn): 3–79.

Derrida, Jacques. 1976. *Of Grammatology.* Translated by Gayatri Chakravorty Spivak. Baltimore: Johns Hopkins University Press.

———. 1979. "Living on: Border Lines." In *Deconstruction and Criticism,* edited by Jacques Derrida, Paul de Man, J. Hillis Miller, Harold Bloom, and Geoffrey Hartman. London: Routledge and Kegan Paul.

———. 1980. *The Archeology of the Frivolous: Reading Condillac.* Translated by John P. Leavy Jr. Pittsburgh: Duquesne University Press.

Didion, Joan. 1983. *Salvador.* New York: Washington Square Press.

Dirlik, Arif. 1994. "The Postcolonial Aura: Third World Criticism in the Age of Global Capitalism." *Critical Inquiry* 20 (winter): 328–56.

Diskin, Martin. 1995. "Anthropological Fieldwork in Mesoamerica: Focus on the Field." *Latin American Research Review* 30, no. 1 (winter): 163–76.

Dorfman, Ariel. 1966. "La última novela de Capote: ¿Un nuevo género literario?" *Anales de la Universidad de Chile* 124:97–117.

D'Souza, Dinesh. 1991. *Illiberal Education.* New York: Free Press.

Duchesne, Juan. 1986. "Las narraciones guerrilleras: Configuración de un sujeto épico de nuevo tipo." In *Testimonio y literatura,* edited by René Jara and Hernán Vidal, 85–137. Minneapolis, Minn.: Institute for the Study of Ideologies and Literature.

Dussel, Enrique, and Daniel E. Guillot. 1975. *Liberación Latinoamericana y Emmanuel Levinas.* Buenos Aires: Editorial Bonum.

Eagleton, Terry. 1990. *The Ideology of the Aesthetic.* Oxford: Basil Blackwell.

———. 1992. *Ideology: An Introduction.* New York: Verso.

Edmonson, Munro S. 1971. "Introduction" to *The Book of Counsel: The Popol Vuh of the Quiché Maya of Guatemala.* New Orleans: Tulane University Press.

Elizondo, Salvador. 1965. *Farabeuf.* 2d ed. Barcelona: Montesinos.

El Sa'adawi, Nawal. 1983. *Woman at Point Zero.* Translated by Sherif Hetata. London: Zed.

———. 1984. *Memoirs from the Women's Prison.* Translated from the Arabic by Marilyn Booth. London: Women's Press.

Eltit, Diamela. 1989. *El padre mío.* Santiago de Chile: Francisco Zegers.

Enzensberger, Hans Magnus. 1992. *Die grosse Wanderung. Dreiunddreissig Markierungen: mit einer Fussnote "Ueber einige Besonderheiten bei der Menschenjagd."* Frankfurt: Suhrkamp.

Escobar, Arturo. 1992. "Culture, Economics, and Politics in Latin American Social Movements." In *The Making of Social Movements in Latin America: Identity, Strategy, and Democracy,* edited by Escobar and Alvarez, 62–85. Boulder, Colo.: Westview Press.

Escobar, Arturo, and Sonia E. Alvarez. 1992a. "Introduction: Theory and Protest in Latin America Today." In *The Making of Social Movements in Latin America: Identity, Strategy, and Democracy,* edited by Escobar and Alvarez, 1–15. Boulder, Colo.: Westview Press.

Escobar, Arturo, and Sonia E. Alvarez, eds. 1992b. *The Making of Social Movements in Latin America: Identity, Strategy, and Democracy.* Boulder, Colo.: Westview Press.

Eysteinsson, Astradur. 1990. *The Concept of Modernism.* Ithaca: Cornell University Press.

Farah, Douglas. 1992. "Beer Baron Spends Millions in Drive to Rule Bolivia." *Washington Post,* 31 March.

Felman, Shoshana, and Dori Laub. 1992. *Testimony: Crises of Witnessing in Literature, Psychoanalysis, and History.* New York and London: Routledge.

Fish, Stanley. 1981. "How to Recognize a Poem When You See One." In *American Criticism in the Poststructuralist Age,* edited by Ira Konigsberg, 102–15. Ann Arbor: University of Michigan Press.

Foley, Barbara. 1986. *Telling the Truth: The Theory and Practice of Documentary Fiction.* Ithaca: Cornell University Press.

Ford-Smith, Honor. 1986. *Lionheart Gal: Life Stories of Jamaican Women.* Toronto: Women's Press.

Fornet, Michel. 1977. "Al ajuste de cuentas: Del panfleto autonomista a la literatura de campaña." *Casa de las Americas* 146 (January–February): 49–57.

Foster, David William. 1984. "Latin American Documentary Narrative." *PMLA* 99:41–55.

Foucault, Michel. 1977. "Language to Infinity." In *Language, Counter-Memory, Practice: Selected Essays and Interviews,* edited by Donald F. Bouchard, 53–67. Ithaca: Cornell University Press.

——. 1981. "The Order of Discourse." In *Untying the Text,* edited by Robert Young. Boston: Routledge and Kegan Paul.

Fraire, Isabel. 1983. "Testimonial Literature: A New Window on Reality." *American Book Review* 9, no. 6:4–5.

Franco, Jean. 1991. "¿La historia de quién? La piratería postmoderna." *Revista de crítica literaria latinoamericana* 17, no. 33:11–20.

Fraser, Nancy. 1990. "Rethinking the Public Sphere: A Contribution to the Critique of Actually Existing Democracy." *Social Text* 25/26:55–83.

Galeano, Eduardo. 1984. "Quito, February 1976: I light the fire and beckon it." In *Poems,* by Roque Dalton, 85–87. Translated by Richard Schaaf. Willimantic, Conn.: Curbstone Press.

——. 1987. "The Resurrection of Miguel Mármol." *Soberanía* 21:16–21.

——. 1988. *Memory of Fire: Century of the Wind.* Part 3 of a trilogy. Translated by Cedric Belfrage. New York: Pantheon.

Gale Chevigny, Bell. 1986. "Twice-Told Tales and the Meaning of History: Testimonial Novels by Miguel Barnet and Norman Mailer." *The Centennial Review* 30, no. 2 (spring): 181–95.

Galich, Manuel. [1949] 1985. *Del pánico al ataque.* Guatemala City: Editorial Universitaria.

Galván, Manuel de Jesús. [1882] 1976. *Enriquillo.* Mexico City: Porrúa.

Garcia Espinosa, Julio. 1982. *Una imagen recorre el mundo.* Havana: Letras Cubanas.

Glowinsky, Michal. 1987. "Document as a Novel." *New Literary History* 18, no. 2:385–401.

Gómez-Peña, Guillermo. 1993. "From Art-Mageddon to Gringostroika: A Manifesto against Censorship." In *Warrior for Gringostroika,* 55–63. Saint Paul, Minn.: Graywolf Press.

González de Cascorro, Raúl. 1978. "El género testimonial en Cuba." *Unión* 4:78–89.

González Echevarría, Roberto. 1980. "*Biografía de un cimarrón* and the Novel of the Cuban Revolution." *Novel: A Forum on Fiction* 13:249–63.

——. 1985. *The Voice of the Masters: Writing and Autobiography in Modern Latin American Literature.* Austin: University of Texas Press.

Gramsci, Antonio. 1983. "The Formation of the Intellectuals." In *Selections of the Prison Notebooks,* edited and translated by Quintin Hoare and Geoffrey Nowell Smith, 3–23. New York: International Publishers.

Greenblatt, Stephen, and Giles Gunn, eds. 1992. *Redrawing the Boundaries: The*

Transformation of English and American Literary Studies. New York: Modern Language Association.

Greimas, Algirdas Julien. 1989. "The Veridiction Contract." *New Literary History* 20, no. 3:651–60.

Groden, Michael, and Martin Kreiswirth, eds. 1994. *The Johns Hopkins Guide to Literary Theory and Criticism.* Baltimore and London: The Johns Hopkins University Press.

Gugelberger, Georg. 1986. *Marxism and African Literature.* Trenton, N.J.: Africa World Press; London: James Currey.

———. 1994. "Postcolonial Cultural Studies." In Groden and Kreiswirth, eds., 581–84.

Gugelberger, Georg, and Michael Kearney. 1991. "Voices of the Voiceless: Testimonial Literature and Latin America." *Latin American Perspectives* 18, no. 3:3–14.

Gugino, Vincent F. 1991. "On Ethos." Ph.D. diss., SUNY-Buffalo.

Guha, Ranajit. 1983. *Elementary Aspects of Peasant Insurgency in Colonial India.* New Delhi: Oxford University Press.

Guillory, John. 1993. *Cultural Capital: The Problem of Literary Canon Formation.* Chicago: University of Chicago Press.

Gusdorf, Georges. 1980. "Conditions and Limits of Autobiography." In *Autobiography: Essays Theoretical and Critical,* edited by James Olney, 28–48. Princeton: Princeton University Press.

Habel, Janette. 1991. *Cuba: The Revolution in Peril.* Translated by Jon Barnes. London: Verso.

Hammond, Dorothy, and Alta Jablow. 1970. *The Africa That Never Was: Four Centuries of British Writing about Africa.* New York: Twayne.

Harlow, Barbara. 1987. *Resistance Literature.* New York and London: Methuen.

———. 1991. "*Testimonio* and Survival: Roque Dalton's *Miguel Mármol.*" *Latin American Perspectives* 18, no. 4 (fall): 9–21.

Hegel, Georg W. F. 1970. *Grundlinien der Philosophie des Rechts.* Vol. 7 of *Werke.* Frankfurt: Suhrkamp.

———. 1977. *Phenomenology of Spirit.* Translated by A. V. Miller; with analysis of the text and foreword by J. N. Findlay. Oxford: Oxford University Press.

Hernández Pérez, Jesús. 1983. "Viaje a las entrañas de la escoria." In *La leyenda de lo cotidiano,* edited by Jesús Hernández Pérez, 11–21. Havana: Letras Cubanas.

Herr, Michael. 1977. *Dispatches.* New York: Knopf.

Hesse, Douglas. 1989. "A Boundary Zone: First-Person Short Stories and Narrative Essays." In *Short Story at the Crossroads,* edited by Susan Lohafer and Jo Ellyn Clarey, 65–105. Baton Rouge: Louisiana State University Press.

Heyne, Eric. 1987. Review of *Telling the Truth,* by Barbara Foley. *The Journal of the Midwest Modern Language Association* 20, no. 1:111–14.

Hitchcock, Peter. 1993–94. "The Othering of Cultural Studies." *Third Text* 25:11–20.

Huyssen, Andreas. 1986. *After the Great Divide: Modernism, Mass Culture, Postmodernism.* Bloomington: Indiana University Press.

James, C. L. R. 1989. *The Black Jacobins.* New York: Vintage.

Jameson, Fredric. 1976. "Criticism in History." In *Weapons of Criticism: Marxism in America and the Literary Tradition,* edited by Norman Rudich, 31–50. Palo Alto, Calif.: Ramparts Press.

———. 1977. "Reflections in Conclusion." In *Aesthetics and Politics,* edited by Ronald Taylor. London: New Left Books.

———. 1984a. "Postmodernism, or the Cultural Logic of Late Capitalism," *New Left Review* 146 (July/August): 53–92.

———. 1984b. "Foreword." In *The Postmodern Condition: A Report on Knowledge,* by Jean-François Lyotard, vii–xxi. Translated by Geoff Bennington and Brian Massumi. Minneapolis: University of Minnesota Press.

———. 1986. "Third World Literature in the Era of Multinational Capitalism." *Social Text* 15:65–88.

———. 1987. "A Brief Response." *Social Text* 17:26–27.

———. 1992. "De la sustitución de importaciones literarias y culturales en el Tercer Mundo: El caso del testimonio." *Revista de crítica literaria latinoamericana* 36:117–33.

———. 1993a. "On Literary and Cultural Import-Substitution in the Third World: The Case of the Testimonio." *Margins* no. 1 (spring): 11–34.

———. 1993b. "Americans Abroad: Exogamy and Letters in Late Capitalism." In *Critical Theory, Cultural Politics, and Latin American Narrative,* edited by Steven Bell, Albert H. Le May, and Leonard Orr. Notre Dame: University of Notre Dame Press.

———. 1993c. "On 'Cultural Studies.'" *Social Text* 34:17–52.

Jara, René, and Nicholas Spadaccini, eds. 1989. *1482–1992: Re/Discovering Colonial Writing.* Minneapolis: Prisma Institute.

Jara, René, and Hernán Vidal, eds. 1986. *Testimonio y literatura.* Minneapolis: Institute for the Study of Ideologies and Literature.

Jauss, Hans Robert. 1959. "Ursprung und Bedeutung der Ichform im *Lazarillo de Tormes.*" *Romanisches Jahrbuch* 10:297–300.

Jiménez, Mayra, ed. 1980. *Poesía campesina en Solentiname.* Managua: Ministerio de Cultura.

Jorgensen, Beth E. 1991. "Framing Questions: The Role of the Editor in Elena Poniatowska's *La noche de Tlatelolco.*" *Latin American Perspectives* 18, no. 3 (summer): 80–90.

Kamenka, Eugene, ed. 1983. *The Portable Karl Marx.* Middlesex, England, and New York: Penguin.

Kant, Immanuel. 1952. *The Critique of Judgment.* Oxford: Clarendon.

Kaplan, Amy, and Donald E. Pease, eds. 1993. *Cultures of United States Imperialism.* Durham: Duke University Press.

Kearney, Michael. 1991. "Borders and Boundaries of State and Self at the End of Empire." *Journal of the Historical Society* 4, no. 1:52–74.

Khaled, Leila. 1973. *My People Shall Live.* Edited by George Hajjar. London: Hodder and Stoughton.

Khare, R. S. 1992. "The Other's Double—The Anthropologist's Bracketed Self: Notes on Cultural Representation and Privileged Discourse." *New Literary History* 23, no. 1:1–23.

Kiddle, Mary Ellen. 1984. "The Non-Fiction Novel or 'Novela Testimonial' in Contemporary Mexican Literature." Ph.D. diss., Brown University.

Kristeva, Julia. 1982. *Powers of Horror: An Essay on Abjection.* Translated by Leon S. Roudiez. New York: Columbia University Press.

Lacan, Jacques. 1977. *Ecrits: A Selection.* New York: Norton.

——. 1978. "Tuché and Automaton." In *The Four Fundamental Concepts of Psychoanalysis,* edited by Jacques-Alain Miller, 53–64. New York: Norton.

——. 1983: *Feminine Sexuality.* Edited by Juliet Mitchell and Jaqueline Rose. New York: Norton.

——. 1992. *The Seminar of Jacques Lacan.* Book 8. *The Ethics of Psychoanalysis.* New York: Norton.

Laclau, Ernesto. 1977. *Politics and Ideology in Marxist Theory: Capitalism, Fascism, Populism.* London: New Left Books.

——. 1980. "Populist Rupture and Discourse." *Screen Education* 34 (spring): 87–93.

——. 1990. *New Reflections on the Revolution of Our Time.* London: Verso.

Laclau, Ernesto, and Chantal Mouffe. 1985. *Hegemony and Socialist Strategy: Towards a Radical Democratic Politics.* London: Verso.

Lamming, George. 1953. *In the Castle of My Skin.* London: Michael Joseph.

Langness, L. L. 1965. *The Life History in Anthropological Science.* New York: Holt, Rinehart, and Winston.

Lanser, Susan Sniader. 1981. *The Narrative Act: Point of View in Fiction.* Princeton: Princeton University Press.

Larsen, Neil. 1995. *Reading North by South: On Latin American Literature, Culture, and Politics.* Minneapolis: University of Minnesota Press.

Latin American Subaltern Studies Group. 1993. "Founding Statement." *boundary 2* 20, no. 3:110–21.

Laye, Camara. 1953. *L'enfant noir.* Paris: Plon.

Leduc, Violette. 1964. *La bâtarde.* Paris: Gallimard.

Lefebvre, Henri. 1988. "Toward a Leftist Cultural Politics: Remarks Occasioned by the Centenary of Marx's Death." In *Marxism and the Interpretation of Culture,* edited by Cary Nelson and Lawrence Grossberg, 75–88. Urbana: University of Illinois Press.

Leiris, Michel. 1948–76. *La règle du jeu.* Paris: Gallimard.

Lejeune, Philippe. 1971. *L'autobiographie en France.* Paris: Gallimard.

——. 1973. "Le pacte autobiographique." *Poétique* 14:137–62.

——. 1975. *Le pacte autobiographique.* Paris: Seuil.

Lohafer, Susan. 1983. *Coming to Terms with the Short Story.* Baton Rouge: Louisiana State University.

Lovell, W. George. 1988. "Surviving Conquest: The Maya of Guatemala in Historical Perspective." *Latin American Research Review* 23, no. 2:25–57.

Loveman, Brian, and Thomas M. Davies Jr., eds. 1989. *The Politics of Antipolitics: The Military in Latin America.* 2d ed., revised and expanded. Lincoln: University of Nebraska Press.

Lugones, María, and Elizabeth Spelman. 1983. "Have We Got a Theory for You? Feminist Theory, Cultural Imperialism and the Demand for 'The Woman's Voice.'" *Women's Studies International Forum* 6:573–81.

Luis, William, ed. 1994. *Dictionary of Literary Biography: Latin American Fiction Writers.* Detroit: Gale Research.

Lukács, Georg. 1983. *The Historical Novel.* Translated by Hannah Mitchel and Stanley Mitchel. Preface by Fredric Jameson. Lincoln: University of Nebraska Press.

Lyotard, Jean-François. 1984. *The Postmodern Condition: A Report on Knowledge.* Translated by Geoff Bennington and Brian Massumi. Minneapolis: University of Minnesota Press.

——. 1988. *The Differend: Phrases in Dispute.* Translated by Georges Van Den Abbeele. Minneapolis: University of Minnesota Press.

Manz, Beatriz. 1988. *Refugees of a Hidden War: The Aftermath of Counterinsurgency in Guatemala.* Albany: SUNY Series in Anthropological Studies of Contemporary Issues.

Mao Tse-tung. 1957. *On the Correct Handling of Contradictions among the People.* New York: New Century Publishers.

Maran, René. 1921. *Batouala: Véritable roman nègre.* Paris: A. Michel.

Marcus, Steven. 1983. "Freud and Dora: Story, History, Case History." In *Literature and Psychoanalysis,* edited by Edith Kurzweil and William Phillips, 153–74. New York: Columbia University Press.

Marín, Lynda. 1991. "Speaking Out Together: Testimonials of Latin American Women." *Latin American Perspectives* 18, no. 3:51–68.

Marks, Elaine. 1975. "I Am My Own Heroine: Some Thoughts about Women and Autobiography in France," In *Teaching about Women in the Foreign Languages: French, Spanish, German, Russian,* edited by Sidonie Cassirer, 1–10. Prepared for the Commission on the Status of Women of the MLA. Old Westbury, Conn.: The Feminist Press.

Mármol, José. [1851] 1971. *Amalia.* Mexico City: Porrúa.

Mascia-Lees, Frances, et al. 1989. "The Postmodernist Turn in Anthropology: Cautions from a Feminist Perspective." *Signs: Journal of Women in Culture and Society* 15, no. 11:7–33.

Mato, Daniel. 1993. "Construcción de identidades pannacionales y transnacionales en tiempos de globalización: consideraciones teóricas y sobre el caso de América Latina." In *Diversidad cultural y construcción de identidades: Estudios sobre Venezuela, América Latina y el Caribe,* edited by Daniel Mato, 13–20. Caracas: Fondo Editorial Tropykos/Centro de Estudios Postdoctorales, Universidad Central de Venezuela.

Mayorga, Fernando. 1991. *Max Fernández: La política del silencio.* La Paz: Cochabamba ILDIS-UMSS.

Meese, Elizabeth. 1990. "(Dis)Locations: Reading the Theory of a Third World Woman in *I, Rigoberta Menchú.*" In *(Ex)Tensions: Re-figuring Feminist Criticism,* edited by Elizabeth Meese. Urbana: University of Illinois Press.

Meiseles, Susan. 1981. *Nicaragua.* New York: Pantheon.

Menchú, Rigoberta. 1983. *Me llamo Rigoberta Menchú y así me nació la conciencia.* Mexico: Siglo XXI; Havana: Casa de las Americas.

———. 1984. *I, Rigoberta Menchú: An Indian Woman in Guatemala.* Edited and introduced by Elisabeth Burgos-Debray. Translated by Ann Wright. London: Verso.

Michaels, Walter Benn. 1992. "Race into Culture: A Critical Genealogy of Cultural Identity," *Critical Inquiry* 18 (summer): 665–85.

Mignolo, Walter. 1989. "Literacy and Colonialization: The New World Experience." In *1482–1992: Re/Discovering Colonial Writing,* edited by René Jara and Nicholas Spadaccini. Minneapolis: Prisma Institute.

Miller, Nancy. 1988. "Writing Fictions: Women's Autobiography in France." In *Subject to Change: Reading Feminist Writing,* 47–64. New York: Columbia University Press.

Millet, K. 1987. "Framing the Narrative: The Dreams of Lucinda Nahuelhaul." In *Poética de la población marginal,* edited by James Romano. Minneapolis: Prisma Institute.

Molloy, Sylvia. 1991. *At Face Value: Autobiographical Writing in Spanish America.* Cambridge and New York: Cambridge University Press.

Montejo, Esteban. 1968. *The Autobiography of a Runaway Slave.* Edited by Miguel Barnet and translated by Jocasta Innes. New York: Pantheon Books.

Montejo, Victor. 1987. *Testimony: Death of a Guatemalan Village.* Translated by Victor Perera. Willimantic, Conn.: Curbstone Press.

Moreiras, Alberto. 1990. "Transculturación y pérdida del sentido: El diseño de la posmodernidad en América Latina." *Nuevo texto crítico* 8, no. 6:105–19.

Moretti, Franco. 1987. *The Way of the World: The Bildungsroman in European Culture.* London: Verso.

Moura, Jean-Marc. 1992. *L'image du tiers monde dans le roman français contemporain.* Paris: Presses Universitaires de France.

Neruda, Pablo. 1946. *Alturas de Macchu Picchu.* Ilus. de José Venturelli. Santiago de Chile: Librería Neira.

———. 1961. *Canto general.* Edited by Enrico Mario Santí. Madrid: Cátedra.

Ngugi wa Thiong'o. 1986. *Decolonising the Mind: The Politics of Language in African Literature.* London: James Currey.

Norris, Christopher. 1986. *Deconstruction: Theory and Practice.* London: Methuen.

Olney, James, ed. 1980. *Autobiography: Essays Theoretical and Critical.* Princeton: Princeton University Press.

Payeras, Mario. 1980. *Días de la selva.* Havana: Casa de las Américas.

———. 1983. *Days of the Jungle: The Testimony of a Guatemalan Guerrillero. 1972–1976.* Translated by Lita Paniagua. Introduction by George Black. New York: Monthly Review Press.

———. 1987. *El trueno en la ciudad: Episodios de la lucha armada urbana de 1981 en Guatemala.* Mexico City: Juan Pablos.

Poniatowska, Elena. 1969. *Hasta no verte, Jésus mío.* Mexico City: Era.

———. 1971. *La noche de Tlatelolco: Testimonios de la historia oral.* Mexico City: Era. Translated into English by Helen R. Lane as *Massacre in Mexico* (New York: Viking Press, 1975).

Pozas, Ricardo. 1952. *Juan Pérez Jolote: Biografía de un Tzotzil.* Mexico: Fondo de Cultura Economica.

Pratt, Mary Louis. 1986. "Scratches on the Face of the Country; or, What Mr. Barrow Saw in the Land of the Bushmen." In *"Race," Writing, Difference,* edited by Henry Louis Gates Jr., 138–62. Chicago and London: University of Chicago Press.

———. 1992. *Imperial Eyes: Travel Writing and Transculturation.* London and New York: Routledge.

Pring-Mill, Robert. 1983. "Mayra Jiménez and the Rise of Nicaraguan 'Poesía de Taller.'" In *La mujer en la literatura del Caribe,* edited by Lloyd King. Trinidad: University of the West Indies.

Rama, Angel. 1984. *La ciudad letrada.* Hanover, N.H.: Ediciones del Norte.

Randall, Margaret. 1972. *La mujer cubana ahora.* Havana: Instituto Cubano del Libro. Published in English as *Cuban Women Now.* Toronto: Women's Press.

———. 1979. *El pueblo no solo es testigo: La historia de Dominga de la Cruz.* Rio Piedras, Puerto Rico: Huracan.

———. 1981a. *Cuban Women Twenty Years Later.* Brooklyn, N.Y.: Smyrna Press.

———. 1981b. *Sandino's Daughters: Testimonies of Nicaraguan Women in Struggle.* Vancouver: New Star Books.

———. 1983. *Christians in the Nicaraguan Revolution.* Vancouver: New Star Books.

———. 1985a. *Women Brave in the Face of Danger.* Tromansburg, N.Y.: Crossing Press.

———. 1985b. *Testimonios: A Guide to Oral History.* Toronto: Participatory Research Group.

———. 1991. "Reclaiming Voices: Notes on a New Female Practice in Journalism." *Latin American Perspectives* 18, no. 3 (summer): 103–13.

———. 1992. "Qué es y cómo se hace un testimonio?" *Revista de crítica literaria latinoamericana* 36:21–45.

Randall, Margaret, with Angel Antonio Moreno. 1979. *Sueños y realidades de un guajiricantor.* Mexico City: Siglo XXI.

Retamar, Roberto Fernández. 1989. *Caliban and Other Essays.* Translated by Edward Baker. With an introduction by Fredric Jameson. Minneapolis: University of Minnesota Press.

Rial, Juan. 1986. *Las Fuerzas Armadas: ¿Soldados-políticos garantes de la democracia?* Montevideo: CIESU.

Rice-Sayre, Laura P. 1986. "Witnessing History: Diplomacy versus Testimony." In *Testimonio y literatura,* edited by René Jara and Hernán Vidal, 48–72. Minneapolis: Institute for the Study of Ideologies and Literature.

Richard, Nelly. 1994. "Bordes, diseminación, postmodernismo: Una metáfora latinoamericana de fin de siglo." Paper presented at the International Coloquium on "Las culturas de fin de siglo en América Latina," Yale University, April 8–9.

Richards, Michael. 1986. "Cosmopolitan World View and Counterinsurgency in Guatemala." *Anthropological Quarterly* 3:90–107.

Ricoeur, Paul. 1980. "The Hermeneutics of Testimony." In *Essays on Biblical Interpretation,* edited by Lewis S. Mudge, 119–54. Philadelphia: Fortress Press.

Rivera, José Eustasio. 1944. *La vorágine:* Dibujos de Julio Vanzo. Buenos Aires: Editorial Pleamer.

Rivero, Eliana S. 1985. "Testimonios y conversaciones como discurso literario: Cuba y Nicaragua." *Literature and Contemporary Revolutionary Culture* 11, no. 1:218–28.

———. 1991. "Testimonial Literature and Conversations as Literary Discourse: Cuba and Nicaragua." *Latin American Perspectives* 18, no. 3 (summer): 69–79.

Rodriguez, Richard. 1982. *Hunger of Memory: The Education of Richard Rodriguez: An Autobiography.* Boston: D. R. Godine.

Rosenblatt, Roger. 1980. "Black Autobiography: Life as the Death Weapon," In *Autobiography: Essays Theoretical and Critical,* edited by James Olney, 166–75. Princeton: Princeton University Press.

Rouquié, Alain. 1987. *The Military and the State in Latin America.* Translated by Paul E. Sigmund. Berkeley: University of California Press.

Said, Edward. 1978. *Orientalism.* New York: Random House.

———. 1993. *Culture and Imperialism.* New York: Alfred A. Knopf.

Saldívar, José David. 1991. *The Dialectics of Our America: Genealogy, Cultural Critique, and Literary History.* Durham: Duke University Press.

Santí, Enrico Mario. 1961. "Introducción." In *Canto general,* by Pablo Neruda. Madrid: Cátedra.

———. 1992. "Latinamericanism and Restitution." *Latin American Literary Review* 20, no. 40:88–96.

Saporta Sternbach, Nancy. 1991. "Re-membering the Dead: Latin American Women's 'Testimonial' Discourse." *Latin American Perspectives* 18, no. 3 (summer): 91–102.

Sarduy, Severo. 1972. *Cobra.* Buenos Aires: Sudamericana.

Sareika, Rüdiger. 1980. *Die Dritte Welt in der westdeutschen Literatur der sechziger Jahre.* Frankfurt: R. G. Fischer.

Sarmiento, Domingo Faustino. 1931. *Recuerdos de provincia.* Barcelona: Ramón Sopena.

Sartre, Jean-Paul. 1966. *Being and Nothingness: A Phenomenological Essay in Ontology.* Translated and with an introduction by Hazel E. Barnes. New York: Washington Square Press.

———. 1976. *Critique of Dialectical Reason.* Translated by Alan Sheridan-Smith, edited by Jonathan Ree. London: New Left Books.

Scannone, Juan Carlos. 1979. "Theology, Popular Culture, and Discernment." In *Frontiers of Theology in Latin America,* edited by Rosino Gibellini and translated by John Drury. Maryknoll: Orbis Books.

Scheper-Hughes, Nancy. 1993. *Death without Weeping: The Violence of Everyday Life in Brazil.* Berkeley: University of California Press.

Scott, James C. 1990. *Domination and the Arts of Resistance: Hidden Transcripts.* New Haven: Yale University Press.

Séjourné, Laurette. 1977. *El Teatro Escambray.* Havana: Editorial de Sciencias Sociales.

Shaw, Donald. 1993. "On the New Novel in Spanish America." *New Novel Review* 1, no. 1:59–73.

Sklodowska, Elzbieta. 1982. "La forma testimonial y la novelística de Miguel Barnet." *Revista/Review Interamericana* 12, no. 3:368–80.

———. 1991. "Hacia una tipología del testimonio hispanoamericano." *Siglo XX/20th Century* 8, nos. 1–2:103–20.

———. 1992. *Testimonio hispanoamericano: Historia, teoría, poética.* New York and Frankfurt: Peter Lang.

———. 1994. "Spanish American Testimonial Novel: Some Afterthoughts." *New Novel Review* 1, no. 2:32–41.

Smith, Carol, and Jeff Boyer. 1987. "Central America since 1979." *Annual Review of Anthropology* 16:197–221.

Sommer, Doris. 1983. *One Master for Another: Populism as Patriarchal Rhetoric in Dominican Novels.* Lanham, Md.: University Press of America.

———. 1988. "Not Just a Personal Story: Women's *Testimonios* and the Plural Self." In *Life/Lines: Theorizing Women's Autobiography,* edited by Bella Brodzky and Celeste Schenck. Ithaca: Cornell University Press.

———. 1989. "Foundational Fictions: When History was Romance in Latin America." *Salmagundi* 82–83:111–41.

———. 1991. "Rigoberta's Secrets." *Latin American Perspectives* 18, no. 3:32–50.

———. 1992a. "Sin secretos." *Revista de crítica literaria latinoamericana* 36:135–54.

———. 1992b. "Resistant Texts and Incompetent Readers." *Latin American Literary Review* 20, no. 40:104–8.

———. 1993. "Resisting the Heat: Menchú, Morrison, and Incompetent Readers." In *Cultures of United States Imperialism*, edited by Amy Kaplan and Donald E. Pease, 407–32. Durham: Duke University Press.

Spivak, Gayatri Chakravorty. 1983. "Displacement and the Discourse of Women." In *Displacement, Derrida and After*, edited by Mark Krupnick, 169–95. Bloomington: Indiana University Press.

———. 1987. *In Other Worlds: Essays in Cultural Politics*. New York and London: Methuen.

———. 1988. "Can the Subaltern Speak?" In *Marxism and the Interpretation of Culture*, edited by Cary Nelson and Lawrence Grossberg, 271–313. Urbana: University of Illinois Press.

———. 1990. *The Post-Colonial Critic: Interviews, Strategies, Dialogues*. Edited by Sarah Harasym. New York and London: Routledge.

———. 1993a. "Extreme Eurocentrism." *Lusitania* 1, no. 4:55–62.

———. 1993b. *Outside in the Teaching Machine*. New York: Routledge.

Sprinker, Michael, ed. 1992. *Edward Said: A Critical Reader*. Oxford, England, and Cambridge, U.S.A.: Blackwell.

Steele, Cynthia. 1992. "Testimonio y autor/idad en *Hasta no verte, Jesús mío* de Elena Poniatowska." *Revista de crítica literaria latinoamericana* 36:155–80.

Steiner, George. 1975. *After Babel: Aspects of Language and Translation*. London and New York: Oxford University Press.

Stephanson, Anders. 1987. "Regarding Postmodernism: A Conversation with Fredric Jameson." *Social Text* 17:29–54.

Stoll, David. 1990a. "*I, Rigoberta Menchú* and Human Rights Reporting in Guatemala," unpublished manuscript.

———. 1990b. "'The Land No Longer Gives': Land Reform in Nebaj, Guatemala." *Cultural Survival Quarterly* 14, no. 4:4–9.

Taussig, Michael. 1987. *Shamanism, Colonialism, and the Wild Man*. Chicago: University of Chicago Press.

Tyler, Stephen. 1984. "The Poetic Turn in Postmodern Anthropology: The Poetry of Paul Friedrich." *American Anthropologist* 86, no. 2:328–36.

Vargas Llosa, Mario. 1986. "Thugs Who Know Their Greek." *New York Times Book Review*, 7 September.

———. 1987. *El hablador*. Barcelona: Seix Barral.

Vera León, Antonio. 1992. "Hacer hablar: La transcripción testimonial," *Revista de crítica latinoamericana* 36:181–99.

Vidal, Hernán. 1993. "The Concept of Colonial and Postcolonial Discourse: A Perspective from Literary Criticism." *Latin American Research Review* 28, no. 3:113–19.

Villaverde, Cirilio. 1971. *Cecilia Valdés; o, La Loma del angel; novela de costumbres cubanas.* Edited by, and with a prologue and notes by, Olga Bloudet and Antonio Tudisco. Madrid: Anaya.

Wald, Karen. 1978. *The Children of Ché: Childcare and Education in Cuba.* Palo Alto, Calif.: Ramparts Press.

Walsh, Rodolfo. 1957. *Operación Masacre.* Buenos Aires: Ediciones Sigla.

Weschler, Lawrence. 1990. *A Miracle, a Universe: Settling Accounts with Torturers.* Harmondsworth: Penguin.

Whisnant, David E. 1989. "La vida nos ha enseñado: Rigoberta Menchú y la dialectica de la cultura tradicional." *Ideologies and Literature* 4, no. 1 (spring): 317–43.

Williams, Gareth. 1993. "Translation and Mourning: The Cultural Challenge of Latin American Testimonial Autobiography." *Latin American Literary Review* 21, no. 41:79–99.

Williams, Raymond. 1980. "The Writer: Commitment and Alignment." *Marxism Today* 24 (June): 22–25.

Wittgenstein, Ludwig. 1953. *Philosophical Investigations.* Translated by G. E. M. Anscombe. New York: Macmillan.

Young, Robert J. C. 1995. *Colonial Desire: Hybridity in Theory, Culture and Race.* New York: Routledge.

Yúdice, George. 1985a. "The *Testimonio* as Historical Discourse," unpublished manuscript.

———. 1985b. "Central American Testimonial," unpublished manuscript.

———. 1986. "Introduction" to special issue, *Contemporary Cuban Culture. Social Text* 15:iii–xii.

———. 1988. "Marginality and the Ethics of Survival." In *Universal Abandon? The Politics of Postmodernism,* edited by Andrew Ross, 214–36. Minneapolis: University of Minnesota Press.

———. 1991a. "*Testimonio* and Postmodernism." *Latin American Perspectives* 18, no. 3 (summer): 15–31.

———. 1991b. "El conflicto de posmodernidades." *Nuevo Texto Crítico* 7:19–33.

———. 1992a. "Postmodernity and Transnational Capitalism in Latin America." In *On Edge: The Crisis of Contemporary Latin American Culture,* edited by George Yúdice, Jean Franco, and Juan Flores, 1–29. Minneapolis: University of Minnesota Press.

———. 1992b. "Testimonio y conscientización." *Revista de crítica literaria latinoamericana* 36:207–27.

———. 1993. "Postmodernism in the Periphery." *South Atlantic Quarterly* 92, no. 3:543–56.

———. 1996. "Testimonial Literature as Popular Culture in Central America: An Alternative to Hegemonic Postmodern Aesthetics," unpublished manuscript.

Zambrano, María. 1987. "La confesión: género literario y método." *Anthropos-suplemento* (March–April): 57–79.

Zimmerman, Marc. 1991. *"Testimonio* in Guatemala: Payeras, Rigoberta, and Beyond." *Latin American Perspectives* 18, no. 4 (fall): 22–47.

——. 1992. "El *otro* de Rigoberta: Los testimonios de Ignacio Bizarro Ujpán y la resistencia indígena en Guatemala." *Revista de crítica literaria latino-americana* 36:229–43.

Žižek, Slavoj. 1992. *The Sublime Object of Ideology.* Verso: New York.

——. 1993a. "From Courtly Love to *The Crying Game.*" *New Left Review* 202:95–108.

——. 1993b. *Tarrying with the Negative: Kant, Hegel, and the Critique of Ideology.* Durham: Duke University Press.

Index

Contributors

John Beverley teaches at the University of Pittsburgh. He has published extensively on testimonial literature and is the author of *Del Lazarillo al sandinismo: Estudios sobre la función ideologica de la literatura española e hispanoamericana* and *Against Literature*. With Marc Zimmerman he published *Literature and Politics in the Central American Revolutions* and with José Oviedo he edited *The Postmodernism Debate in Latin America*.

Santiago Colás teaches Spanish and Latin American literature at the University of Michigan, Ann Arbor. He is the author of *Postmodernity in Latin America: The Argentine Paradigm*.

Georg M. Gugelberger teaches comparative literature at the University of California, Riverside, and presently directs the University of California's Education Abroad Program at U.N.A.M. in Mexico City. He is the editor of *Marxism and African Literature* and editor and translator of *Nama/Namibia: Diary and Letters of Nama Chief Hendrik Witbooi, 1884–1894*. He was one of the editors of the special issue on testimonial literature, "Voices of the Voiceless," for the journal *Latin American Perspectives,* on whose editorial board he serves.

Barbara Harlow teaches English at the University of Texas, Austin. She is the author of *Resistance Literature* and *Barred: Women, Writing and Political Detention*.

Fredric Jameson is William A. Lane Professor of Comparative Literature and Director of the Graduate Program in Literature and the Duke Center of Critical Theory, Duke University. He has published widely on Marxism, literary theory, poststructuralism, postmodernism, and film. His books include *Marxism and Form, The Political Unconscious, The Ideologies of Theory: Essays 1971– 1986, Late Marxism: Adorno, or, The Persistence of the Dialectic,* and *Postmodernism, or, The Cultural Logic of Late Capitalism*.

Alberto Moreiras teaches Spanish and Latin American literature at Duke University and is the author of *Interpretación y diferencia*. Two other books by him are forthcoming: *Tercer espacio: Poética de duelo en América* and *Latin Americanism or Cultural Practice.*

Margaret Randall is a writer, photographer, teacher, and activist who lived in Mexico, Cuba, and Nicaragua before returning to the United States in 1984. Among her numerous books are: *Sandino's Daughters, Women Brave in the Face of Danger, Testimonios: A Guide to Oral History,* and *Walking to the Edge: Essays of Resistance.*

Javier Sanjinés C is at the Facultad de humanidades y ciencias de la educación of the Universidad Mayor de San Andrés in La Paz, Bolivia, and presently teaches at Duke University. He is the author of *Estetica y carnival: Ensayos de sociologia de la cultura* and *Literatura contemporanea y grotesco social en Bolivia.*

Elzbieta Sklodowska teaches Spanish literature in the Department of Romance Languages and Literatures at Washington University in St. Louis. She is the author of *Testimonio hispanoamericano: Historia, teoría, poética* and numerous articles on testimonial literature.

Doris Sommer teaches Latin American literature at Harvard University. She is the author of *One Master for Another: Populism as Patriarchal Rhetoric in Dominican Novels* and *Foundational Fictions: The National Romances of Latin America.*

Gareth Williams teaches Latin American literature at North Carolina State University in Raleigh, North Carolina. His forthcoming book is entitled *José Donoso and the Eruption of the Real.* He presently is working on another book entitled *Postmodernity and the Ends of Utopia in Latin America.*

George Yúdice teaches Latin American literature and literary theory at Hunter College and the Graduate Center, CUNY. He is the author of a book on Vicente Huidobro and numerous articles on literature and theory, and a coauthor with Juan Flores and Jean Franco of the book *On Edge: The Crisis of Contemporary Latin American Culture.* He is also the translator of the Brazilian novel *Stella Manhattan* by Silviano Santiago.

Marc Zimmerman teaches Latin American studies at the University of Illinois at Chicago. Among his publications are *El Salvador at War: A Collage Epic, Nicaragua in Reconstruction and at War: The People Speak, Literature and Resistance in Guatemala: Textual Modes and Cultural Politics from "el señor presidente" to Rigoberta Menchú,* and with John Beverley, *Literature and Politics in the Central American Revolutions.*

Library of Congress Cataloging-in-Publication Data

The real thing : testimonial discourse and Latin America/
Georg M. Gugelberger, editor.
p. cm.
Includes bibliographical references and index.
ISBN 0-8223-1851-2 (cloth : alk. paper). —ISBN 0-8223-1844-X (pbk. : alk. paper)
1. Spanish American literature—20th century—History and criticism. 2. Report-
age literature, Spanish American—History and criticism.
I. Gugelberger, Georg M.
PQ7082.P76R43 1996
860.9'98—dc20 96-41261 CIP